Fantasy Girls

Gender in the New Universe of Science Fiction and Fantasy Television

Edited by
Elyce Rae Helford

ROWMAN & LITTLEFIELD PUBLISHERS, INC.
Lanham • Boulder • New York • Oxford

ROWMAN & LITTLEFIELD PUBLISHERS, INC.

Published in the United States of America
by Rowman & Littlefield Publishers, Inc.
4720 Boston Way, Lanham, Maryland 20706
http://www.rowmanlittlefield.com

12 Hid's Copse Road, Cumnor Hill, Oxford OX2 9JJ, England

British Library Cataloguing in Publication Information Available

Library of Congress Cataloging-in-Publication Data

Fantasy girls : gender in the new universe of science fiction and fantasy television /
edited by Elyce Rae Helford.
   p. cm.
  Includes bibliographical references and index.
  ISBN 0-8476-9834-3 (alk. paper)—ISBN 0-8476-9835-1 (pbk. : alk. paper)
   1. Women on television. 2. Fantasy television programs—United States. 3. Science
fiction television programs—United States. I. Helford, Elyce Rae, 1962–

PN1992.8.W6 F36 2000
791.45'652042—dc21

00-027848

Printed in the United States of America

♾™ The paper used in this publication meets the minimum requirements of
American National Standard for Information Sciences—Permanence of Paper
for Printed Library Materials, ANSI/NISO Z39.48-1992.

Contents

Acknowledgments

Bringing this collection together has taken a great deal of time and energy and has been a great pleasure for me as well. I am grateful for the help and support of many colleagues, students, friends, and others. Thanks first to Jill Rothenberg, my original editor, for her enthusiasm and support for this collection. Thanks also to Christine Gatliffe, Dean Birkenkamp, Janice Braunstein, and Patti Waldygo, all at Rowman & Littlefield, who helped bring this book to print. Thanks to all the contributors to the volume, without whose critical and creative efforts there would obviously be no book. Thanks in particular to Kent A. Ono and Sarah Projansky for multiple e-mail and phone conversations that helped me to be the best editor I could, and to Kent and Rhonda Wilcox for making the time to offer thoughtful responses to my chapter. Thanks to Chad Crouse, my partner in television-viewing and the rest of life, for sharing his insights on reading images of women in speculative television and for the time and energy he spent reading and listening to me read multiple drafts of my chapter, the introduction, and my responses to other contributors' chapters. Thanks to Middle Tennessee State University's Faculty Research Grant program, which provided me with some reassigned time from my teaching responsibilities during the 1998–1999 academic year to work on the book. Thanks to Laura Davis, LeAnn Garner, and Meagan Rikard, who worked with me as graduate assistants, reading chapters and providing personal responses and editorial assistance. And, finally, thanks to Lane Crouse Helford, who fulfilled his role admirably as a devoted profeminist son (in the womb and out) by participating in a relatively easy pregnancy and not being too terribly difficult while I was doing the time-consuming writing and editing of this book.

Fantasy Girls

Fantasy Girls

Introduction

Elyce Rae Helford

When American television offers its pleasures in the form of women in entertainment programming, what do we get? Certainly, this question cannot be an-
swered in any simple or unified fashion. Over its fifty-plus years of broadcasting,
television has given us complex and contradictory female characters who reflect,
direct, and occasionally critique America's fantasies and anxieties about historical gender roles and norms. Early television images of womanhood emphasized
the white, middle-class ideals of post–World War II America, giving us the infamous "perfect" wives and mothers of '50s and '60s sitcoms, such as *Father Knows
Best* and *Leave It to Beaver*, as well as the idealized domestic worker, usually
African American, who "happily" yielded her family life and any other of her own
ambitions to care for these white, middle-class others, as seen in *Beulah* and
Hazel, for example.

Of course, even in its early years, television did not offer a unified picture of
idyllic middle-classness through its images of women and domestic life. *I Love
Lucy*, for example, gave us a wife in a cross-cultural marriage who neglected her
housewifely duties in hopes of becoming a performer at her husband's nightclub.
Actress Lucille Ball distorted normative white feminine beauty and grace
through Lucy's clownish antics on every episode. Thus, though she remained
largely confined to a housewife's role in a domestic setting, Lucy both revealed
and pushed the boundaries that television placed on women's lives.[1] Other early
characters, such as Alice Kramden of *The Honeymooners*, pushed similar boundaries within representations of working-class families, complaining about the
limitations of their lives, the dominance of the husband in the home, and the
elusiveness of the American Dream.

While the domesticated middle-class woman remained a staple of entertainment programming for many years, as television restrictions relaxed in alignment
with cultural norms of the late '60s and '70s, sexual objectification became an-

other strategy for portraying "proper" femininity. Many female characters of the
'70s and '80s fit well into the category of objects of the "male gaze"—film critic
Laura Mulvey's term for the dominance of a masculine/patriarchal perspective
in representation, or "woman as image, man as bearer of the look" (27). Examples such as *Laugh-In's* "sock it to me" girls, shimmying to psychedelic music in
their string bikinis as the camera panned over the slogans and images painted on
their bodies, come to mind. And, even when sexual objectification is not the only
possible reading for a female character, it has often played a significant role in
the popularity of a representation. Though *Charlie's Angels* offered strong female
role models to young, white, middle-class '70s girls, for example, it also limited
how we could think about the relationship between power and attractiveness to
men and about the importance of fitting cultural expectations of age, race, class,
and sexual orientation if we wanted to push the boundaries of feminine behavioral norms.

In the '60s and '70s, another innovation in the representation of women in entertainment television also began to develop, that of incorporating speculative or
fantasy images into programming. In the '60s, before much diversity in format
occurred, the domestic sitcom is where women would most often appear during
prime-time hours. How could television producers of the era address the changing role of women in America—as more and more white, middle-class women
joined the employed masses of working-class white women and women of color
who never had the privilege of a Donna Reed suburban lifestyle—without risking a reduced viewership among conservative, white, middle-class viewers or
making plain that the culture was losing faith in the post–World War II American Dream?

Together, *Bewitched* and *I Dream of Jeannie* offer one of television's answers
to this dilemma. Neither *Bewitched's* Samantha nor *I Dream of Jeannie's* Jeannie
work outside the home, but both can be read as symbolic articulations of
women's (at least white, middle-class women's) aspirations for respect in roles
other than wife and mother.[2] Samantha, the witch, and the magical Jeannie
weekly displayed intelligence and power far beyond that of the mortal men
whom they called husband and "master," respectively. Yet this intelligence and
power was tempered: at the request/demand of the men in their lives, both
women resisted using their magical abilities freely, especially if use occurred at
the expense of the men's masculine egos. Some differences did emerge between
the programs and their methods of negotiating women's power. Samantha, for
example, generally did not use magic to do the dishes or make meals and often
used her witch skills to undo the meddling into her marriage of her more radical and less femininely assimilable mother, Endora. However, few episodes went
by that did not show Samantha saving her husband, Darren, from making a fool
of himself with his boss or clients. Jeannie, by contrast, was generally inept at
housewifely duties and, while she called Major Anthony Nelson (the man who
freed her from her bottle and with whom she lived) "master," she generally did
not hesitate to use her magic whenever she felt it appropriate. Again, though,

with emphasis on balance and containment, Jeannie's magic was always performed in the service of Major Nelson, never for her own pleasure or independence, and her costuming and dependent role identified her as a sexual object. Thus, in both programs, we see evidence that some women of the '60s were gaining power and prominence but also that this change could easily be contained by women's willingness to obey patriarchal authority.

The late '60s also gave us a speculative representation of "empowered" womanhood beyond the boundaries of domesticity: the futuristic space traveler Uhura of *Star Trek*. Here we see not only gender but racial difference addressed, and *Trek* has been credited with bringing more women viewers to the genre of science fiction than any other individual text. Uhura represented the ideal of women finding meaningful work outside of marriage and family and the potential for Blacks, and Black women in particular, to participate fully in the achieved promises of the American Dream. Yet, of course, "fully" is in many ways an overstatement. Uhura served primarily as a receptionist aboard the *Starship Enterprise,* and her role never grew significantly, even as the '60s television series moved to the big screen in the numerous *Star Trek* films of the late '70s and '80s featuring the original cast. That part of Uhura's role was to satisfy the male gaze is evident in her repeated placement in the visible background of the ship's bridge, sitting in silence, her go-go boot–clad legs exposed all the way up to her micro-miniskirt. Though Uhura may have superficially represented the successes of the Civil Rights era, she was clearly placed within what cultural critic Herman Gray identifies as assimilationist discourse (85–86): Uhura was the only Black woman on board, and issues of ethnic difference and/or racism were displaced via the series' science fictional format onto alien species difference (often through the character of Mr. Spock, who was portrayed by a white—if Jewish American—actor). *Trek* thus illustrates, as Barbara Omolade argues, that

> [s]cience fiction films record and mirror the white man's vision of future life [. . .] in which he has assigned himself centrality and placed people of color at the periphery and margins. [. . .] In this future world people of color will have been divested of their cultures and disconnected from their communities. Women of color will be like Lieutenant Uhura, communications specialist of the Starship Enterprise under Captain James Kirk, functioning within the culture and machines of Western man. (203)

Though *Bewitched, I Dream of Jeannie,* and *Star Trek* are forms of programming with differing agendas and representational styles, together they exemplify well the promises and limitations of '60s speculative television for women. Similar programs that followed in the '70s, such as *Wonder Woman* and *The Bionic Woman,* continued the ambiguity of entertainment television's gendered representations. These superwoman programs did follow *Star Trek*'s lead in removing women from the domestic sphere and offered even more, portraying female heroes as wielding both physical and intellectual power. Yet these later series also relied on the containment features of sexual objectification, white dominance, heteronormativity, and obedience to white male authority. Through these tumultuous political decades, then, we see that while television fantasy can be used to challenge the boundaries of lived experience through speculative metaphors (such as the female djinn, witch, space adventurer, and superhero), to display female potentialities, and/or to address patriarchal structures that oppress women, such strategies may simultaneously labor to contain the radicalness of the challenge, encouraging the praise of many viewers and critics while leaving the actual status of women unchanged.

As compromised as '60s and early to mid '70s representations of women in U.S. science fiction and fantasy television were, the late '70s and much of the '80s offered even less. The *Star Wars* films did continue the "plucky" but compromised heroine theme (through Princess Leia), but this big-screen phenomenon did not affect the small screen's offerings significantly. A few years later, film began a new trend of female representation within the science fiction genre, marked by tough, buns-of-steel heroines, such as Sigourney Weaver's Ellen Ripley and Linda Hamilton's Sarah Connor of the *Aliens* and *Terminator* series, respectively. However, the small screen centered on the prime-time soap opera and male-dominated action-adventure series. The speculative programming that did air at this time shifted from single-character vehicles, such as *Wonder Woman* and *The Six-Million Dollar Man,* to ensemble casts, with white men always leading the way. The women of *Battlestar Gallactica* and *Buck Rogers,* for example, are hardly memorable.

The most significant speculative television event for women in the '80s was *Star Trek: The Next Generation* (TNG). Here, again, the white male-dominated ensemble cast strategy held sway, yet TNG did offer multiple women to replace the more obvious tokenism of the original *Star Trek.* Though I can clearly remember deep personal disappointment when the cast first appeared on the screen with a white male captain and first officer, *again,* TNG did offer a female head of security, a female chief medical officer, and a female counselor. Though all these women were young, thin, "beautiful," heterosexual, and white, they did at least suggest that women would emerge as more than receptionists in this brave new era of *Trek's* high-tech militarized future. Nevertheless, the degree to which the female characters of TNG fulfilled traditional feminine roles rendered their presence sadly typical of television's compromised fantastic women. Tough Chief Security Officer Tasha Yar lasted only a season, yielding her position to the more easily assimilable Black warrior stereotype of the Klingon Worf. Dr. Crusher may have been chief medical officer, but she also well exemplified the role of woman as nurturer and healer. Counselor Troi, meanwhile, enabled the dominant white men of the series to neglect their emotions as she felt everything for them, and she clearly fulfilled the role of sexualized object in her corseted and clingy dresses and pantsuits. And the token Black woman of TNG, Whoopi Goldberg's Guinan, may have challenged beauty norms and given advice to the captain as she served drinks and managed the ship's bar, but she remained entirely outside the chain of command and emerged as more Mammy than empowered alien.[3]

Now that we have entered a new millennium, it is important to ask what science fiction and fantasy television have done for us lately. Did the '90s offer any challenge to or complications of past speculative televisual images of women? Certainly, as the scope of this collection's eleven chapters makes plain, the '90s did offer a wider array of fantastic women than ever before and none remains solely in the domestic sphere as wives or mothers (in fact, most are single). By the sheer number of science fiction and fantasy series featuring women in primary roles in the '90s, we can conclude that the tokenism of the past has given way to a recognition of a significant and appreciative audience for speculative programming that includes images of strong, independent women. However, how celebratory we should be as viewers requires a greater depth of examination of these images and programs. Though we now have female warriors, ship's captains, witches, aliens, and superheroes, they remain overwhelmingly white (or at least portrayed by white actresses), heterosexual, and silent on such issues as class disenfranchisement. To be sure, even speculative programming is far more about the present than the future—it is descriptive rather than predictive. Yet, even as description, recent science fiction and fantasy television has retained much of the focus of earlier television (realist or fantastic) on women who are young, white, "beautiful," heterosexual, and economically comfortable. Does it give us anything more?

In addressing this question, we must take the particular cultural context of '90s America into careful consideration. Unlike the 1970s, the word *feminism* will hardly be seen on television (not that it was often seen even back then), yet an assumption that women can succeed in traditional male occupations and roles is plain. (*Xena: Warrior Princess* provides an antidote to the traditional dominance of the male action-adventure hero, for example, while *The X-Files* makes clear that women can be objective, rational professionals.) And, unlike the "backlash" era of the 1980s in which feminism was openly attacked as irrelevant and/or dangerous to women's (and men's) lives, television now more openly offers the "freedom" to question past representations (as a series such as *Lois and Clark: The New Adventures of Superman* invites). Furthermore, offering role models to America's white, middle-class, female youth has become a profitable marketing opportunity (as the popularity of *Buffy the Vampire Slayer* and *Sabrina, the Teenage Witch* illustrates). In addition, there is another quintessentially '90s lens through which to interpret the dominance and success of female-centered speculative programming: the "Don't Ask, Don't Tell" politics of the early Clinton era.

Though the president's sexual exploits, possible criminal activities (some regarding sexual harassment and even rape), impeachment hearings, and role in military actions (such as those involving Iraq, Bosnia, and Kosovo) may come to dominate interpretations of his role in American history, Clinton's early attempts to initiate liberal social reforms (alongside his pro-corporate stance, as seen in his pushing of NAFTA) offer a significant lens through which to understand U.S. cultural politics in the 1990s. Most relevant for an interpretation of the role of women in science fiction and fantasy television of the era is what has come to be called a politics of "Don't Ask, Don't Tell," an early '90s sound bite indicating the compromise made surrounding the issue of gays in the military. As conservative and reactionary voices from within and outside the military swarmed over the president's push to increase superficial tolerance for diversity of sexual orientation within the armed forces, he modified his position until we were left with a policy that allows gays to serve in the military as long as they do not declare their sexual orientation. Ultimately, nothing really changed: homosexuals have always served in the military in closeted form. Nevertheless, many interpreted the "Don't Ask, Don't Tell" stance as an appearance of greater tolerance for difference.

This construction of "change" (sameness reconstructed to appear as progressive shift) arguably dominates American televisual representations of women in the '90s, both realist and fantastic. For example, in the generally realist realm we have *Ally McBeal,* a young, white, middle-class woman lawyer who illustrates the excitement and stresses of being a respected professional in a competitive field. The program makes use of fantasy moments to comment on her struggles (as when, in one episode, she agonizes of feeling "cut off at the knees" by a judge's decision, and we see this literalized on her body, as she stands in the courtroom with no legs from the knees down). Yet Ally also exemplifies the lack of changes in women's lives in the past few decades, for she is young, anorexically thin, obsessed with her looks, and desperate for men's attention. Finding dates and selecting the right outfit are generally of far greater concern to Ally than her role in attaining justice in the courtroom.

Similarly, in the realm of speculative television, women's intellectual, technical, and/or physical skills may pale in comparison to the way they wear their costumes. Xena's leather corset and Buffy's revealing clothes and incessant hairstyle changes (toward ever greater blondeness) exemplify this well. Such change-without-out-change can also be seen through readings of multiple female character clusters, as found in *Star Trek: Voyager,* for example. Here the strong and empowered older white female Captain Janeway and bispecies female crew member of color B'Elanna Torres have failed to ensure the series' popularity as has newer crew member Seven of Nine, the blonde female cyborg in skin-tight catsuit.

Generally speaking, the late '90s offered some of the most developed and compelling (if contradictory and sometimes even reactionary) televisual representations of gender politics and debates over (and within) feminism. Yet U.S. media culture at the millennium is dominated by superficial applause for liberal tolerance combined with an abhorrence of dogma, labels, or presumed restrictions on behavior (as seen in the glorification of "political incorrectness," for instance). The '90s was about retro-style and postfeminism, about celebrating the return of the smiley face and the bell-bottom and proclamations of "girl power" to substitute for the deeper politics of rebellion of the Civil Rights, Vietnam, and (second-wave) Women's Movement eras. With such constellations in mind, the representational style best suited to the media culture of the '90s is therefore one that offers superficial tolerance without deeper commitment and uses subtext or indirection to avoid appearances of authoritarianism. As the "out" episodes of the sitcom *Ellen* and the series' quick demise thereafter demonstrated so well, direct representations of progressive politics are a '90s no-no, even if this is the era of "lesbian chic." *Xena: Warrior Princess,* with its ancient fantasy setting and "optional" lesbian subtext, is what sells.

In many ways, of course, this cultural moment is similar to the representational politics of television throughout broadcast history. Producers' goals are to ensure advertising dollars by alienating as few viewers as possible and targeting specific audiences by appealing to their tastes/politics without pushing the boundaries too far. However, television (like all mass media) must negotiate the particular cultural mood of the era to do so. In terms of gender representation and feminist concerns, the '90s was a decade of careful arbitration of '70s activism and '80s backlash. Science fiction and fantasy programming with strong central female characters is one of the most important media results of this arbitration. From the distancing devices of alternate time frames or alien worlds to the display of contained superpowers, the women of '90s speculative television articulate more suggestively than any other group of character types the cultural mood of '90s America.

In the following chapters, the contributors to this volume examine the gender politics of the diverse-yet-connected offerings of '90s U.S. science fiction and fantasy television and draw some tentative conclusions about what speculative genres offer viewers, especially those invested in a more egalitarian, just, feminist future. The book is organized by the general sites of excursion for the various programs: the present, the future, and fantasy realms. In part I, "Speculating on the Present," authors Projansky and Vande Berg, Matthews and Mendlesohn, Badley, and Wilcox examine the gender politics of series that rely on generally realist, present-day scenarios with specific speculative elements. Sarah Projansky and Leah R. Vande Berg study *Sabrina, the Teenage Witch* to draw conclusions about the ways in which potentially subversive power is contained by traditional feminine norms within the program. Nicole Matthews and Farah Mendlesohn investigate the function and limitations of gender play and performance through the alien mind/gendered human body split in *Third Rock from the Sun.* Linda Badley challenges the popular notion that *The X-Files'* Scully represents the height of feminist television representations of women through a study of the series' reliance on more compromised postfeminist and cyborg feminist/posthumanist politics. And Rhonda V. Wilcox argues that, though the character of Lois received top billing in *Lois and Clark: The New Adventures of Superman,* the series ultimately preserved inequality because the apparently lesser office partner, the male, is mythically the superior member of the duo.

In part II, "Dabbling in the Fantastic," authors Royer, Helford, Ono, and Barr look at programs centered in speculative realms that, despite great differences in premise and setting, establish a similar containment of women. Jessica A. Royer takes readers on an adventure into the white, male-dominated space of *Mystery*

Science Theater 3000 to discover that the humorous '90s voice-over commentary offered by the series' characters serves mainly to further control and condemn the women of the '50s and '60s films screened in the series. Elyce Rae Helford critiques feminist and queer enthusiasm for *Xena: Warrior Princess* through an argument that reads stereotypical butch/femme typing as responsible for turning demonstrations of female power into domestic violence. Kent A. Ono offers a reading of *Buffy the Vampire Slayer* that rejects the superficial girl power message of the series to address its racist marginalization of characters of color. And Marleen S. Barr draws skeptical conclusions about the "color-blind" positions presented in Disney's 1997 remake of Rogers and Hammerstein's *Cinderella*.

In part III, "Projecting a Future," authors Roberts, Ney and Sciog-Lazarov, and Kanar investigate the feminist promises of science fiction television's future worlds of women scientists, ship's captains, and alien diplomats. Robin A. Roberts applauds the promise of a cooperative feminist science in the racially significant relations among female characters of *Star Trek: Voyager.* Sharon Ney and Elaine M. Sciog-Lazarov examine the gender politics of *Babylon 5* to discover that beneath the competence and independence of the series' powerful women lurks a definition of feminine gender identity firmly rooted in and subordinate to the superior male. Finally, Hanley E. Kanar makes plain that the utopian *Trek* future ineffectively masks an oppressive gendered politics of disability through a close reading of the *Deep Space Nine* episode "Melora."

What may be the most compelling aspect of this collection is how the chapters speak to trends within '90s feminist criticism and to each other. For example, multiple chapters address such "hot" topics as girl power (Projansky and Vande Berg, Helford, and Ono), postfeminism (Projansky and Vande Berg, Badley, and Helford), gender play/performance (Mendlesohn and Matthews, Helford), and feminist science (Badley and Roberts). Key themes also echo among chapters, such as sexuality (in most chapters, but especially Mendlesohn and Matthews, Badley, Helford, and Ney and Sciog-Lazarov), the relationship of gender and race (Ono and Barr), and the status of women in the workplace (Badley and Wilcox). In addition to shared emphases, there is also striking diversity among the chapters, including focuses on recent theories of cyborg feminism and posthumanism (Badley), queerness (Helford), neocolonialism (Ono), and disability (Kanar).

Of course, readers will necessarily find that not all of their favorite science fiction and fantasy television series of the '90s are covered within this collection. Some programs only began their first season as this collection was being produced; thus, there is no chapter on *Charmed* or *Farscape,* for example. Simply put, this collection has been assembled to bring together the most thought-provoking and well-written pieces I could find on significant U.S. science fiction and fantasy programming of the '90s that features central women characters and/or foregrounds gender issues. My contributors and I must leave to other writers and other books the task of addressing the series, characters, and issues we have necessarily neglected. Ultimately, all we do offer aims to provide ample critical food for thought for scholars, teachers, students, and fans invested in reading the "trivial" spaces of entertainment television with an eye on understanding the powerful political ways in which media culture affects our daily lives and worldviews.

NOTES

1. See Spigel, 152–154.
2. See Douglas, 126–138.
3. For more on women and *TNG*, see Harrison et al., *Enterprise Zones: Critical Positions on Star Trek*, especially chapters by Projansky, Hastie, and Barr.

WORKS CITED

Douglas, Susan J. *Where the Girls Are: Growing Up Female with the Mass Media.* New York: Random House, 1995.

Gray, Herman. *Watching Race: Television and the Struggle for "Blackness."* Minneapolis: University of Minnesota Press, 1995.

Harrison, Taylor, Sarah Projansky, Kent A. Ono, and Elyce Rae Helford, eds. *Enterprise Zones: Critical Positions on Star Trek.* Boulder, Colo.: Westview Press, 1996.

Mulvey, Laura. "Visual Pleasure and Narrative Cinema." *Screen* 16, no. 3 (1975): 6–18. Reprinted in *The Sexual Subject: A Screen Reader in Sexuality.* Edited by John Caughie, Annette Kuhn, Mandy Merck, and Barbara Creed. London: Routledge, 1992, 22–34.

Omolade, Barbara. *The Rising Song of African American Women.* New York: Routledge, 1994.

Spigel, Lynn. *Make Room for TV: Television and the Family Ideal in Postwar America.* Chicago: University of Chicago Press, 1992.

Part I

Speculating on the Present

1

Sabrina, the Teenage . . . ?

Girls, Witches, Mortals, and the Limitations of Prime-Time Feminism

Sarah Projansky and Leah R. Vande Berg

> *I have to be a witch. I have to be a mortal. I have to be a teenager, and I have to be a girl all at the same time. That's what's the matter!*
>
> —Sabrina, in "Sabrina through the Looking Glass"

> *Adolescence is a time of epistemological crisis.*
>
> —Gilligan, Ward, Taylor, and Bardige (viii)

According to Lyn Mikel Brown and Carol Gilligan, during adolescence girls experience increased uncertainty and loss of confidence and self-esteem while looking to their social environment for guidance and information. As Carol Gilligan puts it, "Girls' initiation or passage into adulthood in a world psychologically rooted and historically anchored in the experiences of powerful men marks the beginning of self-doubt and the dawning of the realization, no matter how fleeting, that womanhood will require a dissociative split between experience and what is generally taken to be reality" (xxi). Indeed, only 47 percent of the 272,000 teens[1] in a 1998 *USA Weekend* survey reported feeling really good about themselves, only 25 percent were satisfied with their looks, and 42 percent had friends who either had tried to commit suicide or had discussed committing suicide (Baldwin and Schoen, 1, 8).

Lisa L. Duke and Peggy J. Kreshel explain that during adolescence young women are bombarded with social messages, many of which come through the media, about the traditional ideal feminine role. According to Martin S. Fiebert, this role has four dimensions: fulfilling cultural standards of beauty and fashion, performing domestic/family skills, caring for and satisfying the needs of others, and acquiring male attention. In her best-selling book, *Reviving Ophelia: Saving the Selves of Adolescent Girls,* Mary Pipher makes a similar argument: she suggests that in order to "revive" troubled girls "we" (i.e., parents, mothers, and teachers) need to help girls transition into a feminine adulthood without losing a cohesive sense of self that presumably characterizes their preadolescent, pre-media culture lives.

Other recent scholarship on girls, however, is less worried about media culture and less pessimistic about the fate of the female adolescent as she approaches adulthood. Lyn Mikel Brown, for example, looks at girls' anger rather than girls' despair and argues that working-class girls in particular are able to maintain a commitment to their own sense of self and experience of the world, despite media and teachers that, she argues, address them as troubled, yet idealized, feminine subjects. The most recent report commissioned by the National Council for Research on Women takes a similar perspective: it points out that most "research on girls [. . .] has focused on risks and negative trends, rather than exploring positive aspects of their lives" (Phillips, xii) and, in response, offers a more balanced analysis of girls' experiences. For example, the report points out that "Girls themselves are venturing into new realms—developing curricula, starting their own teen magazines, creating their own websites, becoming peer advocates, and engaging in political activity in their communities and beyond" (2).

Regardless of their differing conclusions, each of these studies works with the assumption that, as Sandra L. Bartky notes, "the disciplinary power that inscribes femininity in the female body is everywhere and it is nowhere; the disciplinarian is everyone and yet no one in particular" (74).[2] Each of these studies also suggests that among the most pervasive and relentless sites of discipline are media images, regardless of how girls respond to those images. For example, Duke and Kreshel's study of girl readers (ages 12–13) of teen magazines *Seventeen, Sassy, YM,* and *Teen* found that while the girls actively interacted with these media texts in negotiating the meanings of some of the magazines' messages, these girls "were effectively being taught through magazine content to analyze their bodies and identify ways in which they deviate from the ideal" (65) and also to accept as "just the way it is" the "magazines' sexist convention of having boys communicate as voices of authority without providing a similar forum in which girls could voice their opinions about boys" (67).[3]

Contemporary culture provides depictions not only of femininity generally, but also of *girls,* in particular. The fact that some of the research we discuss here has achieved economic success, such as *Reviving Ophelia*'s multiple-month stint on the *New York Times* best-seller list, is one indication of a contemporary intensification of a cultural fascination with girls. In *Reviving Ophelia*'s case, a study of the relationship between damaging and demanding media images of girls, ironically, has ended up contributing to the proliferation of those images through its own mass-marketing and subsequent cultural references to the figure of "Ophelia" as a typical, troubled contemporary girl. Like the *USA Weekend* survey we cite here, *Reviving Ophelia* is part of a set of media texts that depicts adolescent girls as endangered.

The recent explosion of television shows about girls is another illustration of a general cultural fascination with girls. In addition to *Sabrina, the Teenage Witch* (hereafter *Sabrina*), recent television series include *Buffy the Vampire Slayer; The Secret World of Alex Mack; Clarissa Explains It All; The Mystery Files of Shelby Woo; The Adventures of Shirley Holmes: Detective; Clueless; Sister, Sister; Two of a Kind; My So-Called Life; Moesha;* and *Daria.* In film we have seen *Harriet the Spy, Matilda,* and the rerelease of *The Wizard of Oz.* Furthermore, in *Newsweek,* Nadya Labi reports that "by some estimates, more than 60 teen-oriented movies are in production or active development, many of them with seriously empowered heroines" (61). Thus, the general contemporary anxiety about and representation of girls that we describe here is one context in which *Sabrina* can be understood. From this perspective, we examine the series in order to explore the particular version or versions of teenage girl identity that it offers.

Another context within which we can understand the teenage girl identities that *Sabrina* offers is what both Judith Mayne and Bonnie J. Dow have termed "prime-time feminism." As these and other scholars have shown, 1980s and 1990s television has made particular aspects of feminism ubiquitous: it has drawn on ideals of equality, inclusion, and "free" choice to define a contemporary moment in which women have achieved various feminist goals and thus in which feminist activism is supposedly no longer necessary. From this critical perspective, feminism is absorbed and supplanted by "postfeminism" in such a way that the complexity of contemporary feminist theories and activisms is lost.[4]

As the popular press constantly claims and as we argue here, *Sabrina* draws on and contributes to these kinds of representations of feminism. For example, Susan Orlean argues that Sabrina "is independent, spunky, friendly with boys but not obsequious toward them, moderately athletic, unabashedly sentimental, and assertive in the way that only girls who have grown up taking feminism for granted are able to be" (54). Also claiming the 1990s as a particularly feminist moment, Susan Spillman quotes Paula Hart (an executive producer of *Sabrina* and the mother of Melissa Joan Hart, who plays Sabrina) as saying that *Sabrina* differs from the earlier television show *Bewitched* because "Samantha [of *Bewitched*] had to use her magic on the sly, while Sabrina is encouraged by her aunts to use hers to the fullest" (28). Likewise, Debbie Stoller draws on the concept of "girl power" in discussing *Sabrina* in relation to *Buffy the Vampire Slayer, Xena: Warrior Princess,* and *The Secret World of Alex Mack.* Taking a particularly optimistic tone, Stoller writes that "these characters all share a common strength: the ability to leap over sexist stereotypes in a single bound" (42). She argues that these shows "are hinting that there's a wellspring of untapped girl power out there, with the potential to change the world if it could only be released. You go, girls" (45). The photograph that accompanies Orlean's article also invites this interpretation of *Sabrina* and Melissa Joan Hart: it pictures Hart and her mother wearing matching leather jackets and baseball caps printed with the words "girls RULE" (54).[5]

Moreover, Orlean links this version of feminism to *Sabrina*'s popularity.

Sabrina, the Teenage Witch is shown Fridays at nine o'clock on ABC, and this year [the 1997–1998 television season] the network also broadcasts a re-run on Fridays at eight. The nine-o'clock *Sabrina* is watched by more young women, teens, and little kids than any other television program in that time slot, and [as of May 1998] both the eight-o'clock and the nine-o'clock episodes rank in the top-ten shows among all kids. For millions of people, the embodiment of modern girlhood is Sabrina the Teenage Witch. (54)

The popularity of the series (which leads in the ratings for girls 12–17 and is fourth among boys that age),[6] the common suggestion in popular discourse that Sabrina offers feminism to today's teens, and our anecdotal experience with teens and young women who tell us that they "just love Sabrina" prompted us to undertake this analysis of the first two seasons (1996–1998) of the series' network run. Specifically, we believe that *Sabrina*'s location at the intersection of two central aspects of contemporary media culture—a fascination with girls and the incorporation of (some aspects of) feminism—marks it as a particularly important text for understanding what versions of femininity (what *kind* of gendered identity) and feminism (what *kind* of liberatory discourse) are marketed to girls.

Keeping in mind the complexity and intensity of girls' relationships with popular culture (which we briefly discuss earlier), we resist making a definitive argument about *Sabrina*. Rather, we approach the series as feminist critics actively looking for any feminist aspects of the text we can find, but also asking how the text contains or undermines other aspects or versions of feminism. Through our analysis, we argue that the text offers empowering representations of independent girls who have access to equality and engage in cross-gender behavior *and* that it simultaneously contains those representations within narratives that emphasize beauty, male attention, and taking responsibility for others. Through these multiple meanings, the series offers a version of feminism that seeks to value women and disempower gender categories, while simultaneously using narrative and costume to locate this version of feminism within a traditionally feminine world. Thus, we argue that there is a *tension* between feminism and containment in the text, rather than that one *overshadows* the other.[7] Finally, in the last section, we look more closely at the *kind* of feminism that is offered through the text, arguing that it is often race- and class-privilege that allow Sabrina to resist the series' containment of her independence. Thus, the prime-time feminism of the text is simultaneously antifeminist from the perspective of much contemporary feminist activism and theorizing that Ella Shohat, for example, defines as polycentric multicultural feminism.

SABRINA, THE TEENAGE WITCH: AN OVERVIEW

The made-for-cable movie *Sabrina, the Teenage Witch* premiered on the Showtime cable channel in April 1996.[8] The following September, the series *Sabrina* premiered on network television as part of ABC's "TGIF" Friday night lineup. The show centers around events in the life of the title character, sixteen-year-old Sabrina Spellman, who lives with her two aunts, Hilda (a concert violinist) and Zelda (a scientist), both of whom are witches. Sabrina's parents are divorced and appear only rarely on the series. Her father, also a witch, lives in "the other realm," and her mother, a mortal archaeologist, is on an extended dig in South America.

The series' pilot opens on the morning of Sabrina's sixteenth birthday, with her aunts watching her unconsciously levitate in her sleep. Initially, she finds their birthday gift—a small black cauldron—rather odd, but she attributes it to her aunts' eccentricity. When she returns from school, however, Sabrina finds a family birthday party awaiting her. Her big present is an old book. She opens it and discovers that her father "lives" in this book. Her aunts tell her that she and they are witches, that her father and their cat Salem (who is doing a one-hundred-year penance as a witches' familiar for trying to take over the world) are also witches, and that her mother is a mortal. Furthermore, Sabrina learns that she is not allowed to see her mortal mother until after she gets her "witch's license," otherwise her mother will turn into a ball of wax. While this fact does not explain why Sabrina does not live with her father, it does help to naturalize her aunts' custody of her.

In addition to her regular interactions with her aunts and Salem, Sabrina spends a great deal of time with mortals, including her best friends, Jenny (in the first season) and Valerie (in the second season), and her boyfriend, Harvey. She also has an enemy at school, Libby, a vain and self-involved cheerleader who enjoys taunting Sabrina. Several teachers at school have occasional recurring roles, but Sabrina interacts most often with her vice principal, Mr. Kraft, who is self-serving and inevitably takes Libby's side over Sabrina's. Much to Hilda's dismay, he also has a crush on her and pursues her in several episodes.

All of the characters we have mentioned so far are white. In fact, Sabrina's entire world—in both the mortal and the other realm—is overwhelmingly populated with white characters. Generally, when people of color appear on the show, they are guest stars. During the second season, however, African American men play two characters from Sabrina's world of magic. The first to appear is her Quiz Master, who arrives from time to time to test Sabrina as she prepares for receiving her witch's license. Toward the end of the second season, Sabrina begins to date Dash, a young man who, like Sabrina, has one mortal and one witch parent. At the beginning of the third season, Sabrina chooses Harvey over Dash as her steady boyfriend. Dash subsequently leaves the show, thereby maintaining the centrality of whiteness in the series.

Most episodes take place, at least in part, in the Spellman's large Victorian home, at Sabrina's school, or in the Slicery, a local teen hangout. Sabrina's magic, however, takes her to a variety of other locations throughout the series, including the other realm. There she often confronts the witches council, headed by Drell (played by Penn Jillette of Penn and Teller). Sabrina and her aunts access the other realm through their upstairs linen closet.

LIVING IN A FEMINIST WORLD

Sabrina's feminist world includes both gender equality and the crossing of gender and sexuality boundaries. She both expects and is committed to undifferentiated treatment of women and men, girls and boys. Furthermore, Sabrina is open to play and pleasure that depends on both magic and her gender-blind worldview. Her aunts are supportive role models, encouraging her in both contexts.

Independence and Equality

"Inna-Gadda-Sabrina"[9] has perhaps the most numerous explicit references to Sabrina's feminist perspective. In this episode, Sabrina and her entire world time-travel back to the 1960s, where she confronts and challenges a series of sexist experiences. For example, at a college fair at her school, a representative from the college she had been considering attending when she was still in the 1990s informs her that she cannot attend in the 1960s because they do not accept women. Sabrina argues against the policy. In another 1960s scene, Valerie hitches up her skirt after the teacher who has been measuring its length walks away. When Sabrina suggests that wearing jeans might be easier, Valerie replies that girls never wear pants to school. Later, Sabrina mentions to Valerie that she is the editor of the school newspaper, to which Valerie replies that that is not possible because she is a girl. Even Harvey, who is particularly accepting and encouraging of Sabrina's independence in the present and in every other episode, calls her "my lady" when he is trapped in the 1960s. He also tells her she does not need a college education; instead, he suggests that they travel across the country together in his van. Sabrina is not interested, and in fact, she refers to Harvey's attitude as a reason for her aunts to help them all return to the present. This episode endorses a view of feminism that includes equal access to education and freedom of choice in fashion. Furthermore, that Sabrina is surprised by these examples of discrimination in the 1960s implies that they no longer exist for her in the 1990s.

In this episode, and in the series generally, discrimination—whether on the basis of gender or something else—is often criticized through humor and irony. For example, in "Jenny's Non-Dream" the man who comes to fix the other-realm clothes dryer happens to have a tail. Sabrina expresses surprise, but her aunts tell her not to be a "rumpist": someone who judges others by their rear ends.

Discrimination against witches, in particular, can be understood as discrimination against women who challenge social norms (Becker-Cantarino, 169–170). In addition, however, in this series discrimination against witches often stands in for discrimination against lesbians and gays. For example, in "A Halloween Story," when Sabrina gets a Halloween gift of being able to see one person of her choice who is now dead, she chooses her grandmother. When she tells her mortal grandmother that she now knows she is a witch, her grand-mother responds, "Well, dear, as long as you're happy"—an idealized response to a child's disclosure that she or he is lesbian or gay to a parent or grandparent. This association of lesbian and gay closeting/coming out with being a witch is even more explicit in "To Tell a Mortal." In this episode, Sabrina has the opportunity to tell one mortal that she is a witch because it is a special holiday: Friday the 13th. Her aunts caution her not to take advantage of this opportunity (even though the person she tells will lose the new knowledge after one day) because she may be unhappy with her friend's response. Sabrina, however, decides to tell Valerie because, as she says, she wants to "come out of the linen closet." As is typical for the series, Valerie and Harvey (to whom Valerie tells Sabrina's secret) not only accept Sabrina, but love her for who she is. Furthermore, when Libby (who overhears Valerie telling Harvey that Sabrina is a witch) attempts to make a spectacle out of Sabrina by bringing the news media to her house, Valerie and Harvey lie to protect Sabrina by denying that she is a witch.[10] This episode illustrates how the series raises the possibility of discrimination—against witches/homosexuals—but then emphasizes the pervasiveness of acceptance and equality in Sabrina's world.

Sabrina often not only articulates a feminist or antidiscrimination position, but she also draws on her experiences of equality to enact self-confident and independent behavior that specifically represents girls/women as powerful. For example, in "The Troll Bride" Sabrina ends up saving herself from her own captivity, in contrast to the sexist narrative line of male rescue in traditional fairy tales. In this episode, when Sabrina cannot find her biology notes, she goes to her magic book and calls up the Finder of Lost Things, a troll named Roland. Desperate to find her notes for the upcoming final exam, she quickly signs a contract that (she finds out later) says that if Roland finds them for her, he can have anything in the room. He does, and he picks her. Roland holds Sabrina captive in his tower while he and a professional wedding planner arrange his wedding to Sabrina. Meanwhile, her ever-resourceful aunts hire an other-realm lawyer who discovers that Sabrina can be rescued by a prince she desires, so they send her mortal boyfriend, Harvey (whose dad's business sobriquet "The Termite King" makes Harvey the "Termite Prince"). Harvey arrives and fights with Roland. When, rather than saving Sabrina, he ends up about to be run through with a sword, Sabrina drops her biology books on Roland and thus saves herself (and Harvey).

Contrasts between Sabrina and other girls and boys, both mortal and magical, highlight Sabrina's self-confident feminist attributes. One recurring contrast in the series is between Sabrina and Libby. Libby is a rich, shallow, selfish cheerleader. She calls Sabrina and Jenny "freaks" during the first season and Sabrina and Valerie "freaks" during the second season, torments other students who do not "fit"—like the intellectual members of the science club ("Geek Like Me")—and steals a teacher's diamond ring and plants it on Sabrina to get her in trouble

Sabrina saves herself and Harvey from Roland in "The
Troll Bride."

("As Westbridge Turns"). In contrast, Sabrina constantly tries to help others, often through her magic. While her use of magic only makes things worse if she is helping others avoid facing their fears, anxieties, pitfalls, seeming social inadequacies, or any other of life's problems, such turns of events end up forcing her friends to confront their problems. In these episodes, whether or not her magic works, Sabrina not only functions as an idealized caring and giving person, but she also ends up helping others become stronger and more self-confident as a result. For example, in "Terrible Things" Sabrina arranges for Jenny to win the class president election, only to have Jenny learn that she cannot make a real difference. Sabrina also causes a minor accident to Harvey's competitor so that Harvey gets selected for the first string of the football team, only to have Harvey get crushed in the game. Both Jenny and Harvey learn that they do not need the mark of status they thought they desired.

Again, in contrast to her friends Jenny and Valerie (and in stark contrast to her enemy Libby), Sabrina is generally less concerned with feminine than with feminist matters. For example, "Sabrina through the Looking Glass" sharply contrasts Sabrina's and Harvey's academically focused meeting in the school library to discuss their science project with Jenny's feminine concerns over appearance when Jenny rushes up with a burning question for Sabrina: Should she cut her hair? Likewise, in "Dummy for Love," while Sabrina is concerned about freedom of speech issues surrounding her editorial against the sports obsession in the school (which Mr. Kraft first indirectly pressures and then orders her to retract), Valerie is obsessed with getting a date with Kirk. At their hallway lockers, Valerie explains to Sabrina, "I know my mother says I'm too dramatic, but this time I'm serious. If I don't talk to Kirk soon, I will not be able to take in another breath." Then, later, after Sabrina has used her magic to call on Cupid to help Valerie, Valerie rushes up to Sabrina in the lunchroom and gushes, "You'll never guess who just asked me out—Kirk! [. . .] I'm so excited I can't eat. I can't even sit down. I think I'm gonna throw up."

Sabrina's adult female role models normalize her general assumption of gender equality and her antidiscrimination perspective. All these women are independent professionals who encourage Sabrina to follow their examples. Her mother, an archaeologist, is quite happy to be pursuing her career interests and to leave the raising of her daughter to Zelda and Hilda. Despite their more domestic role as "Sabrina's parents," these aunts are strong, capable, powerful, professional, and successful women. Particularly for Zelda, episodes repeatedly emphasize the importance of women's careers. In various episodes, Zelda either talks about physics or actually engages in giving a physics lecture, having a scientific breakthrough, enjoying her scientific research, hoping for a Nobel prize, curing common allergies, and encouraging Sabrina in her own math and science abilities. Indeed, in almost every episode we see Zelda working out some theoretical problem on her computer. In the second season she not only has a laptop computer, but she also has an even more powerful magical "labtop" in which she concocts various magical/scientific potions. Hilda also regularly talks about enjoying her music. She tries out for and sometimes gets positions with professional orchestras, and she is committed enough to her career to take a job playing nonclassical music in a restaurant when she is temporarily unable to gain a position with an orchestra.

Beyond their professions, the aunts specifically articulate feminist ideals and demonstrate through their words and actions (both magical and mortal) that women indeed are powerful and smart and have a right to use all their powers (magical or not) fully. "Meeting Dad's Girlfriend" provides an example of the series' use of these powerful women's ironic, humorous comments to critique traditional gender notions and to affirm feminist perspectives. The episode opens with first Sabrina, next Hilda, and then Zelda each struggling unsuccessfully for a few moments to open a spaghetti sauce jar. When Zelda, too, fails to open the jar, she comments, "You know it's great having supernatural powers, but for some things we could really use a man around the house." Hilda grimaces at this and says nothing, but later when she tries again to open the jar and Zelda tells her, "Give it up. Ted [Sabrina's father] will be here soon and he'll open it," Hilda cannot let this blatantly sexist statement go unchallenged. "Why?" Hilda asks, "Because he's a man?" When Zelda says, "Well, yes," Hilda retorts, "That is *so* sexist!" Zelda, the scientist, then adopts a defensive posture, and asserts, "Men happen to have more upper-body strength than women." The text does not allow this claim to stand for long, however. When Sabrina's father arrives, he, too, struggles to open the jar. When Sabrina comments, "You've been working on that jar for two hours!" Hilda then takes the opportunity to point out to Zelda and Sabrina, "See, men aren't stronger. They just keep trying longer than any sane woman would." Here, Hilda not only uses evidence to disprove Zelda's "scientific" claim, but she does so while articulating an argument about culturally (as opposed to biologically) produced gender behavior.

Even though the aunts sometimes initially express a lack of confidence, as Hilda does when she tries out for the first chair of the symphony, they soon regain their self-assurance. Only occasionally, and then only temporarily, do they express any reluctance about using their particular gifts (magic) to gain an advantage. Thus, these story lines teach the spectator, Sabrina, and the aunts about women's power. In one episode in which this occurs, for example, Hilda does not use her magic for the symphony placement tryouts, and she is given the second violin chair while an obnoxiously arrogant and sexist male (who has the advantage of having a Stradivarius violin) is awarded the first chair. This reminds Hilda that there are all kinds of advantages and that everyone uses his or her unique advantages to achieve his or her goals. If he has a special instrument, she has the power to take that (unfair) advantage away from him. Thus, on the night of the symphony concert, Hilda uses her magic literally to blow the first violinist away and then steps in to fill the first chair position with ease ("Sweet and Sour Victory").

Furthermore, when Sabrina tries to reject her aunts' unusual behavior, the influence of magic in her life only increases. Indeed, whenever Sabrina tries—unsuccessfully—to conform to conventional realist notions of "normal" life, the aunts' lives get in the way. For instance, in "Jenny's Non-Dream" Sabrina talks with her aunts about the wonderful time she had at a sleep-over at her friend Jenny's house: "It was so much fun to be in a normal house with a normal family doing normal things." And when her aunts press her about why she never invites Jenny home for a sleep-over, Sabrina has to admit that it is because she worries that Jenny thinks her aunts are "weird." Just as Zelda promises that they will try to be "normal" if Sabrina invites Jenny over, in rides Hilda on a polo pony.

Sabrina tries very hard to prepare her aunts for this evening of conformity to the grand narrative of white middle-class normalcy, including going to the extreme step of preparing a list of possible dinner conversations on such mundane topics as towels. Of course, her attempt to simulate "normalcy" collapses incrementally. First, the dryer repair person (who has a large bushy tail) arrives from

Hilda uses her magic to take over first-chair violin in "Sweet and Sour Victory."

the other realm to fix the dryer, which is plagued by a lint gremlin who dashes around the house and just barely escapes Jenny's notice. Then Hilda emerges, prepared for the role of mother/housewife in an over-the-top costume and hairstyle that parody those of 1950s sitcom housewives. This is followed by the arrival of "the brains" (disembodied brains) who participate in Zelda's book club. The final element in the demise of this simulated normalcy occurs when Jenny goes in search of a towel in the linen closet and is whisked off to the other realm where Drell turns her into a grasshopper. Sabrina's desire for normalcy, in fact, *causes* Jenny's trip to the other realm: it is, after all, Sabrina's insistence that her aunts discuss domestic things like towels that leads to Jenny's interest in their linen closet.

In sum, Zelda and Hilda provide models of self-confident, talented women who are perfectly willing to use their talents (including their magic) to accomplish their goals and to fulfill their desires. Sabrina follows their model, and in doing so she herself functions as a role model for the many teens with whom she interacts, while at the same time she learns to use her magic in ways that increase women's independence and self-confidence. In all these ways, the series provides Sabrina with a utopian feminist world, marked by equality and independence.

Gender Play

In addition to gender equity, the series' apparent acceptance—at least temporarily—of playful gender instability also marks it as feminist. Any number of episodes upend heterosexuality and gender binaries, using humor and irony to suggest lesbian, gay, and transgender experiences.

The aunts, for example, can be read not only as feminist role models but also as lesbian role models. While the aunts *are* sisters who sometimes talk about men and dating, they are *also* lesbian-coded in that they are two women living and raising a child together. Furthermore, except for Hilda and Mr. Kraft in the second season and references to Hilda's past jiltings by Drell, the aunts never date the same man twice. And even the dates they do have never go well. For example, in "Sweet Charity" Zelda worries about dating a younger man. Ironically, he turns out to be a mortal in his eighties, which technically is much younger than the immortal Zelda but which seems particularly inappropriate because Zelda appears to be in her thirties. In addition, although Hilda has several dates with Mr. Kraft, she does not particularly like him and she is constantly trying to avoid his advances.

The lesbian-coding begins in the pilot, in fact, which opens with the two aunts sharing proud, intimate, parental smiles with each other as they watch Sabrina levitate in her sleep for the first time. In "The Great Mistake," we see a flashback of Hilda and Zelda in their life together before Sabrina arrives. In this flashback they return home together from an evening out in gorgeous gowns and sit down for a post-theater intimate soiree: The dining room table is formally set—with a white linen tablecloth, candles, and champagne—just for the two of them. They are seated and served by three young, attractive liveried male servants (Silvio, Lance, and Derrick) who stand at attention behind the table while the two women drink and talk about how their lives will change after the child comes: they will have to give up Formula 1 racing and weekends in Tuscany, and they will have to turn the second floor disco into the child's room. The setting and dialogue here suggest a lesbian couple about to become parents for the first time. In "Sabrina's Choice," Hilda and Zelda even "separate" (i.e., divorce) to teach Sabrina a lesson about pitting them against each other to get what she wants.

While each of these examples can be read as being about "sisters," they also can be read as being about "lesbians." Indeed, the series seems to anticipate this reading; at least one episode in each of the first two seasons explicitly represents others' perceptions of Hilda and Zelda as "a couple." In the first season episode "The True Adventures of Rudy Kazootie," the aunts attend parents' night at Sabrina's school. Before going, Zelda makes a joke that some people may find it "weird" that two women live alone in a Victorian house. Once at the school, she returns to what can be read as her own anxiety about her lesbian-coding when she assures the teacher and the other parents that she and Hilda are *really* Sabrina's aunts: she explains that they are *"sisters,* not an alternative couple," thus evoking the very possibility that she so strenuously denies. "A Doll's Story" emphasizes this again in the second season. This episode opens with Hilda and Zelda in an escalating battle to annoy each other. Sabrina's demand for a little peace and quiet makes them realize that they have not bickered this much since they chose different sides in the Civil War and that they need time apart from each other. They decide to go away—to the same spa, because it has a two-for-one special. However, when they arrive they discover that the concierge has put them in the same room, having assumed they would want to be together since they have the same last name. While the incest taboo ensures these characters are not *really* lesbians, that same taboo makes it possible for the text to represent an all-female lesbian household in which gender boundaries are constantly dismantled and multiple sexualities are celebrated. As Alexander Doty argues in relation to a number of television shows that focus on pairs or groups of women, the more the show insists on heterosexuality in the face of close female relationships, the more material there is available for a spectator who reads from a "queer" perspective.[11]

Harvey is also an important figure in Sabrina's feminist and gender-playful world. He does not feel threatened or jealous of Sabrina's independence, courage, and intelligence; furthermore, he repeatedly rejects traditional hegemonic masculine behavior. For example, Harvey is delighted when Sabrina performs better than even the white male teacher in what they call their "Kung Fu" P.E. class ("Sweet and Sour Victory"). In "Dummy for Love," when the football coach is particularly hard on Harvey at practice in an effort to use Harvey to get

Sabrina to retract her school newspaper editorial arguing that the school inappropriately emphasizes sports over academics, Harvey and Sabrina have this conversation:

Sabrina: Maybe I should just write a retraction.

Harvey: No. It would be wrong for you to write something you don't believe in—no matter how it affects my spine!

Beyond Harvey's general acceptance of Sabrina's independence, the series codes him as feminine and even sometimes as female, as in "Rumor Mill" when he miraculously becomes pregnant as a result of magic rumors Sabrina spreads and inadvertently makes come true. In "Mars Attracts!" Harvey gives Sabrina "mitten minders" so her hands will not get cold on her skiing trip. Furthermore, it is Harvey who waits alone in his room at home for Sabrina to call him on the telephone, while Sabrina is out dancing with her ski instructor. Harvey paces back and forth, saying to the telephone, "Ring, ring," and eventually he leaves a message with Salem for Sabrina, who has been having such a good time she forgets to call. When Sabrina does call Harvey, he lies and tells her, "Hey, don't worry. I wasn't, like, waiting by the phone."

In general, when Sabrina and Harvey are together, they often do typical "girl things," as in "Sabrina and the Beanstalk" where Harvey braids Sabrina's hair for her. In "The Band Episode," Harvey makes his anti-binary gender thinking clear when he suggests that Valerie and Sabrina wear "unitards" while performing as a band as "a comment on an asexual society." Concomitantly, just as Harvey accepts Sabrina's independence, Sabrina accepts Harvey's gender-crossing. For example, in "To Tell a Mortal" Harvey and Valerie are sucked into a vortex from which they emerge wearing each other's clothes. Neither is uncomfortable with this cross-dressing, and, at the end of the episode when Sabrina looks at photographs of the day, she expresses pleasure as she pauses over one of Harvey and Valerie posing in each other's clothes.

The series often associates traditionally masculine things with Sabrina directly, as well. For example, Sabrina is particularly good at math and science: she wins an award for a paper she wrote in a math class in "Fear Strikes Up a Conversation," and she successfully challenges the all-male membership of the science club in "Geek Like Me." In "Sabrina's Choice," Sabrina uses Zelda's commitment to science to trick her aunt into letting Sabrina go to a party by implying it will be a science club meeting. Zelda not only gives her permission, but she also encourages Sabrina to go, saying, "Women in science, Sabrina, that's the future. You go, and you be the brightest one there!"

The series also uses the body as a source of gross humor and spectator pleasure. While this aspect of the series can be read, in part, as addressing male and/or very young audience members,[12] the series also defines gross body humor as pleasurable for various women in the show, particularly when the jokes and humorous situations involve food. In the pilot, for example, Sabrina mistakenly turns Libby into a pineapple while she is trying to learn to control her powers. While Sabrina and Zelda work on turning Libby back into a person, Hilda suggests slicing her up and eating her. In "Dante's Inferno," when Sabrina asks for ice cream Hilda conjures some for her, but when Sabrina opens the freezer door she is confronted by a screaming eye. It turns out Hilda has "punitis," and the entire episode is peppered with jokes in which Hilda's puns, such as "cat got your tongue," are literalized. For this pun, Zelda loses her tongue to Salem, who holds it in his paw and says, "Imagine the grooming possibilities." And in "Dummy for Love," Sabrina and Salem eat waffle after waffle while looking for the prize that is advertised to be in at least one box.

The aunts participate in this kind of body humor as well. Nonfood body jokes include a moment when the aunts literally ground Sabrina by burying her up to her neck in sand and also their making jokes about diaper powder for an adult-sized cupid who appears in several episodes (e.g., "Dummy for Love"). "Hilda and Zelda: The Teenage Years" opens with Hilda and Sabrina discovering that Zelda has put a booby trap on her clothes to keep them from borrowing them. Zelda's trap is literally a "booby trap": anyone who goes into her drawers/closets and "borrows" any piece of her clothing gets big boobs—as both Hilda and Sabrina, who have grown to about a size 46 and 40 respectively, discover.

While these individual moments of body jokes maintain a consistent association between Sabrina and what the series itself defines as typically masculine pleasure in grossness, the entire narrative of "Sabrina, the Teenage Boy" focuses on Sabrina's masculinity. This gender-playful episode begins with Sabrina and Valerie at the Slicery.

> *Valerie:* Sabrina, what took you so long? [. . .]
>
> *Sabrina:* I stood by my locker for twenty minutes waiting for Harvey, but then he decided to go hang out with the guys at that stupid garage.
>
> *Valerie:* Let's face it. We've been ditched for loud things that go fast.
>
> *Sabrina:* What do you think guys talk about when we're not around?
>
> *Valerie:* Girls?

Not exactly, as the next scene reveals when Harvey and three other teenage boys in a garage (an extremely rare gathering in the series) work on a car and talk about what is "grosser" in movies, guts or pus.

Later, when Sabrina asks her aunt: "What's the mystery of men?" Zelda replies, with feminist irony, "Let me get my calendar and see if I can clear the next decade." Hilda tells Sabrina that the only way to learn how men think is to be accepted by men as one of them, which can only be done if one uses a "turn yourself into a boy" spell. However, when Zelda forbids Sabrina to try such a spell, Hilda, also with feminist irony, explains the reason: "The last time [Zelda] tried a boy spell she got lost for fifty years because she refused to ask for directions." Neither Sabrina nor Hilda are dissuaded. Hilda helps Sabrina make a potion that casts a "boy spell" over her and turns her into a male for two hours. After Sabrina drinks the potion, Hilda asks, "Do you feel different?" Sabrina answers, "Yes and no. I mean, I still feel like me, but for some reason I also sense that *SportsCenter* is on."

Sabrina takes on the body and identity of "Jack Sprattsky" and goes to the garage where his/her initiation test by Harvey and the guys is a belching contest. Later, even though Sabrina has returned to her girl-body, she eats pork rinds and watches sports with Salem and Hilda, who also drank some "boy" potion and turned herself into a bearded motorcycle biker to avoid Mr. Kraft. Even Zelda can no longer resist the desire to change genders: at the end of this scene she emerges from the kitchen as a man. And, Sabrina purposefully maintains at least one aspect of her masculine identity in order to charm Harvey: when she and Harvey are reunited, he is delighted when she begins a conversation with "You know what's really gross? Pus."

In conjunction with this masculinization of Sabrina, a variety of moments during the episode highlight gender as a constructed social category that works to the detriment of feminine people, whether female or male. For example, when Hilda explains what will happen to Sabrina if she uses the spell, she makes a joke about the inadequacy of genetic explanations for gender: "You'll just look like the guy you would have been if one of your chromosomes lost a leg." And Salem, who as a man doing penance as a cat knows quite a bit about bodily transformation, teaches Sabrina about the dangers of anti-gay hate crimes for feminine men. For example, when Sabrina starts to put on perfume after she has turned into a boy, he warns him/her that he/she will be beaten up. And, when Sabrina initially chooses the name "Kirby" for her boy identity, Salem again warns him/her that this feminine indicator may lead to violence against him/her.

As these many examples suggest, *Sabrina* depicts an independent young woman living in a world where she is encouraged to use her strength, self-confidence, and magical powers and where she is accepted and loved for who she is, even when who she is takes her across binary gender and sexuality boundaries. She learns and teaches lessons about a variety of types of discrimination, yet she always has a safe world of gender equality to which she can retreat and on which she can depend. These are the versions of feminism that we see the series as providing for its audience.

THE CONTAINMENT OF FEMINIST PLEASURE

Nevertheless, despite providing many potential moments for particular kinds of prime-time feminist pleasure, the series' affirmation of traditional patriarchal feminine concerns with physical beauty, acquisition of heterosexual male attention, and responsibility for others undermines Sabrina's access to independence and contains her feminist potential as a role model. We turn now to an examination of the limits the series places on girl power, and on Sabrina as a girl, specifically.

Cultural Standards of Fashion and Ideal Feminine Beauty

According to Bartky, "Normative femininity is coming more and more to be centered on woman's body—not its duties and obligations or even its capacity to bear children, but its sexuality, more precisely, its presumed heterosexuality and its appearance." Moreover, she notes that what is new about this in contemporary society is "the spread of this discipline to all classes of women and its deployment throughout the life-cycle" (80). As a result, women are taught to view themselves as objects of a dual gaze—their own and others'—and to compare themselves, and to be compared by others, to culturally defined standards of ideal female beauty.

That Sabrina has learned this lesson well is evident in the prologue of *every* episode. In these moments, while the series' theme song plays in the background, Sabrina stands in front of a full-length mirror and tries (zaps) on various outfits. On occasion, she even directly addresses the audience with comments that acknowledge that she knows others are watching her look at herself. Furthermore, each week her clothing displays her as a fashionable body. For instance, even in a Christmas episode that emphasizes the winter season, Sabrina wears an extremely short miniskirt ("Sabrina Claus").

"Sabrina, the Teenage Boy," which we discuss earlier as crossing and undermining binary gender boundaries, literalizes the distinction between boys as actors (even if they mostly have burping contests) and girls as objects-to-be-looked-at when Sabrina's body begins to turn from a boy back into a girl. While Jack/Sabrina is hiding in the men's bathroom, Harvey enters and notices that Jack's mascara is running. In his usual "unisex" way, Harvey says, "Personally, I don't have a problem with it, but the guys will be all over you." This liberatory moment is undermined, however, by the fact that the makeup seems to be an *internal* aspect of Sabrina's female body: the mascara appears spontaneously when her "boy potion" begins wearing off. As the potion further dissipates, Sabrina runs into the women's bathroom where first half of and then the rest of her girl's body appears—including long shiny hair (as opposed to Jack's dull and poorly cropped hair) and skintight clothes (as opposed to Jack's baggy work shirt). Not only are her pants a slimming black, but her skintight shirt is Caucasian skin-*colored* so that, during the moment in which the episode invites us to look most closely at Sabrina-as-female-body, that body (almost) appears to be naked from the waist up, thereby drawing an equivalency between her body/self and her clothes/fashion.

The importance of adhering to cultural standards of heterosexual fashion and beauty is a recurrent source of narrative action and conflict in many other episodes, as well. For example, in "Sabrina through the Looking Glass" Sabrina

Sabrina/Jack in "Sabrina, the Teenage Boy."

looks in the mirror and discovers that she has a wart on her forehead. Her aunts insist that, despite the wart, she has to go to school. To hide her sudden lack of feminine beauty, Sabrina wears a baseball cap only to have Libby steal the cap and expose the wart. Sabrina then turns Libby into a goat and creates a snowstorm. At home, she stomps off to her room and talks to her alter ego in the mirror. When she steps through the mirror for some quiet reflection, she finds that she is trapped in that alternative mirror world where everyone is unhappy. Although Sabrina eventually escapes, one of the lessons this episode teaches is how excruciatingly important it is not to violate traditional standards of beauty, such as having flawless skin. Furthermore, if one's lack of feminine beauty is exposed, the narrative trajectory suggests, it is equally important to maintain demure feminine behavior by controlling one's emotions/witchcraft.[13]

Male Attention and Heterosexual Partnerships

The series further undermines Sabrina's girl power and its own feminist propensities by narratively assenting to the traditional feminine notion that the whole purpose of striving for beauty is to acquire the attention of males.[14] So, while Sabrina's relationship with Harvey is relatively egalitarian in many ways, especially given his comfort with the feminine and cross-gender aspects of his identity, Sabrina still ponders and dwells on their relationship much more often than does Harvey. For example, in "Bundt Friday" we see Sabrina writing in her diary about Harvey (but not the reverse). "Trial by Fury" is one of many episodes that illustrates this dimension of normative femininity. In this episode, in the middle of a math test—which the teacher, Mr. Rothwell, gives the class because he is irritated with Sabrina for asking a question about a concept he has already explained—Sabrina's mind again wanders from the math problem to heteronormative romantic concerns. In a voice-over she says: "Why did I study with Harvey? Because he's cute. I wonder if we'll get married. Never mind. Pay attention. Negative B+ or −; I hate Rothwell." Eventually, in order to have enough time to work out the problem—given her wandering (toward Harvey) mind—she freezes everyone in her math class.

A particularly vivid enactment of this dimension of traditional femininity occurs in "As Westbridge Turns." In this episode, Sabrina opens a can-of-worms spell in which her life turns into a soap opera and all emotions are heightened. Harvey asks Sabrina to go steady and gives her an engraved bracelet (which says "Harvey digs Sabrina 12:36" [12:36 is the time they first speak on her first day of school and the time at which he gives her the bracelet]). As he leaves, he gets hit in the head with a ladder and loses his memory. Libby seizes the opportunity presented by Harvey's amnesia to persuade him that she is his girlfriend (a relationship she has wanted since the pilot and one of the main reasons she has always resented Sabrina). However, because male attention is so very important, Libby wants to flaunt her acquisition of Harvey's attention publicly. She uses Harvey's passive, eager-to-please nature to persuade him to be her escort at the annual Drake Department Store fashion show. To ensure that Sabrina does not interfere, Libby steals a diamond ring from Mr. Poole, the science teacher (he keeps it in his briefcase for the moment when he will find the courage to ask Nurse Nancy to marry him), and plants it on Sabrina. Sabrina is arrested for theft and loses her bracelet in the process, but her aunts persuade the police to let her go to school to find the bracelet (which will give her an alibi for the time the ring was stolen). Eventually, Sabrina finds the bracelet, dons a fashionable gown, and flits down the fashion show runway just in time to prevent Harvey from kissing Libby.

Harvey: Aren't I supposed to kiss you now? [to Libby at the end of the runway]

Libby: Oh, Harvey, you remembered!

Sabrina: Stop! You can't kiss him! Harvey's *my* boyfriend!

Libby: What are *you* doing here? I thought I sent you to juvey!

Sabrina: Your little scheme failed, and now I'm back to reclaim what's rightfully mine! [she turns to Harvey, and holds out the bracelet] Look!

Harvey: [looks at the bracelet and reads aloud] Harvey digs Sabrina. I'm Harvey and I dig Sabrina. You're Sabrina! That's right, and Roger Clemens signed for the Blue Jays. It's all coming back to me.

[. . .]

Libby: [to Sabrina] You're going down, Spellman!

Sabrina: And I'm taking you with me. [They begin to push and shove each other until they fall off the runway and land in a water pond at the end of the runway. As they fight, they alternatively yell at each other—"Tramp!" "Freak!" "Super freak!" "Super tramp!"—while Harvey looks on in astonishment and the aunts cheer for a while and then intervene to break up the fight.]

Zelda: Why are you fighting with Libby when there's a guy over there who just remembered he's crazy about you?

Sabrina: Good point. [now soaking wet, she turns to Harvey] Harvey.

Harvey: Sabrina.

Clearly, this episode illustrates that girls not only will compete, but also will fight other girls—and even lie, steal, and plant false evidence—in order to gain the attention of boys. The conclusion Angela McRobbie derives from the images and messages in *Jackie,* one of the best-selling teen magazines in Britain, aptly describes this episode and, indeed, one of the major themes running through *Sabrina:* "The consensual totality of feminine adolescence means that all girls want to know how to catch a boy, lose weight, look their best and be able to cook" (84). Of these four behaviors, only cooking eludes Sabrina; however, the series adds "compete with other girls" to McRobbie's list.

Responsibility for Others

A third aspect of traditional femininity to undermine the series' feminist potential is the cultural notion that caring and taking responsibility for others is expected of females. As Julia T. Woods explains, "most females are socialized to be sensitive to others and to understand that caring is an ongoing expectation of them, though not of males" (5). Sabrina's investment in heterosexual male attention extends to her taking more responsibility than does Harvey for maintaining their relationship and for managing their sexuality. "First Kiss" focuses on this responsibility. Early in the episode, Sabrina discovers that any mortal whom she kisses romantically will turn into a frog. While she is aware of her own desire, knowing that she wants to kiss Harvey, she initially resists her impulse to do so. When she finally does give in to her desire and initiates a kiss, hoping that her identity as witch-mortal (rather than only witch) will protect Harvey, she discovers that her sexual desire is as dangerous as her aunts warned her it would be: Harvey promptly becomes a frog. To release him from the spell, Sabrina has to prove her "true love" for Harvey, eventually rescuing him by proving—in a series of tests provided by the witches council—both that they are friends and that she is faithful to him. While the series has already established repeatedly that Sabrina and Harvey are great friends, the test of fidelity is particularly ironic, given that in the episode that directly precedes "First Kiss" Sabrina engages in a flirtation with her older ski instructor. Although she eventually chooses Harvey over the ski instructor, when she tells Harvey about her momentary lack of fidelity he responds by telling her that he just does not want to know about it if it happens again. Thus, while the previous episode ends with Harvey's typical acceptance of all aspects of Sabrina's independence, the subsequent episode not only insists on fidelity between

Harvey and Sabrina, but also forces Sabrina literally to walk through fire (the test provided by the witches counsel) to prove that fidelity.

In addition to specific episodes such as "First Kiss," the dominant narrative structure for the series repositions Sabrina's magic and independence within the context of morality and relationality. The overarching narrative, which is repeated week after week in individual episodes, begins with Sabrina's decision to use her magic in a way either Hilda, Zelda, Salem, or her conscience warns her is inappropriate. Nevertheless, she uses it, sometimes at Salem's urging, sometimes despite his warning. Inevitably, this causes a series of events that produces much of the playful gender-crossing and independence we describe earlier, but it also wreaks havoc that Sabrina must try to fix. The trouble caused by Sabrina's inappropriate use of her magic then takes up the bulk of the story line. At the end of the episode, Sabrina succeeds in returning things to normal—sometimes with her aunts' or Quiz Master's help, and sometimes simply through her own ingenuity. Toward the end of most episodes, either Sabrina or another character actually articulates the lesson she has learned as she has moved from problem to confusion, complication, and eventual resolution of both the initial problem and the subsequent instability caused by her inappropriate use of her magical powers.

This narrative structure overwhelmingly teaches Sabrina to care for, protect, and value others; to trust authority and family; and to resist gratifying her own desires, emotions, and self-involved pleasures. To offer just a few examples: she learns lessons about doing good for others rather than for oneself ("Sweet Charity," "Sabrina Claus," "Rumor Mill"); controlling herself so that she does not affect others with her excesses of emotion/magic ("Pilot," "Sabrina through the Looking Glass," "Oh, What a Tangled Web She Weaves," "Fear Strikes Up a Conversation"), even when the emotion is one of empathy and she uses her magic to bring good to others ("The Equalizer"); and being responsible rather than procrastinating ("Sabrina and the Beanstalk") or fulfilling her own desires ("My Nightmare, the Car"). The narrative structure of problem-complication-confusion-resolution and return to stability is standard for sitcoms, of course.[15] What we are pointing to here is how, in this series, Sabrina herself uses her magic or expresses her personal desires in ways that cause the problem and the escalation of the problem. The typical situation comedy narrative structure thus helps the series to define Sabrina's independence as problematic and to respond to it by supplanting it with repetitive lessons about sublimating self and prioritizing responsibility toward others.

ESCAPING CONTAINMENT

Thus far we have offered two arguments about *Sabrina:* we have pointed out the ways the series simultaneously empowers *and* contains Sabrina and, through her, independent young women who are willing and able to trust in their own self-confidence and powers (whether magical or not). As adult feminist cultural critics, we tend to see the containment of Sabrina as more dominant in the series overall, particularly because of its link to the narrative structure of the episodes. However, we also acknowledge the importance of Sabrina's constant self-confidence and independence as she moves through her gender-equal world. These pleasures and moments (although not overarching narratives) of independence and competence offer a version of teenage adolescence that can be empowering for the many young women and girls who watch this show.

In this last section, however, we push past this polysemic reading to ask: *In what ways* does Sabrina escape the containment of the text? In addition to her general feminist identity, the series provides many moments in which, at least temporarily, Sabrina escapes the heavy consequences of the moral lessons she is supposed to be learning as well as the heavy-handed morality of prime-time feminism that insists on gender-blindness and equality. Sabrina's containment, then, is only partial, not only because she has an independence that "needs" containment in the first place, but also because that containment never really holds. Sabrina escapes that containment both across episodes (when she uses her magic "inappropriately" yet again, despite the "lesson she learned" in the previous episode) and also *within* episodes (when she or the text responds to the lesson of containment with sarcasm). However, as we argue here, many of Sabrina's routes of escape depend on a co-optation of cultural difference, a celebration of consumer capitalism, and a sense of entitlement based on the identity provided to her by her magic as a "special" (i.e., privileged) teen, all of which, from our critical perspective, make *both* the series' feminism *and* its containment problematic.[16]

Co-opted Multiculturalism

Sabrina's magic and play often take her across national and race boundaries in ways that articulate a tourist identity and neocolonial position for her in the world. For example, when Sabrina's father, Ted, comes for one of his rare visits and they decide to eat Chinese food for dinner, Ted not only zaps a dining table filled with multiple Chinese dishes, he also zaps them all into "traditional" Chinese costumes. Nondiegetic orientalized music emerges briefly, and the characters spontaneously begin speaking what is presumably a Chinese language, translated into English by subtitles. This national boundary crossing does not *challenge* racial and cultural distinctions but instead provides access to a stereotyped "Chinese culture" as just one more aspect of Sabrina's pleasure and class-privilege. Literalizing what bell hooks calls "Eating the Other," this scene allows the Spellmans both to be and to consume "Chineseness," while *Sabrina* simultaneously marks itself as multicultural (by including "Chinese culture") and reaffirms the centrality of the white middle-class family (by focusing on the Spellmans).

The aunts and Sabrina constantly access racialized cultures, bringing them into their lives through their use of magic. In "Trial by Fury," when they celebrate Cinco de Mayo in January simply because they want to, they empty it of any specific cultural meaning and free it to signify simply "pleasure for magical women." In "Sabrina through the Looking Glass," Zelda tries to persuade Hilda and Sabrina to practice yoga with her. Zelda's costume seems to suggest that she thinks of yoga as a form of exercise: she wears relatively simple tights and a leotard. Sabrina and Hilda, however, engage in the experience as a form of play, dressing in ornate orientalist costumes and joking throughout the process of trying to do the exercises. In "A Doll's Story," when Sabrina's cousin traps her in her toy box along with a series of other characters whom she previously had also shrunk and collected in the box, Sabrina uses racialized platitudes such as "it takes a village," "cry freedom," and "power to the toys" in order to persuade her fellow prisoners to help her escape so that she can save them all. These few examples emphasize the way the series repeatedly recenters whiteness and empties references with specific meanings in various cultures in order to re-code them as objects of pleasure for Sabrina and her aunts.

The entire episode "Sweet and Sour Victory" emphasizes Sabrina's sense of entitlement and her "difference" from racialized others when she uses her magic to help her win what her teacher defines as a "Kung Fu" contest. Although she initially learns the sport in an explicitly Eurocentric, male context at her school, when she attends a contest she encounters an Asian American male contestant whom she recognizes as an actor from action films, perhaps signifying that the contest is more "real" than the class at school. Because of her magic, she is able to beat this more "authentic" athlete. However, because of her guilty conscience, her trophy begins to talk to her. The figure on the top of the trophy who speaks to her is played by an Asian American actor who is en-tirely covered in gold body paint. He marks the sport as both masculine and Asian, thereby suggesting to both Sabrina and the spectator that, while Sabrina can use her magic to enter his world, this is only a play world for her, one she borrows from Asian/Asian American men and in which, when she is being "fair," she should not remain.

Quiz Master, played by an African American actor, also can be read as a co-opted character. As the only recurring nonwhite character on the show, his out-rageous costumes, clownish manner, occasional use of Black vernacular, and basic incompetence as a Quiz Master (a theme that is dealt with directly in "Quiz Show") draw on a long tradition of stereotypes of African Americans. Fur-thermore, when Sabrina goes to visit her mother (whose absence is based on ar-chaeological tourism in South America) in "Mom vs. Magic," the episode repre-sents the archaeological dig with references to beetle stew and with a generic dark-skinned, long-haired presumably "native" man in the background, one of the few representations of people of color on the show.

Class-Privilege and Consumerism

Bringing multiculturalism into their home as a form of pleasure and humor in these ways is a form of consumption for Sabrina, Zelda, and Hilda. In this context, magic provides instant gratification and helps to transcend material boundaries. In addition, Sabrina and her aunts engage in a privileged tourism, traveling whenever and wherever they wish. We see them travel to Mars ("Mars Attracts!") for a skiing weekend, to Paris for the day to shop and visit the museums ("Third Aunt from the Sun"), and to Tuscany to bask in the sun for a weekend ("The Great Mistake"). Once they surprise Sabrina by taking her and Salem on an around-the-world weekend trip when she gets particularly good grades on her final exams ("The Troll Bride"). This traveling is a mark of their pleasure and freedom in the world, but it also highlights how class-privilege enables that freedom. Furthermore, despite the fact that both Hilda and Zelda are employed at least most of the time, it is their magic and not their occupational talents and success that really enables their class-privilege and sense of entitlement to and in the world. With their powers they have no travel costs, of course, and even their mortal house comes with an other realm five-hundred-year, 1-percent interest mortgage.

In "Oh, What a Tangled Web She Weaves," Hilda suggests that, not only can she travel the world, she literally can shape the world. When Sabrina realizes that her "make everything new spell" has gotten out of hand, Hilda explains that she has had a similar experience. Having once used a "make everything round spell," she transformed the earth so that "you can thank me for Columbus Day." Although Hilda is trying to teach Sabrina a lesson (be careful how you use your magic), it does not seem to occur to her that perhaps Sabrina (or her spectators) might want to blame her, rather than thank her, for Columbus Day. The aunts' obliviousness to class and race politics is clear in yet another episode when they delight over their new magical furniture, which simply appears in their living room, because "it's always delivered on time *and you don't have to tip anybody*" ("A River of Candy Corn Runs through It," emphasis added).

Class jokes that draw on stereotypes of poor whites also abound on the series. In "Witch Trash," Sabrina's cousins come to town in the hope of taking Sabrina's magic book away from her. They seem to have walked off the set of *The Beverly Hillbillies,* except that they are actually poor as a result of their own mismanagement of a sizable fortune left to them by their great-grandmother. Furthermore, they are depicted as "mortalist" (i.e., racist) because they argue that the fact that Sabrina's mother is mortal means Sabrina does not have the right to the witch family's magic book. Similarly, excessive class stereotypes appear in "Rumor Mill" when Hilda and Zelda decide to take a vacation in "middle America," dressing in T-shirts that say "I'm with stupid" and renting a pickup truck. "Sabrina Claus" depicts Sabrina's self-absorption by showing how Sabrina's use of magic to conjure a baked potato for herself takes that potato off the plate of a poor man, presumably in Russia. While Sabrina learns in this episode that such selfishness is wrong, by the credit sequence of "Rumor Mill" she seems to have forgotten the lesson. Her last costume portrays her as (presumably) Marie Antoinette, whose class-blindness Sabrina takes even further by saying not only "Let them eat cake," but also "save me some."

CONCLUSION

On some level, we do want to acknowledge the possibility that *Sabrina* is providing young women and girls with ways of understanding themselves as independent and powerful, with images of play and pleasure that cross and destabilize gender binaries. We would like to hope that Sabrina, like, for example, Nancy Drew before her, will inspire young women to choose futures as lawyers, researchers, librarians, detectives—indeed, as anything they want to be.[17] But we fear that this may not be the case, especially for viewers who are not white and middle-class, for the series does link Sabrina's breathless freedom to class- and race-privilege, all the while reminding her that that freedom is temporary and that she must always come back to her responsibility to others and her pursuit of feminine beauty and masculine attention. Thus, while the popular discourses on *Sabrina* celebrate girl power, our analysis suggests that the series' more powerful ideological work is the revelation of the role that popularized feminism plays in *maintaining* rather than undermining gender, race, and class hierarchies.

Ultimately, we read Sabrina's escapes from containment as co-opted multiculturalism and seductive consumerism, and therefore as antifeminist. Of course, our interpretation of the series should be understood as one potential interpretation of *Sabrina,* just as our readings of feminism and containment in the text are two contradictory but mutually existing potential interpretations of the series. However, as Dana L. Cloud has noted and we have argued here in relation to *Sabrina,* often "instead of polysemy (openness to multiple oppositional interpretations), popular texts offer viewers a multiplicitous but *structured* meaning system in which instances of multivocality are complementary parts of the system's overall hegemonic design" ("The Limits," 313).[18]

Adolescence is an uncertain time, and as Brown and Gilligan have pointed out, girls do look to the media, among other social sources, for help in negotiating their changing roles and relationships and their developing identities. And the media are looking for them, too: a recent *Electronic Media* headline noted, "Television [Is] Desperately Seeking Teen-Agers" because, as the article goes on to explain, "teens age 13 to 17 are a highly appealing demographic audience: emerging consumers" (Spring, 14, 20). These teens are not dupes, but they also are not often invited by the media to engage with them critically. For that reason, we believe that we, as critics, must continue to explore popular media texts and the particular social messages about (girl) power they invite us to create.

NOTES

The authors would like to thank Laura Schooling, Andreana Clay, and Lena Carla Gutekunst for research assistance. In addition, Sarah Projansky would like to thank the University of California, Davis, Humanities Research Institute for a fellowship to work on a larger project of which this essay is a part.

1. Fifty-seven percent of the survey respondents (155,000) were girls.

2. Bartky is drawing on Michel Foucault here.

3. Duke and Kreshel argue further that "These girls saw the initiation, maintenance, and repair of relationships as one of their primary jobs, and magazines guide them to ever higher levels of sophistication in the performance of these interpersonal tasks" (67).

4. In addition to Dow and Mayne, see, e.g., Elyce Rae Helford; Tania Modleski; Elspeth Probyn; Amelia Jones; Thomas B. Byers; Robert Goldman, Deborah Heath, and Sharon L. Smith; and Shelley Budgeon and Dawn H. Currie. We have both written previously on postfeminist culture, as well. See Leah R. Vande Berg and Sarah Projansky.

5. See also Ginia Bellafante.

6. In late 1996, the series drew 1.34 million girl and 928,000 boy viewers aged 12–17 each week, which is more teens than viewed *Friends* and only slightly less than viewed *Home Improvement* (Mifflin).

7. This doubleness in the text, perhaps not surprisingly, corresponds with a doubleness in the scholarship we discuss briefly earlier, suggesting both girls' resistance to traditional notions of femininity and media's pervasive feminine, heterosexist address to girls as concerned with beauty and their relationships to others, particularly boys and men.

8. Sabrina has a long history as a character. She first appeared in Archie Comic's *Archie's Madhouse*, no. 22, in October 1962. In December 1969, Sabrina appeared as one of the leading characters in a new comic series, *Archie's TV Laughout*, no. 1, which featured a group of teens from Riverdale High. In April 1971, the first issue of *Sabrina, the Teenage Witch* comic series appeared in print. In September 1971, *Sabrina, the Teenage Witch* appeared as a CBS Saturday morning animated series, and the character Sabrina also made a number of guest appearances on the animated series *The Groovie Ghoulies*. In September 1977, a new Saturday morning cartoon series featuring Sabrina appeared on NBC. This series, *Sabrina, Superwitch,* was combined with Archie cartoon episodes later in the year to form *The New Archie/Sabrina Hour.* In September 1993, a 48-page special comic book appeared, titled *Sabrina's Halloween Spooktacular;* the title was changed in 1994 to *Sabrina's Holiday Spectacular.* Then, as noted earlier, in April 1996 the live-action made-for-cable movie *Sabrina, the Teenage Witch* appeared on Showtime. Its strong reviews and ratings led ABC to commission the series that is the focus of this analysis, *Sabrina, the Teenage Witch* (Lancon, "What Is"). In the fall of 1999, "Sabrina, the Animated Series" premiered. *TV Guide Online* called it "The colorful escapades of the sorceress from *Sabrina, the Teenage Witch* as a pre-teen who brews trouble with her two aunts and wisecracking kitty, Salem."

9. Most of the *Sabrina* episode titles are humorous, ironic, or suggestive and could be analyzed along with the actual episodes. However, because these titles do not appear on the screen and can only be known by spectators who have access to extratextual material, such as World Wide Web sites, we will not discuss the titles here. We include them only for clarity, and we invite our readers to engage with them analytically. We drew the titles from Donald Lancon Jr.'s "STTW Episode Pages" website.

10. This "recloseting" raises a contradiction in the episode's allusion to lesbian and gay experience because Sabrina previously stated that she wanted to "come out of the linen closet," a contradiction *Sabrina* does not address.

11. Doty specifically discusses shows such as *I Love Lucy, The Mary Tyler Moore Show, Laverne and Shirley,* and *Designing Women.*

12. As we discuss further on, "Sabrina, the Teenage Boy" explicitly links "grossness" with masculinity as opposed to femininity.

13. Duke and Kreshel's study of adolescent girls' reading of teen magazines supports Patricia A. Adler, Steven J. Kless, and Peter Adler's conclusion that "in adolescence, girls focus on their looks, clothes, and weight as they never have before, with good reason: evidence shows that at this age, a female's popularity with her peers is closely linked to her appearance" (62).

14. As Duke and Kreshel's study of teenage girls' readings of adolescent magazines found, "At a time in their lives when girls look to others to reinforce positive assessments of self, the 'other' is too often male" (59).

15. See, for example, Horace Newcomb's genre study of situation comedies.

16. While most scholarship on postfeminism and prime-time feminism does not substantially address its representation of race (whiteness) and class (free access to "choice" and a culture of consumption), Byers and Jones are exceptions to this rule in terms of race and Helford is an exception in terms of class. See Projansky for a development of this argument.

17. For a discussion of Nancy Drew as feminist icon, see Carolyn S. Dyer, Carolyn S. Dyer and Nancy T. Romalov, Carolyn G. Heilbrun, and Bobbie Ann Mason.

18. For a discussion of the potentialities and limitations of polysemic texts and polyvalent readings, see the extended colloquy played out in the works of Dana L. Cloud and Celeste M. Condit. For a discussion of semivalence, see Naomi R. Rockler.

WORKS CITED

Adler, Patricia A., Steven J. Kless, and Peter Adler. "Socialization to Gender Roles: Popularity among Elementary School Boys and Girls." *Sociology of Education* 65, no. 3 (1992): 169–187.

Baldwin, Jennifer, and Gwen Schoen. "A Look in the Mirror." *Sacramento Bee* (1 May 1998): Scene 1, 8.

Bartky, Sandra L. *Femininity and Domination: Studies in the Phenomenology of Oppression.* New York: Routledge, 1990.

Becker-Cantarino, Barbara. "'Feminist Consciousness' and 'Wicked Witches': Recent Studies on Women in Early Modern Europe." *Signs: Journal of Women in Culture and Society* 20, no. 1 (1994): 152–175.

Bellafante, Ginia. "Bewitching Teen Heroines." *Time* (5 May 1997): 82–84.

Brown, Lyn Mikel. *Raising Their Voices: The Politics of Girls' Anger.* Cambridge: Harvard University Press, 1998.

Brown, Lyn Mikel, and Carol Gilligan. *Meeting at the Crossroads: Women's Psychology and Girls' Development.* Cambridge: Harvard University Press, 1992.

Budgeon, Shelley, and Dawn H. Currie. "From Feminism to Postfeminism: Women's Liberation in Fashion Magazines." *Women's Studies International Forum* 18, no. 2 (1995): 173–186.

Byers, Thomas B. "History Re-membered: *Forrest Gump,* Postfeminist Masculinity, and the Burial of the Counterculture." *Modern Fiction Studies* 42, no. 2 (1996): 419–444.

Cloud, Dana L. "Concordance, Complexity, and Conservatism: Rejoinder to Condit." *Critical Studies in Mass Communication* 14, no. 2 (1997): 193–197.

———. "Hegemony or Concordance? The Rhetoric of Tokenism in 'Oprah' Winfrey's Rags-to-Riches Biography." *Critical Studies in Mass Communication* 13, no. 2 (1996): 115–137.

——. "The Limits of Interpretation: Ambivalence and the Stereotype in *Spenser: For Hire.*" *Critical Studies in Mass Communication* 9, no. 4 (1992): 311–324.

Condit, Celeste M. "Clouding the Issues? The Ideal and the Material in Human Communication." *Critical Studies in Mass Communication* 14, no. 2 (1997): 197–199.

——. "Hegemony, Concordance, and Capitalism: Reply to Cloud." *Critical Studies in Mass Communication* 13, no. 4 (1996): 382–384.

——. "Hegemony in a Mass-Mediated Society: Concordance about Reproductive Technologies." *Critical Studies in Mass Communication* 11, no. 3 (1994): 205–230.

Doty, Alexander. *Making Things Perfectly Queer: Interpreting Mass Culture.* Minneapolis: University of Minnesota Press, 1993.

Dow, Bonnie J. *Prime-Time Feminism: Television, Media Culture, and the Women's Movement since 1970.* Philadelphia: University of Pennsylvania Press, 1996.

Duke, Lisa L., and Peggy J. Kreshel. "Negotiating Femininity: Girls in Early Adolescence Read Teen Magazines." *Journal of Communication Inquiry* 22, no. 1 (1998): 48–71.

Dyer, Carolyn S. "The Nancy Drew Phenomenon: Rediscovering Nancy Drew in Iowa." In *Rediscovering Nancy Drew.* Edited by Carolyn S. Dyer and Nancy T. Romalov. Iowa City: University of Iowa Press, 1995, 1–9.

Dyer, Carolyn S., and Nancy T. Romalov, eds. *Rediscovering Nancy Drew.* Iowa City: University of Iowa Press, 1995.

Fiebert, Martin S. "Dimensions of the Female Role." *Psychological Reports* 67, no. 2 (1990): 633–634.

Foucault, Michel. *Discipline and Punish: The Birth of the Prison.* 1975. Translated by Alan Sheridan. New York: Vintage, 1979.

Gilligan, Carol. *In a Different Voice: Psychological Theory and Women's Development.* Cambridge: Harvard University Press, 1982.

Gilligan, Carol, Janie V. Ward, Jill M. Taylor, and Betty Bardige, eds. *Mapping the Moral Domain.* Cambridge: Harvard University Press, 1988.

Goldman, Robert, Deborah Heath, and Sharon L. Smith. "Commodity Feminism." *Critical Studies in Mass Communication* 8, no. 3 (1991): 333–351.

Heilbrun, Carolyn G. "Nancy Drew: A Moment in Feminist History." In *Rediscovering Nancy Drew.* Edited by Carloyn S. Dyer and Nancy T. Romalov. Iowa City: University of Iowa Press, 1995, 11–21.

Helford, Elyce Rae. "Postfeminism and the Female Action-Adventure Hero: Positioning *Tank Girl.*" In *Future Females, The Next Generation: New Voices and Velocities in Feminist Science Fiction Criticism.* Edited by Marleen S. Barr. Lanham, Md.: Rowman & Littlefield, forthcoming.

Hooks, bell. "Eating the Other: Desire and Resistance." In *Black Looks: Race and Representation.* Boston: South End Press, 1992, 21–39.

Jones, Amelia. "Feminism, Incorporated: Reading 'Postfeminism' in an Anti-Feminist Age." *Afterimage* 20, no. 5 (1992): 10–15.

Labi, Nadya. "The Next Generation: What Do Girls Want?" *Newsweek* (29 June 1998): 60–62.

Lancon, Donald Jr. "STTW Episode Pages." <http://www.obkb.com/info/mjhpages/sttwepis.html#epis> (25 July 1998).

——. "What Is *Sabrina, the Teenage Witch?*" <http://www.obkb.com/info/mjhpages/sttwinfo.html> (24 July 1998).

Mason, Bobbie Ann. *The Girl Sleuth: On the Trail of Nancy Drew, Judy Bolton, and Cherry Ames.* Athens: University of Georgia Press, 1995.

Mayne, Judith. "*L.A. Law* and Prime-Time Feminism." *Discourse* 10, no. 2 (1988): 30–47.

McRobbie, Angela. *Feminism and Youth Culture: From "Jackie" to "Just Seventeen."* Boston: Unwin Hyman, 1991.

Mifflin, Lawrie. "Teens Swept under Network Rug: TV Programmers Do Little to Turn Young Viewers into Lifelong Fans." *Sacramento Bee* (6 December 1996): Scene 1, 5.

Modleski, Tania. *Feminism without Women: Culture and Criticism in a "Postfeminist" Age.* New York: Routledge, 1991.

Newcomb, Horace. *TV: The Most Popular Art.* Garden City, N.Y.: Anchor Press/Doubleday, 1974.

Orlean, Susan. "Girl Power: Has Sabrina the Teenage Witch Worked Her Magic on a Generation?" *The New Yorker* (18 May 1998): 54, 56–59.

Phillips, Lynn. *The Girls Report: What We Know and Need to Know about Growing Up Female.* New York: National Council for Research on Women, 1998.

Pipher, Mary. *Reviving Ophelia: Saving the Selves of Adolescent Girls.* New York: Ballantine, 1995.

Probyn, Elspeth. "New Traditionalism and Post-Feminism: TV Does the Home." *Screen* 31, no. 2 (1990): 147–159.

Projansky, Sarah. "Working on Feminism: Film and Television Rape Narratives and Postfeminist Culture." Dissertation, University of Iowa, 1995.

Rockler, Naomi R. "From Magic Bullets to Shooting Blanks: Reality, Criticism, and *Beverly Hills, 90210.*" *Western Journal of Communication* 63, no. 1 (1999): 72–94.

Shohat, Ella. "Introduction." In *Talking Visions: Multicultural Feminism in a Transnational Age.* Cambridge, Mass.: MIT Press, 1998, 1–62.

Spillman, Susan. "Her Magic Touch." *TV Guide* (19 October 1996): 26–29.

Spring, Greg. "Television Desperately Seeking Teen-Agers." *Electronic Media* (24 February 1997): 14, 20.

Stoller, Debbie. "Brave New Girls: These TV Heroines Know What Girl Power Really Means." *On the Issues* (Fall 1998): 42–45.

TV Guide Online. <http://www.tvguide.com>

Vande Berg, Leah R. "*China Beach,* Prime Time War in the Postfeminist Age: An Example of Patriarchy in a Different Voice." *Western Journal of Communication* 57, no. 3 (1993): 349–366.

Woods, Julia T. *Who Cares: Women, Care, and Culture.* Carbondale: Southern Illinois University Press, 1994.

2

The Cartesian Novum of *Third Rock from the Sun*

Gendering Human Bodies and Alien Minds

Nicole Matthews and Farah Mendlesohn

In the opening sequence of the pilot episode of *Third Rock from the Sun* ("Brains and Eggs"), four alien visitors to Earth sit in a car discovering the peculiarities of the human forms to which they have been assigned. For these sapients, the body is literally not linked with the mind and the mind is not a product of human physiology. Instead, their bodies are uncharted territory that they must learn to control or that, alternatively, they will be controlled by. From this very first episode, too, it is the female body—in particular, the security officer's breasts— that seem particularly odd to these alien minds. Sexed bodies and gendered identities are from these beginnings flagged as central to the playing out of the show's underpinning idea.

From this moment the show's creators expect us to understand that the central paradigm, or novum, of this piece of science fiction television is that the mind and body are inherently separate. For our resident aliens, the body and mind are entirely different entities, and the disjunction between alien minds and human bodies provides much of the show's comedy. Here we find a convergence between the show's basic premise and the dualism of mind and body that has been fundamental to Western understandings of the self since Descartes. *Third Rock's* novum—the show's central science fiction idea— echoes Cartesian assumptions about the separation (and hierarchy) of mind and body. This convergence would, on its own, be intriguing enough for feminist analysis. But the creators of *Third Rock* are also peddling an ambiguous message about the nature of gender. This ambiguity might seem to allow for poly- semous, or multiple readings, of this show and points to the care with which the

41

researcher needs to approach programs that might appear at first to be feminist in rhetoric and theme.

The separation of mind and (sexed) body in *Third Rock* allows the show to point up the artifice and absurdity of many conventions of gender. On numerous occasions, the show takes issue with the idea that particular kinds of sexed bodies naturally lead to appropriately feminine or masculine behavior. In particular, the character of Sally, the crew's warrior, bears out the assertions of many first-wave feminists that "ownership" of a female body need not prevent women's engagement with a whole range of activities such as fixing a car, playing with guns, or hitting men. *Third Rock* also demonstrates some of the reasons for the recent popularity within feminist theory of an understanding of gender identity as performed.[1] In place of an essentialist view of femininity and masculinity as naturally inhering in sexed bodies, *Third Rock* often appears to be presenting gender as performed. As aliens, the crew of *Third Rock* is shown to be quite deliberately, if ineptly, acting out familial and gender roles. The defamiliarization of femininity that Sally's engagement with womanhood provides underscores the way that many women experience femininity as a drag performance—a deliberate acting out through appropriate costumes and gestures of a female role. However, we will argue that the show also indicates some of the problems of a performative view of gender. The direction of our argument is signaled in the comic moment with which we started this chapter.

Of the four aliens in the car, only three fully enter the ideological battlegrounds of gender: the high commander, Dick, as he learns to be a patriarch and a lover; Sally, the security officer, who plays the role of Dick's sister; and the information officer, Tommy, passed off as Dick's son, who is quite literally learning to be a man as he negotiates puberty. Harry, who pretends to be Dick's younger brother, is the fool, usually presented as either asexual or the victim of others' predatory advances. However, as the show proceeds through the second and third season, the performances of masculinity required of Tommy and Dick become sidelined, while Sally comes into focus as the character most vividly wrestling with a sexed body: just as in the car in the pilot episode, the female body comes to represent embodiment itself.

PERFORMANCES OF GENDER IN *THIRD ROCK*

One of the pleasures of *Third Rock* springs from the defamiliarization of conventions of gender that the novum of the show provides. The alien characters are often confused by the absurdity or injustice of gender roles, articulating what might be interpreted as radical and socialist feminist points of view. For instance, in the aptly named episode "I Enjoy Being Dick" (season one), Sally makes an observation about the servile nature of women's paid and unpaid work.

> *Dick:* Sally, is there anything you'd like to tell me, as a woman, because I think I'm enlightened enough now to hear it.

Sally: Well, men are always bossing you around, no one ever says thank you, and you're expected to clean up after everyone.

Dick: Are you talking about being a woman or a waitress?

Sally: Waitress, woman, same thing.

Along a similar line, Sally later comes out with an insight that might have been drawn from Gayle Rubin's critical account of women as a commodity for exchange between men (201). In the episode "Post Nasal Dick" (season one), when Dick is explaining to Sally the moment in a wedding ceremony when the bride is being given away, she bursts out, rather in the vein of feminist critiques of marriage, "Excuse me, given away? Like an object? As in free girl with every large fries?"

As we will argue later, it would be a mistake to overgeneralize from these moments of critique: neither Sally nor the show as a whole is consistent in advocating the point of view of any variant of feminism. If the producers wish to maintain a wide audience base, they need to play to feminists, antifeminists, and the merely indifferent. So, despite her protestations at the formalities of wedding ceremonies, in the season two episode "A Dick on One Knee," for instance, Sally reveals herself eager to enjoy the prerogative of a large and expensive wedding. What these protofeminist remarks do point out is that in attempting to fathom the depths of the human sex/gender system, the aliens demonstrate that being male or female is not just a matter of inhabiting the appropriate kind of body, but also consists of acting in manly or womanly ways. This representation of gender as a performance offers a more systematic way in which the show picks up on recent feminist understandings of gender.

Throughout the three seasons of the show, the alien crew members are shown quite explicitly trying to work out how to do this, looking to their neighbors, workmates, and partners for instruction. However, it is important to be aware that in pursuing the notion of gender as performance, the producers are acknowledging the multiplicity of performances that are available. Although Dick will settle, eventually, for some form of the male college professor type, he first has the opportunity to try other modes of masculinity on for size. In "Big Angry Dick" (season one), the crew members study their neighbors, the Mullers. Dick remarks to Frank Muller, "We're so fascinated by you. We've never met someone of your economic class before!" This blue-collar couple is employed as an exemplar of masculinity and femininity by the Solomons: Dick "proves" his masculinity by discussing ball-bearings and fighting with Frank, while Sally is ordered (by Dick) to demonstrate her femininity by learning to cook from Frank's wife, not dignified with a name of her own.

Tommy and Dick are also given some help in performing appropriate gender roles from the directions, respectively, of August (Tommy's sometime girlfriend) and Dick's partner, Mary Albright. Through his courtship of Mary, Dick learns that what Mary seems to want (despite a momentary aberration when she falls for an evil replacement for Dick sent by the Big Giant Head, who seeks to woo her through dominance and a lot of tango) is not adult manliness, but a form of boyishness that can be reduced to child-like simplicity and emotional dependence. In this environment, Dick "performs" the childish man who wants to be mothered. In a similar fashion, Tommy's performance of gender is shown to be shaped by August. In "Dick Behaving Badly" (season two), Dick responds to comments that he is under Mary's thumb by announcing that he is going to fight back:

> *Dick:* She'll just have to accept it. Because I'm the man. I'm stronger than she is. I have a larger cranium. I'm far more likely to go to prison. I'm the man! Now if I can just find someone to teach me how to act like one [. . .]. Tommy!
>
> *Sally:* [laughing] I'm sorry, but before you teach him how to be a man, shouldn't you get August's permission first?
>
> *Tommy:* [looking disgruntled] She told me not to call her 'til after dinner.

The inference is that manliness is something that women permit. If men act like brutes, it is because women wish them to do so. While masculinity is represented as performative here, it is women who are seen as responsible for generating this kind of masculinity, as demonstrated most vividly by Mary's enthusiastic response to evil-Dick in the episode "See Dick Run" (season one). Similarly, in "Assault with a Deadly Dick" (season one) Tommy is fed up trying to meet August's fluctuating expectations:

> *Tommy:* If that redefines the parameters of our relationship [mimicking her style], you're just going to have to accept me for who I am.
>
> *August:* [looks puzzled and then shocked, and then smiles] You know, I kind of like it when you're assertive like this?
>
> *Tommy:* You do?
>
> *August:* But not all the time.
>
> *Tommy:* Well, how often do you think I should be assertive?
>
> *August:* If I told you that—
>
> *Tommy:* Ok, ok, I'll figure it out—is now a good time?
>
> *August:* Sure.
>
> *Tommy:* Come on, then [leads August out of the room, she ironically compliant].

In this sequence we are clearly reverting to a 1950s scenario, in which women are supposed to enjoy being bossed around while maintaining the real control, confusing men with their apparently illogical demands. While containing an element of parody, the parody is of the supposedly liberated feminist who secretly enjoys patriarchy, a point reinforced by Mary's enjoyment of evil-Dick's masterful attentions. Taking their cues from female responses, the men thus perform their masculinity for an appreciative audience.

The performative relationship par excellence of the show is that between Sally and the rather large Officer Don, a local policeman. In a knowing, intertextual fashion, Sally and Don act out roles from film noire and 1950s cop shows: she the femme fatale, and he the hard-boiled detective. Don is attracted to Sally for much the same reasons that other men are attracted to her, but she is attracted to him almost entirely for the role he plays, ignoring him when he is out of uniform. Thus, it is not Don's "inner" personality that appears to appeal to Sally, but his performance of a macho masculinity "donned" with his policeman's outfit. Don and Sally's interaction is stagy, with Sally often acting with coy, girlish charm while under Don's eye. This hyperfeminine persona is juxtaposed against and undermined by the fact that it is Sally's warrior relish for brutality and violence that is explored in Don's company. Like the femme fatales of noire, Sally takes on the persona of a naive girl who needs protecting only when it suits her more dangerous intentions.

Sally's stagy relationship with Officer Don is just part of the way in which she underscores the performative nature of gender. The fact that an experienced extragalactic warrior is inhabiting the body of a human woman is emphasized by the casting of Kirsten Johnson, an exceptionally tall and leggy actress who walks with a bold, even swaggering, step. While this body in some senses conforms to the highest ideals of supermodel-style femininity, as demonstrated in "36-26-36 Dick" in which super-beautiful alien women take over the town, it is also signaled as not a properly or naturally feminine body. While Harry is misidentified as a gay man (in the episode "Lonely Dick") and Tommy's long hair and talents as a flower arranger bring accusations of both homosexuality and looking like a girl (in "A Dick on One Knee"), none of the male crew-members are ever genuinely mistaken for women. In contrast, Sally in the episode entitled "World's Greatest Dick" is taken for a cross-dresser when she is picked up in a gay bar, while in "The Dicks They Are a Changin'," Tommy, under pressure to provide the "family" with a past, invents a history for Sally in which she was a stockbroker who underwent a sex-change operation in 1988. In each case Sally is represented as aspiring to be or acting as a woman rather than naturally inheriting femininity with a female body: her femininity is a drag performance.

Throughout the three seasons of the show, Sally, in order to be recognized as a woman, must actively take on the costume and the social rituals of femininity. This performance of femininity is visibly signaled in the show through the contrast between Sally's habitual attire around the Solomon's apartment—usually trousers, shirts, and a leather jacket—and the short and slinky cocktail dresses she wears for dates and trips into the wider world. Preparing for one of her first dates in "Dick Like Me," Sally suffers a crisis of confidence in her performance of desirable womanhood. "Sure you can put on a tight little dress and look sexy and adorable, but you know what men are like. All they care about is how you dance," she sobs. "Go out there and be a girl!" Dick commands. The order parallels Judith Butler's writings on gender as performance. Butler notes that "acts, gestures and desire produce the effect of an internal core or substance, but produce this on the surface of the body" (136). Like Butler, Dick's comment in this episode suggests that "being a girl" is less to do with a natural femininity springing from the soul or the body, and more to do with the kind of clothes one wears and the gestures one uses.

Sally performs the feminine body.

Episodes of the show that focus on the cosmetics industry reiterate this point. We are very far from a natural, essential femininity here. For example, the work that goes into performances of femaleness is central to the plot of "36-26-36 Dick." In this episode Sally is able to infiltrate an occupying army of supermodelesque Venusian invaders, thanks to her height and bone structure, but is forced to undergo a series of tortuous procedures (exfoliation, eyelash curling) and adopt the obligatory revealing costume in order to performer her role as hyperfeminine seductress. In "36-26-36 Dick," then, we have an alien mimicking yet other aliens who are themselves copying a select group of abnormally young, tall, and thin humans, who in turn serve as unattainable models for ordinary women. These perversely interlocking masquerades illustrate Butler's point that parody of gender "implicitly reveals the imitative structure of gender itself" (137). By showing that femininity must be worked on and acted out, this episode suggests that we shouldn't see Sally's performance of gender as "fake" while other women are "real." Instead, like Sally and the Venusians, ordinary female consumers perform femininity by emulating the fantastic bodies of supermodels. There are no "real" women, no natural or normal femininity here. Rather, it is the constant attempts of ordinary female consumers to play out the role of women properly that keep the wheels of the cosmetics and fashion industries turning.

But if the Cartesian novum of *Third Rock* renders strange human bodies and the rituals in which they engage, it seems that female bodies are in every way more remarkable, more evident, and more prominent than male bodies. After all, in the pilot episode we do not see the male occupants of the car probing their underwear to marvel at their genitals. In this episode, however, Sally *is* asked to bounce up and down so that the men can watch her breasts. Although she refuses, these breasts are almost immediately put on display in a tight-fitting, low-cut black dress. As we will argue in the following paragraphs, bodies in *Third Rock,* especially the prominent female body, suggest a reading of the show that is considerably more problematic for feminists than the progressive reading we have provided so far.

It has been argued that the sitcom is one of the most ideologically flexible of television forms, offering within one text a range of characters and political positions with which to identify (Marc, 1984, 65; see also Hanke, 84). We would argue that not only the gallery of characters and the somewhat episodic plotting of the show (Basic, 72) but also the comic form of *Third Rock* give some scope for articulating complex and contradictory points of view. The show's polysemy, or capacity to be interpreted in many ways, has significant consequences for its representations of gender.

THIRD ROCK AS A COMEDY OF CONTAINMENT

Third Rock frequently parodies or spoofs arbitrary conventions of gender. In series one, the Solomons are often seated, notepad and paper in hand, in front of the television. However, the familial roles that they attempt to perform in the show often seem to recall less contemporary television families, such as those of *Roseanne* or even *Dallas,* than the sitcom families of the '50s and '60s. A running "gag" in *Third Rock* is the family's insistence that Sally undertake all domestic tasks while everyone simultaneously denounces her competence. In "Angry Dick," for instance, Dick exclaims, "You must learn to cook. How far do you think you're going to go with just a fabulous body and the intellect of a genius?" No one ever suggests that the male aliens could cook instead, although in "Dick and the Other Guy" Dick reveals that he can barbecue. When Sally is away attempting to infiltrate the invading Venusian forces that threaten to impoverish the Earth in "36-26-36 Dick," the remaining Solomons call their landlady, Mrs. Dubcek, upstairs to wash some plates, as a last-ditch attempt to fend off starvation—they have not yet worked out that you do not need plates and cutlery to eat. Sally and her neighbor Mrs. Muller may quip about inflicting realistically detailed tortures on their menfolk, but they do so while picking out ripe tomatoes at the supermarket and preparing roast chicken (in the episode "Angry Dick").

Perhaps the most extreme parody of the housewife of 1950s and 1960s sitcoms is through the character of Janet in the episode "Fun with Dick and Janet," which takes up the first two slots of season three. The family returns from its trip home with a wife for Dick: Janet (played by Roseanne Barr), the Big Giant Head's niece, an excessively coy and feminine woman, is easily tricked by Sally into taking on the domestic work as her "right." Janet has the last laugh, however, as Sally comes to resent being usurped by a more competent woman, and Janet discovers through the pages of glossy magazines that she is entitled to love, not just financial support, and goes off to find herself a toy boy. So it is Sally who takes up the paradigmatic activities of television's middle-class woman: shopping, cooking, and finding a man.

Fundamentally, although stuck in the kitchen, Sally is not the mother of the 1950s sitcoms but the elder sister as described by Susan Douglas, whose principle role is to get married. However, in keeping with the "dizzy" characterization usually accorded this role (see the Andy Hardy films and a recent construction such as *The Wonder Years*), she can be trusted neither to time these events suitably nor to select the right man. In "A Dick on One Knee" Sally accepts a marriage proposal from an attractive Frenchman. During the sequence, Dick reminds her that she is on a mission and that this may be a distraction. Sally retorts, "Dick, this is my mission. It's what women are supposed to do." Inevitably, the Frenchman turns out to be marrying for citizenship rather than love, and Sally is left feeling a failure once again, just as she is after Mr. Randall rejects her in "Big Angry Virgin from Outer Space." Dick reprimands her: "You think you can just walk out of here and find another man? I mean really, just look at yourself. Those comically long legs, that blindingly shiny hair, those unruly breasts!"

The joke in the previous line is, of course, that Sally is, by most current standards, distinctly desirable. As with much of *Third Rock*, this line points to the absurdity of Dick's high-handed criticisms of Sally's "failures" but at the same time, within the context of the show it articulates an accurate criticism of Sally, that she is unable to find and keep a man. It could scarcely be argued that *Third Rock* is simply espousing an ideology of domestic femininity, but neither is it wholeheartedly offering a critique. Dick's attack on Sally invites the audience both to laugh at and with Dick, as we will explore further later in this article when we examine the extent to which Sally's body is used against her. In the meantime, Sally's consistent failure to perform the stereotyped feminine role that is her mission within the show, suggests the narrative pattern of the "'zany housewife' sitcom" (Marc 1987, 107): sitcoms like *I Dream of Jeannie, Bewitched,* and their ultimate model, *I Love Lucy.*

As Patricia Mellencamp has argued, *I Love Lucy* presents the audience with a paradox. The "situation" of the show involves Lucy desperately attempting to become a performer on her husband Ricky's variety show, while inevitably finding herself unable to get out of the house and onto the stage or punished for attempting to do so. The irony here is that each episode of *I Love Lucy* hinges on the actress Lucille Ball's virtuoso physical comedy (Mellencamp, 88). On one level, Lucy is contained in a conventional middle-class feminine role, while on another, she is already the performer she aspires to be. As Mellencamp argues, this structure allows the expression of the pleasures of female success, the frustrations of domestic containment, and the ideological norms of '50s television to be expressed in the same program. Andrea Press, in her work on women viewing *I Love Lucy,* demonstrates the fact that some viewers focus on the character of Lucy in her failed attempts to escape the kitchen, while others see Lucille Ball as a successful performer and business woman (125).

However, while it is reasonable to suppose that eccentricity created social and public space for the 1950s woman, it is not so clear why this should be necessary for a woman of the 1990s. Theoretically, Sally is not restricted in her choices in the manner that structured Lucy's life: there is no reason she should be financially dependent (although she apparently chooses to be so for much of the time), and the range of public behavior approved of for contemporary women is relatively broad. Sally's eccentricities, rather than carving her out additional space, seem at times to be employed to restrict her further by, as we shall see, undermining her relationships with those around her and shaping her as a target for ridicule. Thus, the polysemy of the meanings articulated in the "zany housewife" sitcom around femininity and domesticity may point to one of the key ways in which *Third Rock* perpetuates conventions of gender even as it occasionally subverts them.

THE RETURN OF THE NATURAL BODY

Perhaps the clearest indication of the way that *Third Rock* hedges its ideological bets is through the recurrence of the determinative body at certain points throughout all three seasons. In various episodes, hormones or other physical traits seem to dominate the behavior of the character in such a way as to emphasize the irrationality of human "nature." In these moments the human bodies come to shape and even entrap the alien personalities within them in a way that is familiar from both Western and Eastern conceptualizations of the body as a limitation on the soul. A good example occurs in the second-season episode "My Mother the Alien." Mrs. Dubcek, the Solomons' landlady, asks Sally to baby-sit her grandson. The alien spirit of inquiry leads Dick to ask, "Why do you assume Sally will be taking care of the baby?" Mrs. Dubcek responds, "She's a woman," to which Sally remarks with heavy irony, "Yet another perk." The Cartesian novum of the show makes it possible for the show to defamiliarize gendered expectations of nurturing through the scarcely feminist voice of High Commander Dick. However, as the episode progresses, it begins to appear as if Sally is indeed the most capable of the foursome in the role of baby-sitter. While Dick, Tommy, and Harry are unable to get the infant to eat or stop crying, Sally instantly lapses into baby talk, knows what food helps with teething trouble, and is attuned to the child's every need. "Mrs. Dubcek was right!" Sally exclaims delightedly. "I am great with the kid!" If we are in any doubt about the reasons for this affinity, Sally clarifies it for us:

Sally: Hush, I think I hear the baby turning over.

Dick: I don't hear anything.

Sally: Of course, you don't, you're a man.

When questioned by Dick on her enthusiasm for this new mission, she says tentatively, as if surprising herself, "I mean, I know I complained at the start, but this is the first assignment when I actually feel like I'm using all of me." There are certainly plenty of textual indications to suggest that Sally is referring to well-springs of maternal feeling emerging from her female body. However, as the previous dialogue suggests, Sally's maternal behavior is seen as becoming a little obsessive, yet again conforming to the traditions of the zany housewife of the sitcom. She puts the baby in Dick's bed, leaving him to sleep in the cot; won't allow the phone to ring more than once while the baby is in bed; sees mortal danger in the pit of colorful balls that the toddler plays in at the supermarket; and finally refuses to return the infant to Mrs. Dubcek. Her behavior parodies the over-intense maternal feelings of baby snatchers.

If Sally's behavior in this episode is largely represented as an instinctive maternal reaction issuing from her female body, the responses of the other aliens, and Dick in particular, appear to be at the other end of the Cartesian dualisms of mind and body, logic and emotion. He is stereotypically cold and calculating. Dick agrees to the baby's arrival in the attic flat because it will be an opportunity to observe a young human. Later, he offers the baby to Mary Albright as a substitute for the pet fish he killed in her absence, treating the baby as a token in a wider game plan and brushing over both Sally's and Mrs. Dubcek's attachment to the baby as well as Dr. Albright's affection for her fishy friends. The comparison between Dick, who is unable to look after a pet, and Sally, with her uprush of maternal feelings, is clearly offered.

In case we have missed the point that the desire to nurture comes programmed into the female body, Sally's nurturing skills are once more on display in "Post-Nasal Dick." When the whole family gets sick, the male members of the household retreat to bed, demanding attention. Once again, Sally is surprised by her own (natural) reaction: "All I want to do is curl up into a ball, yet somehow I'm compelled to nurture you." Sally herself comes to consider that she is behaving in a way driven by natural or innate female instincts. Early in season one, she returns from explaining to her ex-date that she now understands his limitations—his failure to phone, his inability to interpret her desires, his rejection of her when he is not immediately offered sex—and realizes that she has expected too much. A starting point in her discussion with Dick of the differences between men and women is his assumption that her earlier (read feminine) behavior was somehow defective.

Dick: You're fixed!

Sally: I'm not fixed! I'm supposed to be this way. I'm a woman.

Dick: Yes, and—?

Sally: Tell me, Dick—what kind of shampoo do you use?

Dick: I don't know.

Sally: Exactly. And do you have the urge to have an eight-pound screaming larvae rip its way out of your abdomen?

Dick: No, I think I can do without that.

Sally: You see! Here you and I are completely different life forms and it's just some sick cosmic joke that we have to share a planet.

Dick: You know, I've been thinking about your assignment. Maybe it wasn't fair of me making you the woman?

Sally: I'm alright! I can handle the mood swings, the emotional issues, the cat-calls, the punitive underwear—because frankly, when I think of the alternative [looks him up and down] I just have to laugh. ("Dick Is from Mars . . .")

At points during the first series of the show, the peccadilloes of Tommy and Dick's male bodies also come into focus as impinging upon or constraining their identities. In the pilot episode "Brains and Eggs," Tommy protests that he can't help his adolescent lechery toward girls on his school volleyball team. A disbelieving Dick looks into his mind: "That's disgusting!" he comments with sympathy. Dick, too, is shown to be subject to masculine rushes of lust and anger that appear to take the alien by surprise. In "Lonely Dick," for instance, catching sight of Sally glammed up in pearls, frock, and make-up, he bursts out, "Oh, mama!" then wonders, "Why did I say that?" Similarly, when the Solomons' neighbor Frank Muller tows Dick's car in "Angry Dick," Dick, having already come to see his car as an extension of his identity, is consumed by a fit of rage and slugs him, then marvels at the feelings he is experiencing: "I feel better! And powerful! This is why people have friends. This is incredible. It's the best I've ever felt!" The mutual respect that this punch brings between Frank and Dick indicates that this, like their excited discussion of ball-bearings earlier in the episode, is appropriate and natural male (bonding) behavior.

THE FEMINIZING OF THE HUMAN BODY

As we have already argued, *Third Rock* presents gender as both an arbitrary performance of conventional familial and sexual roles and as naturally springing from sexed bodies. By offering these two perspectives on gender side by side, the show's viewers can choose to come away with any number of interpretations of the relationships between mind and body, sex and gender. Some of these interpretations are consistent with feminist positions, while others fit neatly into an antifeminist worldview. More worrying perhaps, from a feminist perspective, is the way that the objectified human body comes to be feminized, especially through the later seasons of the show, while the male bodies of Tommy, Dick, and Harry are increasingly invisible.

The Cartesian novum of the show increasingly allows the disembodied alien mind to be presented as masculine. This can be seen in the way that Dick's behavior often converges with stereotypically masculine traits, despite the fact that he is apparently behaving simply like an alien in a human body. Dick's performance of masculinity is a rather peculiar combination of '50s and '90s stereotypes of fatherhood. On the one hand, he attempts to play the patriarch, ordering the family about, and "providing for the family"; on the other hand, he is "in touch with" his emotions, enjoying the novel sensation of crying when it is for joy, riveted by his attraction for Mary, and demonstrating all the narcissistic, attention-seeking behavior of the media representation of the "new man," as described by Rowena Chapman and others. However, as the secretly superior alien, Dick inadvertently finds himself replaying much of the behavioral stereotype of the unreconstructed, self-obsessed male (see Hearn, 204, 206). He belittles Dr. Mary Albright's academic achievements, he begs for attention when experiencing unaccustomed sickness, and he makes direct and often insulting comments about women's physical appearance. Even at his most tender, Dick contrives to emulate the worst achievements of the "new man," using his desire to know Mary better to draw attention to himself. All this, however, is technically in his persona of alien.

While Dick's characteristic qualities as an alien in a human body converge with stereotypes of masculinity, there are other indications that the show inadvertently offers a gendering of its Cartesian novum. For example, a review of the pilot episode in SFX magazine describes Sally as "a male alien who drew the short straw" (Basic, 172): the writer assumes a male identity for Sally's alien self that is never confirmed by the show's script. The mind, here, is implicitly masculinized in a way that is in keeping with Western traditions of philosophy.[2] The body is, in contrast, feminized both in Basic's review and in the show itself. The SFX review goes on to pick out "[Actor Kirsten] Johnson's exploration of her new body" as a key element of *Third Rock*'s plot, while the remaining Solomons' experiences of male bodies are not mentioned (Basic, 72). This exemplary reading of the show gives a hint to the way that *Third Rock* increasingly equates the strangeness of the human body with the female body of Sally. One of the few moments of the show in which the male body is mentioned provides an internal comment on the way the male body is treated as invisible. In "Dick Is from Mars . . . ," Dick asks Tommy about his first day at school; Tommy replies: "Man, you can't compliment anybody in the shower!" Just as the homophobic, macho atmosphere of the high school boys' shower room makes it dangerous to remark on the display of male bodies, the show itself seems reluctant to point out the potential for comedy in the male body on screen.

We repeatedly see Sally ordered how to present herself in public. She does not learn how to be gendered, she is directed to be gendered and to a great extent this means physical display. In contrast, for example, Dick's masculinity is indicated in part by his refusal to diet. As the seasons progress, *Third Rock* seems to conform with Dick's Cartesian view of body and mind, allowing the male body to become invisible; while Sally's body is increasingly subject to scrutiny and control.

THE HUMILIATION OF SALLY

The implicit masculinity of the mind of the aliens and the feminization of the human body are most clearly evident in the way that Sally comes to be controlled and humiliated by the characters around her. As we have seen, from the pilot episode we are in a universe in which it is the female body that is considered the primary object of humor. The fascination of the male aliens with Sally's cleavage points to the way that the male body is represented as private, while the female body is presented as a legitimate arena for public commentary and appropriation. Not only, however, is the female body placed firmly in public space, its construction within the show is almost always negative, even while we are expected to admire (or salivate over) Sally's body. Our very first introduction to femaleness as a construct is negative:

Sally: Why am I the woman?

Dick: Because you lost.

This joke, like many in *Third Rock,* can be interpreted as both feminist and profoundly misogynist, recognizing the disadvantages attached to a female body but leaving it up to the audience to decide if this disadvantage is natural or socially organized. Our supposedly ungendered aliens have already, through their preparatory research, come to understand that to be feminine is to be inferior. Furthermore, they already comprehend that to be female is to be an object of the male gaze and that this is not only instinctive but proper. Tommy, on his first day among other young people, makes overtures to a girl on the volleyball team. Reprimanded for altering the life of a human being, he responds, "Yeah, but some of them are just asking for it!" While this is funny, its humor rests in part on the fact that this objectification is not corrected and that we recognize its relationship with the date-rape debate. In a later episode, "Lonely Dick," Tommy's girlfriend, August, protests when he tries to look down her blouse:

August: I don't know how I could have expected a fourteen-year-old boy [. . .] to separate my body from my mind.

Tommy: Wait, August, they're attached!

If the female body is presented as always on display to male onlookers, it is also shaped for us as a body to be controlled and directed by the men of the house. At the end of the pilot episode, Dick decides to go to a staff party to further his fascination with Mary:

Dick: Which reminds me, I command you to shave under your arms.

Sally: Do-able. I'm sorry you find me so offensive. [starts crying]

The uncontrolled female body is an object of shame: in the episode "Dick Is from Mars . . . ," Dick asks Sally to say something personal to practice for a date she has been ordered to make:

Sally: Once every lunar month my uterine lining sloughs itself.

Dick: [covering his ears] That may be too personal.

The exchange reinforces the point that shame is restricted not merely to display of the female body but to discussion of it. While the female is considered controlled by her body, she is, paradoxically, to be shamed by it. As late as the season-three episode "Eleven Angry Men and One Dick," Sally is incapable of stepping beyond this sense of shame about her body. In response to a pretentious English poet, Seth, she changes her appearance drastically, wearing nothing but black "grunge" clothing, leaving her hair unwashed, and omitting to shave. However, first, this decision is taken solely to please Seth; it is not an autonomous action. And second, when Seth turns out to be a fraud, she reverts quickly back to conventional "femininity" and confesses herself relieved to have shaved again: the implication is both that the human female is "meant" to be shaved and powdered and that much femininity, while performative, is performed at the behest of men. As she complains in "Lonely Dick," "While we're on the subject of bodies, why is mine so much higher maintenance than yours?" Tommy: "I think the economy relies on it." Much the same is true for the internal economy of the show.

By contrast, Dick maintains autonomy over his physical body, if not always as completely as he might like. In "Moby Dick" a rare reference is made to Dick's physical condition; the humor is based in the revelation that men (including Dick) react to depression in much the same way as women: they eat. Dick's waistline is expanding rapidly, the result of comfort eating after the breakup with Mary, and initially this leads to fruitless attempts to diet. However, the purpose of this episode is to confirm Dick's masculinity. This is portrayed in the context of the mind-body split. Dick tries to order his body to lose weight but discovers he has no control over it (it is "animal"): "It has a stupid design flaw. It thinks it can fill a gaping emotional hole with food." But the real issue is that men are privileged to accept their own bodies and their own body image to a far greater extent. Faced with a lifetime of controlled eating, Dick prefers the expedient of a larger pair of pants. He does not share the sense of failure that Mary displays at the "Fat Losers" club and he declares loudly: "My body is just the vehicle that carries my mind around. My brain deserves a smooth ride." In contrast, as Sally points out, women are only allowed to gain weight when they are pregnant.

While Dick may be concerned about how he looks, there is little evidence that he feels his outward appearance to be at the root of either his personality or how he is perceived by others. In fact, in the season-three episode "Just Your Average Dick," both Dick and Tommy eventually reject outward normality as an option; only Sally, whose gendered self is constantly subject to remodeling from those around her, finds it both easy and invigorating to take on this new role and personality. Although the connection is obvious, Sally's belief in order and discipline is never linked with her role as a military officer. Interestingly, adherence to the social norms of the apartment block to which they move allows Sally to take far greater control over the family lifestyle than does their usual eccentricity. The message seems to be that women both gain from adherence to social norms and are responsible for their construction. The implication is that if men are eccentric, it is because women—despite their protestations—secretly prefer this. This is exemplified by a line reiterated in "Dick and the Other Guy," in which Dick finds himself competing for Mary's affections with a man more eccentric than himself. Sally's failure to convince the family that being average is desirable results in a successful conspiracy to publicly undermine her in order that the men of the family can return to their preferred lifestyle. That we are clearly expected to identify with the men in this sequence should draw our attention again to one of the more disturbing aspects of the show, the carefully structured and long-term program of humiliation that Sally endures and at which the audience is expected to laugh.

Much of the humor in *Third Rock* is focused on the fact that Sally does not see herself as attractive, takes sarcastic comments seriously, and maintains a low level of self-esteem. The further the series travels, the more we are accustomed to Sally attempting to accept other people's dismissive judgments of her. Dick's (unwittingly funny) criticism of Sally's "comically long legs [. . .] [and] unruly breasts" in "Big Angry Virgin from Outer Space" is a good example of the way Sally is undermined. When Mary makes a similar comment apparently as a compliment, Sally is upset. But then, it may be an insult: in "Will Work for Dick" Sally has been playing with Barbie dolls with a neighbor's child.

> *Nina:* I always had Barbie tea parties.
>
> *Mary:* Ah, Barbie, blond hair, tiny waist, legs up to her neck. Who grows up to look like that?
>
> *Nina:* Yeah, who?
>
> *Sally:* Yeah, who?

At the end of this exchange, Mary and Nina look daggers at Sally, reinforcing a point made continually throughout the show, and despite the close relationship of Mary and Nina, that women are principally competitors, not friends and allies. While this episode shows, in a potentially progressive way, the contribution of men to female low self-esteem and the arbitrary nature of standards of beauty, it manages to turn feminist critiques into a restatement of women's competitive bitchiness.

All too often potentially empowering moments are later used to undermine Sally. As a military officer, Sally is unabashed about taking control of the supposedly masculine role of captain when Dick goes missing in "Dick Smoker" (season one). When the car breaks down, she pushes it one-handed to the garage. However, collecting the car later, Sally has that all-too-common experience: the mechanic talks to Harry (the dim one), not to Sally. Sally points out it is her car and Harry agrees.

> *Harry:* I just stand here and nod.
>
> *Mechanic:* Well, you gotta humor 'em. [laughs and starts an anecdote about a redhead]

The mechanic's humor dries up when he realizes that Sally has walked around him and has his balls (literally) caught in a wrench. Harry, clueless as usual, shrugs:

Harry: Women, huh?

Sally: Hello! I'd like my car ready in half an hour. I don't want a 200 percent mark up on parts, and I'd like it washed. Thank you.

However, when Dick's absence continues, Sally realizes she is on her own and panics. In tune with the conventions of the zany housewife, the little lady over-reaches herself and has to be rescued by the patriarch who sends her back to her kitchen sink.

As we have already argued, Sally spends much of the three seasons of *Third Rock* in a domestic context, trying (and often failing) to rebel against the strictures with which she is surrounded. In keeping with this, when Sally does work, she works not to support herself or to enhance her self-esteem, but for "pin-money" to spend on make-up and accessories. This, inevitably, shapes her choice of employment. Throughout the course of the show, Sally holds down a number of minimum-wage jobs, as does Harry, but in season three, Tommy encourages Harry to go to night school to obtain his high school diploma. No one ever even mentions to Sally (who is clearly much more intelligent) that education is an option and, as if validating the family's lack of faith in her, she proves herself unable to stick at any job for long. Furthermore, her employment often ends in fiasco. In "Tom, Dick, and Mary," for instance, Sally gets a clerical job on the basis of looks alone and finds herself the subject of sexual harassment. At first she sees it as her fault, viewing herself as the temptress, but when Nina corrects her, she reacts "inappropriately" and hits her boss. The consequence is that she loses her job and we receive a lesson that violence, while a bonding experience for men (in the episode "Angry Dick"), is unsuitable for women. As with Lucille Ball's exploits, we are allowed to cheer the "zany" eccentricities of a woman, but we are not allowed to believe that a woman can win.

As the seasons progress, we are less and less permitted to see Sally's assertiveness represented in any positive way, and the emphasis is all too often on her "innate" femininity and limited female body. We see the first indications in "Dick Is from Mars . . .". When Sally does not receive the promised call from her date, she becomes frantic, referring to an indefinable pain, and starts sobbing that although a decorated veteran, she cannot handle the pain of being a woman; it is not clear whether she means the physical nature of femaleness or the social structure into which she is thrust. From this point on, Sally becomes more conciliatory and increasingly bashful with prospective boyfriends; often with little real understanding of what she is doing, she leaves chaos in her wake.

In the early episodes of the show, Sally is shown to be outgoing and confident, despite, or perhaps because of, her ignorance of the conventions of small talk and sexual by-play. Her approach to Mr. Randall, for example, is direct and to the point, without any acknowledgment of the rules of the dating game that would assign to her the role of prey, not predator: "Excuse me," she says suddenly in the course of a parent–teacher interview, "there's something about the thickness of your neck and the broadness of your shoulders that makes me think you'd be an agile hunter and provide well for our children" (in "Dick Like Me"). Her attempts to maintain this confidence, however, are undermined by the demands made by Mr. Randall that she maintain a performance the criteria for which are never clearly stated. In the season-two episode "Big Angry Virgin from Outer Space," Mr. Randall begins to protest Sally's assertiveness. In response, Sally enthusiastically embraces passivity. The principal sign of Sally's submissiveness is a pink dress, accompanied by a continuous response of "You decide," no matter what Mr. Randall asks. Unsurprisingly, he thinks he is being mocked:

> *Mr. Randall:* Look, if there's a problem here, just say so.
>
> *Sally:* Oh, there's no problem, I'm just trying to please you.
>
> *Mr. Randall:* Would you drop this, OK?
>
> *Sally:* Something's wrong, isn't it?
>
> *Mr. Randall:* You like to play naive, but you know exactly what you're doing. [Sally's pose changes from prim and ladylike as she moves to sit astride her chair—gestures forcefully]
>
> *Sally:* Back up! Is naive a good thing in a woman or a bad thing?
>
> *Mr. Randall:* Are you trying to drag me into some neofeminist debate?
>
> *Sally:* I don't know, you decide!
>
> *Mr. Randall:* Fine, I've decided, lunch is over! [gets up and leaves]

At least one uncomfortable implication of this exchange is that there is something undesirable about a feminist, a suggestion only mildly counteracted by the inconsistent feminism of August and Mary. Furthermore, Sally's experiences with Mr. Randall offer a different twist on the suggestion that women enjoy playing with patriarchy. For Sally, the game is only fun while it is still recognizably a game—hence the greater success of her relationship with Don.

A DEFINITIVE READING OF *THIRD ROCK*?

We have argued throughout this chapter that the Cartesian novum of *Third Rock*—the occupation of human bodies by alien minds—allows the show both to articulate incisive criticisms of contemporary practices of gender and to reproduce nostalgic, hyperconventional representations of domestic femininity. *Third Rock* often represents gender as less a matter of sexed bodies and their hormones than an acting out of gender conventions. However, the way that Sally, like her predecessor Lucy, is so frequently humiliated or brought low by her association with a (shameful) female body is, we would suggest, an indication of some of the problems of understanding gender as a performance. There is a long-standing convention of attributing a gendered hierarchy to the Cartesian dualisms of mind and body and, as writers like Susan Bordo have shown, the idea that gender is acted out through the body is vulnerable to a reading that sees the (implicitly feminized) body as an instrument or as a trap of the rational (implicitly masculine) mind. In *Third Rock* this is illustrated in the undercutting of Sally's rational military officer by the imperatives and desires of the female body. While we have explored the textual evidence for each of these apparently contradictory interpretations of the show, our purpose is not to propose either as definitive. The ambivalence toward gender roles portrayed in the series is sufficient that at times a separate interpretation may be required for each episode, as the shows switch between conservative and radical conceptualizations of gender. Thus, the success of both this program and the sitcom genre of which it is a part can be in some ways attributed to its polysemy: the way it allows both feminist and conservative understandings of the relationship between mind and body, gender and sex. However, the longer the show continues, the more evident it becomes that potential feminist interpretations are being undercut both by the show's inconsistent ideology—its continual flirtation between the ideas that gender is innate and that it is culturally constructed—and its inability to move beyond the objectification and humiliation of the female body as its primary source of humor.

NOTES

1. Notably Butler, 1991; also Harries; Ramet; Straub.
2. See Grosz; Gatens; Bordo.

WORKS CITED

Basic, Todd. "TV Review: *Third Rock.*" *SFX* (13 June 1996): 72.

Bordo, Susan. *Unbearable Weight: Feminism, Western Culture and the Body.* Berkeley: University of California Press, 1993.

Butler, Judith. *Gender Trouble: Feminism and the Subversion of Identity.* New York: Routledge, 1991.

Chapman, Rowena. "The Great Pretender: Variations on the New Man Theme." In *Male Order: Unwrapping Masculinity.* Edited by Rowena Chapman and Jonathan Rutherford. New York: Lawrence & Wishart, 1988.

Douglas, Susan J. *Where the Girls Are: Growing Up Female with the Mass Media.* London: Penguin, 1994.

Gatens, Moira. "Towards a Feminist Philosophy of the Body." In *Crossing Boundaries: Feminism and the Critique of Knowledges.* Edited by Barbara Caine, E. A. Grosz, and Marie de Lepervanch. Sydney: Allen and Unwin, 1988, 59–70.

Grosz, Elizabeth. *Volatile Bodies: Towards a Corporeal Feminism.* Sydney: Allen and Unwin, 1994.

Hanke, Robert. "The 'Mock Macho' Situation Comedy: Hegemonic Masculinity and Its Reiteration." *Western Journal of Communication* 62, no. 1 (1998): 74–93.

Harries, Dan M. "Camping with Lady Divine: Star Persona and Parody." *Quarterly Review of Film and Video* 12, nos. 1–2 (1991): 13–22.

Hearn, Jeff. "Is Masculinity Dead? A Critique of the Concept of Masculinity/Masculinities." In *Understanding Masculinities.* Edited by Mairtín Mac an Ghaill. Buckingham: Open University, 1996.

Marc, David. *Comic Visions: Television Comedy and American Culture.* London: Blackwell, 1987.

———. *Demographic Vistas: Television in American Culture.* Philadelphia: University of Pennsylvania Press, 1984.

Mellencamp, Patricia. "Situation Comedy, Feminism and Freud: Discourses of Gracie and Lucy." In *Studies in Entertainment: Critical Approaches to Mass Culture.* Edited by Tania Modleski. Bloomington: Indiana University Press, 1986, 80–95.

Press, Andrea L. *Women Watching Television: Gender, Class, and Generation in the American Television Experience.* Philadelphia: University of Pennsylvania Press, 1991.

Ramet, Sabrina Petra, ed. *Gender Reversals and Gender Cultures: Anthropological and Historical Perspectives.* London: Routledge, 1996.

Rubin, Gayle. "The Traffic in Women: Notes on the 'Political Economy' of Sex." In *Towards an Anthropology of Women.* Edited by Rayna R. Reiter. New York: Monthly Review Press, 1975.

Straub, Kristina. *Sexual Suspects: Eighteenth Century Players and Sexual Ideology.* Princeton: Princeton University Press, 1992.

3

Scully Hits the Glass Ceiling

Postmodernism, Postfeminism, Posthumanism, and *The X-Files*

Linda Badley

INTRODUCTION: ANTI-PAM

"It isn't *Baywatch*," says Gillian Anderson about playing Dana Scully, *The X-Files'* fiercely intelligent, scientific, and stoic FBI agent. "I'm sort of the anti-Pam" ("50 Most," 141), she adds, referring to *Baywatch* babe Pamela Anderson Lee. As *X-Files'* creator Chris Carter tells the story, the network wanted Scully to be "someone who might look sexy in a bathing suit" (Janssen), but Carter chose the "formidable"-looking Anderson instead ("50 Most," 141). "Gillian had that stare," he explains, "and a kind of mysterious aura about her" (Janssen).

The ambiguity in Carter's comments typifies the problem that Scully presents in any discussion of women in television. A groundbreaking character in one of the most popular and controversial shows of the 1990s, Scully has challenged television's portrayal of women and changed the way we think and talk about it. Naming her after Vince Scully, the Los Angeles sports announcer he grew up associating with "the voice of God" (Bischoff, 44), Carter empowered her to an unusual degree, giving her the authority, the language, and the tools associated with male-dominated institutions, including medicine and the law. Through her looks (as opposed to her appearance), and whether wielding a scalpel, a laptop, or a gun, Scully has reversed and traversed female stereotypes. She has brought feminist issues such as the objectification of the female body and the gaze (the male look or perspective that dominates cinema, television, and science) into popular consciousness. Consider the words of William Leith of the London *Observer*:

"She is an attractive woman, but not a sex object, or even overtly sexual. A forensic pathologist, she examines bodies, rather than being an examined body" (Leith).

Yet in spite of (or because of) this desexualization, however, Anderson is voted in poll after poll as the "sexiest" woman on television, the "centre of [a] 90s male obsession" (*Empire*). *The Guinness Book of Records 1999* lists her as "Most Popular Cult TV Star" ("TV Stars," 10), with Alta Vista presently listing some 49,502 Internet websites devoted to her. A June 1998 *Details* magazine cover, captioned "Lust in Space with Gillian Anderson," features a close-up of her face digitally altered into a futuristic silver-metallic mask that sets off the huge eyes and perfect mouth (Janiak). One effect of this "glacial allure" (Janssen) is a Scully/Anderson face fetish. According to Ed Lake, Anderson holds the record—"at least 500" in 1998—for bogus nude photographs (forged by attaching a head shot of the star to a nude model). Says Lake, "[Scully's] always dressed in a suit, so that makes people's imaginations run" (quoted in Beachy). As the "anti-Pam"—the woman who looks—she more potently embodies the mystery of the universe, as woman traditionally has.

Out of such paradoxes, the star's "legions of admirers have been crafting [. . .] a feminist icon," notes the *Village Voice*'s David Kushner:

> For the fans, she's a blessed chemical reaction of actress and character: she's Gillian Anderson, a 29-year-old single mother who tattoos her ankles with blue turtles [. . .] and acts her heart out in a genre ruled (and mostly written) by men; she's Dana Scully, skeptical and spiritual, athletic and scientific, intelligent and sexy. Madonna, Missy Elliott, Lara Croft: none could fight the conspiratorial feds, dissect a spleen, and still be so damn IDDG [Intellectually Drop Dead Gorgeous]. (61)

As Kushner says, the transference of "feminist" connotations between character and star is unusually strong—to the extent that a discussion of the one must refer to the other. And Anderson/Scully is instantly recognizable as an icon of popular feminism. But how does her/their "feminism" hold up under scrutiny? And is feminism consistent with or even possible within the narrative, gender, and genre codes operating in *The X-Files*?

In addressing these questions, I will explore Scully's (and, when relevant, Anderson's) iconography from three perspectives that describe our present cultural condition: postmodernism, postfeminism, and posthumanism. While *postmodernism* has an enormously broad and complex field of reference, I will use the term to mean contemporary texts and discourses that participate in a culture of mass-mediated self-awareness, that assert conventions or ideas primarily to subvert them, thus de-naturalizing (deconstructing) what we take for granted—including capitalism, patriarchy, gender, humanism, and even the human body. Postfeminism and posthuman or "cyborg" feminism I will discuss as "postmodernized" feminisms—movements of the 1980s through the present that have elicited compromises between activist second-wave feminism and postmodern culture, especially Marxist, cultural, and psychoanalytic thought. The redundancy of "posts" is deliberate. I mean to suggest the way these terms tend to collapse into one another. All three are like *The X-Files,* moreover, in sounding more progressive than they really are. In this essay, then, the prefix *post* will mean "after" and "beyond," as might be expected, but *post* will also denote a marker or signpost along the way: the term will point out invisible barriers that Scully bumps up against from episode to episode, season to season.

"*X-FILES* POSTMODERNISM": ANTI-MULDER

We must, of course, look further than Scully. The foregoing discussion ignores the "relationship," as X-Philes call it, and one-half of the equation that determines *The X-Files* formula, David Duchovny's Fox Mulder. *The X-Files* is based on a partnership of two agents devoted to uncovering and comprehending an international/government/corporate conspiracy involving alien/human hybridization. This relationship is thought to be remarkably egalitarian, challenging traditional gender roles as portrayed on television. As Rhonda Wilcox and J. P. Williams argue, the show advocates "an ideology in which Mulder and Scully are free to invert traditional male/female characterizations," presenting them as "gender-liminal" (99). Scully, the skeptic, stands for the rational-empiricist worldview of male science; Mulder stands for nonrational, intuitive ways of knowing often designated as feminine and subversive. He trusts his instincts, offers supernatural explanations, and bases his life's work on the memory of a paranormal experience in which he saw his sister abducted by aliens. An Oxford-educated psychologist, Mulder believes what he feels and has undergone regression therapy of the sort advocated in women's self-help books; Scully, trained as a doctor, is an expert in two areas traditionally off-limits for women, medicine/forensic science and the law.

The gender shifting extends to the representation of male and female bodies and to what psychoanalytic film critic Laura Mulvey defined as the issue of the gaze.[1] *The X-Files* objectifies the male body rather than the female. The camera lingers as hunks such as Mulder and Assistant Director Skinner strip down to their Speedos. Scully, by contrast, keeps her clothes on—a "suggestive" Scully scene is one in which she wears pajamas. The power of the gaze is often transferred from the guys to the gals. Mulder watches X-rated videos the audience never sees instead of watching Scully, who possesses what in this series is the most privileged and invasive gaze of all—that of the medical scientist who examines and manipulates alienated (objectified, feminized) bodies. She is also allowed the leisurely, body-assessing "male" gaze (for instance, at handsome Sheriff Harwell in "Bad Blood"). Between Mulder and Scully, as Wilcox and Williams note, the gaze becomes a dialogue based on the question "What do you think?" Looking into each other's eyes, Mulder and Scully "acknowledge each other as subjects rather than fetishizing or denying the other person" (Wilcox and Williams, 120). In these reversals and variations, the camera deconstructs the gendered gaze. Walking "a heroic path" along the margin of the conventionally gendered romance (120), Mulder and Scully represent 1990s ideals of gender equity and awareness.

It is a given that "If they shag, the show's over" (Cornell, Day, and Topping, 2). The "lack" in the narrative's central relationship produces UST (fanspeak for "unresolved sexual tension") and more, a space for sublimated discourse about body and gender politics, sexual identity, and the "strange" attractions of "alien"—cross-species or trans-human—sex. The dialectic of the main characters takes on resonances from the monster or issue of the week—as in "Jersey Devil" (a female Bigfoot), "Genderbender" (gender-shifting mutants or aliens [or both] who mate with humans, lethally), and "Alpha" (a romance between a male werewolf and a female dog lover who also has an intense online connection with Mulder). If the Scully–Mulder relationship were consummated, the show would lose this resonance, becoming just another heterosexual romance.

The gender bending is amplified by the series' equally well-known "genre bending." "[P]art police procedural, part suspense thriller, part action adventure, part medical drama, part science fiction and part horror," as Paula Vitaris describes it, *The X-Files* is "akin to one of its own mutant characters, with its own eclectic heritage" (17). Eleanor Hersey proposes the term "*X-Files* postmodernism" to account for this eclecticism, arguing that the series' "combination of social critique and aesthetic complexity [. . .] challenges the logic of mainstream television" (109). Layered with allusions directed toward different levels and groups, shape-shifting, resisting category or meaning, *The X-Files* "defies casual viewing" (Flaherty and Schilling, 38). It demands that its audience perform multiple, alternative "guerrilla readings" that provoke discussion and rearrange relations between the marginalized and the powers that be (Hersey, 112). Rather than one truth "out there," *The X-Files* proposes "multiple truths based on cultural, racial, and gendered perceptions" (110). Scully is not merely a "strong" female protagonist in a television series; she is, as Peni R. Griffin says, "a walking gender issue" (30).

The discourse surrounding Mulder/Duchovny and Scully/Anderson is extended into cyberspace and beyond by the show's vast, vociferous, and heterogeneous fan culture. There are Mulderists and Scullyists, groups of fans who claim to think like and identify with one or the other of the characters, regardless of gender, a process that may or may not be consciousness-raising. In an article about the online fan culture, Susan Clerc analyzes how the character of Scully gives women entry into the community of discourse; after gaining a "foothold," they are "free to move into other areas of the series" (49)—and further. The Order of the Blessed Saint Scully the Enigmatic [OBSSE], on the other hand, is devoutly focused, with weekly meditations and penances for all "Sisters." Proclaimed by the Gillian Anderson Testosterone Brigade to be "Intellectually Drop Dead Gorgeous" (IDDG), the "thinking man's" sex object, the star has equally vocal advocates in the Gillian Anderson Estrogen Brigade (GAEB), composed of lesbians and bisexual women. The GAEB home page displays double file cabinets with a drawer labeled "Women's Resources" and links to *Queer XF*, "Index of Gay-Themed *X-Files* Fan Fiction." GAWS, *The Official Gillian Anderson Web Site*, champions Anderson over Duchovny as "the star" of *The X-Files* with sophisticated graphics, Web ring, and an archive with some two hundred transcripts of articles and interviews.[2] GAWS features links to *The Feminist Majority Foundation Online* and an action line to "Stop Gender Apartheid in Afghanistan!"

We might conclude from the previous discussion that *The X-Files* phenomenon invites a vigorous, intellectually challenging, politically engaged, and equitable reading of gender. But what kind of feminism (if the term can apply at all) is it?

X-FILES FEMINISM: SURVIVING IN THE BOYS' CLUB

One kind of feminism was clearly in the minds of *The X-Files* creators in the planning and casting stages. Scully's "independent woman" character is derived from the popular feminist iconography of the late 1980s and early 1990s. As Wilcox and Williams argue, she descends from the hard-bodied fighting woman of science fiction/horror film—from Sigourney Weaver's Ripley in the *Alien* series to Linda Hamilton's Sarah Connor in *Terminator 2*—and more directly from Jodie Foster's petite, intense Clarice Starling, FBI trainee and protagonist of *Silence of the Lambs* (102–103).

Scully is "a woman trying to survive in the boys' club," as she says of Detective Ryan, one of her former students, in the first-season episode "Soft Light" (Wilcox and Williams, 119). She has worked to align herself with a power structure that threatens to use her ambition and innocence, much as the FBI uses Clarice Starling's, as bait. (Starling is assigned to "seduce" Hannibal Lecter into revealing information about a serial killer; Scully is brought onto the X-Files to "debunk" Mulder's paranormal hypotheses.) Like Starling, the diminutive Scully regularly faces down and tongue-lashes a power circle of broad-shouldered, dark-suited men. Unvaryingly serious for reasons women know well, she plays the straight "man" on the team.

Enhancing Scully's character as a woman fighting for her rights is Gillian Anderson's reputation (according to *Entertainment Weekly*) as "the toughest TV diva in town" (quoted in "Gillian Files"). "There's a lot of testosterone on the set," Anderson comments in an interview. While "guy-friendly," she claims to be "*very* independent. I can take care of myself, I don't feel left out. But when it has to do with work, and my input on the work [. . .] I will not tolerate not being heard" (quoted in Tannenbaum, 137–138). In December 1996, she made only half of Duchovny's salary (Lipsky, 33) but negotiated for an equal $110,000 per episode and an equal $4 million for her role in *The X-Files* film (Strauss).[3]

Oddly, the "feminism" associated with Anderson's fight for equity has rubbed off on *The X-Files* phenomenon, which is thought to be progressive. This perception was enhanced beginning with season two, when what eventually became the core narrative—the story of Scully's abduction, near death, and gradual recovery of her memories—began to resemble that subgenre of popular feminism, the abuse survival narrative. Like Starling with her mission to "save" women victims (and woman-as-victim), Scully became dedicated to a cause larger than herself.

In short, *The X-Files* draws on four key tenets of liberal second-wave feminism: (1) recognition of women as an oppressed group; (2) commitment to social and political change; (3) emphasis on sexual/body politics; and (4) a woman-centered perspective.[4] The alien abduction scenario central to *The X-Files* is a rape narrative; it echoes the countless stories in which women are abducted by sky gods with agendas. It is also a contemporary version of Mary Shelley's *Frankenstein*. Subjected to experiments with superovulation and hybridization that render her infertile, Scully is represented as every woman exploited for her body by patriarchy and power, as revealed in season three's "Paper Clip," "Nisei," and "731." These episodes reveal that a group of powerful white (and white-haired) men, an international consortium involved originally in a continuation of Nazi and Japanese eugenics experiments, are ultimately responsible for this medical rape. The crime extends to other women when Scully's sister is mistakenly assassinated in Scully's place ("Paper Clip"). Scully's quest, if she has one, is less for Mulder's truth than for justice.

Particularly in season four, when Scully and a group of twelve other female abductees are revealed to be dying of identical nasopharyngeal cancers and deemed "expendable," like women's bodies/health in general, the series expanded the scope of its cultural and sexual politics. Unable to recall memories of her abduction, Scully suffers from the equivalent of hegemonic or culturally imposed repression. The third through fifth seasons are the story of her increasing consciousness of her exploitation and gradual identification with the group of victim-survivors. When Scully is told she is dying, she seeks out Penny Northern, the last survivor other than herself, separating herself, her values, and her goals from Mulder and what she now comes to define as his quest. In "Emily," a fifth-season episode in which she discovers she is the mother of a hybrid daughter who will die without transfusions of alien blood (toxic to humans), she makes what Paul Cornell describes as "a powerful pro-choice polemic, with Scully controlling the destiny of her ovum" (Cornell, Day, and Topping, 404). She decides to let this child, which was "not meant to be," die.

The X-Files regularly exposes patriarchal "family values" as the biggest lie of all. The home offers no protection in *The X-Files* and the family very little comfort. In "The Beginning," a sixth-season episode, the Consortium of patriarchs are revealed as having given their wives and children over to Project Purity Control, turning the nuclear family into a front for their breeding program. The abduction of Mulder's sister Samantha was engineered by two fathers—her biological father, the infamous Cigarette-Smoking Man, together with her nominal father William Mulder—and condoned by her mother. The purpose of this biological collusion with extraterrestrials is to ensure the survival of a few select human families after colonization, and more: to extend and enhance the patriarchal line in a superhuman species, an *Übermensch*. As the plot surrounding the Project makes increasingly clear, the family is potentially fascist. As the "sacrifice" of Samantha, Scully, the twelve women, and the Cigarette-Smoking Man's wife, Cassandra, suggests, the fathers are collaborating with the colonist powers to control reproduction, turning women into breeders.

X-FILES POSTFEMINISM: "MULDER, WHY DON'T I HAVE A DESK?"

The X-Files is weighted with feminist issues, and Scully's political position seems cut out for her. But the scenario changes when we assess Scully in other terms. The epistemological romance between Mulder and Scully flatters the notion of postmodern gender equity. But postmodernism privileges Mulder, using him to demonstrate male science's failure to access truth. Scully's position as a scientist is consequently "precarious," argues Lisa Parks: her rational empiricism has been introduced as the program's "sitting duck—that which it is out to challenge and dislocate" (124). Indeed, the token scientist's femininity is one sign of science's weakness.

Of course, Scully's role shifts during the early episodes from antagonist/debunker to collaborator, a Dr. Watson to Mulder's Holmes (Wilcox and Williams, 105–107). She provides a sounding board and furnishes the physical evidence for Mulder's hypotheses. More often than not, the two operate on the basis of a compromise in which Scully discovers in testing Mulder's paranormal hypothesis that her forensic evidence supports it.[5] Scully is therefore the perfect partner, Mulder's "other half," his "human credential" (as Duchovny puts it in *The X-Files Movie Special*), or what the Cigarette-Smoking Man, in the feature film, calls "The one *thing* in the world that [Mulder] can't live without" (*X-Files: Fight*, emphasis added). She is the ultimate tool. In this marriage of true minds, Scully plays a traditional female role.

Technically, Scully may be named for the voice of God and may have medicine and the law on her side, but Mulder's vision is validated by Chris Carter, as the prologue to nearly every episode reminds us. The opening teaser typically depicts the paranormal event that Mulder will prove to be truth. Scully's virtue is that she is "grounded," as *U. Magazine* puts it (Fulbright, 30); she brings Mulder back to earth. "Grounded" also describes Scully's limitations. The qualities that make Scully a "good" feminist, according to popular stereotype, turn her into a one-trick pony, "a woman enslaved to logic and science" (Day, 467). Thus, winking at X-

Philes and showing novices the rules of the game, the film ends as Mulder, shielding Scully from the wind, looks up and sees the vast shadow of a spaceship (in which Scully has recently been imprisoned) under the Antarctic ice. Scully misses seeing it—both the spaceship and her imprisonment—as usual. Weakened by her infection with an alien virus, exhausted after cryogenic suspension and a painful resuscitation (that has included the dubious pleasure of being carried out by Mulder for upward of half an hour), her eyes rolling inward and downward, lids fluttering, she looks finally at the ground. The film was a low point for the feminist Scully, one from which the series has not recovered. But anyone could have predicted it. In every opening sequence, we see Mulder entering a doorway, followed by Scully a step behind.[6]

Scully is often left in the shadows. Until the Cigarette-Smoking Man burned it down, Scully worked out of Mulder's office. In the opening frame of the fourth season's "Never Again," in a brilliant non sequitur, she asks, "Mulder, why don't I have a desk?" Mulder points to a dark corner of the office and says, "I always assumed that was your area." The frame of "Never Again," like much of the Mulder–Scully banter, is self-deconstructing parody. Alluding on one level to Anderson's demand for equal pay, it comments thoughtfully and wittily on sexism in the workplace by exposing its own. But while endearingly self-aware, the wit is cavalier. It is designed to deflect *serious* attention away from what it pretends to acknowledge, a sexism embedded in the series' premises.

Scully not only lacks the space, light, and vision to apprehend the truth; as a career scientist (an imitation man) who is secondarily a woman, she is characterized as divided against her "feminine" self. As her New Age sister Melissa tells her in "The Blessing Way" when she refuses to talk about or remember her abduction, "You're so shut off. It's like you've lost all touch with your own intuition." And when events in seasons three through five eventually force her out of her denial, she achieves neither wholeness nor understanding.

In season five's "Redux II," the boundaries of the two principals' avowed roles are confused as they reverse positions. As the depth of the FBI's involvement in the conspiracy is revealed, a disillusioned Mulder becomes the avowed skeptic, while Scully, whose abduction-induced cancer goes into remission (due to prayer and/or the Cigarette-Smoking Man's "cure," the reinsertion of a microchip), regains her childhood faith in miracles. But the role reversal does not validate Scully. Like her science, Scully's faith is conventional (based in organized religion, ritual, and authority), regressive (a return to her religious "roots" brought on by her struggle with cancer, grief, and family pressure), and inconsistent with her science. In contrast, Mulder has chosen as the situation has demanded from a spectrum of modes of knowing. In his bypassing of science and organized religion, he resists assimilation into patriarchy and demonstrates independent thinking. His life's search is an attempt to reconcile his knowledge with his intuition, to achieve consistency. Mulder therefore possesses rational intelligence *and* intuition, leaving Scully a second-rate believer (in her religious mode) and a straw "man" (in her rational mode). The gender bending makes Mulder fully and authentically human and makes Scully an "imitation man." Only in her position as Mulder's partner and disciple can she define her independence from the Father.

In the end, the brilliant, Oxford-educated Mulder appropriates "women's ways of knowing," leaving Scully with nothing he cannot also claim, and disallows her subjectivity as a woman. Her figuration in *The X-Files* demonstrates how easily markers we consider "feminist" can be co-opted. This loaded sort of gender bending, or male feminism, Tania Modleski calls "feminism without women" and attributes to the absorption of feminism by (male) postmodern culture and poststructuralist theory. Like feminist thought, postmodern thought challenges universals and presumptions of identity—a term that "carries with it an assumption of gender and a heterosexual imperative" (Modleski, 15) opposed by early feminists such as Simone de Beauvoir. Women are now taught by postmodern theorists from Derrida to Lacan and Foucault that we are constructed as "women" by language and history rather than born as such, and "the once exhilarating proposition that there was no 'essential' female nature has been elaborated to the point where it is now used to scare 'women' away from making *any* generalizations about or political claims on behalf of a group called 'women'" (15).

The X-Files' "feminism" is one of several ideological by-products of the series' postmodernism, through which it assimilates a vast range of timely issues, popular causes, positions, epistemologies, and marginalized or alienated groups.[7] But while the series deconstructs television stereotypes, it remains indifferent to the issues that it raises or the ideologies it appropriates. In *The X-Files*, all markers—whether of gender, race, nationality, species, or mortality—are unstable and relative, as Adrienne McLean has noted. The series at times seems a "televisual display of ideological virtuosity" in which the shape-shifting of aliens and mutants is merely one type (McLean, 9). In *The X-Files'* universe of postmodern, post-McLuhan cool, gender is finally a matter of individual lifestyle or consumer's choice, and a "real" feminist would be an anachronism.

In treating gender in terms of lifestyle choices or commodities, "*X-Files* postmodernism" is consistent with "postfeminism." The latter term suggests, among other things "post," that as a progressive movement, a sexual politics and a group identity, feminism is over, its goals accomplished, leaving in its wake the assumption of gender equity and cultural heterogeneity we see celebrated and played out in *The X-Files*. The term also refers to a backlash, originating in the 1980s, to second-wave feminism, and a compromise with patriarchal culture that reinstates "family values" and individualism. Postfeminism rejects feminism's first principle that women as a group are oppressed and that the "personal is political," stresses Judith Stacey (562). Instead, the political is personal, with women's autobiography and self-help replacing theory and activism. Above all, postfeminists avoid "all forms of direct struggle against male domination" (562).

As we have seen, *The X-Files* concerns urgent political issues and is in some sense "about" Mulder and Scully's and other small fringe groups' subversion of the powers that be. Through its overwhelming complexity, its web of conspiracy and cover-up, and its paranoia, however, the series makes the very idea of direct struggle—and certainly group activism—seem futile. After all, the series says, Aliens "R" Us. And as the conservative partner to Mulder's renegade, Scully is relatively apolitical, especially where women are concerned; for much of seasons two through four she cannot see the forest—the conspiracy and the power that science represents—for the trees—her scientific methods. As her father's daughter, a woman intent on proving herself in "a man's world," she refuses to see herself as a victim. She cannot remember the details of her abduction and clings to denial. Scully's rationalism and repression, in part, are devices for the show's primary teaser. At least partly because of her gifts and limitations as a woman/scientist, the precise identity and purposes of her abductors remain unknown, even at the end of the sixth season.[8]

Even after she becomes aware of the causes of her cancer, her means of dealing with it are primarily to internalize what the series presents as urgently political. Scully makes a show of stoic "courage" for a time, "fight[ing] this thing" medically, using science against what she learns is science-induced. But the women she might join with and advocate for are dead, with one exception, and when she joins the dying Penny Northern, the scene is quietly conventional, the mood resigned: one woman comforts another at the end. Scully's battle becomes a "spiritual" journey toward decorous acceptance of Everywoman's melancholy fate ("Memento Mori").

Scully's resignation to death as her reward for choosing guns and autopsies over a more womanly life's work of "healing" therefore informs and qualifies her choice of letting Emily, her alien-human hybrid child, die. Her reasoning is that this child "was not meant [by God or fate?] to be." Thus, while Scully assumes custody and asserts the power of choice over her ovum, her reaction can hardly be described as pro-active. With Emily's situation, as with her own, what should have been moral outrage and political consciousness are domesticated, redirected in part by her family into her grief and guilt throughout several episodes, notably "A Christmas Carol," "Emily," and "All Souls." Scully expresses primarily sorrow and morbidly sentimental religiosity. It is Mulder who (like a "good" husband) expresses her repressed rage in terms of gender and body politics: he names the issue and points the finger at the scientists who are "abducting women and stealing their unborn children [. . .]. Medical rapists, that's what you are" ("Emily").

Throughout the series, rather than challenge patriarchy directly or join forces with women activists, Scully channels her anger/ambition into fitting into the system, showing up her father (a naval officer), justifying her choices and, in the process, trying to prove Mulder "wrong" (according to Lyda, the perceptive ghost in "How the Ghosts Stole Christmas"). Beginning with season one's "Beyond the

Sea," the series probes the patriarchal roots of Scully's fascination with male authority. In contrast to Mulder's "anti-family" (a nest of conspiracy, betrayal, abduction, and uncertainty concerning parentage and identity, gender, and species), as we have seen, Scully's is a bastion of traditional values, grounded in the military and the Church. We learn that from her childhood on, Scully (a "tomboy") learned to define herself in relation to powerful men—in the military, the medical profession, and the government. She moved up the ladder by being a "good girl." And while her parents think she chose the FBI over a medical career as an act of rebellion, as she explains to Mulder in the pilot episode, "I thought that I could distinguish myself in the FBI." Her choice was her way of showing Daddy that she could tote a gun and play on his team. Scully's "feminism" is indeed *very* personal.

As the conspiracy is gradually revealed in seasons five and six and Scully moves toward Mulder's position, her politics become indistinguishable from Mulder's. Survival in the boys' club depends on pleasing as well as emulating Daddy, however. Scully's dependence on male approval has its dark side in her susceptibility to dominating and often "dangerous" men—psychotic serial killers, rapists, and a vampire (who is also a sheriff). This pattern makes clear that Scully's "feminist" characteristics are based not in her identification with women as a group but in her assumption of male superiority—her desire to *be* like a man and to *please* the man—and her guilt over her inability to do both at the same time. This pattern begins with "Beyond the Sea," in which Scully's unresolved conflict with her father, who has suddenly died, makes her vulnerable to a death row inmate who claims to be a medium. In another one of these weaker moments, in a bar with a man in "Never Again"—the episode that begins with Scully's overdue question, "Mulder, why don't I have a desk?"—Scully confesses to her attraction to "authoritative" men. She mentions her father and the fact that, after his death, "authoritative figures came into my life and part of me liked it [. . .] and then, along the way, there are other fathers." The pattern is repeated also, for example, in season two's "Irresistible," season three's "2Shy," season four's "Small Potatoes," season five's "Bad Blood," and season six's "Milagro."

"Scully episodes" frequently disempower Scully while offering a pseudo-feminist twist or "reward." In "Irresistible," in which she is captured by a necrophiliac fetishist who kills women for their fingernails and hair, the centerpiece is a sequence in which Scully zips open a body bag and sees that the face of the victim is her own. "2Shy" has a more overtly "feminist" angle: chasing a vampire-like serial killer who subsists on fat and uses Internet chat rooms to prey on lonely, overweight women with body-image problems, Scully is ambushed in a bathroom, but she and the intended victim catch the killer.

Two of these episodes figure Mulder as the man to whose authority Scully is ultimately vulnerable. In the whimsically toned "Small Potatoes," Scully is very nearly seduced by rapist Eddie van Blunt, a loser whose only gift is his ability to assume other men's identities and who impersonates a "romantic" Mulder with considerable success. One fan commented that the episode "made her look fairly, well, stupid, not to put too fine a point on it [. . .]. Basically, you have to assume that Scully *wanted* this kind of behaviour from Mulder bad enough that she put all the warning signs out of her mind [. . .]" (Helwig, "Small Potatoes").

In "Never Again," Scully protests Mulder's indifference by cutting short her field assignment and picking up a man (Ed Jerse) at a tattoo parlor. Taking Ed's dare and imitating his behavior (behavior he admits to regretting), she gets a tattoo. After telling him her life's story and sleeping with him, she discovers that recently divorced Ed is attracted to *and* threatened by strong women. This proclivity becomes psychotic when he is affected by a hallucinogen in the red dye in his 1940s pinup girl tattoo named "Betty." Like Norman Bates's mother in *Psycho*, Betty drives him to kill when "she" senses his attraction to "other" women. The tattoo is another wildly mixed message. Men think women relate to each other primarily through jealousy in their quest to possess a man, it says.[9] But guest-starring as the voice of the tattoo was Jodie Foster, who portrayed a primary model for Scully's "feminist" character. The collision of stereotypes—including Scully's woman in peril, Betty's femme fatale, and Foster's feminist fighting woman—is calculatedly disturbing. When Scully escapes with bruises and a battered ego, the behavior pattern the episode confirms is doubly troubling. As she slouches into Mulder's office looking like a parody of a battered wife, an incredulous Mulder asks, "All of this because I didn't give you a desk?" and congratulates Scully on "making a personal appearance in *The X-Files* for the second time." Thus he announces the defeat of her "feminism."

One might argue that Scully's retort, "It's not always about you, Mulder," allows her the last laugh. Episodes such as this acknowledge Scully's parallel but independent existence as a woman and give lip service to issues of sexual politics. In a witty allusion to Anderson's campaign for equity as a co-star, "Never Again" shows Scully's recognition of the continuation of patriarchy, the "glass ceiling" that precludes her having a desk. But the episode raises these issues only to put Scully back in her place with a doubly sexist combination—of the "Scully-almost-seduced" episode with the "Scully-in-peril" motif. Finally, it relegates the political issues Scully raises—and the "Scully episode" in general—to the dark, outlying regions of the office, to the no-man's land of the personal. While the metaphors are brilliantly consistent, revealing writers Darin Morgan and James Wong's sophisticated knowledge of feminist theory (seen in "Humbug" and "Jose Chung from Outer Space"), they also suggest that Scully will never get a desk as long as her role in this narrative means *being* rather than solving X-Files.

As this discussion has shown, Scully is the "thinking man's sex symbol," not simply because she is smart and independent but because she is the necessary Flesh to Mulder's (and Carter's) Word. She is his and the series' muse, as shown in Carter's teleplay for season six's darkly provocative, metafictional "Milagro." Phillip Padgett, an unemployed writer, stalks and nearly seduces Scully as part of his plan to tap her repressed passion, write the story of her inner life, and, by revealing it to her, "possess" her heart. Lured into his apartment, absorbed by his words, Scully is almost overcome by the perception and power of his fantasy— until Mulder barges in, saving her from her emotions.

The episode's return to the "Scully-almost-seduced" pattern provoked lively Internet discussion. Yet the most provocative element is its self-consciousness. Here is "The Author's" self-deconstructing allegory of his co-option of the female subject. (Indeed, "Milagro" may have been suggested by Roberta Flack's song about a singer "telling [her] whole life with his words," thus "killing [her] softly." This author's seductive words literally kill: Padgett creates a surrogate, a character who comes to life and grotesquely enacts his desire by wrenching out women's hearts and grasping them triumphantly in his hands.) But the episode's obvious effect, especially on the casual viewer, is to reinforce the stereotype, à la *Fatal Attraction*, of independent women as lonely, neurotic, and nostalgic for sexual attention from men.

Gillian Anderson, who often expresses for her character a respect that borders on awe, also admits to wishing Scully would loosen up a little. At media fan convention Expo 3, a young teenage fan gushed that "Scully IS the epitome of womanhood because, not only can she kick ass but she also [. . .] works with Mulder without jumping him [. . .]." Anderson, laughing, replied, "So the epitome of womanhood is SEXUAL RESTRAINT? [. . .] I don't think so" ("The *X-Files* Expo"). Because Scully is desexualized, it seems Anderson "rounds out" the character by posing provocatively for magazine covers and photo spreads. The cover story foldout for the May 16, 1996, *Rolling Stone* depicts Anderson (in a lacy black negligée) lying between Duchovny and Carter in a satin-sheeted bed (Montalbetti/Campbell, 38–39). The image comments on how successfully the three have made their bed together, accumulating mutual profits. It just misses saying that Anderson/Scully is Carter and Duchovny's whore. But because she is in the center of the picture, with her chest covered (Carter's is completely exposed) and her eyes wide open, coolly smoking a cigarette as the men sleep like babies against her shoulders, she *appears* to be in control.

Scully/Anderson's "feminist" iconography is a very mixed phenomenon. If the "feminism of the '60s and '70s was steeped in research and obsessed with social change, [post]feminism today is wed to the culture of celebrity and self-obsession," explains Ginia Bellafante of *Time* (57). In an interview for *Jane* magazine, Anderson comments: "I think it's miraculous that these young girls have been attracted to such a strong and independent female character [. . .]. [A] lot of girls [. . .] have pushed themselves in school [out of] admiration for her" (quoted in Kelly). "Frightening how a TV character could have such power," reporter Christina Kelly acerbically observes.

Emulating Scully has affected Anderson just as "powerfully." In a foreword to *Girl Boss,* the "1999 Official Book of *Ms.* Foundation for Women—Take Our Daughters to Work," Anderson explains that Dana Scully

> has taught me about strength and self-worth and personal power. In early episodes, when I was called upon to address large groups of male FBI agents with authority and self-assurance, I felt so scared and weak that my voice would come out high-pitched and shaky. But the more I "acted as if" I was self-assured, the more I felt powerful. And believe it or not, it can be that simple.

Indeed, she claims to have carried her Scully-role-playing, self-help feminism "into other areas of [her] life," enabling her to confront "high-powered directors and producers" (Anderson).

Anderson justly takes pride in holding her own with the boys and in creating a private space for herself and (now a single mother) her daughter. She has made wise career choices, choosing small character roles in independent films (in direct contrast to Duchovny's ill-fated lead in *Playing God* in 1996). Yet, taken together, the values represented by Anderson and Scully are postfeminist. With few exceptions, the two are consistent: they/she stand for individual effort and reward in a context of career as opposed to working for social change, and for setting a high-profile example in a world of men rather than discovering her commonality with other women.[10]

X-FILES POSTHUMANISM

In posthumanism, the postmodern and postfeminist "gender bending" and identity politics of the sort discussed previously are taken to another stage. The term refers to our current and future condition of moving beyond the concept of the human. Posthumanists describe and advocate a symbiosis between the human and the "alien" in all senses, including the machine and other species. Abandoning humanist—hence masculinist—models, they identify with cybernetic and microbiological models (Halberstam and Livingston, 13). Like postmodern deconstructions of gender, only more so and more literally, posthuman, "cyborg," or "cyber-" feminism promises to deliver women from the essentializing equation of female anatomy with female destiny.

According to "cyborg" feminist Donna Haraway, both the human and the feminine are no longer "natural" states; we are made rather than born. This is true not only in the metaphorical sense of being socially or culturally constructed but also physically—we are wired and rerouted in cyberspace, implanted, transplanted, refigured, and transfigured by surgery and drug therapies. "By the late twentieth century," Haraway reflects, "we are all chimeras, theorized and fabricated hybrids of machine and organism: in short we are cyborgs" (193). As we become less and less bound to anatomy, gender (along with family, race, nationality, species, identity, and even mortality) becomes noncompulsory. Cyborg feminism, like postmodernism and postfeminism, makes old-fashioned feminism (as sexual politics) archaic.

Cyborg space is electronic, mediated space, subjecting us to what Vivian Sobchack calls "pervasion" (*Screening Space,* 229). We are not ourselves: identity in the old humanist sense is "terminal," puns Scott Bukatman (iv). In keeping with this perspective, as Adrienne McLean explains, Mulder and Scully are "both literally and figuratively alienated, penetrated, and probed to the molecular level by omniscient and omnipotent forces that have infiltrated, like television and, now, computers, virtually everything in our lives" (8).

A posthumanist perspective helps to explain why *The X-Files* has been celebrated as the "sexiest show on the air" when "the relationship between the lead couple is almost wholly nonphysical" (Rapping, 34). As Duchovny explained to Audette Fulbright, Mulder "thinks about UFOs the way other men think about sex" (30),[11] and Mulder and Scully represent an idealized cybersex, "the Internet Generation writ glamorous" (Cornell, Day, and Topping, 2). "Kill Switch," a fourth-season episode written by cyberpunk inventor William Gibson and Tom Maddox, is about a "man" (David) and a "woman" (Rachel) who consummate their relationship through "uploading" ("transferring of memory, consciousness, to the distributed system maintained by the AI [artificial intelligence]"). Their relationship is on one level a variation on the sexless, intellectual, dialogic, gender-and-body-transcending partnership of Scully and Mulder. Says Rachel to Scully, "Imagine being merged so completely with another that you no longer need your physical self."

Frohike, the "dirty old man" of the Lone Gunmen team of hackers/conspiracy theorists, whose distinguishing characteristic is his lust for Scully, gives us the cue. He finds Rachel, who wears a nose ring, has a sleek, muscular body, and talks like a brilliant machine, "hot." His mindset seems sexist, but it is also (perhaps more so) in tune with Haraway's. Scully the scientist is a cyborg, according to Haraway's feminist vision of the woman who has transcended her anatomical "destiny" and defines herself in connection with technology.

Haraway's "cyborg politics" proposes, as an alternative to the masculine fantasy of technology as domination familiar in dystoptian films from *The Terminator* to *Gattaca,* a utopian technological symbiosis where people affirm "their joint kinship with animals and machines [. . . ,] partial identities and contradictory standpoints" (196). But Haraway's utopianism begs the question in regard to politics and class. Carol Stabile points out that the cyborg feminist "need not *do* anything in order to be political." Politics are "embedded" in the cyborg's body, so that simply in signifying cross-species and biomechanical kinship, the cyborg's politics are "guaranteed" (512). Cyberfeminism coincides with the shift from an activist feminism, which asks "What is to be done?" to identity feminism, based in "the more passive and individualistic 'Who am I?'" (Stabile, 513).

Likewise, whose or what interest the cyborg serves is not at issue. Cyborgism can result, as Rosi Braidotti notes, in Dolly Parton, Elizabeth Taylor, Michael Jackson, and Jane Fonda (522): all "culturally enforced icons of white, economically dominant, heterosexual hyper-femininity—which simultaneously reinstate huge power differentials while denying them" (524–525). Speculating about what cyborgism might really mean in terms of class, specifically the Third World, Stabile makes an important distinction between First World feminists, who "assume the cyborg position through active, creative practices," and the Third World woman who "has cyborg status conferred on her through a [First World] reading of her body and actions" (512). The latter is "made" a cyborg, a tool, in much the same way that one is "made" a woman under patriarchy.

In the alienated world of *The X-Files,* Scully alternates between First World and Third World positions. The series introduces her as a cyborg in the privileged First World sense, as a scientific cybercop—a forensic scientist who conducts autopsies on alien bodies or monsters. But regardless of Scully's cyborg feminist progressivism, *The X-Files* is dystopian and becomes increasingly so. As he often asserts, Chris Carter's aim is to scare people, and *The X-Files* has become a catchword for a culture of premillennial paranoia. And for Scully and women, although not quite in the way Carter imagines it, the paranoia may be warranted. As Parks notes at the end of season two, Scully's position in *The X-Files* is "more dystopian" than Haraway imagines: in fact, "her technologized body and skills typically serve the interests of the state or of Mulder rather than any overtly feminist agenda" (128). In the third through sixth seasons, Scully increasingly has (or is shown to have had) posthumanism forced on her in the Third World sense. She is the abductee, the body implanted with alien seed, hypersexualized, unknowingly a slave to the machine state—to the extent that in "The Red and the Black," the microchip in her neck is used by rebel aliens as a homing device. An analysis of Scully's situation, with specific reference to the representation of her body, shows how posthumanism for women is as likely to result in alienation and hyper-embodiment as in transcendence of gender. Scully's characterization tells us much about the limitations, as well as the potential, of cyborg feminism.

SCULLY AND THE MOMMY TRACK;
OR, THREE MEN AND X DOZEN SCULLYBABIES

The X-Files "mythology" was engendered by the crisis of Gillian Anderson's pregnancy, shortly after her marriage to *X-Files* art director Clyde Klotz halfway through the show's first season.[12] Her pregnancy "forced Chris and the writers to come up with an arc, which they had never done before," Duchovny has said (*X-Files Movie*). The arc focused on Scully's abduction "by forces unknown," as Carter explains, and became "crucial to the rest of the show" and "the telling of the mythology [. . .]. Those three episodes were the core of the first arc and all of the subsequent arcs [. . .]. It was hell at the time but also one of the luckiest things that happened" (*X-Files Movie*). In the shocking final episode of the first season, the X-Files investigation was closed down and the partnership dissolved, with Scully sent back "home"—to lab work and teaching—and Mulder out in the field. The first seven episodes of the second season would be narrated "around" Scully's body in ways that made sense of (and reminded fans of) its absence and return.

The "story arc" was founded in, and would prove always in some sense to be about, Anderson's biology and Scully's body's absence, and it was plotted in an obviously gendered way. Even the camera work and the mise-en-scène took their shape from the disavowal of Anderson's anatomy, turning Scully into an X-File, a de-naturalized, fractured body, on the one hand, and a hyper-embodied "Third World" cyborg, on the other. As a seven-month-pregnant Anderson explained to reporter James Glave in 1994, "I'm not a sex symbol. I'm a reproduction symbol! This is the least sexiest [sic] character I've ever played." To X-Philes, Anderson's "secret" pregnancy lent a special resonance to Scully's lab-coated, bespectacled cybersensuality that the writers cultivated with subtextual allusions.

Scully replaced Samantha as Mulder's lost sister or twin, becoming less the partner/co-star than the chief representation of the absent female body, the signifier of the most potent meaning; the "alien" desire for female reproductive "technology" made it prime currency. Like Samantha and other mysteries, but more so, the abducted Scully could be represented through association and metaphor only: as the enlarged fragment of a photograph taken by a police car's hidden camera, as in "Duane Barry," or in Mulder's dreams and fantasies. She became pregnant with signification. In "Ascension," Mulder imagines Scully's experience on an alien operating table under blinding white light. A drill descends, the next shot framing Anderson's wondrously swelling abdomen. Vicari-

Shooting around Anderson's pregnancy led to Scully's representation as a tool-wielding, ultrawired Harawayan icon.

Scully is sighted in an enlarged photo of Duane Barry's car taken by a hidden police camera.

The pregnant Anderson is fully visible only in Mulder's fantasy of the abducted Scully undergoing superovulation on an alien ship.

ously, Mulder experiences what he has always wanted: her/his body is filled with alien presence, impregnated with the alien Word. Touched by the sky gods, implanted with a microchip, having immaculately conceived, Scully is transfigured, Mulder enraptured. At the end of the episode, he stands, gazing at the stars, waiting for a sign.

As Mark Leiren-Young notes, abduction by aliens is "*The X-Files*' version of maternity leave," returning Scully to the show with a worldview open to "extreme possibilities" (21). In "One Breath," Scully is mysteriously returned in a coma, her body's functions operated by machines. In her "out of body" experience, she is depicted in a northern forest, at times drifting in a rowboat on a lake, loosely tethered to the shore by a (life-supporting) rope. Her elements are "natural" and organic: earth, trees, and water, her "soul" or essence represented as a body. By contrast, in *his* near-death experience in "The Blessing Way," Mulder drifts (supernaturally) among the stars on a regal bier, surrounded by dark patriarchal "gods." His elements, as is appropriate to his questing hero role, are transcendental: air and fire.

The pregnancy more generally changed Scully in another way: shooting around Anderson's body meant representing Scully almost exclusively as a technician and accounts partly for her soaring popularity on the Internet. She became a tool-wielding, ultra-wired Harawayan icon in the "First World" sense. Hooked up to a computer terminal, green light reflecting off her goggles, gazing alternately into a microscope and a screen, she became, as Bernstein notes, "about as connected as a person can get. Proficient with laptops [. . .] and covert government databases, she is one of the few television characters equipped for the '90s and beyond" (68). As they connected covertly by cell phone and code, meeting in shadowy parking garages or on park benches after dark, the famous Mulder–Scully "chemistry" came to be associated, as in cyberpunk, with wired connections and technological augmentation.

Scully became, almost literally, a wirehead. For instance, shooting around her body in "The Host," the camera put half of her face in shadow, elongating and exoticizing it, abstracting her into a "sexily" disembodied head. Similarly, the June 1998 *Details* cover photo equating Anderson's digitalized face with "Lust in Space" says that Scully's mystique is posthuman. Her image morphs the feminine with the alien, clone, and cyborg to represent technology as empowering sensual play, safe and exotic cybersex (Janiak).

The face fetish is equally important for what it disallows. It is an icon to which viewers may attach any body and any fantasy. Hence Anderson's role as queen of the fake nudes. Pamela Anderson Lee represents "sex"; Gillian Anderson is "sexy"—meaning that she may be invested with whatever sexual content the viewer desires. Through Anderson's body's absence, Scully's face becomes superhumanly potent. The camera's replacement and fragmentation of her body can also, more sinisterly, be seen as an extension of the medical technology that uses dissection, fragmentation (isolation of reproductive organs and parts), sterilization, and radiation to induce superovulation and steal Scully's eggs.

Scully's body's absence during Anderson's pregnancy intensified the need for projection. The sexual subtext and the feminine in general became increasingly displaced onto *The X-Files'* mise-en-scène (dark and moist to begin with), special effects, and plot: onto the monsters, aliens, mutants, and vamps encountered by Mulder in various action sequences. *The X-Files'* "alienation effect" became doubly eroticized as female innerspace was projected onto the world at large. "Sex," especially in the early second-season episodes filmed during Anderson's pregnancy, is voraciously oral and anal. In episodes like "3," the vampire story filmed during the week Anderson gave birth, the viewer first notices a different color coding: blood red clouds above a blackened skyscape, red fingernails caressing a glass of red wine, red light, and so forth. "The Host" is shot in muddy greens and browns from an excremental perspective, taking spectators on an alimentary *Fantastic Voyage* via Mulder's descents into the Newark sewers.

In psychoanalytic terms, such visually embodied episodes provide regression, a view from the womb that is erotically charged—and that came to typify the series as a whole. Sex is deferred, shifted from skin shows to the interiors of the body, to the deep truths Scully both seeks and (increasingly) represents. In the first season's "Genderbender," there were the flesh-colored caverns where the sect members mine/absorb animal vitality and change sex. These caverns are marked on the earth's surface by crop circles. In other alien landing sites, the setting and mise-en-scène alternately signify and conceal layers of the deeper truth within the feminine and the body—for instance, the mountain (in "Paper Clip") that contains tunnels of medical records, tissue samples, and childlike aliens, who feyly peer at Scully before scampering into the darkness, or the underground hives tended by Samantha clones in "Herrenvolk." The film revealed that the truth for which Mulder had for so long been seeking "out there" was in a virus buried in the earth and which required a human host in which to mature into a gray. After Scully's abduction, Mulder's refrain shifts from "The truth is out there" to "The truth is in there" to "That truth is in you"—referring first to the literal X-Files, and increasingly to something contained or represented in Scully's body. Variously, this is the microchip and her memories ("The Blessing Way"); her cancer ("Memento Mori"); her stolen, alienated, and reproduced ova; and the whole mystery surrounding her abduction that formed the series' mythical core ("The Red and the Black").[13]

As Parks argues, Scully's role is consistent with Barbara McClintock and Evelyn Fox Keller's account of the feminist scientist. She discovers truths about a body by becoming "part of the system" she is scrutinizing, empathizing with the organism under scrutiny, rather than standing outside of it (McClintock, quoted in Parks, 126). In "Fearful Symmetry," such intimate investigation means literally going into the body to do the work, as Scully performs an autopsy on a pregnant elephant, dictating her findings from the animal's gaping abdominal cavity. But her intimacy with her subject has less than empowering implications. Concerned with aliens' abduction of animals for experimentation at a zoo near a UFO spot, "Fearful Symmetry" alluded to Scully's recent abduction and Anderson's equally recent cesarean section. The episode also extended the association between Scully and the female body as simultaneously vulnerable and "monstrous" (engulfing, massive, out of control).

Scully's "feminist" science is not always empathetic science, either. It is just as often depicted as scientific *de*sensitization. Scully's "strong stomach," in which she departs from gender stereotype, is a running joke. Referring to "Bad Blood," an episode about vampires, David Kushner quips, "When Agent Dana

Scully finds undigested pepperoni in a cadaver, she doesn't want to puke, she wants to order a pizza" (and does). Performing two autopsies in the same episode, she is depicted as a butcher, lugging heart, lungs, and intestines onto a scale and recording condition and weight in routinized monotony. In other episodes, Mulder teases her about her eagerness to "snap on the latex" and dig in, and critic James Wolcott stresses her "forensic zeal" (98). With the same eagerness with which she carves up corpses, Scully eats meat "like a man." (Mulder tends to be queasy and is rarely shown eating anything other than sunflower seeds.)

Like most signs, this one works in contradictory ways. Scully's "unfeminine" appetite for blood and guts lends her a carnivorous promiscuity that identifies her with the devouring and devoured Mother. In "Red Museum," where teenage males have been inoculated with bovine growth hormones and/or alien DNA, making them aggressive, and members of a vegetarian sect at odds with the cattle industry have been accused of local abductions, Scully enthusiastically consumes a local restaurant's barbecued ribs. Similarly, at the poultry processing plant in "Our Town," where a worker dies in a trough of chicken by-products, human bones are dragged from the blood-red river, and the townspeople will be exposed as cannibals, Scully is carrying her lunch, a half-empty bucket of the local product, as she examines the forensic evidence. (Having thus partaken, it is no surprise when Mulder has to save her from being stewed in the community pot.)

Whether configured as the empathetic scientist or the butcher-cannibal, Scully is allied with the female body. Being a "cyborg" (a female scientist) does not free her from gendered embodiment; instead she becomes hyper-embodied in forms that reinstate femininity. In its dark fascination with inner spaces and reproductive technology, a fascination shared with Victor Frankenstein, *The X-Files* has produced a charged variant on Haraway's cyborg, one in which Scully epitomizes its "monstrous" contradictions. She is the body *and* the doctor, the healer and destroyer, colonized and colonizer, maternal mystery and the gaze whose phallic technology opens what Linda Williams describes as "the fleshy secrets of normally hidden things" (191).

The woman scientist, having violated boundaries of identity and function, is in particular threatened and threatening. She embodies the "unnatural" union of two powers of reproduction, maternity and technology, in a monstrously denaturalized maternity, the feminine out of control, the machine run amok. Thus Scully's technologized body begins to function in the story as a wild card or coyote—an agent of nature's revenge. Her eggs, separated from her and treated as commodities, have been cloned, resulting in (at the very least) two dozen red-headed sons. However, beyond even the control of their "fathers" (the scientists and the Consortium), they are conspiring with other clones to develop research to "save the mothers" ("Memento Mori"). Scully is also the mother of an unknown number of alien-human hybrid children who, like Emily, were "conceived" in vitro, nourished in canisters, brought to term in the bodies of nursing home residents, and are now living with Project-approved "adoptive" parents. These hybrids have blood that is toxic to humans and (without continuous inoculations) to themselves. Scully is thus associated indirectly with Dr. Sally Kendrick, a brilliant but psychotic geneticist (of the first season's "Eve") who has replicated herself and her disease in a dozen female killer clones. The proliferating "Scullybabies" (as the fans like to call them) or "Über-Scullies" (as Mulder prefers in "Home") have the potential to be part of a dystopian/gothic nightmare or Haraway's posthumanist utopia. At this late point in the series, near the end of season six, while presented in the light of Scully's medical rape trauma and maternal grief and guilt, they remain ambiguous: "male" and "female," victims and monsters, rebels and drones.

In her cyborg, Haraway tries to reclaim the monstrous feminine in her "utopian dream" of "a monstrous world" beyond gender (223), beyond the family, beyond death. She finds in the salamander an alternative biopolitical model. For it, "regeneration after injury [. . .] involves regrowth with the constant possibility of twinning or other odd topographical productions [. . .] . The regrown limb can be monstrous, [. . .] potent. We have all been injured [. . .] [and] require regeneration, not rebirth" (223). The monstrous, like the bio-mechanical, is a posthuman norm and goal. In *The X-Files,* it is grotesquely encouraging that Leonard Betts, a literal "cancer man" who is composed of and subsists on cancer cells and who can regenerate even his head, informs Scully of her terminal disease. Seen from Betts's perspective, cancer is not a disease, much less terminal ("Leonard Betts").

But women in *The X-Files* rarely have Betts's luck; they are trapped in their anatomical destiny, and that destiny is not usually pretty. Betts, for example, devours the tumor in his mother's breast, allowing him to escape mortality once again. Self-sacrificing Mom is taken to the hospital. The entwined motifs of maternal sacrifice and maternal monstrosity run throughout the series, peaking in the mythology and the monsters of the week in seasons four and five. In the most horrific episode to date, the fourth season's "Home," the Peacock family is the product of generations of inbreeding, as three grown sons keep their limbless mother/communal wife under the bed—totalizing her, reducing her to all female functions simultaneously. "I can tell you don't have no children," Mrs. Peacock says to Scully upon being found. "Maybe one day, you'll learn—the pride—the love—when you know your boy will do *anything* for his mother." The real horror of "Home," as noted by Cornell, Day, and Topping, is "the grotesquely willing mother who has lost any sense of individual purpose" (288). In the fourth season's "The Post-Modern Prometheus," women mysteriously impregnated by the Great Mutato are merely grateful. Appearing on the *Jerry Springer Show* with her/their offspring, and asked how she feels about the experience, Shaineh Berkowitz, who is visually defined as the monstrous (obese) mother of monstrous children, replies, "What's not to love."

Both of these episodes predict Scully's fate as the mother of "immaculately" (technologically) conceived and monstrous progeny—destined to embody and reproduce male culture. When Scully is distressed upon examining a deformed Peacock baby, Mulder tells her to "find yourself a man with a spotless genetic make-up [. . .] and start pumping out the little Über-Scullies" ("Home"). Having just bragged about the Mulder line, our hero may be thinking of himself. (Later in the episode, he teasingly calls Scully "Mom.") Yet, as the next story arc will fully reveal, and thanks to a collective "man" whose goal is Purity Control, Scully has been pumped, harvested, sterilized, commodified, and Übermensched already. It will also show how her life depends on the microchip inserted in her neck, which mysteriously regulates her alien-ated body chemistry, reads and guides her mind, and tags her for future projects.

The "Mommy track," which proposed that corporations create a path that allowed women to take lower-paying jobs with flexible schedules in order to work around their domestic lives, has not done much for women, argues Judith Dobrzynski (162). One view, the "paranoid" but probably accurate one, according to Heidi Hartman, director of the Institute for Women's Policy Research in Washington, D.C., is that "family friendly policies are a way to keep women in their place and not let them rise too far, that the policies that allow for advancement may also limit advancement" (quoted in Dobrzynski, 162). Thus the fate of Anderson/Scully. When the pregnant Anderson was put on the Mommy track as far as the story and the camera were concerned (the story arc working around her absence and the camera working around her body), Scully was put on a parallel course. Carter and his writers came up with a family-friendly arc indeed; however dystopian, it made the maternal function represented in Scully's body and progeny the holy grail of Project Purity Control and the mythological core of *The X-Files*. Now, four years later, in a review of season six's "Terms of Endearment" (in which several women give birth to "transhuman" children fathered by the devil), Maggie Helwig notes how frequently "issues around children, baby-stealing, birth defects, violence against women, interference with women's reproductive systems, and so on and on resonate in Scully's life."

"I don't want to see Scully left behind to look after children any more times this season," Helwig concludes in a review of "The Beginning": "It's happened enough now." Indeed, the pattern began in a then atypical episode in season three, "Revelations," in which Scully, spiritually altered by her abduction, suddenly feels "called" by God to protect the stigmatic child Kevin Kryder after his mother has been killed. The three male authors of *X-Treme Possibilities*, noting a tinge of jealousy in Mulder's line "You never draw *my* bath," find "Scully getting all maternal [. . .] strangely arousing" (Cornell, Day, and Topping, 224). In season five, this divinely maternal inflection increasingly defines Scully's characterization. As she becomes an icon of reactive maternal sorrow, Mulder acts as the father-protector who comes and goes, performing the covert and dangerous actions. In "Emily," as Scully is nursing her daughter, it is Mulder who finds the physical evidence behind Emily's gestation, birth, and origins; he sees the canisters containing Scully's other "children" and steals a vial of Scully's ova. Scully, in the meantime, gives, loves, and loses. In "All Souls," Scully is again designated to protect "special" children—disabled female quadruplets allegedly fathered by angels. (Like the girls, she has beatific visions, including one of her angelic, dead daughter.) Season six opens as a misty-eyed Scully nurtures the alien-human hybrid chess prodigy Gibson Praise, a victim of torturous tests ("The Beginning"). She has become the Divine Mother "special" children instinctively seek out.

The underlying message of this maternal melodrama validates what her mother, brother, and priest repeatedly advise, that outside the patriarchal family Scully is incomplete. Just before the last scene of "Emily," Scully lies with her face next to the dying child. Then, in a match cut, the camera pauses on a stained-glass Madonna and child, panning down to Scully, alone in a chapel, mourning. Scully's sister-in-law, pregnant through most of the episode, shows Scully her new baby. Mulder enters to join Scully at the casket. Suddenly, Scully brightens into the scientist—a scientist not unlike the abstraction she condemned earlier when she said, "This child was born to fill an agenda." As the subject of an "alien autopsy," Emily can provide evidence of the Truth. Scully opens the small coffin. But the body of proof is, as always, gone. Whether in the role of scientist or in the role of mother, Scully is thwarted.

The Mommy track, *X-Files* style, seems a very mixed blessing. The arc leading from Scully's abduction to Emily allowed Anderson to bring "a new dimension" to the character, as she notes in the *Movie Special*. It also made for outstanding acting, especially in season four, handing Anderson the 1997 Golden Globe, Screen Actors Guild, and Emmy awards for Best Actress in a drama series. But it left Scully with the most traditional of roles: that of the monstrous and sorrowful mother, her body out of her control, unconsciously proliferating, belatedly discovering and then grieving her children on their way. Thus, another effect of this depiction of posthuman, extrafamilial motherhood was to reinforce postfeminist family values so obviously at the heart of Chris Carter's other (and comparatively puny) FOX Network baby, *Millennium*. Scully's cyborg version of the Virgin/Madonna is "classically" postfeminist in its strategy of making a feminist statement and retracting that statement in the same gesture. It says that, liberated by technology, women have the right to choose what happens to their bodies, but it asserts this claim against the backdrop of a Madonna with Child. In *The X-Files'* dark take on cyberfeminism, Scully is taught a very old "profamily" lesson, that a scientist cannot be a mother, that a woman scientist is a contradiction in terms, and that a female (pregnant) scientist reproduces monsters. In contrast to Haraway's ideal cyborg, Scully's biology is her destiny with a posthuman vengeance.

The image of a "family-friendly" 1990s is a facade for what *X-Files* horror stories tell us. The fetus (now figured as the alien) has become one of our most "anxious" cultural images, comments David Skal, as "political hysteria over abortion and reproductive issues [. . .] converge with millennial anxiety over what we're giving birth to and what we're becoming—our collective gestation in the womb of science" (228). As its popularity attests, *The X-Files* reflects such anxiety brilliantly, thanks to Scully in her dual role as Scientist and as Woman, pregnant with alien and alien-ating technology. Sadly, she is made to carry the symbolic weight of that anxiety rather than comprehend it fully, much less address the issues it raises.

It is true that the audience may be subtly brought to realize the truth that is "in there"—and that Scully is often too immersed in to see. I still believe that *The X-Files* has changed the way many of us watch television. And Scully's *has* been a ground-breaking role. But at the end of the sixth season, its more obvious effect is to reinforce some of the most traditional gender stereotypes we can think of. These are expressed as some of the most vividly imagined and influential images on television. Scully therefore has much to say to us, the readers of this text, about the similarities, powers, dangers, and limitations of postmodern, posthuman feminisms.

EPILOGUE: POSTMARRIAGE

Anderson may have been joking in 1994 when she claimed to have become an unsexy yet hypersexualized "reproduction symbol." The alienation and subversion of the patriarchal family that runs as a motif through *The X-Files* has produced similar repercussions. According to Halberstam and Livingston, posthuman "[e]xtrafamiliar desire exposes the family as a magic trick pulled by science and sustained by social science. Mommy and daddy are not sexy, and the Freudian family sitcom isn't funny anymore" (13). Mulder and Scully's extrafamiliar desire, standing for where we live now, together with that exhibited by the fringe groups with which they are linked, have provided posthuman alternatives to the nuclear family structure. Certainly, the family has been radically undermined—most notably in the case of the Mulders. The incestuous Peacocks and the Cigarette-Smoking Man stand for the biological family boiled down to essential impulses—matriarchal self-sacrifice, on the one hand, and patriarchal fascism, on the other—with "purity control" the goal. At the same time, these and episodes with such titles as "Two Fathers" and "One Son" insist on the vestigial survival of the patriarchal model.

This antifamily stance is increasingly countered, moreover, by what must be called teasers: self-referential episodes designed to placate the fans with trappings of romance. After all, the Mulder–Scully relationship has always been drawn in analogies to marriage, from which institution it has taken much of its mythical power. And when we take a long view of Scully's situation, what seemed "the most progressive female character on mainstream television" (Leith) looks increasingly familiar. By the end of the fifth season, Scully has been through posthuman (cyborged, alien-ated, denaturalized) variations on the cycle of a "natural" woman's life: intercourse, impregnation, conception, gestation, multiple births, death, and resurrection.

The show is not over yet, of course, and on *The X-Files* just about anything can happen. But at present, at the end of the sixth season, and having been through it all, virtually speaking, Scully is ready for marriage, posthuman-style. Mulder has already, more or less, proposed—at a turning point in *The X-Files: Fight the Future:* "You've never needed me. I've only held you back," Scully says, biting her lip to keep from crying. "You're wrong," Mulder retorts: "You kept me honest. You made me a whole person. I owe you everything. Scully, you owe me nothing. I don't know if I want to do this alone. I don't even know if I can."

The sixth season is dominated by "virtual marriage" episodes that woo the fans with self-parody, nostalgia, and fantasy romance. These take place in alternative universes or liminal spaces: for instance, a ship caught in a Bermuda Triangle time warp in the 1940s, where Mulder finds a Scully look-alike ("Triangle"), a suburb in Area 51 where Mulder changes identities and acquires a family ("Dreamlands"), and a house haunted by a comically co-dependent ghost couple who talk Mulder and Scully into reenacting their love death ("How the Ghosts Stole Christmas"). All these episodes are nuclear family sitcoms, *X-Files* style. "Arcadia" employs a "feminist" text as a cover for the following fan teaser: Mulder and Scully, investigating mysterious disappearances in an upscale, oppressively conventional gated community (*The Stepford Wives* was one model), pose as a married couple named after the *Dick Van Dyke Show*'s Rob and Laura Petrie. After the requisite clutching and cooing in public, with Mulder furiously overacting his role as protector/possessor and Scully wincing and flinching away, they get ready for bed and fall to bickering. We get the sitcom-ish clichés (the toilet seat dispute, squeezing the toothpaste wrong, wife in the mud mask), with Mulder and Scully reacting as if this were nothing new for them—the point being that Mulder and Scully virtually *are* an old married couple. As Lyda, the ghost, explains to Scully, "Your only joy in life is proving [Mulder] wrong." These episodes broadly mock the Freudian family sitcom but in doing so replicate it in nostalgic detail, reassuring the audience that it is (quite firmly) in place. *The X-Files* has been infected with a virus called *Ally McBeal*.

NOTES

1. Mulvey in 1975 argued that Hollywood film is structured around male vision and narrative point of view ("gaze"), resulting in voyeurism, stereotyping, and objectification of women on the screen. Her position has been amplified and challenged in later theories of female spectatorship. See Williams and Kaplan. On the gaze in *The X-Files,* see Wilcox and Williams, 100–118.

2. I thank the online fans, and especially *The Official Gillian Anderson Web Site,* for helping make this article possible.

3. Like Scully, Anderson was a novice in contrast to her co-star, who had been chosen for the series before she auditioned. *The X-Files* was and still is produced, directed, and written by men—often three and four per episode. Duchovny co-wrote the second-season's "Anasazi," wrote and directed "The Unnatural," and has influenced the writing of the primary narrative. Anderson has had little direct influence on the writing, although she has closed the power gap through her worldwide mystique and her award-winning acting.

4. See, for example, Humm (95) and Whelehan (25–26).

5. As Wilcox and Williams note, although Mulder chooses nonrational knowledge, he, like Scully, employs rational inquiry to arrive at conclusions (106). Cornell, Day, and Topping note that, as the conspiracy has been revealed, Scully's rational inquiry has increasingly "dominate[d]" Mulder's thinking (3). Still, Mulder's premises and quest remain the show's reason for being.

6. Wilcox and Williams note this clip, from the first-season episode "Squeeze" (120).

7. The aliens or "alienated" in this culturally open sense include, for instance, Holocaust survivors, lepers, sideshow performers, the Navajo, Chinese Americans, prisoners in Tungaska, "invisible" Mexicans (illegal aliens), the very old, and the very young.

8. True, Scully's memory has been "wiped," but, until season five's "The Red and the Black," she is characterized as resistant to therapy and reluctant to confront the issue.

9. Betty, the tattoo, may be intended as a stereotype of feminine jealousy, but the series has increasingly resorted to a pattern in which Scully is unable to express her feelings for Mulder except as jealousy of intelligent women—especially scientists, detectives, and agents. Notable examples are season three's "Syzgy" and "War of the Coprophages," season five's "Kill Switch" and "The End," and season six's "Alpha." Diana Fowley, Mulder's former partner and lover, was invented apparently to create extra sexual tension in seasons five and six.

10. In the last year, Anderson has aligned herself with groups, individuals, and causes in a way that suggests a shift in consciousness and politics—for instance, her March 1999 presentation of Anne Heche with a Creative Integrity Award from the Gay and Lesbian Community Center in which she praises Heche's courage in coming out ("Gillian Anderson's").

11. Mulder's abstinence from sex with "real" women is a series joke, signaled in everything from his addiction to pornography to his attraction to "little [gray] men" and girls who remind him of his sister ("Humbug"). This proclivity is a hallmark of science fiction film, Vivian Sobchack argues from a psychoanalytic perspective in "The Virginity of Astronauts." Technological man seeks to transcend the flesh, projects his desire and fear onto objects and spaces (the phallic/womblike ship in *2001* or *Alien*). Hence Mulder is more interested in regeneration ("Lazarus," "Tooms") or reincarnation ("In the Field Where I Died") than reproduction. His heart's desire is his alien Other half—assurance that "We are not alone." This attraction to the "transhuman" involves and aligns him with the Project. Scully, by contrast, is attracted to and stands for the body.

12. Some material in this section was included in a different form in my article "The Rebirth of the Clinic: The Body as Alien in *The X-Files*," in Lavery, Hague, and Cartwright (148–67).

13. In the fifth season's "Redux II," a finally outraged Scully swears to expose

The truth. About the men behind what happened to me, about my abduction and the tests, about being exposed to something against my will, about being put on a table and having something implanted in me, and then having my memory stolen, only to have it return along with a disease that I was given.

WORKS CITED

"The 50 Most Beautiful People in the World 1997." *People Weekly* (12 May 1997): 141.

Anderson, Gillian. Foreword. In *Girl Boss—Running the Show Like the Big Chicks,* by Stacy Kravetz. Los Angeles: Girl Press, 1999. Reprinted in "GAWS Transcripts." *The Official Gillian Anderson Web Site* 1999 <http://gaws.ao.net/transcrp/girlsboss.html> (16 April 1999).

Badley, Linda. "The Rebirth of the Clinic: The Body as Alien in *The X-Files.*" In *"Deny All Knowledge": Reading* The X-Files. Edited by David Lavery, Angela Hague, and Marla Cartwright. Syracuse: Syracuse University Press, 1996, 148–167.

Beachy, Susan Campbell. "Gillian Anderson." *TV Guide Online: News & Gossip Daily Dish* <http://www.tvgen.com/dish/0304a.htm> (19 June 1998).

Bellafante, Ginia. "Feminism: It's All about Me!" *Time* (29 June 1998): 54–62.

Bernstein, Rob. "Gillian's Island." *Yahoo! Internet Life* (July 1998): 68–69, 115.

Bischoff, David. "Opening 'The X-Files': Behind the Scenes of TV's Hottest Show." (Cover Story). *Omni* 17, no. 3 (December 1994): 42–47, 88.

Braidotti, Rosi. "Cyberfeminism with a Difference." *New Formations* 29 (Autumn 1996): 9–25. Reprinted in *Feminisms.* Edited by Sandra Kemp and Judith Squires. New York: Oxford University Press, 1997, 520–529.

Bukatman, Scott. *Terminal Identity: The Virtual Subject in Postmodern Science Fiction.* Durham, N.C.: Duke University Press, 1993.

Clerc, Susan J. "DDEB, GATB, MPPB, and Ratboy: *The X-Files'* Media Fandom, Online and Off." In *"Deny All Knowledge": Reading* The X-Files. Edited by David Lavery, Angela Hague, and Marla Cartwright. Syracuse: Syracuse University Press, 1996, 36–51.

Cornell, Paul, Martin Day, and Keith Topping. *X-Treme Possibilities: A Comprehensively Expanded Rummage through Five Years of* The X-Files. London: Virgin, 1998.

Day, Martin. "'I Want to Believe': *The X-Files* and Faith." In Cornell, Day, and Topping, 467–474.

Dobrzynski, Judith H. "Women on the Corporate Ladder." *New York Times,* 6 November 1996. Reprinted in *Who Are We? Readings on Identity, Community, Work, and Career.* Edited by Rise B. Axelrod and Charles R. Cooper. New York: St. Martin's, 1997, 160–164.

Empire Magazine, September 1998. Reprinted in "GAWS Transcripts." *The Official Gillian Anderson Web Site* 1999 <http://gaws.ao.net/main.html> (24 January 2000).

Flaherty, Mike, and Mary Kaye Schilling. "X-Cylopedia: The Ultimate Episode Guide." *Entertainment Weekly* (29 November 1996): 38–48.

Fulbright, Audette. "Phile under Phenomenon." *U. Magazine* (October 1995): 30.

"Gillian Anderson's Presentation Speech (in honor of Anne Heche's Creative Integrity Award), 6 March 1999. "GAWS Transcripts." *The Official Gillian Anderson Web Site* 1999 <http://gaws.ao.net/transcrp/anneh.html> (16 April 1999).

"The Gillian Files." Narrated by Peter Graves. *A & E Biography.* A&E Productions.

Glave, James. "X-Symbol." *Vancouver Magazine* (September 1994). Reprinted in "GAWS Transcripts." *The Official Gillian Anderson Web Site* 1999 <http://gaws.ao.net/transcrp/xstar.html> (11 May 1999).

Griffin, Peni R. "The Sum of the Partners." *Spectrum* 1, no. 4 (July 1995): 29–30.

Halberstam, Judith, and Ira Livingston. "Introduction: Posthuman Bodies." In *Posthuman Bodies.* Edited by Judith Halberstam and Ira Livingston. Bloomington: Indiana University Press, 1995, 1–19.

Haraway, Donna. "A Manifesto for Cyborgs: Science, Technology, and Socialist Feminism in the 1980s." *Socialist Review* 80 (March–April 1985): 65–108. Reprinted in *Feminism/Postmodernism.* Edited by Linda Nicholson. New York: Routledge, 1990, 190–233.

Helwig, Maggie. "The Beginning." "Maggie Helwig: Season Six." *Maggie Helwig: Reviews, Essays, Commentary* 1999 <http://traveller.simplenet.com/xfiles/helwig6.htm#The Beginning> (16 May 1999).

———. "Small Potatoes." "Maggie Helwig: Season Five." *Maggie Helwig: Reviews, Essays Commentary* 1999 <http://traveller.simplenet.com/xfiles/helwig5.htm#Small Potatoes> (16 May 1999).

———. "Terms of Endearment." "Maggie Helwig: Season Six." *Maggie Helwig: Reviews, Essays, Commentary* 1999 <http://traveller.simplenet.com/xfiles/helwig6.htm#Terms of Endearment> (16 May 1999).

Hersey, Eleanor. "Word-Healers and Code Talkers: Native Americans in *The X-Files.*" *Journal of Popular Film and Television* 26, no. 3 (Fall 1998): 108–119.

Humm, Maggie. "Feminist." In *The Dictionary of Feminist Theory.* 2d ed. Columbus: Ohio State University Press, 1989, 95.

Janiak, Seb. "Lust in Space with Gillian Anderson." Cover photograph. *Details,* June 1998.

Janssen, Jan. "Gillian Anderson Is Never Fazed as *X-Files* Agent Scully—but in Real Life, How Does the New Mum Cope with a Daily Diet of Aliens, Serial Killers and Space Slime?" *The Express on Sunday Magazine,* 16 August 1998. Reprinted in "GAWS Transcripts." *The Gillian Anderson Web Site* 1998 <http://gaws.ao.net/transcrp/express.html> (11 September 1998).

Kaplan, E. Ann. "Feminist Criticism and Television." In *Channels of Discourse, Reassembled: Television and Contemporary Criticism.* Edited by Robert C. Allen. Chapel Hill: University of North Carolina Press, 1989, 211–253.

Keller, Evelyn Fox. "Feminism and Science." In *Sex and Scientific Inquiry.* Edited by Sandra Harding and Jean F. O'Barr. Chicago: University of Chicago Press, 1987, 233–246.

Kelly, Christina. "You Made Gillian Cry." *Jane* (January/February 1999). Reprinted in "GAWS Transcripts." *The Official Gillian Anderson Web Site* 1998 <http://gaws.ao.net/transcrp/jane.html> (11 September 1998).

Kushner, David. "The X Factor: Swooning over Scully at the 'X-Files' Confab." *Village Voice,* 19 May 1998, 61.

Lavery, David, Angela Hague, and Marla Cartwright, eds. *"Deny All Knowledge": Reading The X-Files.* Syracuse: Syracuse University Press, 1996.

Leiren-Young, Mark. "X-Treme Possibilities: How *The X-Files* Built a Franchise on Aliens." *Shift* (November–December 1995): 18–22.

Leith, William. "Space Cadet." *Observer* (UK), 20 February 1999. Reprinted in "GAWS Transcripts." *The Official Gillian Anderson Web Site* 1999 <http://gaws.ao.net.tran­scrp/obv.html> (16 April 1999).

Lipsky, David. "All Gillian Anderson Wants Is Universal Enlightenment and a Decent Paycheck." *Rolling Stone* (20 February 1997): 32–33.

McLean, Adrienne. "Media Effects: Marshall McLuhan, Television Culture, and *The X-Files*." *Film Quarterly* 51, no. 4 (Summer 1998): 2–11.

Modleski, Tania. *Feminism without Women: Culture and Criticism in a "Postfeminist" Age.* New York: Routledge, 1991.

Montalbetti/Campbell. "*X-Files* Undercover." Cover story photograph. *Rolling Stone* (16 May 1996): 38–39.

Mulvey, Laura. "Visual Pleasure and Narrative Cinema." *Screen* 16, no. 3 (Autumn 1975): 6–18.

Parks, Lisa. "Special Agent or Monstrosity? Finding the Feminine in *The X-Files*." In Lavery, Hague, and Cartwright, 121–134.

Rapping, Elaine. "*The X-Files*." *The Progressive* (January 1995): 34–35.

Skal, David J. *Screams of Reason: Mad Science and Modern Culture.* New York: Norton, 1998.

Sobchack, Vivian. *Screening Space: The American Science Fiction Film.* 2d, enlarged ed. New York: Ungar, 1987.

———. "The Virginity of Astronauts." In *Alien Zone.* Edited by Annette Kuhn. London and New York: Verso, 1990, 103–115.

Stabile, Carol. "Feminism and the Technological Fix." In *Feminisms.* Edited by Sandra Kemp and Judith Squires. New York: Oxford University Press, 1997, 508–513. Reprinted in *Feminism and the Technological Fix.* Manchester: Manchester University Press, 1994, 1–7, 51, 54–55, 134–137, 146, 150–152.

Stacey, Judith. "The New Conservative Feminism." *Feminist Studies* 9, no. 3 (Fall 1983): 559–583.

Strauss, Bob. "Gillian Anderson Gets 'Jovial' about Duchovny." *E! Interview,* June 1998. Reprinted in "GAWS Transcripts." *The Official Gillian Anderson Web Site* 1998 <http://gaws.ao.net.transcrp/e1xfp.html> (21 June 1998).

Tannenbaum, Rob. "Scully and Mulder's X-cellent Adventure." *Details* (June 1998): 130–138, 172–173.

"TV Stars." *The Guinness Book of Records 1999.* Rev. American ed. New York: Bantam, 1999, 10–13.

Vitaris, Paula. "*The X-Files*." *Cinefantastique* (October 1995): 17.

Whelehan, Imelda. *Modern Feminist Thought: From the Second Wave to "Post-Feminism."* Washington Square: New York University Press, 1995.

Wilcox, Rhonda, and J. P. Williams. "What Do You Think? *The X-Files*, Liminality, and Gender Pleasure." In *"Deny All Knowledge": Reading* The X-Files. Edited by David Laverys, Angela Hague, and Marla Cartwright. Syracuse: Syracuse University Press, 1996, 99–120.

Williams, Linda. *Hard Core: Power, Pleasure, and the "Frenzy of the Visible."* Berkeley: University of California Press, 1989.

Wolcott, James. "'X' Factor." Review of *The X-Files. The New Yorker* (18 April 1994): 98–99.

"The *X-Files* Expo, New York 1998." 9 May 1998. "GAWS Transcripts." *The Official Gillian Anderson Web Site* 1999 <http://gaws.ao.net/main.html> (24 January 2000).

The X-Files Movie Special. Produced by Chris Carter. Fox Network. 25 June 1998.

The X-Files: Fight the Future. Directed by Rob Bowman. Twentieth Century Fox, 1998.

4

Lois's Locks

Trust and Representation in *Lois and Clark: The New Adventures of Superman*

Rhonda V. Wilcox

Lois Lane has four brass locks on her door. The close-up shot of these locks is one of the most vivid images in the pilot episode of *Lois and Clark: The New Adventures of Superman,* and one of the most frequently recurring shots—both as close-up and backdrop—throughout the 1993–1997 series. These locks serve as an emblem of Lois's lack of trust. This suspicious attitude sharpens her investigative edge as a reporter, yet this same attitude provokes frequent criticism from the man who is soon to be her professional—and later her romantic—partner, Clark Kent: "Does everyone have an angle? [. . .] Pretty cynical, Lois" (pilot). He urges that she trust others even while, in effect, he validates her tendency toward suspicion by deceiving her. He represents himself as merely a mild-mannered reporter and hides his nature as a superhero. Meanwhile his enemy, the mythically villainous business mogul Lex Luthor, misrepresents himself as virtuous and attempts to persuade and possess Lois. As Lois says to Clark in the early (and interestingly titled) episode "I'm Looking through You," "Nobody really knows anybody. [. . .] We all wear disguises—don't you?" While Clark fumbles over his answer, Lois adds, "As soon as you let them see you as you really are, they wind up using it against you."

The "disguises" we all wear, the everyday representation of self that does not precisely relate to the reality of self, is motivated by lack of trust, then. Of all the 1990s women characters discussed in this book, Lois Lane has had the longest history as an icon of popular culture. The '90s Lois of *Lois and Clark*—the character with top billing in the series—represents at first a woman of great independence in her career, but she is later weakened. Her independence is connected to her lack of trust—in effect, her dissatisfaction with the male-dominated contemporary world as well as her means of surviving that world. Erving Goffman, in *The Presentation of Self in Everyday Life,* refers to the "faith" between speaker and auditor that is a proper element of the representation of self when that representation is a facet of the real self (2). In this series, however, both Clark and Lex sharply exemplify the distance between representation and self. The main male characters live out their lack of trust as a way of succeeding in the world, but each of them criticizes the woman's, Lois's, lack of trust.

And the issue of trust is woven through both the professional and the personal world. The first shot of Lois's locks, in the pilot, comes in the context of a discussion of her personal relationships with men. Immediately after she locks the world out of her space, away from her self, her sister inquires about Lois's dating and asserts that she "just wants [Lois] to find a super guy." Over the years of the series, Lois's relationships finally narrow down to that focus, personal and professional partnership being represented by one man, Clark. Relationships with the wrong man or with other women (even her sister) wither and disappear. J. P. Williams suggests that any period's attitude toward Lois Lane reveals attitudes toward women in general (*Evolution*). If that is so, then in the 1990s a popular view (as indicated by this popular series) is that the feminism of many career women is to be seen as excessive and that such women can save themselves by allying with patriarchal power, not other women. And if Xena fights off invasions of territory and Scully confronts the intimate invasion of her own body, Lois deals with turf that women viewers in the '90s could perhaps more directly relate to—the personal space of office and home. In the context of the show's underlying structure, Lois's locks are there to be opened—but only by the right man.

THE MALE UNDERDOG AS MYTHIC SUPERIOR

The right man, of course, is Superman. But "Superman is what I can *do;* Clark Kent is who I *am*," says Clark Kent in a 1995 episode ("Tempus Fugitive"). His remark suggests a paradigm for certain male television characters who are portrayed as seemingly undervalued, especially by their female partners. Occasionally, 1980s television series such as *Moonlighting* and *Remington Steele* presented male-female couples purportedly engaged in work and love as equals. However, superficially dominant females are disempowered by variations on this paradigm (Wilcox). *Lois and Clark* clearly displays this pattern of control. In it, the dominant female does not realize that the lower-caste male is actually heroic; by extrapolation, even outstanding women in the real world's offices do not recognize that their untrained or everyday-seeming male associates are secretly superior. The often-heard complaint of the woman who has to train a man for the job she wishes to hold is echoed in the television situation. The 1995

Labor Department "Glass Ceiling" Report is thus adumbrated by these series. In each case the successful business "superwoman," to use the common hyperbole,[1] fails to see that the term *superman* more properly, perhaps even literally, applies to the man with whom she works.

Lois and Clark does not evince a simplistic sexism: the tensions in the series' presentation (gender reciprocity versus dominance) recreate the tensions in the series' central relationships, and in real relationships. *Remington Steele* co-creator and *Lois and Clark* consultant Robert Butler, in an interview with Stephen Dark, acknowledges a marked malleability of interpretation that applies to both shows. Butler explains, "When I had the original idea [for *Remington Steele*] I couldn't tell whether it was chauvinistic or feminine. [. . .] Because I can see it go both ways. [. . .] It's both there. I guess it's going to come in the eye of the beholder" (Feuer, Kerr, and Vahimagi, 276–277). But a primary pattern of *Lois and Clark* undermines reciprocity, undermines equality: the premise that the apparently lesser office partner, the male, is mythically the superior member of the duo.

Lois and Clark has a long fictional history preceding it in the various incarnations of Superman in comics, earlier television series, and films. One significant element emphasized in the modern movies and television series is that Clark Kent is the neophyte reporter while Lois Lane is the established professional; thus, the female is dominant at least temporarily in business. This sex-role reversal is accentuated in the very first line of dialogue of the series: Lois is shown in the middle of an office party celebrating her exposé of a crime syndicate, and her young colleague Jimmy Olsen says to her, "I still can't believe they thought you were a boy." "Well—the mustache helped," she replies (apparently, it was as effective a disguise as Clark Kent's glasses). When *Daily Planet* editor Perry White assigns Clark Kent to work with her on a space agency scandal, she complains, "He's a hack from Smallville. I couldn't *make* that name up." And to Clark himself she says, "I did not work my buns off to become an investigative reporter for the *Daily Planet* just to baby-sit some hack from Nowheresville." Later she calls him "inexperienced"; later still, "amateur[ish]." She makes it eminently clear that she does not want to have to train someone who will then share the byline and the glory for which she has worked so hard.[2]

And Lois is shown working hard. When, on Clark's second day, he greets her with "Morning, Lois," she says, "Maybe for you—I've been at it for hours" (pilot); and when, in a later episode, they visit Smallville to cover a story, Clark's father, Jonathan, comments, "The girl never stops working, does she?" ("The Green, Green Glow of Home"). Lois pops up in the middle of the night for a fax ("Green, Green"), tests out murder theories in the wee hours ("The Source"), and memorizes city maps in her spare time to be able to move more quickly during an investigation ("Wall of Sound"). And when, as with space program manager Dr. Toni Baines in the pilot, Lois says, "I don't trust her" (or him), she is often on the track of the villain. Lois's determination to keep the credit for her own work is clarified when, believing they are facing death, she tells Clark of an occasion in her early days at the *Daily Planet* when she broke her rule never to sleep with someone she works with because of "Claude. He was French. I must have been in love with him, or thought I was. Anyway, one night I told him about my story and the next morning when I woke up he was gone—so was my story. He won an *award* for that. Didn't even thank me for my *input*" (pilot). Lois's trust has in the past resulted, then, in an abuse of a sexual relationship and power in the workplace.

In something of a rarity for television, Lois's written work is given importance by being displayed: we hear her reports occasionally read aloud. Clark's, too, are occasionally read, and the content of his work reveals some sex-role reversal. In his initial unsuccessful interview, Clark has overheard Lois reject an assignment described as a "mood piece" on "the razing of [an] old theater"; writing this stereotypically feminine human interest story on his own initiative is what gets Clark the job.[3] While Lois, unlike her comic book predecessor (Williams, *Evolution*, 48, 54), continues to prefer crime reporting, Clark in the second season aces out Lois for a journalism award with a story about a nursing home scandal— for telling, as a disbelieving Lois puts it, "the really searing truth about old people" ("Wall of Sound"). Again, the subject is one that would more traditionally be seen as feminine. Clark describes Lois to his parents (in the pilot) as "complicated. Domineering, uncompromising, pigheaded—brilliant"—and he is as determined to be her partner in business as in romance. Clark Kent in this series is attracted to strong women; after all, he is a man who lives on Clinton St. ("Neverending Battle").[4] He must, however, prove himself to the woman professionally. When, at the end of the pilot, he promises not to reveal her secret about Claude and says, "You can trust me," her response is, "Heard that one before."

Clearly, then, the lead female in the series is presented as being overtly dominant in the professional situation. Yet, just as clearly, the audience is aware that the woman is underestimating the man; Lois, in fact, "should" trust Clark. The domineering woman in the office does not appreciate the true worth of her new male associate. And the man is not merely shown to be more and more effective on the job; he is further empowered by mythic underpinnings that are an important element of the series.

In the third episode of *Lois and Clark*, Lois, to her own shame, does something she has never done before: she steals a story—from Clark Kent ("Neverending Battle"). It should be noted that her aggression is counterbalanced by the fact that part of her motivation is desire: the story is about Superman, and "He's mine!" she shouts in a staff meeting—and then, embarrassed, amends, "as in my story [. . .] ". When Clark says that someone should teach her a lesson, Jimmy Olsen replies, "Yeah, but who? Godzilla?" By the end of the episode, Clark, the office underdog, has in fact gotten back at Lois for her "monstrous" behavior by sending her on a wild goose chase through the Metropolis sewage reclamation plant, hunting for information about Superman. Her only reward is a plastic Godzilla figure with a Superman S painted on its chest. In fact, Superman/Clark is the Godzilla who can teach her a lesson (a lesson the series has justified by having her steal the story). A bedraggled, smelly, and mosquito-bitten Lois congratulates Clark: "You got the story, and you took me down a peg in the process—guess I deserved that. You worked hard and you earned your success." Though the male lead is also sympathetic, in part because he is occasionally feminized, the female lead is punished for her assertiveness. And we are not shown Clark working on the story in the same way that we see Lois working, grubbing for clues and grabbing for phones; Clark gets the story because of his innate nature: he gets the story on Superman because he *is* Superman (Williams, *Evolution,* 76–77).

It would be a real distortion to suggest that Clark is never shown working in the normal way. But the man's inner nature establishes him as superior here. Superman is, after all, as another *Daily Planet* reporter puts it, "a god in a cape" ("Witness"); he is, in Richard Gess's phrase, a "flying superego" who obeys all the rules and fights for truth and justice. Joanna Connors, in her essay on the comic books, discusses the power of Superman in terms of the Freudian connection of sexuality and dreams of flying (108–109). Richard Reynolds examines at length the character's fulfillment of the paradigm of the "man-god" (12–14, 16, 61–62). He was invented at a time (1938) when a Depression-weary public longed to identify with such invulnerability (Williams, *Evolution,* 43; see also 83). But in perhaps the single most famous fictional example of the disempowered female gaze, Lois is blind to Clark's real nature (Williams, "It's My Job," passim, and *Evolution,* 26). In a conversation between Clark and a schlemiel scientist who has felt metaphorically invisible to wife and coworkers before he discovered how to make himself literally invisible, the scientist says, "You have no idea what it's like—people pass you by and look right through you. They never see the part of you that you want 'em to see."[5] But Clark answers, "You'd be surprised, Alan. I'll bet a lot of people know what that's like" ("I'm Looking through You"). At the end of the episode Clark implies, in a soliloquizing comment after an interchange with Lois, that he is the real invisible man, his true nature unappreciated, and his earlier comment to Alan suggests that his condition is typical. Alan is a small illustration of the larger pattern of the male who believes he is underestimated in romance and business. And Clark Kent/Superman is the abiding trope.

In this series, then, we are presented with the strongest of females not realizing that the male is, of course, superior after all, even when he seems amateurish or untrained. When the woman complains of problems in the office with the male cohort—even though, based on the information she has, the man's qualifications certainly might be questioned—we in the audience know the woman's judgment to be faulty. The general purport of the series is that the woman is underestimating the man. The presentation of the man, in fact, co-opts women's genuine sociological place as office underdog, while maintaining the man's status as superior in the subtext. The image that begins the opening sequence of every *Lois and Clark* episode tells the tale: Clark Kent is flying across the screen in a business suit.

THE MEN WHO DEFINE HER MISTAKES

Lois's underestimation and mistrust of Clark are shown to be wrong, but this version of Lois (played by Teri Hatcher) is if anything even more mistaken in her relationship to the business mogul of the series. In *Lois and Clark* the popular figure of villainy constituted by the big businessman (e.g., the husband of the weaker Teri Hatcher character in the James Bond film *Tomorrow Never Dies*) is none other than that well-known villain Lex Luthor—well-known as a villain to most of the audience, if not to our heroine. Almost as much as her relationship to Clark Kent/Superman, her relationship to Lex Luthor defines Lois Lane. And, though the audience knows she should not, this incarnation of Lex Luthor is someone whom Lois comes to trust. For this Lex Luthor is someone quite different from the Lex of the old comic books and movies. For one thing, this Lex is not bald; he is a handsome, suave, intelligent, even occasionally tender man. Lex Luthor has the world (except for Clark/Superman) convinced that he is a philanthropist, and he is a self-made man, orphaned in his early teens (pilot, "The Fall of the House of Luthor").

Lex Luthor is one of two major characters leading double lives in this story, the other being, of course, Clark/Superman. Each represents himself as something other than he is, and Lois is tested by her ability or failure to perceive, despite the men's purposeful misrepresentation. While Clark hides mythic virtue, Lex hides almost equally mythic villainy as a criminal mastermind, and the series emphasizes this element. Just as Superman is the "god in a cape," Lex is portrayed as Lucifer, Satan, the fallen angel. In the pilot episode he is connected with snake imagery when the turbaned Indian Asabi releases a cobra into Lex's room. Lex vanquishes the cobra simply with the power of his own snake-like stare, his own version of super-vision. Lex owns a falcon named "Faust," thus also evoking the Mephistophelean connection ("Let's kill some pigeons," says the businessman to his pet ["Neverending Battle"]). Lois complains that Clark thinks the monied "Lex is the root of all evil in Metropolis" ("Barbarians at the Planet"); in fact, Clark accuses her of planning to "get in bed with the devil" by marrying Lex. The last episode of the first season, "The Fall of the House of Luthor," begins with Lex enjoying a virtual reality dream of flying, with an *L* emblem on his chest comparable to Superman's *S*. From the pilot on, Lex has spoken of the necessity to take "the high ground" (tactically, not morally) in order to conquer and of the fact that his penthouse is the highest building in Metropolis. Lex plunges to his death when he leaps from the "top of the world" to avoid capture by the authorities who have discovered his iniquity; he becomes the fallen angel, Lucifer, now known by all to be evil. In the same episode of "The Fall [. . .]," whirling images of newspaper reports from the tabloid *National Whisper* flash upon the screen the news that, first, his body has been stolen, and, next, that he is still alive. Later he is literally revivified in "Return of the Phoenix." Thus Lex, too, is connected with the superhuman, though with its dark, Satanic side.

Lois is in an interestingly ambiguous position: She attracts both the most virtuous man and the most villainous in this fictional world. She has begun to trust each of them, but she fails to perceive fully the true nature of either. The audience can feel itself to be more perceptive than Lois. Yet the audience, of course, is given more information than Lois. She is the focal point in a contest that depends on her gradual education as to whom to trust, as to whom is the most heroic. "Trust me," says Lex, but in the next scene Clark says to Lois, "Prizewinning investigative reporter. You look right at the guy and still don't have a clue who he really is" ("Barbarians at the Planet"). Clark/Superman has not trusted Lex since the pilot episode, in which he tells Lex, "I know who you really are." Clark, too, however, as Superman, has information about Lex to which Lois does not have access. The audience is thus aligned with the male lead in knowing more about the villainy of the business world than the female lead does, even though she is at the top of her profession.

Unlike Clark, Lois gradually comes to trust Lex more and more. In the sixth episode, Lois represents herself as a chorus girl and later a singer at a nightclub as part of her undercover work for a story ("I've Got a Crush on You"). Clark exposes her in order to keep her safe; Lex, meanwhile, has spotted her but kept silent—thus earning her trust by his endorsement of her disguise, her false representation of herself for business purposes. (He also responds to these sexualized representations—scantily clad chorus girl, slinky singer—by telling Lois he sees them as her true self.) Clark, on the other hand, has aroused her jealousy by his involvement with the female owner of the club, so much so that when Lois comes home, she slams her door without refastening the locks. In this vulnerable state (having just said aloud, "I *am* jealous") she is found by Lex, who stands at her door asking to come in—first dipping his finger in the bucket of ice cream she holds and asking for a spoon. This scene's sensual elements illuminate the sexual component of the lock imagery. Lois normally locks away both her body and her emotions; she does not lightly allow anyone to walk through her door, any more than she allows anyone to enter her body. Thus the locks can be seen as symbols of her control over her own body, her own space. In fact, despite Lex's slow and purposeful seduction over many months, he and Lois never make love.

Lois does, however, come to the point of trusting Lex enough to plan to marry him, even though Clark has told her of his own love for her. The regular guy at the office loses out to the business mogul who can offer an engagement ring as violinists play in his private jet while the couple flies back from dinner in Italy. It should be noted that Clark tells Lois of his feelings for her only just before the wedding, and Lois in fact refuses to say "I do" to Lex because images of Clark—not Superman—flash through her mind as she walks down the aisle. But she has failed a test when she turned down Clark and subsequently turned to Superman, saying, "If you were just an ordinary man leading an ordinary life, I would love you just the same." Superman replies, "I wish I could believe that," with her rejection of Clark fresh in his mind ("Barbarians at the Planet").

Lois closes her door but forgets her locks in "I've Got a Crush on You."

This scene confirms condemnation of the woman: at this point she sees her best romantic choices as the man of great wealth (Lex) or the man of great strength (Superman). Many men see women as involved in a self-serving search for such qualities in a husband, and so Lois's choice is presented as almost tragically blameworthy. This scene also provides a rare moment in which Clark/Superman's privileged vision is presented in a sexualized and aggressive fashion: when Superman arrives, Lois is clad in a thin gown. She therefore speaks of getting a robe, but Superman tells her (with an edge to his tone) not to bother unless the robe is "lined with lead." Though Lois gives a slight laugh, the moment is a chilling one. As J. P. Williams notes, "Both the use of the gaze and the way in which the woman's attention is called to it are clearly means by which she is meant to be controlled and punished" (5). This scene indicates the anger that the regular guy, Clark, feels after his rejection in the preceding scene. He is angry that she fails to see him as he really is, even though he does not trust her enough to show her his real self. Once again, Lois's lack of vision is connected to her undervaluing the normal male.

After the wedding is halted, Lois attempts to tell Clark what she felt for him as she walked down the aisle. In those brief moments, she recalled Clark repeatedly in scenes at the office—the place where they work together. Lois is allowed to perceive Clark's full worth in flashes, at a highly emotional moment. For this moment of emotional response, the female is validated by the audience: we see Lois responding appropriately to the hero. Her earlier mistake of rejecting him, however, requires a penalty. Clark precludes her revelation of her feelings by saying (with fingers childishly crossed) that he lied, that he told her he loved her simply in order to prevent her from marrying a villain. He may fear that she will cut off their business partnership and friendship if she feels pressured by his romantic desire. His wish to relieve her of such pressure can be seen as honorable and self-denying. But it is misrepresentation nonetheless, and once again his misrepresentation clouds the relationship.

Consistently and consciously, these men with double lives misrepresent themselves to Lois. While Lois frequently goes undercover as a reporter, misrepresenting herself for business, Clark and Lex fictionalize themselves as a way of life. Both love her and wish to win her love. But neither trusts her to know his secret side. Each man urges Lois to trust him, but neither of them seems able to resist spying on her. Lex provides Lois with a car bugged with a listening device. And while Lex has secretly listened to her, Superman has secretly watched her. He floats outside her apartment at the time of her first date with Lex, seeing that she did come home (pilot). And in a later episode he watches, tormented, through the window as Lex slips the engagement ring onto Lois's finger ("Barbarians at the Planet"). Not using his X-ray vision, but seeing into the window from the darkness outside, Superman seems a lonely voyeur in these scenes. The fact that he does not use his super-vision means he is acting as a regular male might. The episode shows him outside—in the cold, as it were— and thus seems at one level to disempower him. Yet he has chosen this way of interacting with Lois; rather than speaking the truth in trust, he watches her in distrust. Laura Mulvey's seminal work on film suggests that the male objectifies the female through his controlling gaze. Perhaps the emotional power of this moment in the series is due in part to the fact that it displays Clark/Superman's *lack* of control of Lois. However, the scene focuses on her handing over control of herself to another man, Lex, an evil man, so there is no implied praise of Lois's independence here. In fact, Lois's wrong choice can be seen as the reason that Clark/Superman secretly gazes at her, objectifying her rather than entering into a communication of trust with her. "Why doesn't he tell me what he's feeling?" "He shouldn't have to; if you really loved him, you'd know," seems to be the message. In short, the problem with the relationship is the woman's fault.

Another reason for Lois's lack of trust may be found in a third important male figure in her life—Lois's father, Dr. Sam Lane. Early in the series it is established that Sam Lane has been an absentee father. In the fifth episode, "Requiem for a Superhero," Lois and Clark are partnered by Perry on a story about corruption in the world of boxing. When Perry suggests that Lois try talking to her contact in the business, Clark realizes that her father is the reconstructive surgeon Dr. Sam Lane whom, Clark says, "anyone who's ever read the sports pages has heard of."

In other words, though not bearing the mythic power of Clark/Superman or Lex, Lois's father is a man of unusual stature. But his deep involvement with his work has cost him his family life. While Lois is willing to contact a fight manager who is an old family friend (and who, in a fatherly way, calls her "Punkin"), she only encounters her father accidentally, and very apparently has not seen him in months. In a confrontation later in the episode, after the family friend is murdered, Sam Lane says, "I know that you resent me—and you should for those times I let you down. But it doesn't mean I don't care. It was because of my work."

It is clear that Lois's model for allowing work to consume her is her father. Lois complains that as a child, if she got a 98 on a test, her father would remind her that that left 2 percent for improvement ("Requiem for a Superhero"). And throughout the series, other characters joke about Lois's perfectionism, her need always to be right, her workaholic attitude (see, e.g., "Honeymoon in Metropolis"). It is also clear that both father and daughter blur the borders between the professional and the personal. They are able to come to a personal rapprochement when, later in the episode, Dr. Lane agrees to help her professionally, as a source. Despite the risk to his own life, he tells his daughter to do her job as a reporter, and he agrees to cooperate in part because the boxing business owners (including, though Lois does not realize it, Lex) are misusing the prosthetics he has designed as a doctor—misusing his work. The metal-based prosthetics hidden inside the boxers' limbs involve Dr. Lane in a misrepresentation that he comes to find intolerable. And when he rejects that misrepresentation and accepts Lois and Clark's reporting of the truth, he is able, in some degree, to rejoin his daughter emotionally.

Lois is clearly shown as having patterned herself on her male parent. Yet being a workaholic is shown, for both father and daughter, to be a faulty choice. Their overwork has impaired their family relationships. To this extent the series can be seen as criticizing traditional masculine behavior patterns relating to careers. Furthermore, when the father and daughter overcome secrecy and relate to each other more fully and honestly, the emotional rewards are made clear. And the improved relationship is encouraged by Clark, whose strong bond with his parents is one of the mainstays of the series.

However, while the series suggests Lois's need for improvement (and implicitly praises her for steps in that direction), it suggests no such need for Clark. Is Clark a workaholic? No, of course not; though he and Lois are, as reporters, equally productive, he does not have to be a workaholic to achieve the same results: he is the young Superman, not a woman or an older man who has made faulty choices. In episode after episode (especially during opening teasers), we see Clark—unlike Lois—relaxing, watching sports on television, playing basketball, and so forth. For that matter, Lex, too, is shown enjoying life. When Lois, interviewing him in the pilot, asks what he seeks in life, he does not answer "power" (as she expects), but "pleasure." But the woman who is to equal such high-powered men professionally is shown as hyperactive.

Lois shares the blame for this flaw with her failed male role model, her father. Other episodes develop the Lane family history in more detail—particularly the division between Lois's father and mother, which clearly affects her judgment of relations between men and women. The episode preceding the introduction of Lois's father is "I'm Looking through You," which focuses on a man who, as previously mentioned, invents a way to become invisible because he feels he has already become invisible to his wife (and coworkers). During this main plot about a troubled marriage, the audience learns in a brief aside that Lois's parents are divorced. In a conversation in a car, Lois and Clark argue their different perspectives. Continuing the discussion about disguises cited in the introduction of this chapter, Clark says, "Marriage is about sharing everything, even when you don't feel like it," and Lois jokes that her mother made that clear to her father when they divorced.

In later episodes Lois's parents both appear, usually alongside and in contrast to Clark's adoptive parents, Jonathan and Martha Kent, who are the perfect, loving couple. As Lois says in a third-season episode, "Your parents made marriage look like fun; mine made it look like a root canal" ("Ordinary People"). More than once, Lois attributes her difficulty in relationships to her father's being a workaholic and her mother's being an alcoholic, while Clark acknowledges his parents' positive example. In the third season's "Home Is Where the Hurt Is," when the two families get together for Christmas, Sam Lane says, "Jonathan, I want to thank you for being so good to my little girl. It's been tough for her to trust people, and I feel somewhat to blame for that."

Elsewhere in the same episode, Lois's mother, Ellen, even notes that she and Sam had worked together as doctor and nurse. Though the male doctor/female nurse relationship recalls the overt inequality of male-female roles typical of the time period in which Sam and Ellen are supposed to have worked, the fact that they had any working relationship extends the parallel to Lois's relationship with Clark. Thus the multiyear absence of Lois's father is daunting not only in terms of relationships with men in general, but with a working partner in particular. And once again, the woman's quest for professional success is identified with her quest for personal success—that is, a romantic relationship with a man. And trust affects both the personal and professional realm. When, in the second season, Lois and Clark temporarily break up their professional partnership, Editor Perry White condoles with Clark over her behavior, saying, "I've seen her like this before. The doors are locked, the alarms are on, and you ain't gettin' in" ("Wall of Sound").

The desire for the absent father becomes especially significant in the context of the series' repeated association of work and sexual connection. In the pilot episode, Lois makes the comment about her affair with the French reporter Claude and his taking credit for her work. In another first-season episode, "The Rival," she confesses to Clark that in college she wrote a story with the purpose of impressing someone she wanted to date. And, as noted before, throughout the series Lois wants to get both Superman stories and Superman himself ("He's mine! . . . as in my story"). These repeated examples suggest a pattern: if Lois can fully succeed at work, she can satisfy her father—and get her man.

It should be reiterated, however, that Lois is far from a simplistic creation. Whatever complication of unacknowledged motives she may have, she is a reporter for the sake of the work—and that is foregrounded in the series. Her first real date with Clark expresses that point directly. On her first date—or is it an interview?—with Lex (pilot), he invites her to have dessert with the clear implication that dessert suggests sex. She insists that she never has dessert ("Don't know what you're missing," he tells her). On her first date with Clark, however, the camera lovingly dwells on her face as Clark spoons one bite of his dessert into her mouth ("Lucky Leon"). One important reason for their closeness is that Clark pays attention to her feelings about work, which are expressed in the same scene in a quiet, low-key conversation:

> *Lois:* He [her father] was always disappointed that he never had any sons.
>
> *Clark:* So you went out and became a world-famous reporter just to prove him wrong?
>
> *Lois:* Maybe.
>
> *Clark:* So why don't you quit?
>
> *Lois:* I guess I found out I like it.

When Lois assesses their date later, her choice of words is significant: "It just seemed to *work*." Lois does not work solely to be her father's son-substitute, then. But she must learn the right man to trust in the workplace before she can achieve personal success. As her relationship with Clark proceeds in the next episode, there is a shot of Lois's multilocked door, but to Clark, Lois says, "It's open" ("Resurrection").

THE BUSINESS BITCH AS FOIL

Given the intertwining of her identity with her work—Lois quintessentially *is* a reporter—it is perhaps not surprising that there is a commutative intertwining of romance with work. That would, however, mean in part that Lois's love of work is seen as acceptable because it is also love of her love—and major news story—Superman/Clark (only in part, since Lois is already an avid reporter before Superman's appearance). Other working women do not always fare so well in *Lois and Clark*. They may be bitchy, promiscuous, or even depraved. In general, they serve as foils, highlighting the sterling qualities of the good girl reporter, Lois. They externalize the negatives of competitive, aggressive working women, keeping Lois, by contrast, on the positive side of a graph of more acceptable feminist behavior.

First-season regular Catherine "Cat" Grant certainly serves as a foil to Lois. While Lois reports hard news, Cat is a gossip columnist. While Lois almost entirely eschews dating, Cat dates promiscuously. And while Lois dresses in an attractive and very professional fashion (Robinson, 89), Cat wears tight, revealing clothing. She furthermore condemns herself by pursuing Clark; in fact, in a clear sex-role reversal, Cat's pursuit barely misses being sexual harassment, and Clark is forced to ask her to stop misleading other office workers about their relationship: Cat wishes to claim him as a sexual conquest, though he has resisted her appeals ("Strange Visitor from Another Planet"). Lois and Cat are not a simple virgin/whore pairing; thanks to writer and creator Deborah Joy Levine, the audience knows from the pilot (which was re-run at mid-season of the first year) that Lois has had, as noted previously, at least one other sexual relationship. In fact, in another sex-role reversal, it is Clark who is the virgin here (as the audience may suspect and will learn for certain in the fourth season). The situation is not, then, the stereotypical good, relatively experienced male hero's choice between the virgin and the whore. Nonetheless, as she mocks what she sees as Lois's goody-two-shoes behavior, the aptly named Cat serves to highlight Lois's greater professionalism and her choice not to pursue men promiscuously.

After Cat disappears at the end of the first season—and after creator Deborah Joy Levine's loss of creative control—Lois's skirts rise and her clothing becomes less professional. Perhaps it was deemed necessary for at least one female regular to have revealing clothing, and with only Lois and Martha Kent left, the choice was fairly obvious. It might also be speculated that while Lois is not quite a virgin and Cat is not exactly a whore, once Cat has left the series it is not so easy to externalize the sexuality. It should be noted as well that this period is something of a fall from grace for Lois. This is the time period immediately succeeding her rejection of Clark's first proposal and her acceptance of Lex's. She is therefore in some degree a fallen woman. She narrowly misses participating in the "Fall of the House of Luthor," narrowly misses joining herself to that house, and her clothing reflects that fall. In responding to Lex, Lois has in part responded to sex rather than to True Love. The Lex of this series engages in frequent sexual activity and exerts a powerful sexual attraction. The snake imagery associated with him can be seen as phallic in the context of Lex's actions, as well as mythically related to the woman's possible sexual fall. Certainly, then, there may be multiple reasons for the change in Lois's style of clothing. Nonetheless, the absence of bad-girl Cat as a foil may be one of those reasons.

During the first season, the period of Deborah Joy Levine's greater control, there were, in contrast to Cat, some examples of impressive working women who actually seemed to be of an appropriate age and normal appearance, such as Mrs. Powell, manager of the Beckwith School for troubled children ("Smart Kids"), or the physicist Dr. Goodman ("Man of Steel Bars"). But these are distinctly secondary characters. Much more notable are a series of major female characters who explicitly complain of sexism in business. They all turn out to be villains. Thus Levine clearly raises feminist issues, but contains feminism by admonitory tales that show women who make such direct complaints as being blameworthy in their excessive actions.

In "I've Got a Crush on You," for instance, Toni Taylor wants to move her family out of crime into legitimate business through their operations in the nightclub called The Metro Club. A professionally dressed, smart, good-looking woman, she is mocked by her brother for attempting to enter a man's world. She has an M.B.A., yet she is told, "You don't speak at meetings." But she successfully usurps her brother and even manages to begin a relationship of sorts with Clark before being revealed as a criminal herself—a criminal in partnership with Lex Luthor, no less. Lex forces her to take the blame for their crime and enter prison in exchange for the possibility that he will allow her back into the organization after she serves her time. "Welcome to big business," he tells her.

She fares better than the Toni whom Lex partners with in the pilot, however. The name Toni, of course, is a unisex one appropriate to the gender-crossing activities of the women who bear it in these episodes. In the pilot, Levine offers the audience an opportunity to detect itself in sexist assumptions through her method of introduction of the name. The audience first hears a reference to the space station's operations chief Dr. Toni (Tony?) Baines, and only later sees on the television screen within a screen the news report showing the beautiful blonde with the written inset "Dr. Antoinette Baines" who is the primary villain of the pilot, aside from Lex. As with Toni Taylor, Lois's untrusting reporter instincts are right on target when it comes to her suspicions of Dr. Baines—though they are fueled in part by the "very unprofessional" looks Dr. Baines gives to Clark. Lois's perceptiveness as a reporter is thus displayed here. But that perceptiveness is undercut by the implication that it is supported by an emotional, indeed a sexual, response—jealousy over Clark. Toni Baines is strong and smart, and she commends Lois for her similar qualities, acknowledging that a woman needs to be tough nowadays. But she is no role model. This high-powered businesswoman is secretly allied with evil—partnered with Lex sexually and professionally, as so many of the wicked women are. In other words, Toni shows her evil in part by having sex with Lex (a mistake Lois almost makes) and in part by desiring Clark when she has no right to him. And when Lois recognizes a woman wrongdoer in this situation, she is also recognizing a rival. In short, good and evil, professionalism and failure in business, all are explicated by the woman's sexual choices. The wrong choice results in a clear penalty: Lex blows up Toni Baines's helicopter as she leaves the scene of a botched attempt to kill Lois, Clark, and Jimmy.

Another clear case of the feminist who goes too far comes in "Illusions of Grandeur." Here, the daughter of a famous magician resents being kept out of an all-male society. Professionally, she appears to be no more than a beautiful assistant. But she uses a front man, Darren Romick, to gain power in the world of magic and then proceeds to megalomaniacal expansion of her control through her powers as a hypnotist. She actually initiates a plan to rule the world through her hypnotic control (oh, the seductive power of the scantily clad wicked woman!) of world figures from politicians to the Pope. Her complaints are clearly those of a feminist; her solutions, just as clearly criminal. In the revelation scene, she explains: "Darren Romick was a penniless card hustler when I found him. I taught him everything—everything my father taught me. [. . .] No one wanted to see a female illusionist [. . .] so I got myself a front man—who started to believe in his own success. [. . .] There was a secret society that wouldn't let me in. [. . .]" Clark/Superman's assessment is "You had a great talent, Constance. . . . But you're the one who wasted it on revenge." Though he never suggests how she might have pursued a career in magic (and in fact, one struggles to think of female exemplars of this profession), the series arranges matters so that blame can be placed on the overreacting woman and diverted from the systemic problems. She objects to the patriarchal system and, in attempting to circumvent it, becomes simply criminal: she kills people. She endangers both Clark and, in particular, Lois, who works within the patriarchal system to prove her worth and is thus less dangerous—and less simplistically portrayed.

Perhaps the most clearly antifeminist example of a businesswoman comes in the first-season outing "Witness." In this episode, a stylish, fifty-something executive, Barbara Trevino, is set to become the first woman chair of a rain forest consortium, as a large news conference announces. Trevino falls into what Rosabeth Moss Kanter, in *Men and Women of the Corporation,* calls the "mean and bossy woman boss" stereotype (201). To carry the stereotype to absurd extremes, instead of being a powerful, mature female advocate for the environment, she is actually a murderer who plans to sell the rain forest to miners and thus block the development of a drug for "increased male potency" that was discovered by her former lover Vincent Winninger. The castrating bitch will keep us from the natural (rain forest) way of things (male potency). It should be noted that it is almost always a saving grace of *Lois and Clark* that it does not take itself too seriously at the wrong moments; and certainly the scene during which Lois and Vincent Winninger discuss the drug for increased male potency is played in part for humor. But the antifeminist elements are nonetheless clearly present. Having a powerful woman take over a large business will, of course, endanger the potency of males.

The antifeminism is perhaps more noticeable in a scene during which Lois has been invited by Trevino to talk to her alone—so that Lois can be killed. Our Lois, of course, sees through the wicked woman. But the particular form of her sarcasm directly scorns some stock phrases of feminism. Pretending to be deceived, Lois says of Trevino (with a barely restrained sneer), "She wants to talk woman to woman, sort of a sisterhood thing." Lois is certainly given no reason to trust these faulty examples of professional women who decide to work outside the system. Overt feminist criticism of the system is repeatedly translated to criminal behavior, and Lois's choice to work within the system is validated.

THE FAILURE OF WOMEN FRIENDS

Lois's scorn of the "sisterhood thing" might have seemed merely a condemnation of phony dogmatics if the series had shown more sisterlike characters—or more of Lois's own sister—as a counterbalance to this sequence of negative female characters. Lois's sister Lucy was originally set to be a regular on the series and appeared to be living with Lois in the pilot and in the third episode (which should by series chronology have been the second). In that episode, "Neverending Battle," Lucy borrows Lois's clothes, brings her lunch, and in general interacts with Lois in a cheerful, sisterly fashion. She is also not afraid to criticize her successful sister, advising Lois to apologize to Clark for stealing a story. But the actress appeared only once more in the series. The character of Lucy was portrayed by a different actress in a one-time appearance in a subsequent episode ("Metallo," season two) in a very different incarnation, seeming by her language almost to come from a lower social class than her sister—no longer a peer.

Lucy did not even appear at Lois's wedding; her absence was explained for the near-miss third-season faux wedding (during which Clark wed a Lois clone constructed by Lex—an instance of duping the male hero through misrepresentation, which made fans seriously indignant for a variety of reasons), but the character's absence was not even mentioned for the fourth-season actual wedding of Lois and Clark. In effect, Lois's sister dwindles into nonexistence. Her disappearance is part of the gradual isolation of Lois from other strong females—except one who will be discussed later. Thus Lois's "good strength" is presented as unusual for a woman.

As well as being separated from her sister, Lois has very little in the way of a support system through female friends. As with many television characters, her real family seems to be constituted of her coworkers. But more than most, her lack of outside friends seems noticeable. "The Rival," for instance, focuses on her former best friend from college, Linda King, another newspaper reporter who is now Lois's detested competitor (in a relationship suggesting the sexist view that women are often catty competitors masked as friends). In one scene, at a restaurant, Linda asks Clark to walk her to the subway after Lois tells Linda in a women's room conversation, "Clark's good-hearted and he's a little naive." Clark promises he'll be right back, saying, "Trust me." But Lois only waits a few minutes before leaving, certain that he will not return. Thus Lois is shown as mistaken because she does not trust Clark, whom the audience sees resisting temptation offered him by Linda; but, in contrast, the series tells the audience that Lois's mistrust of the other woman is well-founded.

We next see Lois at home, furiously scrubbing the grout in her kitchen. She retreats to female territory, a place she can control. With scrubbing gloves on, she has to angrily open the locks of her door to let Clark in. But the physical byplay between the characters (Lois's accidentally sprinkling Clark with cleanser, for instance) suggests that Lois's anger is a bit ludicrous. Lois proceeds to explain her past with Linda; as Clark sums it up, "She stole a story and she stole a guy"—and Lois is afraid it is happening again. Clark's response, however, is to join Linda at the rival newspaper—another layer of deception beyond the usual baseline Clark/Superman deception: he has decided to infiltrate the other paper but, on Editor Perry White's orders, does not tell Lois. For his part, Perry reassures her: "Lois—it's gonna be all right. Trust me." "That's what *Clark* said," she shoots back.

Once again, though Lois clearly *is* supposed to trust the character of these men, her suspicions that they are deceiving her in this instance are just as clearly correct. And as for her ex-best-friend Linda, as the two women lie on the floor, tied together by the villain and expecting death, Linda asks Lois to forgive her on the grounds that she is weaker than Lois: she is, indeed, not to be trusted. At the end of the episode, Linda leaves town, on her way to make a great deal of money from her movie version of the story, including a bit part playing Lois Lane, one more fillip of misrepresentation by a woman who has tried to play Lois's part with Clark. Linda is a deplorably sexist example of a sexually and professionally aggressive woman who should not be trusted. Clark and Perry, for their part, demand that the good woman trust them even when they are misrepresenting themselves. And Lois herself—though she is the senior reporter—is not trusted enough by the man in charge to be made part of the secret until she discovers it on her own. Men who mistrust are cautious; women who mistrust are cynical.

Another ex-best-friend from college surfaces in season two. Clark is surprised to learn that Lois has gotten completely out of touch with her old friend Molly. When Lois asks if he has kept in touch with all his old college friends, he asserts that he has. But Lois has not; because of Lois's disapproval of Molly's boyfriend, the two women have stopped speaking. Now, for a newspaper story, Lois contacts Molly again, who declares, "It bugs me that my best friend dropped out of my life because of my boyfriend." Later, when, like Lois and Linda King, Lois and Molly are trapped by a villain and facing death, they come to a rapprochement. Says Molly, "I have not met the man yet who was worth giving up a good friend for. Then again, I haven't met Superman." The idea of the importance of friendship between women is raised only to be instantly undercut by the suggestion that, if the woman finds "a really super guy" (to quote sister Lucy from the pilot), then female friends will be unnecessary. Lois and Molly embrace each other, and Molly is never heard from again during the course of the four-year series.[6] Molly is one more piece of evidence that Lois's relationship with her man is not just central but virtually exclusive. If your man is man enough, you won't need any women friends.

Given Lois's lack of old friends, the writers occasionally try to provide her with new ones. In "The Ides of Metropolis," Melanie Mayron (who might be identified by the audience with a lively, independent character from the 1980s series *thirtysomething*) portrays police detective Reed, a woman who seems to share Lois's suspicious nature, though in this case Lois is the one suspected. And in fact, as is often the case with Lois, Detective Reed is right to be suspicious: Lois is hiding a man convicted of murder. As is also often the case with Lois, the bottom line, however, is that the suspicious woman should be more trusting: though he has been convicted, the man Lois is hiding is innocent. "You should trust what's in people's hearts," says Lois, and Clark teases her about her assumption that she has "infallible reporter's instincts."

As Lois and Detective Reed try to outwit each other, the interaction is lively. But when they move toward friendship, the depiction is less successful. Once again, the two women in the case are trapped by the villain so that a tête-à-tête is forced. Without any conversational springboard to speak of, Detective Reed offers, "Must be tough being a reporter—'specially for a woman." And Lois responds, "Not any tougher than being a detective." From this dual peace offering the conversation moves to a ritual discussion of hair and nails. While Detective Reed might indeed have made a reasonable friend for Lois, the relationship was given insufficient time to grow in a natural fashion; instead, the pressure-cooker device of entrapment and imminent death was invoked. Thus, the interaction was not completely successful, and Detective Reed joined the group of Lois-friends never to be seen again. The series' lack of investment in providing her with a steadfast friend translates as Lois's having only ephemeral or failed friendships with women. And once again, Lois is left as the only career woman among the regulars of the series.

In the third season, a serious attempt to provide Lois with a friend came in a character's repeat appearance through several episodes. A psychic neighbor, Starr, moves into Lois's apartment building. Clearly modeled in part on Whoopi Goldberg's character in *Ghost,* Starr is amusing in her ability to talk even faster than Lois. And her open nature allows her to declare to Lois, "Maybe we were friends in an earlier life." Starr does engage in an interesting conversation with Lois in "Contact," her first episode, reaffirming the work/love parallel. She asks Lois, who is doubting her relationship with Clark, "If you're willing to risk your life for work, why not risk your life for love?" Starr is bucking for the role of traditional gal-pal—the one with whom the heroine can discuss her romantic interests. But these two women characters seem to have virtually nothing in common. And although Starr appears in a few other episodes, she seems to serve as a plot device—because of her mind-reading and spirit-channeling abilities—rather than as a genuine companion.

GRAFTED TO THE PATRIARCHAL TREE: MOTHER-IN-LAW AS MODEL

Aside from Lois, then, other major women characters include a trampy one-season coworker, absent or dysfunctional family members, wrong-headed businesswomen who turn out to be villains, or friends who disappear. There is, of course, one major exception to this pattern: Martha Kent. From the beginning of *Lois and Clark,* Martha (partly because of actress K Callan's input) is a lively,

charming woman, not a humdrum, repressed refugee from a Grant Wood paint-
ing. She is an equal work partner with her husband, Jonathan. She also enjoys
creating art; in the pilot, she displays her metalwork sculpture "Too Much, Too
Soon/Tortured Heart, Waning Moon." Though the title directs the audience to
laugh at her, Martha is proud of and takes pleasure in her work. Her artwork occasionally appears in other episodes as well—for instance, when she first meets
Lois and Lois successfully manages to respond to one of Martha's semirepre-
sentational paintings, or when Jonathan fears Martha is having an affair with her
art teacher because she has posed for a nude portrait. Martha does everything
from plumbing to cooking; and we are told in the third season that when
Jonathan was laid up with a back injury and the farm was financially endangered, she took a job outside the home (temporarily, of course) and shortly began
supervising other workers. Other than Lois, Martha is unquestionably the
strongest woman in *Lois and Clark*. The relationship that develops between the
two characters over the course of four seasons seems trusting and respectful. As
the third season wedding plans are under way, Lois confides to Martha Kent that
her own mother is "going to drive me mad." And Ellen Lane later says, "No wonder you turn to Martha" ("I Now Pronounce You").

In fact, Martha Kent is one of the reasons Lois and Clark's relationship comes
to fruition. When Lois finally realizes that Clark is actually Superman (in the last
episode of the second season, "And the Answer Is . . ."), it happens in part because she has offered to risk death in order to save Martha and Jonathan Kent.
The villain of the hour has kidnapped the Kents and demanded in exchange the
ever-popular Lois's dead body, and Lois suggests that Superman temporarily
freeze her in order to convince the villain of her death. Despite the hero's warn-
ings of the danger, she trusts him to revive her. As she closes her eyes and Superman touches her face before chilling her, Lois recognizes the gesture as
Clark's. She later explains that facing death "heightened" her perception, and, of
course, she felt rather than saw his represented self. It is perhaps not surprising
that, after she offers up her life for his parents', Clark (not Superman) asks her
to marry him. And it seems equally appropriate that this is the moment when
she confronts him with her knowledge of his secret identity. "Who's asking—
Clark or Superman?" she wants to know. She has trusted him with her life, but
he has not trusted her with his secret.

"We Have a Lot to Talk About," the third season opener that deals with the
couple's response to this new state of affairs, effectively avoids stridency or over-
done, oversimplified reactions. Lois is not shown as some kind of stereotypically
overemotional female, and Clark is not shown as some kind of—for want of a
better word—superman. The genuine difficulties couples can have when they
have been secretive about important elements of their relationship are explored.
Clark finds it hard to believe that Lois is not angry. She tells him, "I get it—I really do. It's logical; it's even thoughtful. But when you get right down to it, you
made me believe that you were two different people. And you did that by lying.
And that makes me feel like I don't know you—and that really hurts me—and

you know what? I *am* mad." She therefore temporarily rejects his proposal, and he flies off (literally, of course), hurt. Both the woman and the man are allowed to respond emotionally (though Clark clearly tries to repress his feelings in standard Superman style). Despite the episode title, they find difficulty in talking through the problem alone.

Later in the episode, however, Lois, dressed in a homey chenille robe, unlocks her door to allow Martha in to talk. In parallel, intercut scenes (a frequent device in this series), Jonathan advises Clark while Martha talks with Lois. Lois explains that she needs "time to get to know him for who he really is," and Martha reassures her that, of course, her response is "not unreasonable." Then she adds, "But you have to understand that Clark has always been alone." In effect, Martha is explaining the difficulty that Clark has had in trusting Lois with his secret. For while Lois's lack of trust is made an issue of, time and again, Clark's, only hinted at, is basic to the show's structure. As Clark says to Lois in "I'm Looking through You," "Did you ever think that maybe Superman was afraid to reveal himself?" Martha helps Lois to understand Clark's fear, even though it is the fear of a superman. The male—even Clark Kent, the great reporter and wordsmith; even Superman—needs a female translator. And Mother Martha shows us the woman succeeding in that role, a role key to her success as a model woman.

Thus, two strong and admirable women join forces to sort out this complicated relationship. Martha is a true friend to Lois, and in spite of further delaying tactics and complications as the series proceeds, that fact never changes. Lois and Clark's relationship is supported by Jonathan and Martha not just from the first time they meet her (when Martha whispers, "I love her!") but from the first time Clark speaks of her. When, in the two-part closing episode of season one, Clark says he thinks Lois is "the woman that I want to spend the rest of my life with," Martha responds, "Are you just now figuring that out? Your father and I have known that since the first moment you started talking about her." Lois and Clark's relationship is fully endorsed by his family, the central social unit in this series.

Lois and Martha are indeed admirable, in some ways feminist models of intelligence, strength, morals, and caring. But the underlying structure of the situation is that the only woman Lois is truly close to is her mother-in-law. Lois is thus gently but firmly inducted into the patriarchal social system. The two women whom we are allowed to admire are the ones who operate within this system—pushing its edges (plumber mother, investigative reporter), but never really stepping outside of them. Bereft of other female support, narrowly escaping the satanic seductions of a wealthy business mogul, Lois finally lands in the arms of the honest, hard-working guy from the office who is the true hero of our story. It is a commonplace to suggest that the marriage of Lois and Clark reduced the series' popularity because of the loss of sexual tension. But the show might also have drawn fewer viewers because the domestication of Lois was not a popular theme in the '90s—a more positive possibility from a feminist perspective. Lois never stops loving her work, but she works in part to satisfy her father, and her success in work is entwined with success in love. On the home front, her future mother-in-law helps her understand that if she stands by her man and gives him trust, he will respond with his true heroic self instead of feeling he must give a phony representation. Though Clark changes very little, the series has been occupied with showing Lois's education to worthiness. So Lois and Clark at last do get married and move into Clark's place. In the end, Lois not only opens her locks; she gives up the whole apartment.

NOTES

I wish to acknowledge the generous bibliographical advice and expertise of J. P. Williams (media scholarship) and Jo Sloan (sociology) and the videographical work of Leigh Raglan. I also wish to acknowledge the *Journal of Popular Film and Television,* in which one section of this chapter was originally published (see citation further on).

1. Molly Haskell's film criticism contrasts the "superfemale," who is "exceedingly 'feminine,'" with the "superwoman," who "has a high degree of intelligence or imagination, but [. . .] adopts male characteristics in order to enjoy male prerogatives [. . . ,] male freedoms [. . . ,] 'male logic' and ideology to influence people—and who lose[s] friends and [. . .] make[s] enemies in the process" (214).

2. Morrison cites the pattern of the woman's being required to train a male for a job and then defer to him professionally (86–87).

3. Of course, the series deftly suggests that Clark actually gets his initial job interview through networking, when Perry White mentions an old professor who had telephoned on Clark's behalf. Though his lack of experience works against him, the old boy network does help Clark get his foot in the door.

4. The Clinton Street address derives from the comics of pre-President Clinton days; the presidential allusion, however, may be more available for many viewers.

5. This scene closely parallels one between Remington Steele and a schlemiel CIA researcher in the *Remington Steele* episode "Signed, Steeled, and Delivered."

6. Interestingly, the single episode written by Lois's portrayer Teri Hatcher ("It's a Small World after All") includes Lois's high school friends. However, the episode did not appear until late in the series, and it was again an isolated instance, with no recurring characters among the friends.

WORKS CITED

Connors, Joanna. "Female Meets Supermale." In *Superman at Fifty: The Persistence of a Legend.* Edited by Dennis Dooley and Gary Engle. Cleveland: Octavia, 1987, 108–115.

Feuer, Jane, Paul Kerr, and Tise Vahimagi, eds. *MTM: "Quality Television."* London: British Film Institute, 1984.

Gess, Richard. Personal communication. 15 December 1994.

Glass Ceiling Commission. U.S. Department of Labor. *Good for Business: Making Full*

Use of the Nation's Human Capital: The Environmental Scan. Washington: GPO, 1995.

Goffman, Erving. *The Presentation of Self in Everyday Life.* Garden City, N.Y.: Doubleday, 1959.

Haskell, Molly. *From Reverence to Rape: The Treatment of Women in the Movies.* New York: Holt, Rinehart, 1974.

Kanter, Rosabeth Moss. *Men and Women of the Corporation.* New York: Basic, 1977.

Morrison, Ann M., et al. *Breaking the Glass Ceiling: Can Women Reach the Top of America's Largest Corporations?* Reading, Mass.: Addison-Wesley, 1982.

Mulvey, Laura. "Visual Pleasure and Narrative Cinema." *Screen* 16, no. 3 (Autumn 1975): 6–18.

Reynolds, Richard. *Super Heroes: A Modern Mythology.* Jackson: University Press of Mississippi, 1992.

Robinson, Michael G. "*Lois & Clark:* What's New About *The New Adventures of Superman.*" *Studies in Popular Culture* 21, no. 1 (1998): 83–98.

Wilcox, Rhonda V. "Dominant Female, Superior Male: Control Schemata in *Lois and Clark, Moonlighting,* and *Remington Steele.*" *Journal of Popular Film and Television* 24, no. 1 (Spring 1996): 26–33.

Williams, J. P. *The Evolution of Social Norms and the Life of Lois Lane: A Rhetorical Analysis of Popular Culture.* Dissertation, Ohio State, 1986.

———. "'It's My Job to See beyond the Surface': *Lois and Clark* and the Failure of the Female Gaze." Paper presented at the Popular Culture Association in the South Conference, Charlotte, October 20–22, 1994.

Part II
Dabbling in the Fantastic

5

What's Happening on Earth?

Mystery Science Theater 3000 as Reflection of Gender Roles and Attitudes toward Women

Jessica A. Royer

Each week on *Mystery Science Theater 3000* (*MST3K*), a young white man trapped on a satellite with only robot companions is forced to watch B-grade science fiction and horror movies made predominantly in the 1950s and '60s, with the occasional dubbed foreign film or bad '80s flick mixed in. To make the torture more bearable, the man and two of the "bots," Crow and Tom Servo, entertain themselves (and, unbeknownst to them, the viewing audience) with a running commentary on the film's characters, plot, special effects, dialogue, costumes, and anything else they can think of. Among the objects of ridicule are the women in these films. Appearing most often in subservient roles as wives, secretaries, or nurses and occasionally as scantily clad heroines or sidekicks, these women, particularly their attitudes and actions, seem out of place in the cultural context of the 1990s. Their behavior and interactions with male characters are sources of great amusement for the three masculine voyeurs.

This strange scenario has sparked affection and near-obsession in the hearts of many viewers, both male and female. As of the writing of this chapter, *MST3K* has survived ten seasons and transfers to three different cable networks. In the process, its story line has shifted slightly and main characters have changed, but the program's fans have persevered. They voice their opinions about the changes, and about everything else they love or hate about the show, on websites and listservs all over the Internet, and they tune in loyally each week. In addition, the series has been lauded for its clever writing and art direction and has been nominated for eight CableACE awards and two Emmys. It received a 1994 Peabody Award for Outstanding Quality Programming (Cornell and Henry). The Sci-Fi Channel, *MST3K*'s current host, announced that its tenth season would be its last; however, it is difficult to say with certainty that this decision will not be reversed or the series picked up by yet another cable network. In any case, *MST3K* is certain to live on in reruns, as it currently does on the Sci-Fi Channel.

MST3K is creative and quirky, certainly a bit out of the norm for television programming, and intriguing when interpreted through feminist theory. As a genre, science fiction provides a nonrealistic scenario through which to examine and evaluate questions that may be too difficult to address in present time. In *Constructing Postmodernism*, Brian McHale explains that in science fiction "models, materials, images, 'ideas,' etc. circulate openly from text to text, and are conspicuously cited, analyzed, combined, revised, and reconfigured" (12). Furthermore, as contemporary debates over issues such as gender roles, sexual orientation, and changes in the structure of the family and workforce grow more heated, they "seem to have intensified the symptomatic wish to pose and re-pose the question of difference in a fictional form that could accommodate such an investigation" (Penley, vii). In accordance with the practice McHale describes and the goals Penley establishes, both the form and content of *MST3K* provide fertile ground for the exploration of problematic societal issues, especially those pertaining to women.

The show's bizarre juxtaposition of opinionated contemporary characters with films from another cultural era sparks valuable investigation. Feminist literary critics have urged us to revisit old texts and scrutinize "shared cultural assumptions" that are both "deeply rooted" and "long ingrained" (Kolodny, 149). Furthermore, as feminist scholar Annette Kolodny points out, "we appropriate different meanings, or report different gleanings, at different times—even from the same text—according to our changed assumptions, circumstances, and requirements" (153). Therefore, *MST3K*'s setup jolts viewers out of the norm (loud-mouthed robots and B-movies from the 1950s are not the most logical pairing) and provides a unique means of reinterpreting older texts. To make its function clear, this multilayered revisiting process requires some deciphering.

Old cinematic texts are resurrected in each episode of *MST3K*, but they are not offered to audiences in a way that encourages open interpretation. Instead, the films are delivered with a new layer of commentary already added in. It is nearly impossible to separate the film shown on an episode of *MST3K* from the heckling that accompanies it. Although the show's at-home viewers watch the torturous movie right along with the series' main characters, the volume levels of the running commentary and the film's actual dialogue are proportioned so that the "peanut gallery" is dominant. At times, the voices in the movie can scarcely be heard above the series' characters' discussion. The television audience thus receives the film in a new form and in a new context.

Crucial to fully understanding the impact of this added layer is an understanding of its use of humor. *MST3K*'s humor provides a reason, in addition to its form and content, that the show is useful for feminist analysis. Comedy is frequently used to negotiate social change because, like science fiction, it provides a safe atmosphere for the examination of sensitive topics. "Under the guise of play, our most sacred values are opened to reason" (Duncan, 398). In addition, "comedy has often been linked to man's [*sic*] ability to transcend his oppression by laughing at his chains, linked to his satiric facility which enables him to suggest changes for his society, and related to his natural cycles of regeneration and renewal" (Barreca, 11). As television viewers laugh at the movies along with the observers on *MST3K*, an examination of what lies below the show's surface will provide insight as to just what they are laughing at. Does this program's humor live up to its highest political potential?

As outrageous as the outdated clothing, language, and social norms depicted in the films shown on *MST3K* seem to contemporary audiences (both the captive satellite audience of characters and at-home viewers of the series), they do offer insight into the cultural era from which the films come. While the films cannot mirror the era's reality in all its complexity, in hindsight we can see connections between, among other things, the roles society considered appropriate for women during the 1950s and '60s and the gendered typing of the characters women play in these movies. As feminist film theorist Laura Mulvey explains, mainstream cinema's "formal preoccupations reflect the psychical obsessions of the society" that created such films (23). If the films shown on *MST3K* illuminate the culture that produced them, then, is it not possible that the added layer of commentary from the characters on *MST3K* could offer insight into '90s society? After all, television has been declared a mediator of the views of our modern society. Because it is so pervasive, available in the privacy of our own homes, television is able to "articulate the main lines of the cultural consensus about the nature of reality" (Fiske and Hartley, 602). With this question in mind, this chapter aims to discover just what *MST3K* says about American society's perceptions of gender roles and women in the 1990s. Through the close analysis of two episodes, I will offer a feminist perspective on what the commentators on this show reveal about the ways our societal views of women have changed—as well as the ways they have stayed the same—over the years since the films shown on *MST3K* were originally released.

In addition to analyzing the three trapped viewers' comments on and reactions to the film in each episode, I will examine their roles in the plot of *MST3K* itself. Several times in each episode, the characters file out of the theater to take a break. These breaks often include lessons in human nature (taught by the human character, Joel or Mike), conversations with other robots who are not in the theater, and parodic reenactments of scenes from the film. Analysis of these interactions will add insight into the messages *MST3K* sends about gender roles in the '90s.

The two episodes I have chosen for analysis, *"The Amazing Colossal Man"* (from the 1991 season) and *"The She-Creature"* (from the 1997 season), are products of the same producer/director team and also reflect the two versions of the show's story line. In the first six seasons of the show (shown on the Comedy Channel, which later became Comedy Central), evil scientist Dr. Clayton Forrester stranded Joel, a low-level employee he disliked, on a satellite and forced him to watch bad movies as part of an experiment. When the show shifted to the Sci-Fi Channel for its seventh season, a new female writer joined the male-dominated staff, and the character of Pearl Forrester, mother of the late Dr. Clayton Forrester, became the lead foil. Joel also departed, and the tortured victim became Mike Nelson. Mike is described simply as Pearl's "enemy" (Cornell and Henry), and her quest is to destroy him by forcing him to watch bad science fiction movies.

The addition of Pearl has increased the female presence on the show. Prior to her inclusion, the only female on the show (other than those pictured in the films) was Gypsy, a cartoonishly feminine robot with a squeaky "bimbo" voice and bright red lips. She had few lines and little screen time in comparison to her male counterparts (human and robot). Mary Jo Pehl, one of the show's few female writers and the actor who plays Pearl Forrester, also "brings a feminine touch to the male-dominated writing staff, 'like when to draw the line with boob jokes,'" she explains in her online biography for the show's website (*Mystery Science Theater 3000 Page*). The selection of an episode from the pre-Pearl and post-Pearl eras of the show will thus provide fuel for comparison.

THE CRITICS

Before examining what the *MST3K* hecklers' comments reveal about the mores and stereotypes of contemporary society, these critics must be contextualized themselves. Their dialogue is an important element of *MST3K's* subtext, but their identities, chosen by the show's writers, are an equally important factor to be considered in the evaluation of their messages. Of primary relevance is the fact that these deliverers of commentary on the films are all males. Essentially, they are all white males. While Joel and Mike are technically the only Caucasian humans, the comments and points of view put forth by Tom Servo and Crow do little to distinguish their robot perspectives from a white American male's. What they know of life on earth comes from Joel and Mike, their creator (in Joel's case) and companions. During breaks from movie watching, Joel or Mike often give the bots pointers about "human nature" (as they interpret it) and how to act on Earth. Although the bots do not always show the aptitude for human sensibilities their teachers would like (as will be illustrated later in the analysis), it can be assumed that they all get along because they hold similar views.

The role of this white male captive audience, in addition to being cinema viewers, is that of critics. Elizabeth A. Meese describes the "traditional (masculinist) critic" as a "categorizer, interpreter, ameliorator" and as "reactive rather than active." "At worst," she explains, he is a "conservator of Culture" and a per-petuator of the status quo (7). *MST3K*'s critics can be read through this de-scription. In "Visual Pleasure and Narrative Cinema," one of Laura Mulvey's ini-tial premises is that "film reflects, reveals and even plays on the straight, socially established interpretation of sexual difference which controls images, erotic ways of looking and spectacle." The ways men interpret what they see, and per-haps even their interest in watching is influenced, "by pre-existing patterns of fascination already at work within the individual subject and the social forma-tions that have moulded him" (Mulvey, 22). Such a description further helps to elucidate the type of viewer/critic *MST3K* posits.

Gender, however, is not the only issue to be considered in interpreting these critics' messages. Their position as essentially passive observers in a theater also has a unique effect on their perspective. Generally, cinematic conventions "por-tray a hermetically sealed world which unwinds magically, indifferent to the presence of the audience, producing for them a sense of separation and playing on their voyeuristic phantasy" (Mulvey, 25). Even the darkness of the auditorium helps promote a feeling of isolated safety. It is difficult to tell who is saying what on *MST3K* while the film is rolling and the comments are flying, and it does not really matter. The writers have not developed distinct personalities for Joel or Mike and the two bots in the theater. Instead, the three heads are silhouetted at the bottom of the screen and represent a homogenous unit. The three charac-ters are arguably able to say whatever they want, cruel or crude as it may be, be-cause they know they cannot be seen or heard by those on screen and are not responsible to anyone for the opinions they express. Their status as observers gives them a sense of power and superiority. They feel none of the threat or need for politeness they might feel if they were witnessing actual interactions be-tween people or even watching a live performance.

A final point to be considered in interpreting these critics' messages is their veil of humor. As I have already noted, joking often productively cloaks difficult issues in a more acceptable format and allows for their discussion. However, it can serve a number of particularly masculine purposes as well. According to Judith Wilt,

> Women are only just beginning to realise that male humour has various functions, but none of them is intended to please or benefit them. It can be a bonding device, assisting male solidarity (and excluding women). It can be a smoke-screen, set up to dissipate an aura of good humour (distracting and deceiving women). Finally, it can be a form of assault, a teasing attack (putting women in that mythical region, their place). In any event it is used to avoid, to impede, or to deride the possibility of free equal relationships between men and women. (187)

I do not wish to argue, particularly before the episode analyses have been per-formed, that the humor on *MST3K* is solely at the expense of women. As men-tioned previously, no subject is safe from the *MST3K* characters' scathing re-marks, and the films' male characters are targeted for verbal abuse as well.

However, we must not ignore the fact that there are certain perspectives able to be articulated in an all-male situation that are less likely to be voiced in mixed company. None of the female characters on *MST3K* are ever in the theater watching the films. This viewing context is bound to have an impact on the "freedom of speech" practiced by the male characters, as it releases them from accountability to anyone but each other for what they say. The characters' unawareness of the male and female members of the television audience, who watch both them and the films, also contributes to this freedom.

In addition to providing crucial context for the analysis of the *MST3K* hecklers' comments, the writers' choice to make the hecklers all males offers further insight into the gendered conventions of our society. Both men and women write for the show, and, as is explained on the show's website, the goal of *MST3K*'s humor is to allow people the freedom to say whatever they want (Cornell and Henry). Yet despite this "freedom," only male characters deliver the film commentary the writers develop. Society traditionally finds aggression more appropriate for males, and *MST3K*'s sort of humor and criticism can often be seen as aggressive. The sexual and physical nature of some of the jokes also renders them conventionally more appropriately delivered by men. The all-male character audience allows the show's writers to create dialogue with these conventions in mind and also reveals that the writers are not as irreverent to societal roles and rules as they might think.

EPISODE ONE

This episode, which was broadcast in July 1991 on Comedy Central, used 1957's *The Amazing Colossal Man*. "Not even the U.S. Army can keep her away from the man she loved—but only the U.S. Army can save her from the monster he became!" proclaims the movie's original trailer. As the film begins, Colonel Glen Manning, an army reservist, is caught in a nuclear accident while on duty. He is severely burned and hospitalized. His young, blonde fiancée, Carol Forrest, comes to the hospital and is understandably distraught to learn of his near-fatal condition. In the morning, however, Manning's skin has miraculously healed. Soon he begins to grow. The nuclear blast has somehow sped up the cell reproduction inside his body. Manning eventually reaches a height of sixty feet and lapses into insanity in the process. At the end of the film, he attacks the city of Las Vegas and must be destroyed. Loyal to the end, though, is Carol. Despite the efforts of military personnel, most particularly the handsome Dr. Paul Lindstrom, she refuses to abandon her fiancé until all hope is lost.

The Amazing Colossal Man relies heavily on stock footage and bad special effects for its action scenes. It is overburdened in a number of places with lengthy explanations—usually medical or military—about Manning's condition and the actions being taken to control him. Wide-eyed Carol is used conveniently in several scenes as the object through which authority figures disclose this technical information to the audience. Manly military men and attractive, perpetually well-groomed, passive women are the standard for this film.

Interestingly, the story is not placed in the futuristic setting of many sci-fi movies but instead fantasizes about the effects of nuclear radiation on normal, present-day (1950s) life. Because of this "realistic" setting, the makers of the film seem to have worked that much harder to render accurately the cultural conventions of the era, such as Carol's indefatigable willingness to stand by her man. In fact, it is the film characters' stiff social roles that provide the majority of the amusement for the three *MST3K* characters watching it. The viewers alternately ridicule and reinforce these roles through their mocking comments and occasional silences.

The movie begins, and the first round of ridicule consists of an extended riff on the military. Actions that seemed patriotic and respectful in the 1950s are now construed as blind obedience by less-than-intelligent soldiers. "Mind if I smoke, sir?" asks a soldier while hunkered down waiting for a nuclear test blast. "I don't care if you burst into flames," responds the commanding officer in a voice supplied by one of the bots.

Manning then runs across the screen toward a huge nuclear blast. "He runs like a girl," observes a voice from the audience. "Glen, this is your mother," chimes in another viewer in a high, breathy voice. "If you stop, I'll make your favorite dish." While these comments continue the assault on the hypermasculinity of these military characters, they do so using clichéd jokes with women as the butt. To be compared to a "girl" in terms of athletic ability implies weakness and undesirable effeminacy. And while the words of "Glen's mother" ridicule him for being a supposed mama's boy, they also imply that there could be nothing worse than deference or obedience to a female. These are the same insults junior high–aged boys have been using on one another since before the 1950s, yet, even in the '90s, their meanings resonate.

Not long into the film, Carol appears. Her interactions with the male characters throughout the film, or rather their interactions with her, offer the next major object of the commentators' wrath. Distraught Carol meets Dr. Paul Lindstrom in the hospital lobby as she waits. He immediately launches into a vivid description of Manning's condition, only afterward discovering that Carol is the victim's fiancée and is perhaps less than interested in the gory details. He apologizes and asks if he can do anything for her. "Get you drunk maybe?" suggests a voice from the darkened theater. "How long have you known Col. Manning?" Lindstrom asks next. "And what are you doing after he's dead?" supplies one of the bots. Similar satellite audience commentary continues throughout the film and adds sexual overtones to nearly every scene between Carol and Lindstrom. He always seems to be hitting on her, but she makes no acknowledgment of his intentions, real or implied. Only the audience, with its contemporary perspective, renders his actions callous and inappropriate.

The satellite viewers' interpretation of Lindstrom as uncouth and predatory again suggests a preoccupation with the now-unacceptable male role presented in the film. Lindstrom stands a little too close to Carol and is a little too familiar by today's standards, but the characters' comments are focused on supplying his thoughts, rather than on Carol, who it seems could have some equally humorous thoughts about the situation supplied for her. The male critics (and their largely male writers) identify more readily, and display evidence that they feel more comfortable, with the mind of the male film character. While the satellite viewers' comments identify the situation as one that is out of the appropriate contemporary social norm and therefore do critique Lindstrom's sexism, they still prevent Carol from having a voice, both literally and figuratively. The woman's viewpoint is not provided at all. Carol is not given any more chance to express herself in the '90s than she was in the '50s.

The satellite audience's identification with the male perspective while the female's is overlooked can be noted in a number of other scenes in the film. At times, the normally raucous observers are noticeably silent. For example, in an extended flashback scene, Manning recalls a picnic he and Carol had shortly before the accident. She implores him to be careful and think of the future. He replies that he is thinking of both their futures and that they'll get married as soon as his weekend of duty is over. Carol says she won't be happy until he's safe at home. Joel and the bots are silent throughout this entire exchange, and they miss a seemingly perfect opportunity to satirize this stereotypically gendered pairing of adventurous man and passive, nurturing woman. In fact, Carol is more a mother than a partner. Her job is to nurture and worry if she is to meet the white, middle-class 1950s ideal. Only when the couple kisses, on a blanket with their picnic lunch, do the observers comment: "Ooh, hot dogs make her go wild!" The role of passive female from the 1950s apparently does not offend their modern sensibilities as much as the outdated male characters' actions do. Thus, an immature, sexist crack about the phallic shape of hot dogs at Carol's expense is the best they can offer.

In two other instances, Manning and Carol have arguments. He becomes increasingly self-pitying and abusive as he grows (the bots refer to him as the "fifty-foot whining man"), and he vents this frustration freely on the ever-positive and supportive martyr, Carol. A plaintive "Glen, you're bumming me out" is supplied at one point during an argument by a breathy voice from the audience, but even this response is understated and weak. Rather than a true retort, the comment reinforces Carol as trapped and unwilling to get out of what is becoming an unpleasant relationship. A few moments later, when Glen orders Carol to leave, she is given no rebuttal at all. Rather than bringing her character into the '90s by exposing the incongruency of her actions with contemporary conventions or by giving her a chance to fight back through supplied lines or thoughts, Carol is left in the '50s where the public female voice was rarely heard. The critics ridicule her for appearing stupid and shallow by '90s standards—as she is focused only on getting married and supporting her man—but they offer her no alternatives. In the 1990s context of the critics' commentary, Carol is doubly oppressed.

Only on rare occasions do the critics offer Carol any empowerment at all, and when they do so it seems more directly related to ridiculing one of the male characters than to commenting on her character in its own right. During one of the many instances in which Carol is subjected to a long-winded speech about Glen's condition (more for the audience's benefit than her own), Lindstrom asks her if she recalls his last round of explanations. "You put me in a coma," recalls a female-impersonating voice from the audience. "Let me give you a simplified layman's explanation," Lindstrom continues. "He's really big," offers one of the bots. So, while Carol is briefly given a chance to voice her opinion, the focus quickly returns to the pompous, overbearing nature of Lindstrom. Again, this approach offers indirect commentary on gender relations but always from the male perspective. Far more often the comments supplied for Carol during these lectures are "I don't get it" or "He's losing me, but I don't dare say anything." While "I don't dare say anything" at least acknowledges Carol's being trapped in silent oppression, for the most part her character continues to be ridiculed for her passivity and feminine subordination, as no one really cares whether she understands or not.

About the only instance in the movie when Carol's character acts at all assertively is in a scene with another female, the hospital secretary. Carol demands to know Glen's whereabouts and gets the run-around in return. As Carol's tone becomes increasingly aggressive and the secretary's equally snippy in return, a voice from the audience pipes up, "Ooh, I hope they start wrestling!" The viewers supply under-the-breath mutterings of "bitch" and "tart" on behalf of the two women throughout the rest of their exchange. Not only are the women ridiculed for assertiveness as well as passivity (leaving them essentially no correct option), they also are immediately reduced to sexual objects. The satellite audience is clearly distanced from the characters and sees them as objects, not as people. Mulvey describes such a method of viewing as exemplifying the "male gaze," which "projects its phantasy on to the female figure which is styled accordingly" (27). The series argues that viewers on the satellite (and most likely in the television audience as well) have no interest in the emotion or content of the scene. This perspective is encouraged by the selection of movies with horrible stories, actors, and special effects that leave little chance for any suspension of disbelief. Instead, the characters are voyeurs and the audience is rendered as voyeurs, with both parties hoping for a "good show." The film plays easily into these expectations.

Exemplifying this male gaze, a large percentage of the jokes on *MST3K* are sexual in nature, which, according to Mulvey, can be explained by the conventions of cinema itself. As just illustrated by the commentary on the scene between Carol and the secretary, even when the plot of the story has nothing to do with sex, the relationship between viewers and what is being exhibited for their pleasure on the screen is sexualized. Mulvey also points out that films often include interludes that add nothing to the plot and serve no other purpose than providing an opportunity to look (27). In a number of instances in *The Amazing Colossal Man,* the camera lingers over Carol in her bed or putting on her robe to answer the door and receives no complaints from the audience. Toward the end of the film, as Glen is attacking Las Vegas, he pauses for a moment to peer in a window at a woman bathing. "Well, I wouldn't kick her out of my tent," exclaims a voice from the front row. The comment refers to the earlier argument between Glen and Carol when he essentially kicked her out of his tent. Clearly, the pleasure found in observing through the "male gaze" has not changed much since the '50s.

The other element of commentary on this episode of *MST3K* comes during the viewers' breaks. The first one consists of Joel telling the bots that there's "an important lesson to be learned from today's experiment." He replays the scene between Carol and Lindstrom in the waiting room. "Clearly, this is no way to act around the spouse of a horribly disfigured nuclear accident victim," Joel says. "What could you say to make her feel better?" After a few humorous but completely inappropriate replies from the bots, such as "After looking at him, I can better understand the muscle groups," Joel concludes that his robot companions have "no aptitude for human sensitivities." He does not, however, supply any of his own suggestions. The bots proclaim that they are sensitive, and as the scene closes Crow asks Tom Servo, "You cried earlier, what was that about?" While this scene is premised as a lesson in subverting the stereotypical male response, it ends up using humor to further ridicule any male who might show emotion or attempt to be sensitive. Such male humor is used to strengthen the male bond and exclude women (Wilt, 187). The exclusion of all female or feminist voices from this exchange makes impossible any sense of balance or equality between genders.

Not until the very last break does a female presence appear on the show (other than the women in the film). Gypsy, the satellite's lone female robot, finally appears just before the episode's end. She is constructed from "household items," perhaps a hint at domesticity, while the male bots are made from sporting goods and Tupperware (Crow) or toys (Tom Servo) (Cornell and Henry). Gypsy has huge red lips and wears earrings, so there can be no doubt as to her identity as a female. Her voice is a parody of feminine breathiness, and as a result her lone comment is nearly indecipherable. When asked what she would have done if she were Glen, she responds, "I would have taken my head and made a hat," a statement that makes little sense to the television audience and, judging from their confused and dismissive responses, to the other bots and Joel either. "Just smile and nod" seems to be their manner of interacting with Gypsy. Her character is not particularly humorous and does little other than reinforce the idea that women are stupid, completely foreign, and impossible to understand, which has already been driven home by the commentary during the movie.

Information on the official *MST3K* Frequently Asked Questions list responds to this interpretation of Gypsy's character:

> Q: Why does Gypsy talk that way? Is she stupid? And why doesn't she watch the movies with M&TB [Mike and the bots]?
>
> A: Gypsy is probably the most sophisticated robot on the ship. She is responsible for controlling all the "higher functions" of the ship so that M&TB can watch the movies without worrying about it. She talks that way because all of her brain power is being used up in controlling the ship, and she has very little left over for normal conversation. In episode 207, "Wild Rebels," she shut down most of the ship's functions for a little while in order to have a regular conversation, and she spoke perfectly normally (while Joel gasped for oxygen). She does not watch the movies, again, because she is busy elsewhere. (Cornell and Henry)

The average viewer does not have this information to use in interpreting Gypsy's character, and even this explanation serves only as an excuse for sexist representation. Regardless of her alleged intelligence, Gypsy still is kept silent by her duties, which are the traditionally feminine roles of nurturing and being responsible for the lives of everyone on the ship. The line of reasoning that says women are much too tired after fulfilling their household duties even to desire a public forum for their ideas is another relic from the 1950s. Gypsy, despite the futuristic context, is silenced by her work much as the women in the films shown on *MST3K* are silenced by males providing all commentary.

EPISODE TWO

The insights drawn from Episode One can be used to raise the following issues for discussion in the analysis of Episode Two: What has the new story line on *MST3K* done to alleviate the all-male perspective? Has an additional woman writer increased the level of female empowerment for the characters in the films? Has the plot device of Pearl Forrester's control of the film selection made any noticeable difference? Let us examine an episode from the 1997 season on the Sci-Fi Channel to find out.

The She-Creature, a 1956 Ankoff/Nicholson film, is the basis for an episode first shown on April 5, 1997. This movie is the story of Dr. Carlo Lombardi, a greasily sinister hypnotist who has his subject, Andrea Talbott, completely under his power—both when hypnotized and when fully conscious. A terrible sea creature that, according to the bots, resembles a female cross between a Samurai warrior and a giant lobster is terrorizing the beach near the carnival where Lombardi performs. After much bumbling on the part of the police and a number of skeptical (and emotionless) scientific types, it is revealed that the She-Creature is actually a past incarnation of Andrea called into existence at Lombardi's command while she is deeply hypnotized. As the film progresses, Andrea becomes aware of her exploitation and increasingly desires to escape. Finally, with the help of the handsome Dr. Ted Erickson, Andrea is able to free herself from Lombardi's controlling power. The She-Creature kills Lombardi in her last appearance, and Andrea is able to enjoy the rest of her life with Erickson.

The movie is plagued by an unfortunate lack of acting ability. The male characters are unable even to make eye contact with one another, as if this intimacy might compromise their masculinity. The film also relies heavily on close-up shots of King, the family dog, barking wildly to convey Lombardi's evil and the periodic presence of spirits from the past. Rather than focusing their ire on the characters in the film, as they did while watching *The Amazing Colossal Man,* Mike and the bots fixate mainly on the horrid acting and the lousy special effects and lighting. There is no pretense of being even superficially involved with the story. During one of the breaks, the three examine *Do Not Act,* a book supposedly written by one of the film's main actors. Its instructions include "no listening," "no eye contact," and "no emotion."

Nevertheless, *The She-Creature,* even more so than *The Amazing Colossal Man,* illuminates the social conventions of the era regarding women. "Some women keep pets or grow roses for kicks," remarks one husband, ruefully. "My wife supports quack occultists." But, to make everything better, he reassures her, "Well, so long as it amuses you." This same man also does all he can to get his daughter Dorothy (portrayed by Cathy Downs of *The Amazing Colossal Man* fame) a worthy dowry so she can be married successfully. In a party scene, virtually without complaint, Dorothy endures the unwanted drunken affection of a former beau. Even Andrea, the woman who is supposedly "empowered" by her desire to escape Lombardi's evil clutches, is able to free herself only with the assistance of a big, strong man: Dr. Erickson. Her character, along with all the other female characters in the film, is confined by '50s society's concept of femininity.

The three observers' comments again focus largely on ridiculing the men in the film and on injecting sexual innuendo into every possible situation. "He's challenged me publicly and privately to disprove the authenticity of his experiments," Erickson explains to Dorothy about Lombardi. "And to oiled jockstrap wrestling," adds a voice from the front row. In addition, as before, there are a number of instances in this episode where the lack of audience comment is a statement in itself. "You go home and call the police," Erickson orders Dorothy after they stumble upon a murder scene; "I'll wait here for them. Hurry up!" She obeys this instruction without question, and rather than supplying her with a retort to Erickson's bossy command, the satellite audiences' comment refers to the dog, who is not even on-screen. "King is the Scorpio killer," supplies a voice to finish Erickson's statement.

However, there are distinct differences in the commentary on this episode. Pehl's addition to the writing staff does seem to have had some impact. The comments offered during the voyeuristic scenes in the film (which are as plentiful and pointless as those in *The Amazing Colossal Man*) are much tamer in this episode, and in some cases even give the women some recourse. Andrea changes clothes behind a screen as she converses with Lombardi in one scene, and in another she dresses behind a sheer curtain as Lombardi entertains a male guest. Andrea receives no audience comment as she changes shirts behind the screen. But when she comes out, wearing a tight, rather form-fitting scoop-neck blouse, "May I suggest a size up from that?" drifts up from the crowd. "Yeah!" adds another commentator. In contrast to the "the more eye candy, the better" opinion that prevails in the previously analyzed episode, these comments acknowledge the indignity Andrea experiences because of her ill-fitting clothing. Rather than just objectifying her and enjoying the view, this time the male observers seem to recognize Andrea as a person, and they comment on the ridiculousness of her outfit.

The comments during this scene continue in this vein by ridiculing the men on-screen for ogling Andrea. Erickson has a bit of a staring problem and answers the questions he is asked rather distractedly. "Breast," is supplied as his answer to one inquiry. "Boobies, exactly," is offered for another. He then follows Andrea outside. "Look, the Federal Witness Seduction Program," pipes up one voice. Erickson asks her if she'd like to get a cup of coffee. "Would that be a C-cup or a D-cup of coffee?" inquires an audience member. These last two comments do not solely attack Erickson's interest; they ridicule Andrea's sexuality as well. The context of the film does not indicate that she is being intentionally seductive, so the viewer's comments must be examined carefully.

While the viewers seemed to regard Andrea as a person rather than an object during her clothes-changing scene, this view is quickly overwhelmed. Because of her appearance, they attribute sexual behavior and desires to her. This thought process not only occurs in contemporary society; it has occurred for generations. An appearance that triggers sexual thoughts in observers often causes these observers to project those same sexual thoughts onto the person at whom they are looking, a dangerous and sexist jump in logic. Although Andrea's physical beauty gives her some power over her on-screen male counterparts, who have trouble constructing coherent thoughts in her presence, she is ridiculed for being attractive by the men in the satellite audience. These critics, according to Mulvey, are intimidated by the sexual prowess they attribute to her; "the look, pleasurable in form, can be threatening in content" (26). A beautiful woman can be aggressive in all her glamour, and therefore the male satellite viewers verbally attack Andrea, again reducing her to merely an object.

Yet despite this slip into stereotypical reasoning and masculine fear, overall, the comments the observers supply for Andrea are much more empowering than the comments supplied for Carol in *The Amazing Colossal Man*. The power relationship between Andrea and Lombardi is a constant target throughout the film. Compared to her youthful beauty, he is much older, wrinkled, unattractive, and most often glowering or ogling her. He controls her for his own ends but also

*Mike and the bots heckle
Dr. Lombardi during the*
She-Creature *episode.*

says that he "loves her" and that "her beauty must be preserved forever." His interactions with her are sexual in nature; he stands and sits extremely close to her and touches and kisses her (against her will) as well. He speaks to her with her face just inches from his own.

Through the *MST3K* characters, Andrea is given consistent rebuttals to his advances, and her own capacity for selective physical attraction and sexual pleasure is clearly acknowledged. The ridiculousness of her relationship to Lombardi is made obvious. Lombardi leans over Andrea as she reclines on a couch in a hypnotic trance. "You will awake feeling refreshed," he tells her. "You will find neck wattles sexy," adds a voice from the darkened theater. "I shall touch you and soon you'll be asleep," Lombardi says as he hypnotizes her in another scene. "So, like every night," adds one of the bots in a feminine voice. "Where are you now?" Lombardi asks the hypnotized Andrea. "Under a big cloud of your halitosis," replies one of the bots on her behalf. "She should get a Purple Heart for doing this role," adds another after a particularly intimate moment between Andrea and Lombardi.

Regardless of the observers' apparent sympathy for Andrea, she does not escape her own share of the audience's jeers. Marla English's marginal acting and wide-eyed expressions leave the viewers plenty of opportunity to question Andrea's intelligence. Lombardi and Andrea have an argument during which she tells him she hates him and desperately wants to escape. He storms off, and she is left with an oddly wistful expression. "Well, he is kind of cute," says a high, breathy voice from the audience. "I don't know how to love him," sings the same voice, like Mary Magdalene sings about Jesus in *Jesus Christ Superstar*. In the rock opera, Mary Magdalene does not know how to love Jesus because he is God and completely beyond her understanding. To imply the same sort of relationship between Andrea and Lombardi, which the use of this song does, belittles Andrea's character and minimizes her intelligence.

Other interactions between the men and women in this film are ridiculed as well, but, again, some of the comments come from a relatively feminist, rather than hypermasculinist, standpoint. "You're not going out there?" says a frightened Dorothy to Erickson as he prepares to head down to the beach where the She-Creature has been sighted. He brushes past her without answering. "You're a woman, so you deserve no answer to your question," a voice from the audience says for him. The rudeness of his action is acknowledged, and the comment makes clear that his behavior is more unacceptable in the eyes of contemporary viewers than it would have been to the film's original producers.

The "promotion" of Pearl Forrester to a main character on *MST3K* also affects the content of the skits between segments of the film. Simply having a female presence who is able to speak and interact with the other characters adds feminine perspective. However, closer analysis of Pearl's behaviors reveals that she is a rather stereotypical character. Pearl is bossy, actually a bully to her two sidekicks, the Observer (often referred to as "the Brain Guy" by Pearl because he carries his brain in a dish) and Professor Bobo (an escapee from the Planet of the Apes), and she clearly controls the proceedings. Pearl is even able to outsmart Mike and the bots on the satellite, which makes her the most intelligent (or at least cunning and resourceful) character on *MST3K*. Her aggressive, angry behavior and disdain for men may be intended as a counterbalance to the many passive females in the films, but her character veers into the "angry bitch" stereotype. Further complicating a feminist analysis of her character, Pearl exhibits a number of attributes typically associated with radical feminism, including beliefs in the superiority of females and in the individual (namely, herself) as more important than the group (Austin, 6). Furthermore, that Pearl is stout, has "bad" hair, and cannot use make-up "properly" validates the stereotype of the feminist as unattractive and undesirable.

The *She-Creature* episode begins with Pearl speaking to Mike and the bots on the satellite from her base on the Observer's home planet. She has lost control and is being imprisoned while the Observer and others of his kind prepare to dissect Bobo. "I know you guys hate me, even loathe me, but could you help me out?" she asks. She urges them to create a distraction so she can escape. As Tom Servo, Crow, and Mike deliberate on the satellite, Pearl begins to beg. "Pweese?" she says in baby talk as she pooches her lips out and bats her eyes. "Pwetty pweese for Pearl?" "Don't do that!" implores Mike. "God, stop it!" adds Tom Servo. Disgusted by her behavior, the prisoners agree to help her and successfully reinforce the effectiveness of Pearl's feminine ploys. She has feminized herself to the point of being a helpless, passive child so the men will have no choice but to take pity on her, even though they find her actions revolting. This behavior certainly should not be construed as feminist, and its combination with Pearl's more feminist attitudes feeds into the stereotype of women as manipulative and wanting the "best of both worlds"—equality with men and preferential treatment as well.

*Pearl Forrester: new feminism
or old stereotype?*

In a later break segment of the episode, Pearl is penciling her eyebrows (a stereotypical sign of feminine vanity) as Bobo drives her and the Brain Guy around the galaxy in her spacecraft, constructed largely from a VW bus. Again, she appears much smarter than her inept male companions. When the spaceship gets a flat tire, Pearl tries vainly to convince Bobo there's no need to fix it. "We're in space. It doesn't make any difference," she says. "Women!" Bobo replies. "I'll get out and fix it." He promptly opens the door and free falls through space to the surface of the planet below. The lesson? He should have listened to Pearl's advice, which was correct even regarding automotive mechanics, a typically male domain. As a change of pace, this scene indulges a stereotype about males (you can't tell them anything about cars). While humorous, particularly in the opinion of some female viewers, the exchange does little to dispute the social norm.

Though Pearl's character usually belittles and abuses her male companions, she is also nearly always right. At a superficial level, her character seems to offer a distinctively feminist voice to what was previously a male-dominant perspective on the show. However, closer examination of the methods she uses to get her way reveals that her expanded role is merely a new means of exploiting yet another set of stereotypes. Rather than being a legitimately strong female voice, Pearl gains power by mimicking male attributes or by exploiting her femininity. Overt aggression, dominance, and the belittling of those nearby are not healthy means of asserting oneself, and neither is feigning weakness to secure help. Ultimately, while Pearl may seem to score some valuable points for women in the battle of the sexes, her generally annoying qualities and largely masculine means of obtaining power make it impossible to identify her as a feminist character.

CONCLUSION

In a 1990 interview, Joel Hodgson, *MST3K*'s creator, offered this explanation for the purpose of the series: "It's about liberty, in a small, goofy way." Chris Cornell and Brian Henry, authors of the *MST3K Frequently Asked Questions* webpage, add that the show "appeals to an innate human desire to unabashedly say what you think. [. . .] The whole notion of grown-ups in power being heckled and ridiculed for their obvious inadequacies is irresistible." They go on to say that there is even more behind the show than this, otherwise the series "would just be 'Beavis & Butthead.' [. . .] *MST3K* is an object lesson, a demonstration that we don't have to—and shouldn't—passively accept the garbage we are spoon-fed on a daily basis" (Cornell and Henry).

My close analysis of just two episodes of *MST3K* indeed reveals that attention to detail while watching the show pays off with added humor and political depth within the seemingly innocuous words, expressions, and gestures in the films the series screens. However, even as *MST3K* celebrates the ability to comment "freely" and irreverently on the films, it still perpetuates the societal conventions that so often keep women from having an equal say. And, more often than not, the show's characters ridicule the social conventions of the 1950s without straying far outside contemporary social norms. Despite the increased presence of female characters on the show and the shift toward more female-empowering commentary during the films, *MST3K*'s brigade of male critics still filters these comments through their homogenous gaze.

Ultimately, however, the show does provide unique and useful insight into the conundrum that is our society. Even as the satellite critics' commentary provides some progressive critique of gender roles and social mores of the 1950s, there are instances where these dated mores are still more acceptable as they apply to women than as they apply to men. And attitudes toward many of the conventions popular in film during the 1950s, particularly images of women as on-screen sexual objects, remain the same in the 1990s. As we have seen, the humor of the observers' comments is at times productive and empowering but is still used to bond the male critics and exclude women.

In a similar manner, the humor of the break time skits for the most part stays safely within the realms of established stereotypes. Despite her strong female persona, Pearl's character is not particularly likable, nor, as we have seen, is she a good representative of feminism. The character is described by Cornell and Henry as "an almost-too-vividly realized character that seemed to remind just about everybody of their least-liked, most unpleasant and unwelcome female relative or acquaintance." Interestingly, quite a bit of negative fan response has been generated, particularly online, and Pehl has since softened Pearl a bit in the hopes that she might become "more likable in the same way that the evil Dr. Forrester was perversely likable." As a result, Cornell and Henry report "a growing appreciation of her more amusing aspects of the character, and far fewer negative reactions."

To some degree, these mixed reactions to Pearl may provide insight to our society's continuing unresolved feelings regarding feminism and feminists. Not that Pearl—or Pehl, for that matter—proclaims herself a feminist, but the character's actions and attitude clearly indicate that she feels herself superior to her male counterparts. Yet radical feminism is only one incarnation of the wide range of beliefs gathered under the broad umbrella of "feminism(s)." One can be a feminist and actively challenge radical feminist ideology. After all, in late twentieth-century society, "feminism is a loaded word. If a woman chooses to call herself a feminist, she must be ready for all the varied denotations, compounded by a multitude of connotations, that are attached to a word that is a political act in itself" (Woodward, 1).

MST3K makes no claims to be an advocate for women. However, the show remains thought-provoking and amusing to male and female viewers alike. The analysis, at least of these two episodes, reveals that, for good or for ill and whether we like it or not, *MST3K* has a lot to say about the state of contemporary gender roles and societal conventions regarding, among other things, women. Acting out of what they perceive (and perhaps a large portion of our society would perceive) to be "complete freedom," the writers of *MST3K* provide an in-depth look at the multilayered, contradictory nature of what is acceptable in contemporary American culture. But negative examples are as useful for instruction as positive ones, and if nothing else, we can learn as we laugh.

NOTES

I would like to thank Dr. Elizabeth Homan, Ms. Rie Woodward, and Dr. Claudia Barnett for their contributions to this chapter.

WORKS CITED

Austin, Gayle. *Feminist Theories for Dramatic Criticism*. Ann Arbor: University of Michigan Press, 1990.

Barreca, Regina. "Introduction." In *Last Laughs: Perspectives on Women and Comedy*. New York: Gordon and Breach, 1988, 3–22.

Cornell, Chris, and Brian Henry. *Mystery Science Theater 3000 Frequently Asked Questions*. Version 3.3<http://www.mst3kinfo.com/mstfaq/> (6 April 1998).

Duncan, Hugh D. *Communication and Social Order*. New York: Oxford University Press, 1962.

Fiske, John, and John Hartley. "Bardic Television." In *Television: The Critical View*. 4th ed. Edited by H. Newman. New York: Oxford University Press, 1987, 600–612.

Kolodny, Annette. "Dancing through the Minefield." In *The New Feminist Criticism: Essays on Women, Literature, and Theory*. Edited by Elaine Showalter. New York: Pantheon, 1985, 144–167.

McHale, Brian. *Constructing Postmodernism*. London: Routledge, 1992.

Meese, Elizabeth A. *Crossing the Double-Cross*. Chapel Hill: University of North Carolina Press, 1986.

Mulvey, Laura. "Visual Pleasure and Narrative Cinema." In *The Sexual Subject: A Screen Reader in Sexuality*. London: Routledge, 1992, 22–34.

Mystery Science Theater 3000 Page. The Sci-Fi Channel. <http://www.scifi.com/mst3000/>.

Penley, Constance. "Introduction." In *Close Encounters: Film, Feminism, and Science Fiction*. Edited by Constance Penley et al. Minneapolis: University of Minnesota Press, 1991, vii–xi.

Wilt, Judith. "The Laughter of Maidens, the Cackle of Matriarchs: Notes on the Collision." In *Women and Literature*. Edited by Janet Todd. New York: Holmes and Meier, 1980.

Woodward, Anne-Marie. "The Third Wave of Feminism: Reclaiming the F-Word?" Senior thesis, Emory University. May 1995.

6

Feminism, Queer Studies, and the Sexual Politics of *Xena: Warrior Princess*

Elyce Rae Helford

Everybody loves *Xena: Warrior Princess* (*X:WP*). Though critics in the popular press often describe the fantasy-drama series as "schlock" TV (Baumohl, Greenwald, and McDowell, 80; Goldblatt, 32), they simultaneously offer praise for its self-conscious campiness (Kastor, C1; "Legends, Warriors and UFOs," 49; Pozner, 12; Tucker, 60). Whether trashy or hip, the press has been forced to acknowledge the success and popularity of this spin-off of *Hercules: The Legendary Journeys,* both despite and because of its superficial plots, cheap special effects, slapstick humor, anachronisms, and cartoon-like fight scenes. Yet not only the popular press and fans love *X:WP*. Feminists and lesbian, gay, bisexual, and transsexual activists applaud the series for its strong woman-identified and ambiguously sexualized female hero. Because *X:WP* means much to many for diverse reasons, it deserves serious examination as a cultural phenomenon. This chapter will study critical responses to *X:WP*, particularly its alleged feminism and progressive sexual politics, in order to speculate on the political limits of television in the 1990s.

X:WP tells the ongoing story of an ancient Greek warrior woman who is strong, independent, resourceful, intelligent, and committed to righting wrongs in the world, often through violence. In the first episode of the series (beginning its fifth season at the time of this chapter's publication), "Sins of the Past," we learn some of Xena's history, especially that she enjoyed life most as the leader of a ruthless army of mercenaries that plundered and destroyed whole villages of people, down to the last child. On a return visit to her native village of Amphipolis, however, she confronts her past through her mother's accusations and her own concern over threats to the village by Draco, a warlord she once admired. By defending her village, Xena begins to atone and use her strength in the service of the disempowered. Another good deed she accomplishes in Amphipolis is to take a young woman, Gabrielle, along with her when she leaves. Gabrielle seeks to travel the world as a bard, primarily to escape her likely future as a traditional wife and mother in her small village. After this fateful meeting, the series follows Xena and Gabrielle's adventures together and Xena's ongoing internal struggles.[1]

Despite its superficial action-adventure format, many critics celebrate *X:WP* as a mass-culture moment feminists have been dreaming of "since feminism came into being" (Minkowitz, 74). They praise the Warrior Princess's "ability to leap over sexist stereotypes in a single bound" (Stoller, 42) and her "proactive stance" ("Lucy Lawless," 78). She is "the perfect antidote to 'Dr. Quinn, Medicine Woman's' Martha-Stewart-on-the-frontier sanctimony" (Millman). In particular, she offers an antidote for fans of the traditionally male-supremacist superhero genre. Heroes tend to be men in historical accounts and popular texts, yet Xena demonstrates the traditional traits of a hero, from courage and selflessness to intelligence and displays of physical strength—in fights that are never "catty or kinky" (Pozner, 13). Though physical power is Xena's most obvious heroic trait, the series also highlights her experience and wisdom. We see this feature, for example, when she displays healer's skills, even teaching Hippocrates about medicine ("Is There a Doctor in the House?"). Through demonstration of strengths in traditionally male-dominated arenas, *X:WP* challenges societal norms that identify men as the sole creators of history and myth (Meister, "*Xena: Warrior Princess*"). Critics thus assert that the series emerges as "a Hollywood corrective to the ancient world's sexism" ("Why Greek Tunics Are Back," 93). No wonder Secretary of State Madeline Albright has identified Xena as one of her heroes (*CNN Live*, 3 August 1998).

Stepping into the traditional role of hero seems a feminist triumph to many; however, it also arguably masculinizes Xena, suggesting that for women to be heroic they must become, in effect, men. Nevertheless, the series does arguably challenge such a perspective in its emphasis on Xena's moral ambiguity. "Unlike classic superheroes, Xena is not decency incarnate" (Pozner, 13); thus, "the show's greatest innovation may not be the toughness of its female lead, but her deep awareness of her own desire to exploit and intimidate others," making Xena a "hero whose ethical struggles are never over" (Minkowitz, 75). While she is certainly not the only ethically complex hero in contemporary popular culture (comic book heroes Batman, Sandman, and the Crow come to mind, among others), there are potential feminist implications in offering such an ambiguous hero in female form. *X:WP*'s "sophisticated discussion of morality" (Minkowitz, 75) can invite audiences to challenge gender essentialism, to separate (socialized) gender from (biological) sex. Specifically, we may come to see beyond equations of femaleness with moral perfection (woman as goodness incarnate). In other words, in this fantastic world in which female characters are "unique, multifaceted individuals," never "implied to be inherently moral or tender"

(Pozner, 13), women can be recognized as complex beings unconnected to any "natural" (feminine) attributes.

Popular feminist critics invested in America's youth emphasize Xena's function as a role model for teen girls desperate for strong media images of women. Critics celebrate that "Today, girls who enjoy play-acting do not have to compromise their developing intellects to find worthy heroines to impersonate, enjoy and respect. Today, instead of Charlie's Angels, girls play Xena and Gabrielle" (Pozner, 12). *X:WP* seems especially provocative for those whose feminist politics stress compromise with mainstream American cultural norms. Xena can productively be linked with "girl power," a '90s media-focused "movement" invested in increasing girls' self-esteem and personal empowerment without "sacrificing" preoccupations with beauty, boys, and consumerism. Says Sarah Dyer, editor of *Action Girl* comics, Xena "really appeals to younger, post-feminist women and girls. She wears a skirt and she proves you can fight really good in a skirt. She has cool-looking hair, but she kills people" (Dyer, quoted in Kastor, C1). In this context, *X:WP* makes "the traditionally male superhero genre cool for girls without hollowing out the strong message" because Xena "compellingly combines action with appearance" (Kingwell, 83). Through this lens, our warrior princess emerges as a superb example of "a new kind of pop culture heroine, one that is at once powerful and undeniably girly" (Stoller, 45). And she can thereby "inspire self-reliance in young female fans, even a kind of new-style power feminism" (Kingwell, 83).[2]

Feminist perspectives less compromised than that of girl power also appear in popular *X:WP* criticism, however. Some critics note that Xena's sexiness can be read as reworking the female body "as an active and aggressive subject": "After Xena punches out some mealy-mouthed enemy guys, she has the chutzpah to raise her arm, sniff her pit, and sigh, 'I love the smell of warrior sweat in the morning!'" (Stoller, 45). And, to the question "Is Xena sexy?," critic Jennifer L. Pozner replies:

> Absolutely, not only because of her lithe, muscular body, but because she is entirely comfortable living, fighting, and loving inside of it. Unlike most television women, she neither denies nor exploits her own sexuality. What better model for positive female behavior could we present to girls maturing amid insistent virgin/whore stereotypes, and in a culture in which eating disorders run rampant? (13)

Indeed, the series provides an important critique of glorifications of women's sexual innocence and of attacks on women's sexual experience because it makes no judgments about the characters' sexual activities—neither Gabrielle's virginity (see Minkowitz, 75) nor Xena's promiscuity (see Meister, "*Xena: Warrior Princess*").

Clearly, for these various critics and countless fans, Xena is a multifaceted feminist icon. In light of such celebration, however, it is important to observe just how a critic can and will bend the series to her own perspective in order to praise it. As journalist Elizabeth Kastor invites: "She is Xena, Warrior Princess. Turn on your TV, tune in her show and interpret her at will" (C1). To illustrate this divergence of opinion, we may note that there is conflict over how to read Xena's "dominatrix-influenced duds" (Pozner, 13). How does one speak of Xena's "formidable leather minidress" ("Lucy Lawless," 78), a costume Xena's portrayer Lucy Lawless describes as leaving her "trussed up like a chicken" (quoted in Jacobs, 86)? While critic Donna Minkowitz, in a *Ms.* tribute to the series, rejoices that Xena's outfit "doesn't emphasize her breasts" (77), this is hardly convincing to anyone who has seen the costume. Kastor makes this particularly plain: "You will notice her breasts. Really, there's no way not to, what with all the swirls and twists of metal buttressing her leather bustier" (C1). Critic Debbie Stoller, similarly, sees "a molded breast-plate contraption that would make Madonna's mouth water," containing a female character who "resembles no one so much as legendary pin-up queen Bettie Page" (44). Meanwhile, Pozner reminds us of RuPaul's statement that we are all born naked and the rest is drag (13). To Pozner, what is important is not whether Xena's outfit is "brief" but that "you won't catch her fumbling with frills or teetering on the stilts so many women have accustomed themselves to from nine to five" (13).

Ultimately, what is most important here is that each critic seems so assured with the Xena she constructs. Surely all of television is available for contrasting readings, and the diversity of perspectives even among critics who share some feminist orientation clearly reveals that *X:WP* is an excellent example of a polysemic text. Polysemy (the availability of a text for multiple interpretations) allows us to understand why a series that some may see as revolutionary may be identified by others as reactionary or even as a complex blend. As an example, consider the previous discussion of feminist interpretations alongside the popularity of *X:WP* among men. *Playboy* announces that there is "plenty" in the series "for guys who appreciate a postmodern kick-ass warrior gal" (Rensin, 144). According to series producer Rob Tapert, Xena is a "hero for women" and a "hero *and* a sex symbol for men" (quoted in Minkowitz, 77). Tapert denies lesbian attraction to Xena here while asserting that some men will appreciate women's strength, as long as it is accompanied by hetero/sexual availability.

Science fiction writer and critic Gregory Feeley further develops Tapert's implicit argument, reading Xena through retro images of pulp fiction's well-endowed women warriors, those "chick in a brass bra" types (quoted in Kastor, C1). He contends that when read through the sexist pulp magazine tradition, Xena is not about "older gay women or young girls seeking good role models." Instead, she is the fantasy of the insecure, "relatively unsophisticated, uneducated male [. . .] who would be deeply bothered by a strong woman in his real life, [but] could get off on a sword-wielding damsel wearing hip thongs and a brass bra" because the conventions of the pulp genre allow him to feel safe with this familiar character type (quoted in Kastor, C1). Thus, though their positions are not identical, the nonfeminist viewer who praises *X:WP* for its recognition that women should always be sexy (whether they are heroic or not) and the feminist viewer invested in seeing a strong and independent woman may overlap in their readings of the text. Even if the "eye candy element is a factor" in the popularity of *X:WP* among straight men, one can still ask, "[H]ow fabulous is it that a strong, confident, and valiant woman can finally be seen as sexy?" (Pozner, 13).

Of course, there are even more highly divergent perspectives than these. Some viewers apparently enjoy *X:WP* without addressing female heroism or power at all. In his study of *X:WP* fandom, Mike Flaherty cites an anonymous male fan who makes his objectification quite plain: "What's not to like? [. . .] Xena's a total babe. Not only that, she's a babe who likes other babes . . . It's a babe-fest" (41). Moreover, some lesbians may be invested in celebrating sexual desire without a more explicit political agenda. Says Heather Findlay, Xena fan and editor of lesbian-oriented *Girlfriend* magazine, "A figure like Xena can come along with great cleavage and beautiful legs and we can enjoy lusting after her" (quoted in Kastor, C1). The key point is that the program is available for all these readings—and more. In fact, to some, polysemy may seem the very point of the program. Kathleen E. Bennett argues that *X:WP* is groundbreaking because, above all, it "provides an example to creators of television programs of a way to make use of open spaces inherent in television texts."

LESBIAN TEXT AND SUBTEXT

What Bennett is specifically referring to in her praise of the use made of "open spaces" is perhaps the most compelling aspect of *X:WP* for fans and critics: the program's statement(s) on sexuality. The anonymous male fan quoted by Flaherty shares with Bennett, Pozner, Minkowitz, and a vast army of Xena critics and fans an appreciation of what is often called the lesbian "subtext" of the program. Most generally, the subtext of *X:WP* refers to specific aspects of the program that can "be used to support a reading hospitable to desire between women" (Bennett). These elements are generally not overt expressions or demonstrations but relatively subtle hints. Much is available within the program to enable (or, for those who agree with Bennett, to actively encourage) such a reading. In a number of episodes, Xena and Gabrielle share intimate experiences; they sleep on the same blanket or take a bath together, for example. They also engage in displays of affection, such as hugs, kisses, and shared tears. And they exchange ambiguous dialogue, including sexual innuendo and *double entendre,* as well as overt and direct declarations of love. That Xena has had relationships with men in the past and some romances since meeting Gabrielle and that Gabrielle has actually married a man while adventuring with Xena does not disprove that the program can be read as bisexual or even lesbian.[3]

For fan critic Melissa Meister, the importance of the series' homoeroticism is not simply its challenge to heterosexual dominance on television and throughout U.S. culture. The "extraordinary feat" of *X:WP*, she argues, is that it is "one of the first shows on TV that can satisfy both a straight and gay audience" (Meister, "Academic Theorisms"). *X:WP* "transcends and expands on the ways that homoerotic love can be shown on TV" because in Xena we have a "homosexual icon [. . .] that is not always concerned with their [*sic*] sexuality." Meister explains that

> Xena and Gabrielle's sexuality is not an issue on the show. They don't [. . .] have long, drawn out conversations about what it's like to be with another woman. They simply are what they are, and we love them for it. They show a comfortable, loving relationship between two women that doesn't have to be justified, questioned, or explained. ("Academic Theorisms")

With such a perspective in mind, Meister can conclude by wholeheartedly praising the series for helping viewers to "stop and think that it is okay and great for women to be so close. That it is okay if a leading character on prime-time has a homosexual relationship. That it is okay to be lesbian and a role model. These are ground-breaking ideas [. . .]" ("Academic Theorisms").

Just how truly groundbreaking a homosexual (or even bisexual) lead character on television is should not be underestimated. Thus, the subject deserves some attention before we proceed with analysis of *X:WP* in particular. As cultural critic Larry Gross argues, "[T]he visible presence of healthy, non-stereotypic lesbians and gay men does pose a serious threat: it undermines the unquestioned normalcy of the status quo, and it opens up the possibility of making choices to people who might never otherwise have considered or understood that such choices could be made" (137). Generally, the history of lesbian, gay, bisexual, and transsexual (LGBT) representation on U.S. television has been one of invisibility, victimization, and demonization (135–136). There have been rare exceptions (such as Jody on the sitcom *Soap*); however, more often we have been given either no LGBT characters or stereotypical and offensive ones. Even a groundbreaking sitcom such as *Roseanne,* which did effectively address the subject of homophobia within its lead characters, relied on the stereotypes of the male-hating dyke and the "swishy," effeminate gay couple (see also *Northern Exposure*'s gay couple). The '90s have arguably been somewhat kinder, giving us relatively inoffensive minor gay and lesbian characters (such as those on *NYPD Blue* and *Friends*); however, the development and fate of the sitcom *Ellen* offers perhaps the most relevant explanation for the popularity of *X:WP*'s "subtextual" approach to LGBT representation.

Although Chrysler and Wendy's avoided advertising during the episode and Rev. Jerry Falwell "exhorted his flock to boycott the show's sponsors," the "coming out" episode of *Ellen* garnered awards, high ratings, and much critical praise ("Ellen DeGeneres," 56). After this revolutionary event, however, the ABC network, fearing audience and sponsor alienation, decided that future *Ellen* episodes representing any physical affection between same-sex characters would feature an on-screen advisory: "This program contains mature content. Parental discretion advised" (Stockwell, 92). An infuriated DeGeneres threatened to quit, asserting, "The only other ABC show that's ever had this label is *NYPD Blue,* and that has nudity and violence" (quoted in Stockwell, 92). Determined not to back away from overt representations of gay life, DeGeneres stayed and continued to chart new territory. However, this open homosexuality on a sitcom actually signaled its demise. Negative response came from all sides.

For those who championed this season of *Ellen,* the cancellation of the series was about paranoia. ABC retreated from support and right-wing Christian groups protested. Anne Stockwell, writing for the gay and lesbian newsmagazine *The Advocate,* reported, "What really aggravates the conservative 'pro-family' groups who oppose the show is the fact that Ellen Morgan keeps getting happier. She's found a special woman, kissed her, held hands in the movies, and, as of November, taken her to bed" (92). As DeGeneres put it, "I'm gay, the character's gay, that's the problem everyone has with the show. It's just too controversial. Nobody wants to deal with it" (quoted in Frutkin, 22). With too little support from the network, attacks from ultra-conservative groups, and declining numbers of viewers, *Ellen* was canceled in 1998.

If we read the trajectory of *Ellen* as a case study in the best that television can presently do with homosexuality, there may be no surprise in acknowledging that more subtle representations can fare better. For example, LGBT characters may be projected into a more tolerant science fictional future, as exemplified by the capable and intelligent bisexual character Commander Susan Ivanova of *Babylon 5.* Yet, even in other worlds, such directness is rare. In the Clinton "Don't Ask, Don't Tell" political era, the ambiguousness of *X:WP* has enabled it to achieve remarkable economic success and popularity.

There are, however, perspectives that refuse the concept of subtext in identifying a series as homosexual. While some critics emphasize that *X:WP* "can be taken in through both heterosexual and homosexual lenses" (Meister, "Academic Theorisms"), a queer studies perspective refuses the notion of viewer's "choice." For Alexander Doty in *Making Things Perfectly Queer,* the concept of subtext identifies not praiseworthy pluralism but obvious heterosexism. When read through Doty's perspective, we might argue that only under the assumption that primary readings are and must be heterosexual will a view of Xena and Gabrielle's relationship as lesbian (or even bisexual) be subtextual. And the problem is not simply mislabeling: "[T]he concept of connotation allows straight culture to use queerness for pleasure and profit in mass culture without admitting to it" (Doty, xi–xii). In other words, subtext means the series never has to "out" its characters and the producers never have to risk the censure and eventual cancellation that might happen with an overtly lesbian program, like *Ellen.* Instead, it can maintain an economic base of homophobic viewers while also endearing queer (LGBT and other sexually minoritized) viewers, often eager for any representations that suggest the existence of nonheterosexuals (Gross, 142).

For example, the *X:WP* episode "A Solstice Carol" features a moment in which Xena gives Gabrielle a Solstice gift. Gabrielle sadly says, "I don't have a gift for you," and Xena replies "Gabrielle, you *are* a gift to me." The text's polysemy means we can read this as an exchange of affection between friends, a declaration of love between partners, or even a sexual innuendo linked to pornographic representations of bisexual women whose sexual activities with one another are primarily in service of men's voyeuristic desires. However we read this scene—from a straight, queer, or sexist/objectifying perspective—as long as we keep tuning in, the producers make money. And if they make money without viewers having to challenge homophobia, neither a LGBT rights nor a feminist agenda will be served. Therefore, such analysis reveals that polysemy is a highly problematic basis for political struggle.

When networks cannot be persuaded to take significant risks (and the cancellation of *Ellen* may mean that few will for years to come), reading subtext may be the only option for viewers seeking a nonheterosexual lead character. However, Doty reminds us that even the queerness we can find in television texts may be "deniable or 'insubstantial' as long as we keep thinking within conventional heterosexist paradigms, which always already have decided that expressions of queerness are *sub*-textual, *sub*-cultural, *alternative* readings, or pathetic and delusional attempts to see something that isn't there" (xii). Nonetheless, many people do not and all of us need not see the world through such reactionary paradigms. Says Doty, "I've got news for straight culture: your readings of texts are usually 'alternative' ones for me, and they often seem like desperate attempts to deny the queerness that is so clearly a part of mass culture" (xii).

With Doty's perspective in mind, the following paragraphs take a voyage through *X:WP*, emphasizing a queer reading as the dominant reading and examining what the series has to offer viewers who are invested in interrogating the feminist promises and (hetero)sexist limitations of television. A queer studies lens can help us to see the pleasures of *X:WP*'s challenges to heteronormativity, but a feminist perspective also requires that we challenge the series to live up to a progressive sexual politics in its queerness. In order to obtain this reading, I first make plain the queerness of *X:WP* and its celebrated subversive pleasures. Then I use a study of the history and politics of butch/femme identities to examine the precise constellations of lesbianism/queerness represented in the series and to construct an argument regarding its statements on gender roles, gender play, and gender performance.

READING QUEERLY

In her "Are They Lovers?" website, fan writer Fanofargo makes plain a belief that Xena and Gabrielle are lovers. A "Do You Believe?" page suggests that if "you don't think you can handle the following material run far, far away and hide under a rock, because you have got some thinking to do because the times, they are a changin!!" This is followed by a series of quotations, images, and sounds that together argue for a lesbian reading of the close bond between Xena and Gabrielle. Fanofargo ends the page with the question "And how could thousands of fan fiction writers be wrong?" and links to a number of websites containing lesbian-focused, fan-written stories. Unlike Doty in his radical reversal of traditional heterosexist perspective, Fanofargo opts to offer space to others who may not agree with her perspective. Her pages are based upon open questions, and the writer even conducts a poll of visitors to the site. Through these questions, Fanofargo reveals an investment in attaining support for a queer perspective, actively seeking to convince others that Xena and Gabrielle are lovers.

Fanofargo's investment is made plain in a "Responses" page, in which the writer has taken the time to type in and post rude and homophobic responses to the lesbian question. Statements describe the website as "stupid and a waste of my time" and "cruel and offensive," demonstrating the threatening nature of identifying even fictional characters in a fantasy setting as nonheterosexual. One respondent in particular perfectly validates the assertion that queer readings can be seen as "delusional attempts to see something that isn't there" (Doty, xii): "I have watched Xena since it first started and I have never seen anything that would give the impression of them being lesbians. In my opinion this whole idea is just wishful thinking on your part. I find it to be an extreme insult that you would try and degrade their close, FRIENDLY relationship by thinking of them as gay." Not only is Fanofargo or any viewer who reads the characters as lovers delusional, such an individual is also insulting all of womankind (and perhaps humankind) with this perspective. This is also made plain by an anonymous respondent from Australia who accuses Fanofargo of "slander" and demands that she stop watching the series.

Certainly, one could argue that nonsexual friendships between women are too rarely seen on television. Most often, the representations center on temporary school roommate relationships (as in *The Facts of Life* or *A Different World*), or dating men plays a major role and men are seen on every episode at the center of women's lives (as in *Living Single* or *Friends*). When women's friendships appear on television and the focus is not on competition for men, traditional femininity may be central to their interactions (as in the dominance of domesticity on *Kate and Allie* or the emphasis on beauty, the decoration of domestic spaces, and "gossip" on *Designing Women*). From this perspective, the friendship between Xena and Gabrielle is arguably feminist, whether lesbian or not, for they reject hyperfeminine norms of behavior in their interactions. Nevertheless, the previously quoted respondent's attack is clearly not about a desire to see a celebration of women's friendships but a reactionary fear of lesbianism, as is made even more plain in the statement "I do not like you and perfer [*sic*] not to hear your homosexual beliefs."

The idea of simply not hearing or seeing someone else's "homosexual beliefs" is central to U.S. culture in the '90s. From the sexual ambiguity of Marilyn Manson videos to Clinton's "Don't Ask, Don't Tell" policy regarding gays in the military, subtlety and subtext sell while directness (being out) does not. A refrain with many variations that lesbians and gays often hear is, "I don't mind homosexuals, as long as they . . . keep it to themselves" or "do it in the privacy of their own homes" or "don't rub it in my face" or "don't come after me." However it is said and whatever taboo desire is (ineffectually) masked in certain of these expressions, the message is clearly that homosexuality is entirely about sex and that it is inappropriate subject matter for polite company. Again, that the sitcom *Ellen* had to feature an "adult themes" warning and was canceled soon after Ellen came out provides apt evidence that homosexuality is most acceptable when homophobic individuals can identify it as morally wrong or pretend it does not exist.

So, one (political) statement this chapter needs to make regarding Xena and Gabrielle is: THEY ARE LOVERS. The best "evidence" of this can be obtained by placing oneself in the position of a queer (or queer-sympathetic) viewer and simply watching, particularly episodes that are centered on the relationship between Xena and Gabrielle. A non-TV route emerges through the Web and its numerous subtext fan sites, such as Xenite's *Xenaquest's Xena Subtext Page* or Cdward's extremely thorough "Xena: Warrior Lesbian" site, both of which review every episode for lesbian (subtext) content. Similarly, one can peruse the AXT Subtexters' "Subtext FAQ [frequently asked questions guide] for alt.tv.xena" or Dswriter's "*Xena: Warrior Princess:* A FAQ for Subtext Fans and the Loyal Opposition." The press also reveals that producers and certain writers of the show sometimes acknowledge the active placement of subtext into the program and even occasionally admit that the characters are not exclusively heterosexual. Typical are ambiguous statements, such as executive producer Tapert's rather pornographic declaration, "All I can say about that [the lesbian question] is that Gabrielle satisfies her [Xena's] every whim" (quoted in AXT Subtexters). However, it is out lesbian producer Liz Friedman who has been most forthcoming. When asked, "How do the actors feel about the sort of gay twist to their characters?" during an October 1996 interview for a Boston lesbian and gay radio program, she replied, "I think they really like it" (quoted in AXT Subtexters). Perhaps most direct of all, in an *Entertainment Weekly* interview, Friedman announced, "I don't have any interest in saying they're heterosexuals. That's just bulls—, and no fun, either" (quoted in Flaherty, 41).

To illustrate the claims made and validate the ample Web materials, we can briefly examine a single episode. Though many would suffice, perhaps the best example is the most famous—or infamous—episode for initiating new fans into queer readings of *X:WP:* "A Day in the Life." Other episodes provide better evidence of the emotional depth and serious conflicts that substantiate an intense emotional bond between the two characters (such as "The Greater Good," in which Gabrielle mourns an apparently dead Xena, or "One Against an Army," in which Xena faces the depth of her emotions for Gabrielle while fighting off an entire army as Gabrielle wastes away from an AIDS-suggestive poisoning). Nevertheless, the playful "A Day in the Life" provides an unmatched glimpse into an "average" day for the questing couple.

"A Day in the Life" is a campy second-season episode that many subtext fans read as absolute proof of a lesbian relationship between Xena and Gabrielle. Xenite, for example, states, "They were behaving like an old married couple" throughout. Even the Universal Studios–sanctioned book *Xena: Warrior Princess: The Official Guide to the Xenaverse* must acknowledge the "alleged signposts" that "fueled speculation about the possibility of a romantic relationship between Xena and Gabrielle" in this episode (Weisbrot, 212). Often, these "signposts" are subtle textual or purely visual cues. For example, Gabrielle suggests that Xena wear less sexy clothes so that men stop falling for her in every village. Xena replies that she will wear a smelly wolf skin and not bathe. Gabrielle informs her that such a plan will work, but that she will also be traveling alone from then on. Xena's reply—"Oh, really?"—cannot fully convey the play occurring between the two as a couple; the look Xena gives along with this question that is not really a question is what has fans saying, "I'm not just making this stuff up . . . it's all there" (Xenite).

Briefly, "A Day in the Life" illustrates the mundane in Xena and Gabrielle's life together, especially quarrels over trivial domestic matters. There is no death-defying rescue or touching utterance of "I love you" (as seen in more serious episodes such as "One Against an Army" and "The Bitter Suite"). However, "A Day in the Life" does feature a shared hottub scene that is probably the single most discussed moment in all of Xena fandom. It takes place when the duo encounters Minya, a devoted Xena fan—until her boyfriend, Hower, develops a crush on Xena. When the two meet Minya, she makes clear that no request is too great to please her hero, Xena. A nude Xena and Gabrielle enjoy her enormous bath together while the eager Minya races in and out of the room, dumping in bucket after bucket of hot water. In what Xenite labels "another screaming subtext example," Xena asks, "Are you sitting on the soap?" Gabrielle replies, "I was wondering what that was." In addition to the sexual suggestiveness of the fact that Gabrielle knew she was sitting on something and the only "things" in the tub are her body and Xena's, the missing soap moment recovers the homophobic joke about men bending over in prison showers. Like queer studies' scholars reclaiming the term "queer" from its degrading usage by homophobes, this *X:WP* scene reclaims the soap joke and simultaneously points to a lesbian relationship between the women. As they touch and rub each others' nude bodies in a manner that may or may not appear sexual to various audiences and audience members, mentioning the soap alludes (albeit through homophobia) to homosexuality and may draw viewers to read queerly.

Later in the episode, we learn that Gabrielle has traded Xena's whip with Minya for a new frying pan because Xena ruined theirs earlier by using it as a

The infamous hot-tub scene.

weapon to fend off bandits. Xena demands to have the whip back, claiming it still belongs to her. Minya, angry because Xena has already "stolen" her boyfriend and now wants the whip that might, if used seductively, entice him back, lays it out clearly: "No, it belongs to me. You don't get that concept real well, do you? The whip is mine. The frying pan's yours. Hower is *mine. She's* [pointing at Gabrielle] yours." Gabrielle, looking on, just smiles. Here it is not just Xena and Gabrielle who act and speak in ways that show they are lovers; even strangers seem to know it.

Though other episodes feature similar moments, none condenses so much into so brief a space. And "A Day in the Life" does more than simply point to a lesbian relationship between Xena and Gabrielle, it also invites us to ask about the specific type of representation of lesbianism *X:WP* offers. Producer Liz Friedman provides a useful and provocative answer. In an interview for *The Advocate,* Friedman calls Xena and Gabrielle "a perfect little butch-femme couple" (quoted in AXT Subtexters). Lesbian fan Kelly Marbury adds to this perspective, arguing that Xena fulfills her expectations of a female superhero by being "so butch" (quoted in Kastor, C1). If this butch/femme label is appropriate for the Xena/Gabrielle relationship, investigating the complexities of butch/femme identities in U.S. culture alongside the specific representational style and patterns of *X:WP* can provide an important angle for interrogating the series' celebrated feminist and queer pleasures.

BUTCH/FEMME IDENTITIES

Butch/femme identities in the United States have a complex political history. During the 1940s and 1950s, these roles were fairly rigid, offering both a "personal code guiding appearance and sexual behavior" and a "system for organizing social relationships delineating which members of the community could have relationships with whom" (Kennedy and Davis, 62). Yet even during this "prepolitical" era of gay and lesbian history (62), roles were not static. During the '40s, for example, a butch lesbian might dress in a traditionally masculine manner and cultivate "masculine mannerisms in the little details of self-presentation—manner of walking, sitting, and holding a drink, and tone of voice." Nevertheless, "the total image, although masculine, was not aggressive or rough" (64). By contrast, during the '50s, the butch "bar dyke" or "bulldagger" "was little inclined to accommodate the conventions of femininity and pushed to diminish the time she spent hiding and to eliminate the division between her public and private selves" (66). In addition, the '50s butch "added a new element of resistance: the willingness to stand up for and defend with physical force her fem's and her own right to be who she was" (66). Despite this increasingly masculinized public identity, however, scholars make clear that being butch was not about trying to be a man. "They did not refer to each other by masculine pronouns," for instance, "and they adopted unisex rather than exclusively masculine names." Ultimately, for these eras as well as earlier and later decades, "to recognize their [butches'] masculinity and not their 'queerness' is a distortion of their culture and their consciousness" (70).

Discourse about butch identity is inseparable from discourse about femme identity. And queerness as part of a butch identity is best exemplified as it relates to a sexual relationship with a femme. The butch may fulfill the role of more physically active partner and of leader in lovemaking; however, "in contrast to the dynamics of most heterosexual relationships, the butch's foremost objective was to give sexual pleasure to a fem; it was in satisfying her fem that the butch received fulfillment" (Kennedy and Davis, 72). Furthermore, "The dangers inherent in sex for heterosexual women in a male-supremacist society—loss of reputation, economic dependency, pregnancy, and disease—were absent in the lesbian community" (73). From such a perspective, it can be argued that "[b]utches challenged rather than reinforced patriarchal rules about women's sexual expression" (73).

Yet butch/femme roles, even if seen as more liberatory than restrictive for lesbians, fell from visibility and from feminist grace in the 1970s. Dominant during this era was the belief that lesbianism offered the purest and highest ideal to which women could aspire in ridding themselves of patriarchal oppression and living an egalitarian life, or "the most clearly marked exit from the phallocracy" (Parkin and Prosser, 447). However, this can be interpreted not as a vision of unification but of co-optation of lesbianism. Most individuals live their sexual identities in some relationship with the political, but desire is not always about doing what is deemed best for the movement. Butch/femme roles, s/m play, and other nonegalitarian sexual practices were deemed harmful to lesbian feminism, leaving some lesbians to wonder, "What happens to the possibilities for sexual pleasure when we've been set up as 'good' feminists precisely because we're not supposed to be concerned with the excesses of sexual pleasure?" (448).

It is important to understand, before condemning what some justly see as oppressive restrictiveness within the '70s lesbian "community," that there was a reason that "likeness and similarity [became] the necessary hallmarks of political change" (Roof, 31). Lesbianism sought to legitimize itself in a sexist and heterosexist culture; lesbians needed to be seen as a "bona fide oppressed group" (30). One way to accomplish this was to forge theoretical links between feminists and lesbians and to find grounds upon which to claim some sort of superiority to both male-dominance and heteronormativity. If lesbianism could be about a celebration of female bodies, egalitarianism, and feminine values, it could become worthy of respect by mainstream feminist activist groups that were often homophobic in the '70s. Nonetheless, in attempting to gain access to respect and validity as an oppressed group, lesbianism had to be sold as a very homogeneous lifestyle/worldview.

Debates over the "purity" of lesbianism as a feminist ideal raged in the '70s and '80s. In the '90s butch/femme identities have again become a visible public presence. One important explanation for the reappearance of butch/femme rests on the division of (biological) sex from (socialized) gender. Being female was necessarily linked to feminine traits, according to '70s radical feminism; being lesbian was the best way to celebrate such traits. Yet we can also see gentleness or nurturance as traits women are taught, not born with. If our emphasis is on detangling sex and gender, then, butch/femme roles can be seen as examples of this separation. A butch woman is still a woman; she may display masculine traits, from cross-dressing to sexual dominance to fighting, but she is still a woman. The '90s have thus revealed that "it is only with the systematic and highly visible rethinking of the relation between sex and gender that butch-femme can return as a viable lesbian practice instead of as a sell-out non-difference" (Roof, 33).

If we adopt a '90s perspective and argue that butch/femme identities are neither emulations of heterosexual pairings nor betrayals of ('70s) lesbian feminist ideals, we find a greater acceptance of diversity within the lesbian experience than political expediency has in the past encouraged. As Judith Butler, a dominant voice in '90s gender theory, asks, "Do the various practices of desire and identity [. . .] not in some way contest and disrupt the internal coherence and dominance of heterosexual normativity itself?" (227). Surely, from such a vantage point, the butch can be reenvisioned as radical challenge, for she reminds us that "sex/gender norms are anything but stable and are in the service of patriarchy" (Roof, 35).

With these complex configurations and questions in mind, we can now return to *X:WP* and ask two questions: (1) How does the series use butch/femme roles in the development of its main characters, Xena and Gabrielle, and their lesbian relationship?; and (2) Is the use of butch/femme roles ultimately progressive (with reference to '70s and '90s political goals, as described previously) or not? On the most superficial level, butch/femme oppositions appear through physical differences within a couple. Xena and Gabrielle certainly exemplify such contrast. Xena is taller and stronger, her voice is lower pitched and less melodic, and her stance and walk are more open and aggressive. By contrast, Gabrielle is shorter and weaker (though in recent seasons she has become more muscular and physical), her voice displays more emotion and vulnerability, and her look is always "softer" and gentler than Xena's. Xena is also dark (as revealed in her make-up, hair color, and clothing) to Gabrielle's light (seen in her pinker make-up and facial coloring, blonde hair, and cool-toned clothing). Gabrielle's blondeness, in particular, links her with idealized femininity.

This oppositional coloring also invokes a type of racial symbolism. Xena has the more brooding, sullen, violent personality, and "evil" is traditionally linked with darkness in the Western cultural tradition. Lightness, in this system of thought and representation, becomes the symbol of "goodness," of purity and kindness. Because *X:WP* offers Xena as a repentant villain who works to overcome her past in altruistic fashion, it is not surprising that, while dark (in fact, Lawless's hair is dyed black), she is portrayed by a white actress with blue eyes. We can thus read both Xena and Gabrielle as "good" while noting their typed differences and the series' inattention to actual racial difference.

The obviousness of butch/femme roles suggested by the physical differences between the two characters remains tempered by the feminized style of their hair and clothing. Both women wear skirts, expose cleavage, and wear their hair long and often femininely stylized (with small pieces tied back or braided). Midway through season four, Gabrielle's hair is cut very short to mark a change in attitude and behavior (toward pacifism), but the style is even more highly coifed and feminine than before. To truly fit a butch stereotype, we might expect Xena to cross-dress or at least wear a costume that seems appropriate for a warrior. The chest is a key area to cover with armor, for example, rather than leave exposed and vulnerable. Instead, both women wear short skirts (Gabrielle's seems to shrink every season) and low-cut necklines. What scholar Judith Roof identifies as the "radical and threatening" nature of the butch (35), then, seems particularly contained in *X:WP* by the degree to which Xena deviates from butch appearance norms through feminized aspects of her hair, make-up, and clothing.

Xena evidences far more butchness in behavior. Unashamedly violent, displaying anger without hesitation and often gleefully, and uncomfortable with verbal or physical displays of emotional closeness or weakness, Xena's actions and attitudes typify the hypermasculine hero. This figure is readily identifiable as linked with a stereotyped butchness when contrasted with Gabrielle's displays of hyperfemininity. Though rational, intelligent, and a good fighter in her own right, Gabrielle is the one who nurtures and comforts, rarely displays anger, follows Xena's lead, and does almost all of the emotional work for the couple. One excellent example of their oppositional butch/femme behavior emerges in their individual responses to parenting. In the ambiguously titled third-season episode "Maternal Instincts," we learn that back in her warlord days, Xena became pregnant and decided to give her baby up to be reared by a surrogate (centaur) father. Though she displays dismay at parting from her infant, she also knows herself to be incapable of childrearing because of her nomadic warrior lifestyle. Later, when she meets her son as a preteen, she is hesitant to form any bond with him, though eventually she decides he can join her on her travels because he can now take care of himself. Gabrielle, by contrast, is far more stereotypically feminine in her parenting style. When she finds herself impregnated by an evil god, she blindly maintains faith that the child will turn out to be good through her influence. She never doubts her mothering abilities and defends the child with her life, even as it becomes increasingly obvious that the child is entirely evil ("The Deliverer," "Gabrielle's Hope," "Maternal Instincts").

If *X:WP*, then, utilizes superficial traits associated with masculinity and femininity to enable readings of the duo as a butch/femme couple, does it also live up to the radical/feminist promises of butch/femme gender play? To answer this question, we must read the series in terms of some of the subtle differences between butch/femme and masculine/feminine that I have outlined. Most generally, *X:WP* does allow Xena and Gabrielle to escape what Elizabeth Lapovsky Kennedy and Madeline Davis identify as the dangers and consequences of sexual activity for women under patriarchal domination. As previously discussed, there are important feminist opportunities for the lesbian (butch/femme) couple, such as the absence of concerns over reputation (Kennedy and Davis, 73). While the heterosexual community standard renders promiscuous women "sluts" while men bask in the status of "studs," this does not occur when the couple is a butch/femme lesbian pair. That Xena and Gabrielle have a bond some characters may acknowledge as more than friendship (such as Minya in "A Day in the Life" and male companions Joxer and Autolycus at times) does not lead to ostracization or ridicule. Xena, the more obviously promiscuous of the couple, may be labeled dangerous and violent, but never whore or slut.

Within the relationship, blame is also never placed on either character for promiscuity or bisexual experiences. Xena, in particular, has a rich history of past male lovers. We meet Petracles, who seduced a young Xena with promises of marriage and then abandoned her ("A Fistful of Dinars"); Barius, Xena's primary lover when she was a warlord ("The Debt") and the man who fathers her only child ("Maternal Instincts"); Marcus, another former lover, temporarily revived from the dead ("Mortal Beloved"); and Caesar ("Destiny"), with whom Xena fell in love during her young days as a pirate. In the series' present, Xena also falls for Hercules ("Prometheus") and Ulysses ("Ulysses"). Gabrielle seems to have had no past lovers, but within the series' present she finds herself romantically inclined towards Hercules' sidekick Iolaus ("Prometheus") and even marries, though her husband, Perdicas, dies during the same episode in which they wed ("Return of Callisto"). We also learn that while Xena may be Gabrielle's first female lover, the same seems not to be true for Xena (as revealed within suggestive moments in the two-part episode "The Debt"). Thus, though bisexual is a more precise label than lesbian for the pair, they certainly maintain primary ties with each other throughout the series. Even more important from a feminist perspective is the way the series reveals that monogamy need not be the defining characteristic of a relationship for a couple to feel generally secure and committed to each other. That Xena and Gabrielle do not become increasingly suspicious or distrustful of one another as their lists of flirtations and romantic interludes with others (generally men) grow illustrates well an alternative relationship pattern to traditional heterosexual monogamy within a system of male supremacy.

Apart from this important aspect, butch/femme complexity is reduced to masculine/feminine stereotype in most of the characters' interactions. Before exploring the limits of butch/femme representation within *X:WP*, however, we can note that such an approach to butch/femme may be linked not only to popular homophobic misconceptions but also to the concerns of lesbian theorists and critics. Chicana lesbian feminist writer and self-identified butch Cherríe Moraga, for instance, hints at significant problems that may be inherent in living within a butch identity. She reveals that her love of being the dominant partner has left her "always needing to be the one in control, calling the shots," and this restriction can keep her harmfully "private and protected" (Hollibaugh and Moraga, 245). Such concern with physical and emotional unavailability and blocked communication reveals the potential for butch/femme to become a more disturbing hypermasculine/hyperfeminine interaction for lesbians. Moraga addresses well the important qualifier that even if there is difference between butchness and masculinity, there can still be a flattening of difference that leads to pain and division within a relationship.

Absolute physical and emotional untouchability identifies a "stone butch" identity. In such categorization, vulnerability is a loss of dignity, a sign of disempowerment. As Moraga argues, "Nobody wants to be made to feel the turtle with its underside all exposed, just pink and folded flesh." Thus, she continues, "In the effort not to feel pain or desire, I grew a callous around my heart and imagined I felt nothing at all" (quoted in Cvetkovich, 162). Of course, attempts to make oneself callous do not erase emotion; rather, emotion becomes repressed. Butches "may suffer from too much feeling rather than too little," butch lesbian writer Ann Cvetkovich asserts. "Butch untouchability establishes a tension between public and private" rather than between feeling and nonfeeling (Cvetkovich, 164). In many ways, Xena exemplifies disturbingly well a stone butch identity. She has serious difficulty revealing any emotional or physical vulnerability, such as expressions of intimacy or grief. She defiantly resists being put into situations in which she will have to display emotions other than anger, and she resents Gabrielle when she feels forced to acknowledge weakness, insecurity, or sadness. Furthermore, Gabrielle must force or pry these emotions from her, creating of Gabrielle the disempowered femme who is made responsible for her butch's emotions— whether gentle or vicious. Even more disturbing than witnessing both Xena's and Gabrielle's anguish when Xena does occasionally release her powerful pent-up feelings, however, is that when Xena does so she cannot relinquish her butch role and Gabrielle becomes the victim of and even martyr to Xena's emotional or physical violence. The ultimate result of the stereotyping of butch/femme roles on *X:WP* is an abuser/victim dynamic and is at the heart of the feminist limitations of the series. To illustrate this claim, I examine this pattern in several *X:WP* episodes, particularly "The Bitter Suite."

VIOLENCE AND GENDER ROLE EXTREMES

The third-season episode "The Bitter Suite" was originally advertised as the most compelling and entertaining episode of *X:WP* that fans could hope for. It offers a climactic resolution to a conflict between Gabrielle and Xena over the death of Xena's son, Solan, at the hands of Gabrielle's evil daughter, Hope. Because of Gabrielle's blind love for a daughter she increasingly knew to be inherently evil and Xena's intolerance of and resentment of this kind of mother love, the two women become deeply alienated from one another. In addition, we learn in this episode that Gabrielle holds a resentment from a past adventure when Xena murdered an evil tyrant but lied about it, breaking her promise to Gabrielle that she would let him live ("The Debt II"). There is no trust left between the women. All they have left is "hurt" and "open wounds," in the words of Gabrielle, and "fury" and "hatred," according to Xena. We see polarized gender roles in the language they use for the pain and distance between them: Xena does not want to admit to feeling hurt; Gabrielle resists admitting to anger. To address their conflict, the two are magically brought to an alternate plane of existence called "Illusia" where they confront each other through song, face their anguish, and resolve it. Without such a manipulative setting, it is difficult to imagine that Xena ever would have expressed her emotions to Gabrielle. And the use of song adds to our awareness as viewers of the alienness in seeing Xena reveal her pain.

There are moments in the episode that arguably challenge rigid butch/femme roles, as Gabrielle gets in touch with her rage and Xena acknowledges her suffering. Both women sing the lines "My heart is hurting beyond words / The pain is tearing up my soul," for example. However, this quickly devolves into mutual blame. To emerge from their pain, the two realize (in a moment in which "subtext" plainly becomes "text") that they must "turn again to love" and "leave this hatred far behind." Together, they sing:

> We'll overcome our damaged pasts
> And we'll grow stronger side by side

> To stand together through the storms
> We're safe 'cause love will be our guide.

Mutual understanding and an admission of love for one another allows the two to put aside their stereotyped butch/femme roles and language, if only for a few minutes.

Struggle over the roles to which they have become accustomed continues throughout the episode, however. A particularly powerful example comes when Gabrielle finds out Xena murdered the dictator Ming Tien, breaking her vow. Xena sings her apology, vacillating between a tone of butch/masculine defensiveness and a more gender-neutral regret. First, Xena adopts the role of (masculine) protector to explain her lies:

> Yes, I lied
> I thought I could protect you from the truth
> Deliver you from evil
> Spare your innocence and youth [. . .]

Then, she admits that she was lying to both Gabrielle and herself. She claims, "I wore a mask to cover my deceit," but now reveals, "I'm left without a mask." Without the blocking of emotions that her stereotyped butch role enables, Xena is exposed and vulnerable. Yet this does not keep her from continuing to place Gabrielle in a femme/feminine role as caretaker. Xena begs,

> I'm sorry, please help me, forgive me
> Don't hate me, don't leave me, forgive me
> Forgive me my debt as only you could
> Forgive me the hate, replace evil with good [. . .]

While Xena does actively apologize here, shedding her hypermasculine invulnerability, she also asks Gabrielle to take responsibility for her. Gabrielle, representing "good" (whiteness/femininity), must save "evil" (Xena's darkness/masculinity). Xena does not actively consider working off her own emotional "debt." Then Xena continues, asking Gabrielle to

> Forgive those who'd harm you
> Do good for those who hate
> Forgive if not forget
> I know it's not too late
> Forgive me and you'll discover too
> That the love of your love is you.

The song ends with Gabrielle reaching out for Xena, who takes her hand. They stand, holding onto each others' arms, eyes locked. Xena briefly breaks away to embrace her son and tell him she loves him before he drifts away to return to the afterlife. Then the scene fades to show Xena and Gabrielle embracing in a similar position. Suddenly, the reconciled companions are lying on their backs on a shoreline, the surf rolling in. They splash around together in it, evoking the famous beach scene in the film *From Here to Eternity*, finally at peace with each other.

While a highly gendered "co-dependent" relationship clearly continues, the episode does push Xena out of her stone-butch extremism. She admits to vulnerability in the private/alternate space of Illusia and emerges in a romantic (equally illusory?) space with Gabrielle, purged of her anger, having mourned and been forgiven. Gabrielle has released her pain and anger as well, though she has been the victim of a great deal more anger than she has unleashed. This victim/martyr experience is the aspect of "The Bitter Suite" that causes me the most concern over *X:WP*'s alleged queer progressiveness and feminism. When Xena asks Gabrielle to "Forgive those who'd harm you," it is not only some speculative others to whom she refers but indirectly to herself. Before the sung expressions of emotion and the reconciliation on the beach, Xena attempts to torture Gabrielle to death and mortally stabs her with a sword.

Before reviewing the extreme violence of "The Bitter Suite," let us return briefly to the previously discussed episode "A Day in the Life." One secondary plot element involves Gabrielle spending much of her time contemplating how to "get" Xena, to strike one successful blow in "combat" against her. While superficially an attempt to show how skilled Gabrielle has become in fighting, it is difficult not to read her efforts as a desire to raise herself from a physically disempowered or, as I will presently illustrate, battered role. Subtext fans may enjoy what they deem "flirtatiousness" (Cdward) when Gabrielle tries to hit Xena, just misses, and Xena says, "You were 'this' close 'cause I let you get 'this' close"; however, the words can also be read as menacing, especially because they are accompanied by Xena's serious and intense gaze. At the end of "A Day in the Life," Xena and Gabrielle lie, side by side, under the stars. The beauty of the moment is broken when Gabrielle does, at last, catch Xena unaware and smashes her in

Xena and Gabrielle's reconciliation on the beach.

the nose with her staff. Gabrielle's face reveals multiple and contradictory reactions: disbelief, dismay, glee. Xena, holding her nose in obvious pain, acknowledges that Gabrielle did catch her off guard then turns fully away from her and sullenly suggests they go to sleep. She clearly does not like this reversal of roles, and we do not see such a moment again between them.

More common are episodes in which Xena dominates in physical scenes. This scripting leads to many images of Xena as protector; however, it also leads to violence against Gabrielle. In the episode "Forgiven," which takes place two episodes after "The Bitter Suite," we meet Tara, a wild and violent teen who admires Xena and seeks to usurp Gabrielle's role as sidekick. She attempts to oust Gabrielle by beating her, ferociously, without provocation. In Tara we see a stereotyped "baby dyke," a hypermasculine butch wanna-be without the knowledge or experience to temper her rage. Gabrielle tries to reason with Tara, to treat her with typical femme/feminine gentleness and nurturance. Disturbing here is not only the graphic violence in the fight scenes that nevertheless erupt between Tara and Gabrielle but also Xena's amusement at this fighting. Xena not only seems to believe that a good beating is the only thing that will teach this child a lesson, but she seems to derive pleasure from watching Gabrielle attempt to provide this lesson. Gabrielle spends much of the episode with a blatantly bruised and bloodied face. In the end, Tara realizes that she need not compete with (beat) Gabrielle to win Xena's attentions and the three emerge as friends. It is tempting to read this resolution in butch/femme terms as the baby dyke coming to the realization that such gruesome beating of the femme is simply more butch/masculine than she needs to be to gain Xena's respect.

"The Bitter Suite," however, belies this message. When the episode begins, Xena and Gabrielle have gone their separate ways. Gabrielle has killed Hope by giving her poison. She then goes to the Amazons to undergo a "ritual of purification." After three days, she seems to be uncured; the loss of Xena's love, her guilt at being the indirect cause of Solan's death, and her own grief over her child's tragic life and death have depleted her of the will to live. Yet she regains some energy when she hallucinates a visit from Callisto, one of Xena's greatest (female) enemies. The violence against Gabrielle in the episode begins when we see a hand softly caress Gabrielle's face, then slap it. Callisto rouses Gabrielle through the slap and an argument that Xena is the one responsible for Gabrielle's pain. At first, Gabrielle refutes Callisto's words, but soon she admits that she does feel hatred for Xena.

Meanwhile, Xena has wandered far, fighting her pain by crying out a song/wail in empty frozen wastelands. Ares, the god of war, suddenly appears. He has always admired (and lusted after) Xena for her inner "fire," a passion for violence and war. He tells Xena to abandon the way of life she has followed since meeting Gabrielle and to return to her glory days as a warlord. He advises her to stop trying to atone for past sins and to seek revenge instead. Though Xena does not respond, in the next scene we see her riding into the Amazon stronghold, eyes wild, seeking Gabrielle. She smiles and sneers throughout this scene, displaying only enjoyment of her furious anger. A weak Gabrielle emerges from a hut in a flowing white gown and in the arms of their friend Joxer. He calls out "Somebody help her!" then attempts to carry Gabrielle off as Xena approaches. The Amazons attack and Xena fights them off with a staff. This is one of the only times we have seen Xena use a staff rather than a sword, and it stands out as likely proof that it is only Gabrielle upon whom Xena wishes to truly "avenge" herself. Gabrielle looks up, shocked, and calls out a meek, questioning "Xena?"; then, seeing the murderous rage in Xena's eyes and flashing teeth, she runs.

Gabrielle's passive role along with her gown clearly identify her in this scene as innocent feminized victim. Xena, meanwhile, displays a hypermasculinity and viciousness toward Gabrielle we have never before seen in the series. Nevertheless, given the stereotyped butch/femme structure of the relationship between the women, such an extreme is not out of character. Xena goes after Gabrielle, lashing her ankles with a whip and pulling her roughly to the ground. As she does this, and throughout the scene, Xena smiles and sneers. She never hesitates to enact her violent retribution on the passive Gabrielle. Xena mounts her horse quickly and drags Gabrielle mercilessly through the Amazon village. We see Gabrielle's body twist and writhe as she is hauled through market stalls, crashed through a bonfire, dragged over rocks, and pulled through water, marsh, and dirt roads. Xena continues to smile bitterly as she tortures Gabrielle over miles and miles of land. At last, they emerge at the edge of a cliff overlooking the ocean. We see Gabrielle's bruised, scratched, and bloodied face close up. We see cut and bloodied feet as well when Xena unties her. More evidence of the gruesome violence done her appears as Xena raises Gabrielle's unconscious body overhead to throw her over the cliff. But at this moment Gabrielle awakens and kicks Xena in the head. In slow motion, the two face each other. Xena smiles. Gabrielle screams, "I hate you!" And the two dive at each other, both plunging off the cliff.

Gabrielle, battered by Xena.

Once in the ocean, Gabrielle looks drowned. A far-away voice speaks of the need for both women to lose themselves in order to find themselves again. Suddenly, Xena awakes in what we come to learn is Illusia. Portrayed by the same actress who plays Callisto, a young woman in a page-like costume begins a light-hearted song reminiscent of a scene from *Alice in Wonderland,* sharply altering the mood and the viewer's attention. Yet the dragging sequence is not the only act of violence Xena commits upon Gabrielle before the climactic confrontation and reconciliation scene at the episode's end. In Illusia, Gabrielle and Xena awaken in separate spaces, but when they are reunited, Xena stabs Gabrielle with her sword and apparently kills her. She soon learns that this was a fantasy and Gabrielle is not really dead; however, her intent was clearly murderous and remorseless.

Ultimately, no matter the power and romanticism of the reconciliation on shore, Xena has committed extreme acts of violence against Gabrielle. Gabrielle does not know about the stabbing, but she did live through the dragging torture. And this act is never directly addressed by either character; no physical evidence of the torture remains on Gabrielle's face or body. The series does not make plain that either woman even remembers the act. Gabrielle's forgiving and apparent forgetting encourage us as viewers to do the same. Yet, can we?[4] I have already discussed the problematic violence against Gabrielle in the episode "Forgiven." Even more disturbing is the continuation of a pattern identifiable as domestic violence, exemplified well in the subsequent episode "Paradise Found."

In "Paradise Found," Xena and Gabrielle experience another *Alice in Wonderland* setting. They find themselves in the enchanted garden and palace of Aidan, a quasi-guru who has found a serenity he wishes to share with others. Xena is skeptical, but Gabrielle desires to learn from this wise man. Gabrielle studies meditation and yoga and finds herself increasingly at peace. Meanwhile, Xena grows more and more agitated and wishes to leave. Soon, we discover that Aidan is a sort of positive energy vampire, sucking the goodness out of his visitors. Gabrielle, because she is wholly good according to the series, becomes drained of energy; Xena's limited goodness, meanwhile, leaves a hostile and dangerous evil side in control. And as she becomes increasingly evil, she hallucinates gruesome acts of violence against Gabrielle. The extreme gendered opposites come into play again here, and with them comes Xena's desire to do violence to Gabrielle. Xena realizes that the only way to save Gabrielle from losing her entire self and ultimately her life to the vampiric Aidan is to release control and give herself over to her "evil" side. She knows this may mean she will hurt not only Aidan but Gabrielle, but this is a risk she is willing to take. The episode thus implicitly argues that a desire to do violence to our loved ones is simply a part of a "dark" side we possess. In this episode, a male character leads Xena to this recognition, yet Aidan's (masculine) intervention arguably exposes rather than truly manipulates her consciousness. When it comes time to act, Xena kills Aidan; unlike the scenes in "The Bitter Suite," however, she does not attack Gabrielle. Nevertheless, the desire to harm her, we learn, is fully a part of Xena's consciousness.[5]

CONCLUSION

When we consider the multiple ways in which we can read *X:WP*, from diverse social positions and through a variety of critical lenses, the series seems to exemplify polysemy perfectly. *X:WP* is a feminist program; *X:WP* is a lesbian text; *X:WP* is queer friendly; *X:WP* engages the politics of butch/femme; *X:WP* is about battering within a lesbian butch/femme relationship. None of these readings is absolute, a "correct" reading that negates the others. However, as popular response to the series has made plain, it is easy and compelling to ignore the degree to which the series operates via unequal power relations. Polysemy allows us to add a reading of power imbalance in *X:WP* to more celebratory readings.

As a cultural critic and *X:WP* fan, I do see what others see as progressive and hopeful for feminist and queer scholars, activists, and fans in the character of Xena and her relationship with Gabrielle. The series does effectively challenge problematic aspects of gender essentialism, such as linking women with passivity, emotionalism, and weakness. It shows friendships between women as positive influences and central to women's lives. And it escapes static notions of sexuality and representations of homosexuality on television by offering characters who can be read as lesbian or bisexual and nonmonogamous without critique of their lifestyles within the narrative. However, if we attend carefully to the violence we see in *X:WP*—particularly the graphic violence in "The Bitter Suite" and that which emerges as a core of the Xena/Gabrielle relationship in "Paradise Found"— we can recognize that the specific scripting of lesbianism in *X:WP* should give us pause. While television offers few strong women to admire and even fewer committed lesbian couples, it is vital that we do not simply accept the superficial bounty of *X:WP* without interrogating its troubling depths. Ultimately, my reading of *X:WP* holds that the series' sexual politics rely on patriarchal myths of gendered identities and relations that belie the feminist and queer pleasures so many critics and fans applaud. Conflating strength with violence and butchness with hypermasculinity leads inevitably to the image of a battered, unconscious woman lying at the feet of her smiling, unrepentant abuser and to the notion that at the heart of butch/femme lesbian relationships is violence. In the end, I am not convinced television can give us truly progressive feminist or queer visions, but I am certain it must do better than this before we praise it so highly.

NOTES

1. As with all criticism of ongoing television series, this chapter's analysis must stop at an arbitrary point in the development of *X:WP*. I discuss episodes and developments that take place up to midway through season four, just before Gabrielle's character makes a major but temporary change toward a more overtly pacifist stance based upon training within a generic style of Eastern spiritualism. This includes a short-lived change in atti-

tude (she makes active efforts to thwart violent conflict) and a significant shift in look (she wears a sari, sports multiple henna-colored tattoos, and has her hair cut very short). These episodes and those shown early in the 2000 season, however, do not suggest any significant shift in the pattern of Xena and Gabrielle's relationship. I see no signs that future episodes are likely to do so.

2. Like girl power, "power feminism" emphasizes "practicing tolerance rather than self-righteousness" and "taking practical giant steps instead of ideologically pure baby steps" (Wolf, 53). Compromise with patriarchal culture is deemed necessary for women to achieve increased social and economic power. For Naomi Wolf in *Fire with Fire: The New Female Power and How to Use It,* this means centering feminist energies on a "new link between sisterhood and capital" and emphasizing "the shared pleasures and strengths of femaleness" over oppression and pain (53). Furthermore, power feminism "welcomes men and honors their place in the lives of women, straight and gay" (53). In this context, from *X:WP* (and other girl power and power feminist fantasy programming, such as *Sabrina, the Teenage Witch; Charmed;* and *Buffy the Vampire Slayer*) girls can learn that they need not give up make-up, sexy clothes, or emphasis on the attention of the opposite sex to have independence, physical strength, and moral courage. Power feminism's other dominant lesson, that embracing corporate capitalism is a feminist goal, is relatively less central to these series.

3. Actually defining a "lesbian" text poses many problems. In the context of literature, Bonnie Zimmerman describes the process in which the critic

> begins with the establishment of the lesbian text: the creation of language out of silence. The critic must first define the term "lesbian" and then determine its applicability to both writer and text, sorting out the relation of literature to life. Her definition of lesbianism will influence the texts she identifies as lesbian, and [. . .] it is likely that many will disagree with various identifications of lesbian texts. (187–188)

Adrienne Rich offers a "lesbian continuum" to assist the critic, focused on varied levels of "woman-identified experience." A lesbian text will, for Rich, emphasize "primary intensity between and among women, including the sharing of a rich inner life, the bonding against male tyranny, the giving and receiving of practical and political support" (quoted in Zimmerman, 184). The strength of such a broad definition is that it de-emphasizes lesbianism as a "static entity" and addresses diverse ways in which women bond; however, "all inclusive definitions of lesbianism risk blurring the distinctions between lesbian relationships and non-lesbian female friendships, or between lesbian identity and female-centered identity" (Zimmerman, 184). For those invested in examining the specific history and development of lesbian theory and criticism, the reductiveness of Rich's formulation may in effect eliminate lesbianism as a meaningful category (Zimmerman, 184).

Somewhat more specifically, literary critic Lillian Faderman suggests these criteria: "two women's strongest emotions and affections are directed toward each other" and "the two women spend most of their time together and share most aspects of their lives with each other" (quoted in Zimmerman, 185). In addition, according to Barbara Smith, the lesbian text should feature a "consistently critical stance toward the heterosexual institutions of male/female relationships, marriage and the family" (9). Writing in 1977, Smith was strongly influenced by radical feminist/essentialist constructions of the woman-identified woman, such as that articulated by the New York Radicalesbians. For this group, a lesbian's primary identity emerges in her resistance of the traditional feminine role. She expresses the "rage of all women" and "acts in accordance with her inner compulsion to be a more complete and freer human being than her society [. . .] cares to allow her," until she is "in a state of continual war with everything around her, and usually with herself" (Radicalesbians, quoted in Smith, 12).

All of these definitions are relevant to discussions of *X:WP*, as Xena and Gabrielle share an intense and intimate bond, spend most of their time together, offer explicit and implicit critiques of women's traditional roles and (some) feminine norms, challenge the marriage imperative, and reconfigure motherhood. Xena, in particular, demonstrates the "rage" and internal "war" of radical feminism particularly well, while Gabrielle encourages within the relationship the "rich inner life" Rich emphasizes.

4. Little reliable data are presently available on the pervasiveness of violence within gay and lesbian relationships, but some unscientific surveys over the past decade claim that battering occurs in 25 percent of relationships (Friess, 50). Nevertheless, it can be difficult to find the issue taken seriously, either within or outside of LGBT communities. Factions of the lesbian, bisexual, and transgender women's community, for example, may not "want to betray or destroy the myth of safety in a 'Lesbian Utopia'" (Wilkinson, 5). Echoing this minimization, outsiders who witness LGBT battering may misinterpret what they see, assuming "the size of a person or the role he/she may favor is a determinate of who may batter" (5). As I read the series, *X:WP* directly bases its representations of Xena's physical abuse upon this myth. Within an already sexist and homophobic cultural climate, then, *X:WP*'s portrayal of battering as a "natural" element of butch/femme relationships contributes to further misunderstandings of abuse in same-sex relationships.

5. In fact, though length constraints prohibit discussion of additional episodes, Xena commits violence upon Gabrielle immediately again in "Devi," the very next episode after "Paradise Found."

WORKS CITED

AXT Subtexters. "The Subtext FAQ for ALT.TV.XENA." Edited by Erin (erin@cts.com) <http://www.xenite.org/faqs/subtext.htm> (7 January 1998).

Baumohl, Bernard, John Greenwald, and Jeanne McDowell. "Barry's Back in Prime Time." *Time* (3 November 1997): 80ff.

Bennett, Kathleen E. "*Xena: Warrior Princess*, Desire between Women, and Interpretive Response." <http://www.drizzle.com/~kathleen/xena/index.html> (2 February 1998).

Butler, Judith. "Afterword." In *Butch/Femme: Inside Lesbian Gender*. Edited by Sally Munt. London: Cassell, 1998, 225–230.

Cdward (Cdward@hotmail.com). "Xena: Warrior Lesbian." <http://www.geocities.com/TelevisionCity/4580> (21 December 1997).

Cvetkovich, Ann. "Untouchability and Vulnerability: Stone Butchness as an Emotional Style." In *Butch/Femme: Inside Lesbian Gender*. Edited by Sally Munt. London: Cassell, 1998, 159–169.

Doty, Alexander. *Making Things Perfectly Queer: Interpreting Mass Culture*. Minneapolis: University of Minnesota Press, 1993.

Dswriter (Dswriter@idir.net). *"Xena: Warrior Princess:* A FAQ for Subtext Fans and the Loyal Opposition." <http://members.aol.com/daxwtesq/FAQ/FAQ.html> (2 March 1997).

"Ellen DeGeneres: Out and About, She's Reshaping TV's Take on Sexual Identity." *People* (29 December 1997): 56ff.

Fanofargo (Fanofargo@hotmail.com). "'Are They Really Lovers?' Web Page." <http://www.geocities.com/TelevisionCity/9300>.

Flaherty, Mike. "Xenaphilia." *Entertainment Weekly* (7 March 1997): 39–42.

Friess, Steve. "Behind Closed Doors: Domestic Violence." *The Advocate* (9 December 1997): 48ff.

Frutkin, Alan. "The Buzz: The End of 'Ellen.'" *The Advocate* (26 May 1998): 22.

Goldblatt, Henry. "The Universal Appeal of Schlock." *Fortune* (12 May 1997): 32.

Gross, Larry. "Out of the Mainstream: Sexual Minorities and the Mass Media." In *Remote Control: Television, Audiences and Cultural Power.* Edited by Ellen Seiter, Hans Borchers, Gabriele Kreutzner, and Eva-Maria Warth. New York: Routledge, 1994, 130–149.

Hollibaugh, Amber, and Cherríe Moraga. "What We're Rollin' around in Bed with: Sexual Silences in Feminism: A Conversation toward Ending Them." *The Persistent Desire: A Femme-Butch Reader.* Edited by Joan Nestle. Boston: Alyson, 1992, 243–253.

Jacobs, A. J. "Toys in Babeland: Lucy Lawless of 'Xena.'" *Entertainment Weekly* (24 November 1995): 86.

Kastor, Elizabeth. "Woman of Steel: Television's Warrior Xena Is a Superheroine with Broad Appeal." *Washington Post,* 21 September 1996, C1.

Kennedy, Elizabeth Lapovsky, and Madeline Davis. "'They Was No One to Mess with': The Construction of the Butch Role in the Lesbian Community of the 1940s and 1950s." In *The Persistent Desire: A Femme-Butch Reader.* Edited by Joan Nestle. Boston: Alyson, 1992, 62–79.

Kingwell, Mark. "Babes in Toyland: Xena versus Sailor Moon." *Saturday Night* (February 1997): 83ff.

"Legends, Warriors and UFOs." *Time* (10 March 1997): 49.

"Lucy Lawless: A Kiwi Actress Breaks the Action-Hero Mold." *People* (29 December 1997/5 January 1998) (Special Double Issue): 78ff.

Meister, Melissa. "Academic Theorisms of the Homoeroticism on *Xena: Warrior Princess." Xenameister's Web Pages.* <http://melissa.simplenet.com/xwp/xg/academic.html>.

———. *"Xena: Warrior Princess* through the Lenses of Feminism." 1997. *Xenameister's Web Pages.* <http://melissa.simplenet.com/xenapaper.html>.

Millman, Joyce. "Yes, 'Xena' Does Rule and Other Answers to TV's FAQs." *Salon Magazine* <www.salonmagazine.com/weekly/tvshows960729.html> (29 July 1996).

Minkowitz, Donna. "Xena: She's Big, Tall, Strong—and Popular." *Ms.* (July/August 1996): 74–77.

Parkin, Joan, and Amanda Prosser. "An Academic Affair: The Politics of Butch-Femme Pleasures." In *The Persistent Desire: A Femme-Butch Reader.* Edited by Joan Nestle. Boston: Alyson, 1992, 442–450.

Pozner, Jennifer L. "Not Your Mother's Heroines." *Sojourner: The Women's Forum* (October 1997): 12–13.

Rensin, David. "Interview with Lucy Lawless." *Playboy* (May 1997): 144ff.

Roof, Judith. "1970s Lesbian Feminism Meets 1990s Butch-Femme." In *Butch/Femme: Inside Lesbian Gender.* Edited by Sally Munt. London: Cassell, 1998, 27–35.

Smith, Barbara. "Toward a Black Feminist Criticism." In *Conditions: Two,* 1977. Reprinted in *Feminist Criticism and Social Change: Sex, Class and Race in Literature and Culture.* Edited by Deborah Rosenfelt and Judith Newton. New York: Methuen, 1985, 3–18.

Stockwell, Anne. "Yep, She Rules; This Year on TV, Ellen DeGeneres Was the Story." *The Advocate* (20 January 1998): 92ff.

Stoller, Debbie. "Brave New Girls: These TV Heroines Know What Girl Power Really Is." *On the Issues* (Fall 1998): 42–45.

Tucker, Ken. "Leapin' Lizards: The People Who Brought You *Gulliver's Travels* Spin Another Tall Tale with *Merlin,* an Equally Spellbinding Treat." *Entertainment Weekly* (24 April 1998): 60ff.

Weisbrot, Robert. *Xena: Warrior Princess: The Official Guide to the Xenaverse.* New York: Doubleday, 1998.

"Why Greek Tunics Are Back." *The Economist* (17 May 1997): 93ff.

Wilkinson, Bernadette. "Similarities and Differences." In *Abuse and Violence in Same-Gender Relationships: A Resource for the Lesbian, Gay, Bisexual and Transgender Communities.* Edited by Wingspan Domestic Violence Project. Tucson, Ariz.: Wingspan Domestic Violence Project, 1998, 5.

Wolf, Naomi. *Fire with Fire: The New Female Power and How to Use It.* New York: Ballantine, 1994.

Xenite (Xenite@webtv.net). "Subtext by Episode." *Xenaquest's Xena Subtext Page.* <http://www.geocities.com/Hollywood/Academy/4316/discuss.html>.

Zimmerman, Bonnie. "What Has Never Been: An Overview of Lesbian Feminist Criticism." In *Making a Difference: Feminist Literary Criticism.* Edited by Gayle Greene and Coppélia Kahn. London: Routledge, 1985, 177–210.

7

To Be a Vampire on *Buffy the Vampire Slayer*

Race and ("Other") Socially Marginalizing Positions on Horror TV

Kent A. Ono

In this chapter, I examine the narrative construction of characters in the popular television show *Buffy the Vampire Slayer* (*Buffy*). Specifically, I examine characters on the show that I will argue are racially marginalized in some way. Unlike articles in the popular press, I do not focus primarily on the central protagonists or antagonists on the show; instead, I opt to think about the role of the nonprimary characters.[1] Thus, in general, I focus on vampires who get killed and other characters whose positions are marginal to those of the show's white star, Buffy (Sarah Michelle Gellar), and her white counterparts.[2] While resistant readings like the one taken in this chapter are of course possible and even prevalent in the representations of *Buffy* on the Web, such readings are still *resistant* ones, meaning they are not the meanings most vigorously championed by the text. Resistant readings are ones that do not seem to be recommended overtly or encouraged by the text itself.[3]

I take this critical approach in order to understand the complex racial dynamics of the show and to comment on specific lessons *Buffy* teaches contemporary viewers about social life—gender and race, specifically. After having studied the series's episodes during the first three seasons (1996–1999), the only ones available at the time at which this chapter was written, I argue here that despite the relatively successful marketing of this television show with a central female protagonist, *Buffy* (often embraced by the popular press for providing liberating images of girls and women) nevertheless conveys debilitating images of and ideas about people of color; in doing so, the show reestablishes what I have defined elsewhere as neocolonial power relations (Ono, "Domesticating" and "Power").

163

Popular discourse about Buffy tends to co-opt the rhetoric of liberation and, by framing its message to appeal to a general desire for gendered political empowerment, ultimately aims to subvert liberatory movements for social change and social justice. *Buffy* ultimately *privileges* an antiseptic white culture and takes part in TV's overall habit of marginalizing people of color and other marginalized groups. In this specific case, the valorization and heroification of a white female protagonist is constructed through an associated villainization and demonization of people of color. The show produces these contrasting representations by drawing distinctions between the heroes whose *marginal position* makes them heroes and the villains whose social *difference* justifies their characters' violent expulsion from the show—the ultimate form of marginalization. However, just because a character is different does not by itself lead to her elimination from the show. In fact, the show represents simple differences as alterable but suggests that other differences, such as those pertaining to race, are not; the show, then, eliminates characters marked as unredeemably different.[4]

As critical media scholars as well as fans, we recognize that even fictional representations that champion liberal values and beliefs or invite active audience members to think critically about what they are viewing nevertheless have other, often problematic, effects. In her study of young male viewers of horror films with female protagonists at the center, for example, Carol Clover suggests that even media representations depicting women as heroes can still function to re-center versions of masculinity detrimental to women.[5] Manthia Diawara argues that films very often construct Black characters for the pleasure of white viewers, and thus, similar to Clover's argument about gender, Diawara suggests characters are racialized in ways that help white viewers make sense of things.[6] Furthermore, as Sarah Projansky suggests, given the proliferation of legislation to limit and control what girls can be and how girls should behave, we must ask what the motivation is behind the media culture's fascination with "girls" and "girlhood." More still, as scholars of postcoloniality, such as Jenny Sharpe, have demonstrated, representations of white women have had an important function within historical colonization projects; white female heroification narratives play a specific role in the negotiation of colonial race relations.[7] Thus, I regard the mass-mediated heroification of white women in contemporary U.S. culture critically and encourage others to do so as well, especially when I consider the powerful role media have played in the long history of social marginalization of white women and people of color in the United States and elsewhere.

BUFFY AND THE POPULARITY OF GIRL POWER IN THE MEDIA

Buffy is currently riding the wave of contemporary girl power discourse that is part of an even larger U.S. media fascination with popular feminism at the end of the twentieth century. The July 1, 1998, cover of *Time* magazine, for instance, reads "Is Feminism Dead?" Alongside cropped black and white pictures of the faces of Susan B. Anthony, Betty Friedan, and Gloria Steinem is a color photograph of Calista Flockhart's face (the actor who plays television character Ally McBeal). A story written by Ginia Bellafante inside the magazine discusses contemporary feminism and even suggests "'girl power,' that sassy, don't-mess-with-me adolescent spirit that Madison Avenue carefully caters to," is evidence that women's struggles for liberation have indeed changed women's lives for the better (58). And while indirectly critical of the marketing campaign targeting girls, another article by Nadya Labi in that same issue of *Time* mentions (to name a few) Buffy, the Spice Girls, Alanis Morisette, the WNBA, Mulan, Brandy, and various women writers as exemplars of the pervasive and lucrative dimensions of girl power commerce (60–62).[8] This issue of *Time* draws on popularized conceptions of feminism and redirects attention away from the degradation and economic exploitation of women worldwide, and away from the need for vigilant social activism and social change; instead, the issue concerns itself with white, middle-class, individualist, and ostensibly pleasurable notions of female identity, most of them produced by commercial enterprises largely responsible for the continuing gendered and racialized exploitation of laborers globally.

In this context, popular media articles have compared *Buffy* to many other contemporary television shows, including *Xena: Warrior Princess, Ally McBeal,* and *La Femme Nikita.*[9] *Buffy* has received widespread popular praise for its positive representations of powerful females. Barbara Lippert compares the popularity of *Xena: Warrior Princess* and *Buffy* and says they follow a line of female action heroes beginning with Sigourney Weaver in *Aliens* (24–26). *Buffy* is included on lists of popular postfeminist characters on television today, which include Xena, Captain Janeway (*Star Trek: Voyager*), and Dana Scully (*The X-Files*) (Rogers 60).[10] Like *Felicity, Dawson's Creek,* and *Sabrina, the Teenage Witch, Buffy* has been praised for reaching out to teen female audiences, specifically. And, while the show's largest audience is in the 18–34-year-old range, with the average viewer being 29 (Rogers, 60), media commentators regularly assume and discuss its specific appeal among teen girls.[11]

In order to address the way race functions in these popular discussions of *Buffy,* I will briefly discuss two articles that address the role of such television shows as part of the popular girl power movement. Debbie Stoller's article draws heavily on research by Carol Gilligan and suggests that as girls reach their teenage years, they lose self-esteem resulting from pressure to give up masculinity and take on limiting feminine roles. Stoller sees Buffy, Xena, Sabrina, Alex Mack, and Mulan as "representatives of this new kind of pop-culture heroine, one that is at once powerful and undeniably girly" (45). Unsurprisingly, given society's pressure to give up masculinity and accept femininity, this idealized heroine is akin to girl-ness associated with the "Riot Grrls" movement. According to Stoller, "Riot Grrls celebrated the fierce, tantrum-throwing little girl as one of the last examples of socially-acceptable female aggressiveness, before girls are taught to be 'perfect little ladies' and instructed to suppress any display of anger" (45). As I will suggest further on, it is necessary to examine the kind of "aggressiveness" Stoller has in mind. The show *Buffy* justifies violence largely in response to dark masculinity; such violence is not unlike U.S. neocolonial military aggression abroad.

Paula Geyh is more skeptical than Stoller about the particular kind of feminism Buffy and other "sexy, powerful and dangerous women" offer. She cites extensively feminist critics Tessie Liu, associate professor of history at Northwestern University, and Ellen Willis, director of the cultural reporting program at New York University, who both discuss the history of feminism and the role the new "bad girls" phenomenon plays within it. Geyh also critiques both *Ms.* magazine's and *Time* magazine's portrayals of feminism and argues that political feminism is hard to hear over the "din of the bad girls" and a bad girl movement premised on the "personal, not political" (5F). She further suggests that the movement distinguishes between feminism and neofeminism, defined as being more concerned with sex than with gender. As examples of this dichotomy, she refers to "'do me' feminism, sex-positive feminism, even babe feminism" (5F). And she criticizes Elizabeth Wurtzel's book *Bitch: In Praise of Difficult Women.* Nevertheless, her article concludes with a gesture of hope that the bad girls movement carries with it a positive rage girls actually do experience in life.

In discussing recent mass murders, like those in Littleton, Colorado, Jackson Katz and Sut Jhally are correct to point out that mass media use the term *youth* in sexist ways in discussions of the "crisis of youth culture." They illustrate that discourse that is really about *male* youth and *masculinity* tends to use the generic term *youth* to talk about kids killing kids, when in fact this contemporary phenomenon of teenage shootings has almost entirely been "boys killing boys and boys killing girls" (E1). However, neither Katz and Jhally nor the entire list of mass media articles about *Buffy* I have read seriously address the fact that whether talking about youth or girls, the mass media rarely concentrate attention on the specific experience of people of color. As I will show with regard to *Buffy,* recuperating white female angst and violent aggressiveness must be understood within the context of a racially gendered perspective that situates the popular co-optation of feminism in relation to the social centrality of white people and the social marginality of people of color.

In the London newspaper *The Guardian,* Melinda Wittstock begins her article about "watching in black and white" by discussing *Sabrina, the Teenage Witch* and *Buffy the Vampire Slayer* as "hip heroines [who are] bright, blonde, precocious and confidently in control" (4). While ostensibly promising to address the racialization of Buffy, the rest of the article focuses on the implications of a nationwide survey of television viewers in the United States conducted by TN Media (a media research group in New York). The article suggests that white viewers over the age of twenty-one in the United States do not watch shows with predominantly black casts, themes, and narratives. It reports that *Friends,* the fourth most popular show for white viewers, ranks 188th for Blacks, and *Seinfeld,* which ranks second among white viewers, ranks only 59th among Black audiences. Nevertheless, the article goes on to say that teenagers are less racially divided than adults. It gives the example of white teenagers who watch *Sister, Sister* and *The Wayans Brothers* as evidence. After discussing the "pressure" the WB, UPN, and Fox are experiencing to move away from airing all Black shows in stereotypical ways, the article ends with a quotation from a white girl who says, "I don't care whether the characters are white or black, just as long as they are funny" (4).

Thus, when race is discussed, as in this article, whiteness is constructed as a default norm. When girls are discussed in articles generally, *girls* is to be read as (white) girls. Such articles do not concern themselves with the experiences of girls and women of color and boys and men of color in evaluating TV's impact on contemporary culture.[12] Those that do, such as the one just mentioned, often rely on a vacuous politics of equal airtime of Blacks on TV, versus a theoretical model that addresses the subtle and complicated function of race in contemporary media culture.

NEOCOLONIALISM ON TELEVISION

What should be evident from my discussion thus far is that the media valorization, even glorification, of girl power discourse ignores, decenters, and marginalizes people of color. Furthermore, discourse about *Buffy,* in particular, avoids discussing many, if not most, of the lessons about race and racialization the show actually teaches. As the previous quotation from the girl interviewed in Wittstock's article testifies, what is praised as liberatory (in this case, colorblindness) often reinforces oppressive relations (in this case, comedic stereotypes of Blacks). Furthermore, Wittstock's article does not discuss Latinas and Latinos, Asian Americans, and Native Americans, even as it raises the rarely discussed (in popular news articles) issue of Black and white race relations on television.[13]

Thus, a careful analysis of the depiction of race on *Buffy* is warranted in order to address racialization of popular feminism on the show. What better way to respond to contemporary social relations than to examine and challenge contemporary popular cultural narratives that, in addition to providing entertainment, also simultaneously represent those social relations? The series constructs what I have suggested elsewhere about other fantasy television texts to be a neocolonial context (Ono, "Domesticating" and "Power"), a context in which marginalized characters in media culture serve a pedagogical function for viewers by affirming contemporary racial, gender, sexual, class, and (in the case of *Buffy*) ability hierarchies.[14] Like *Mighty Morphin Power Rangers,* another show mass media valorized for empowering representations of girls,

Buffy valorizes militant violence by vigilante youths whose purpose is to save "the world" from being destroyed by evil (always "dark") people. As part of the long, continuing history of colonization in what is now called "California," recent popular and nativist California voting initiatives—propositions 187, 209, and 227—have targeted undocumented immigrants, people of color, and non-English speakers throughout the 1990s. *Buffy*, set in a fictional California town called Sunnydale, villainizes people of color both through complex media metaphors and through literal racist representations, and in doing so indirectly and directly shows violence by primarily white vigilante youths against people of color in the name of *civilization*.

I consider the rhetoric of *Buffy* part of a larger contemporary neocolonial rhetoric in media culture. This pervasive rhetoric serves to remind viewers subtly and not so subtly that U.S. culture typically treats any social difference as a justification for waging campaigns of violence, destruction, and annihilation against those labeled *different*. In several essays (e.g., Ono, "Domesticating" and "Power"), I have undertaken a research project exploring what many media pundits conceive of as "progressive" and/or "liberal" films and television shows. After studying such texts carefully, I have found that these media products tend to re-center whiteness and decenter interests of people of color—a strategy I have since defined as neocolonial. For example, on *Star Trek: The Next Generation,* a typical episode, "The High Ground," tells the traditional, colonial rescue narrative of a white female doctor, Beverly Crusher, who is captured by a white (albeit swarthy) male enemy who is also a terrorist. The show concludes with the murder of the male who captures her, the return of Jean-Luc Picard to his patriarchal helm as captain in control of his technologically superior ship, and the punishment and the return of Crusher to her role as doctor and mother on the ship, thus defusing any threat she might pose to white masculine control.[15]

As is illustrated by this example, neocolonial rhetoric, a newer version of colonial rhetoric, exists in contemporary media culture. Unlike so-called "postcolonial" societies such as India, Algeria, and very recently Hong Kong, in which the colonizers abandoned their colonies, those who colonized the United States never relinquished control. And the history of various colonization practices, ranging from the genocide waged against Native Americans, to the expansion of neocolonial outposts in Asia and the Pacific, the transportation and enslavement of African Americans, and the exploitive labor practices such as the *Bracero* programs affecting Latinas and Latinos, continue to be felt today. Indeed, the ideological apparatuses and mechanisms responsible for these abominable campaigns are largely still intact. And, because they have sizable viewing audiences, popular media programs play a very important part in communicating ideas about the history of U.S. colonization efforts as well as their continuing practice and effects. TV programs do not have to come right out and say anything specific about the history of U.S. colonization in order to actually be *saying* something about it; they can either assume audiences already know this or can provide enough of a hint, or a wink, to encourage such understanding. Whether through metaphor or literal historical details, such shows very often justify past oppressive actions taken by the U.S. government and military, insisting that hierarchies of race, class, gender, nation, and sexuality are normal and necessary and that changing those relations would be messy and ultimately undesirable.

Among the many other assumptions I make and goals I have, which are far too numerous to list fully here, I would like to mention that my scholarly approach seeks social justice and affirms liberation struggles; understands that rhetoric of liberation can be (and very often is) co-opted by media institutions for their own ends; recognizes lapses and fissures between media representations and my own understanding of social reality; seeks to expose exclusive and oppressive practices that often work because their oppressiveness is downplayed; encourages diverse ways of thinking, being, and acting; and embraces contradictions as a way not to further marginalize differences.

I will examine episodes of *Buffy* through theoretical and textual analysis (with an awareness and appreciation of fan studies). *Buffy* is interesting to me precisely because it not only contains but allows for particular non-normative readings. Initially, the show was, like the horror films Clover examines, directed toward a white, heterosexual, male viewership. However, after the first few episodes, the show focused more and more on themes in relation to females[16] and, I would argue, queer perspectives. As Joss Whedon, the creator and director of *Buffy*, is quoted as saying, "What interests me is making a hero out of somebody who doesn't (ordinarily) get to be a hero" (Rogers, 60). For this reason, it is all the more important to ask what kind of non-ordinariness is being valorized.

ABOUT THE SHOW . . .

Having just completed its third season, *Buffy*, based on the film by the same name (written by Joss Whedon),[17] appears on the network channel the WB; premiered March 10, 1997; and has tended to occupy the late night, 7–8 p.m., 8–9 p.m., and 9–10 p.m., time slots. Sarah Michelle Gellar, formerly of (among other shows) *All My Children*, plays Buffy, a high school student who wants to be "normal" but is fated to "slay" vampires. By day she is a student, by night the slayer. Her experience of being a teenage woman in "high school" *and* her being a slayer responsible for repeatedly saving her friends, family, town, and society creates much of the dramatic tension of the show. A group of friends accompany her— Willow (a shy but ultra-bright witch and computer "geek"), Angel (Buffy's vampire-turned-good sometimes boyfriend), Giles (her English librarian "Watcher"); Xander (her awkward and sexually frustrated friend who provides sometimes unwanted comic relief); Cordelia (a popular, clothes-conscious, ironic snob), and a string of secondary characters, including the Goth vampire Drusilla and the punk vampire Spike; Buffy's mom, Joyce; Principal Snyder; the third slayer, Faith; Willow's boyfriend and lead singer for a band, Oz; and a second Watcher, Wesley Wyndam-Pryce, who is, like Giles, also an elite British character. Each of the human characters does not feel included in some way and therefore does not meet the standard of what is depicted as popular on the show. For instance, Oz is a werewolf, and historically Giles was a member of a cult. Nevertheless, each also has talents and traits others admire and often wish to emulate. For instance, Cordelia's naiveté often leads to imaginative and effective solutions. And, despite Joyce's common misunderstandings of her daughter's life, her commitment to and love for Buffy are largely unassailable. The dual role of each of the major characters creates an ambivalent fantasy subject position in which the character both feels marginalized and yet occupies a position to which others feel marginal. Together, Buffy and her friends destroy a slew of thoroughly marginalized characters very often coded as biologically *and existentially* different— vampires and other nefarious creatures—"mysterious" and "dangerous" villains. I say "thoroughly marginalized" because Buffy and company literally set out to kill them; as "killable" characters, they hold the most marginalized positions on the show.

Each episode usually begins with a snapshot preview made up of brief clips of the episode to come. Sometimes, at the beginning of a new season or at the beginning of the second of a two-part episode, there will be a review of the previous episode.[18] That is usually followed by commercials and then a very brief voice-over narration with a montage of historical images explaining the overall premise of the show. The brief historical portion leads into the introductory sequence setting up the key characters and the central problem to be solved in the episode. Another set of commercials precedes an establishing shot, usually outside of Sunnydale High School. Sequences usually end with a powerful line delivered by one of the characters *or* with a piece of information that had not been previously provided on the show. After the episodes establish the problem, the search for the solution takes up much of the rest of the episode. Usually, the initial problem becomes more complex before a solution is found. And very often the initial solution is not sufficient and an even more powerful solution must be sought. The next-to-final sequence usually takes place above ground, at school, and in daylight. The friends are reunited, relaxed, and are rehashing what happened to them the night before. The show often ends, however, with a wink to the viewer, implying that while all has returned to normal for now, all is not over. A vampire either is not dead or the extent of the problem has not been fully grasped by the characters in the episode.

The action in episodes usually takes place both above and below ground. Camera shots panning from below ground through dirt to above ground at school cue the reader to the different settings. Below ground, in basements, or in other dark corners of the world, monsters, vampires—generic antagonists—tend to roam. They generally occupy cavernous spaces filled with jagged rocks, jutting stalagmites and stalactites, deep dark fissures, green pools of liquid, candle-lit caverns, mortuaries, or the like. While they regularly appear above ground to threaten normal "humans" and occasionally live above ground, fooling people into thinking they are regular and normal, for the most part they live (at least their days) below ground.

The neutral ground both humans and monsters occupy is the cemetery. There are many scenes in the cemetery of Buffy waiting for and fighting vampires at night. Action also takes place in mausoleums, which inevitably have entrances into the caverns of vampires. A mortuary also is right off of the cemetery. The cemetery is the site at which neither human nor monster rules, although more often than not Buffy wins individual fights in the cemetery.

Protagonists live above ground, where we see typical school images, such as a bus arriving or a long shot of students walking and talking in front of the school. Buffy may arrive with her mother in their car (or minivan) early in the episode or later on at the beginning of a sequence. Or, she may already be there with Willow and Xander, preparing to go to class. Buffy tends to meet up with Willow, Zander, and often Cordelia (sometimes Oz, in more recent episodes) in the library, in which Giles is more or less a fixture or prop, in the hall just walking or stopping at lockers, in the cafeteria, in the locker room (in earlier episodes, mostly the girls' locker room), in an indoor recreation area with tables, in the computer room, or outside on the stairs or at tables. Generally, while they may be in the same room, they tend to be separate while at class, although at times they may converse about their alternative lives. Buffy and Willow very often are engaged in discussions about dating, what to wear, and mother-daughter relationships, which are inevitably interrupted by business, slaying, and responsibilities. Other settings also appear, such as the football field, the gym, an attic in the school, the custodial closet, storage areas, the principal's office, and Giles's office off the library.

At home, we see Buffy sleeping in her bed, often dreaming about monsters, talking with her mother downstairs in the kitchen, chatting on the phone with Willow, getting slaying supplies from her closet and putting them in her bag, or, especially in earlier episodes, before her mother knows she is the slayer, climbing in and out of her window at night or when grounded.

Social scenes usually take place at the Bronze, the local nightclub for high school students. Bands, whose real soundtracks are overtly advertised within each episode, appear on stage. Oz, a guitarist for one of the bands, often meets up with Willow there.

THE RACIALIZATION OF VAMPIRES

Throughout the series, partly because Buffy herself recognizes she is not "normal" because she slays vampires[19] but ultimately longs for a "normal" existence,

the show privileges normalcy. In the first-season episode "The Witch," Buffy
laments, "I will still have time to fight the forces of evil, okay? I just want to have
a life. I just want to do something normal, something safe."

Throughout the show, Buffy's longing for normalcy (not being a slayer) is contrasted with the world of vampires and slaying, both of which are constructed as
abnormal. Normalcy not only regulates Buffy's personal desire to be a normal
human and "having a life" other than being the responsible slayer,[20] but normalcy
also serves as a regulating feature to demarcate appropriate behaviors and privileges affecting all characters. While Buffy, Xander, Willow, and Cordelia occasionally tease each other because of their variance from the norm of white, middle-class, suburban culture, they are in fact the center around which various
degrees of deviation get measured. For instance, Angel's human status is forever
questioned by the show. Even though Buffy has faith in him, both Ms. Calendar
(a teacher romantically interested in Giles and who we later find out is a gypsy)
and a second slayer, Kendra, never fully accept his having overcome vampire status; to them, he cannot be trusted. Giles himself is British (and his accent is not
working class), and the teenage characters at times can be cruel to him by teas-
ing him about what they see as his stereotypical stuffy, uptight, unemotional Eng-
lish-ness. Buffy teases him so much at one point about his attraction to Jenny
Calendar in "Some Assembly Required" that he turns his back on her. They are
forever making fun of his use of English words, his fear and suspicion of computers, and his overall "geeky" behavior (e.g., practically living in the library).[21]

Moreover, even humans who are not vampires or other members of the un-
dead, but nevertheless play the antagonists on the show, are depicted as somehow different from the main characters who represent the norm. Either the antagonists are evil mothers who want their high school glory days back, as in
"Witch"; girls without social skills who become invisible and violent, as in "Invisible Girl"; or a boy with a knack for science who feels so responsible for his
brother's death that he brings him back from the dead only to have to cut up
dead women to piece together a girlfriend for him, as in "Some Assembly Required." The underlying problem with each character is moral in nature, namely,
anything excessive is bad, whether it be greed, self-pity, or guilt—something
from which none of the main characters suffer.[22]

While these examples tend to establish normalcy along a continuum of implicit whiteness, vampires' status as nonhuman only makes this whiteness more
apparent, because the marginalization of vampires on the show takes the place
of racial marginalization in the world outside the show. For instance, when a
character becomes demonized for the first time, his or her eyes often are "blackened." Indeed, vampires on the show appear in what I call *vampireface* when
they kill or are about to kill;[23] otherwise, they simply look human. Because vampires and *other others* are defined as abnormal by the show, it is easy to see them
in general through a racial metaphor, since marginalization of those who are
racialized differently from the white Anglo norm in U.S. society is represented

similarly (e.g., through mass media). Like "aliens" in science fiction films (Ramírez Berg), another popular metaphor for racialized others, vampires lurk in the underworld, live in darkness, and wait to attack and suck the life blood out of an unsuspecting "human." The metaphor relies on a fear of contamination, invasion, being overpowered, and assault. As characters "descend" into evil, something about them becomes darker, usually their clothes.[24] For instance, in "The Pack," when Xander becomes a member of the hyena group, he dons a black trench coat like his fellow members, who are all garbed in black. In "Becoming, Part I," the message deliverer sent to deliver her message and disappear is wearing black as a cue to viewers that something bad, scary, or dangerous is about to happen to the protagonists. And in the third-season episode "Doppelgängland," when an evil "Willow" is brought forth from a different temporal dimension, "good" Willow and "bad" Willow are distinguished centrally by their light and dark clothing, respectively. Indeed, when their clothing is exchanged, their friends briefly misrecognize one for the other. Furthermore, areas that are shaded or are dark in or outside of buildings are coded as mysterious and potentially threatening. The industrial look of the Bronze, the dance club where high school students on the show party and hang out, is often the site of a vampire encounter. Thus, Buffy and company's marginalized normalcy is necessary to be able to *see* the real danger in order to protect those in the center.

It is worth commenting in more detail on a few of the characters on the show in terms of their explicit racial deviation from Buffy as the norm. In the second season's "Becoming, Part I," a second slayer meets with an untimely and ill-fated death. During the earlier second-season episode "What's My Line?" Kendra, a second slayer, appears on the show. Because there can only be one slayer at a time, Buffy et al. speculate that Kendra's emergence is a result of Buffy's brief death on "Prophecy Girl."[25] Also, because there is only *supposed* to be one slayer at a time, Kendra's very existence as another slayer is secondary to Buffy who preceded her and is living (again).[26]

As a woman of color who speaks with what sounds like a Jamaican accent, Kendra counters Buffy's prim and proper attire while simultaneously being more rule-bound, insisting on the letter of the slayer handbook, which Buffy not only has not read but, until Kendra refers to it, does not even know exists. Kendra's rule-bound nature leads her nearly to kill Angel and forever to talk about him as a vampire who must die. In "What's My Line, Part 2," when Kendra suggests that Angel must be killed, after Xander defends Angel's life to her, Buffy then says, with almost out-of-character passion, "You can attack me, you can send assassins after me. That's fine, but nobody messes with my boyfriend."

But Buffy is not only threatened by Kendra's determination to kill Angel. Kendra's very presence as a second, more studious, and more sacrificial slayer poses a threat to Buffy. As a result, Buffy's racism emerges specifically with regard to Kendra and becomes most evident around her discomfort with Kendra's language in "What's My Line, Part 2." When Buffy uses the word *wiggy* and Kendra asks what that means, Buffy responds with a racist comment that, in my experience, is usually made by people who speak only English attempting to mimic and demean those who speak Spanish, Italian, or Japanese. She says, "You know, no kicko, no fighto."

Throughout the series, Buffy has difficulty talking with Kendra about slaying. Later in that same episode, out of frustration, she tells Kendra in front of Giles that the clothing she is wearing is out of style and, when Kendra asks what Buffy means when she says Angel is her "friend," says impatiently: "As in people you hang with, Amigo?" Buffy's own inability to listen to Kendra leads her to misinterpret her purposefully and ascribe blame to Kendra for what Buffy assumes is Kendra's inability to speak the language. Buffy responds to Kendra with impatience and by using the racist language of the day: derogatory comments normally spoken to a person whom the speaker thinks speaks only Spanish.

Buffy goes on to say Kendra's presence "creeps me out." She sarcastically calls her "percepto girl," sarcastically implying Kendra is slow-witted. And at one point in the episode, when Buffy seriously realizes that Kendra might replace her as slayer, Buffy says to Willow, then "Maybe I could even have a normal life," which implies that being a slayer, as both she and Kendra are, is abnormal. In this case, Kendra would become the servant, allowing Buffy to avoid slaying— that "messy" aspect of her life. To read this metaphorically, if Kendra polices those who are dark, Buffy can go on to live a peaceful, bourgeois lifestyle, knowing the dependable Kendra will take care of things.[27]

At the end of the episode, Buffy no longer responds to Kendra's language use by making racist comments. Rather, she begins mimicking Kendra and simply talking over the top of her. After taking it upon herself to teach Kendra how to show emotion and get angry, which Buffy thinks will make Kendra a better slayer (Buffy's way of apologizing to her?), Buffy mimics Kendra's voice by saying, "I tink" rather than "I think" in the sentence "I tink we might make him." In "Becoming, Part I," at one point Buffy interrupts Kendra and answers a question Kendra is asked.

Throughout Kendra's time on the show, characters openly ask questions that border on the real question: "Can there only be one slayer?" In contrast to blonde Buffy, Kendra's presence seems to pose a threat to the uniqueness of Buffy, to her whiteness, and perhaps to her individuality. The fact that Kendra is a woman of color who ultimately and unexpectedly has her throat slit is just one more instance of a woman (of color) who cannot be a hero.

Another example of a woman of color who ultimately dies appears in "Inca Mummy Girl." Ampata, an international exchange student from South America, comes to stay with Buffy.[28] Early in the episode, the characters understand that the visitor, Ampata, will be a young man, which makes Xander jealous, thinking that Buffy might be attracted to him, but later in the episode, while the viewers see action the characters do not, Ampata arrives as a young woman, having killed the real Ampata and taken his place. At that point, Xander begins to become sexually interested in Ampata. The audience knows, and the protagonists later find out, that the young woman is a five-hundred-year-old mummy of a girl who was sacrificed to the gods. Once she is revived by an unsuspecting ne'er-do-well, the young woman awakens, goes to the bus depot, and kills Ampata, taking his place and name as the exchange student. Later in the episode, with the impostor Ampata sitting with Buffy on her bed at home,[29] Ampata confides in Buffy that she feels dead and cramped back home and, thus, came to the United States to feel accepted. She says, "I want to fit in, Buffy, just like you, a normal life."

However, from the very beginning, Ampata's acceptance is put into question. Before they know Ampata is a girl, Xander makes stereotypical observations about "him." He says out of jealousy when Buffy says she has to go see her exchange student, "Making time for some Latin love whose stock and trade is the breakage of hearts," to which Buffy replies, "I don't know how good his English is. He's from South America." The difference in language abilities and sexuality is already marked in the dialogue. Later, Giles asks Ampata to translate Incan words, assuming she can read hieroglyphic symbols because they come from her native land. Thus, she immediately has use value to Giles, and he wastes no time putting her to work toward his interests.

When they approach Ampata at the bus station, Xander says, "So, do we have to speak Spanish when we see him, because I don't know anything much besides Doritos and Chihuahua." But when Xander finds out Ampata is a girl, he immediately shows interest, forgetting his negative assumptions about male "Latin lovers" to take pleasure in his stereotypical view of a female one. When attempting to communicate with Ampata, who speaks English fluently, Xander speaks slowly, uses exaggerated hand gestures as if to help Ampata understand his English better, and tries to use Spanish words as well. In response to Ampata speaking English, Xander patronizingly praises her English skills by saying, "Your English is very *bueno*."

The entire episode, devoted to the exchange student experience of the protagonists, becomes a celebration of xenophobia. Cordelia's exchange student, Sven, who also speaks English, is a source of irritation to Cordelia, who at one point complains, "This whole student exchange program thing has been a horrible nightmare. They don't even speak American," before calling to Sven as if calling to a dog, "Sven, come." In fact, later on at the dance at the Bronze, Cordelia explicitly refers to Sven as a dog and says, "I keep trying to ditch him. He's like one of those dogs that you leave at the Grand Canyon on vacation. It follows you back across four states. See, my own speechless human boomerang." She tells him to get her some "punchy" "fruit drinky." Later on, we hear Sven comment in English on Cordelia's poor English skills. While this moment invites an audience critique of the central characters' xenophobia and racism, because it is brief and functions through humor, because Sven disappears from the episode after this moment, because Sven is white, and because Ampata ultimately turns out to be

Xander, patronizingly, speaks slowly and with exaggerated hand gestures to Ampata, who speaks fluent English.

morally bad (for being willing to kill someone else to bring herself back to life), that minor critique (conducted at the expense of a woman, Cordelia) is subsumed by the larger narrative trajectory that values and protects the central/normal white characters.

Xander later asks Ampata to the dance, and when he shows up at Buffy's door, he introduces himself in costume by saying, "I'm from the country of Leone," pretending to be Italian. And when Joyce sees Ampata descend the stairs in a dress, she utters a line praising Ampata for her early acquiescence to the pressures of assimilation by saying, "Look at that. Two days in America and Ampata already seems like she belongs here. She's really fitting in." In response, Buffy jealously says, "Yeah, how about that," envious of Ampata's ability to fit in.

Later on in the episode, Ampata asks Buffy to borrow her lipstick. This is just one clue that tips Buffy and Giles to the fact that Ampata must be an *impostor*. Buffy says, "Doesn't pack lipstick. How could she be a girl?"

Ampata, who has played the "vamp" in the episode to Buffy's primness, stops herself from kissing Xander and thus draining him of his life. Instead, she tries to kiss Willow, but Xander intervenes and says she will have to kill him first. The whole plot ends when Ampata tries to kiss Xander but cannot bring herself to do so; without his kiss, she turns to stone and crumbles. At a school setting after that, Xander laments having horrible taste in women, and Buffy says that Ampata was "gypped," using a derogatory term referring to gypsies, even though Ms. Calendar, herself, is a gypsy. Then, thinking of the similarity of Ampata to herself, Buffy says, Ampata "was just a girl but had her life taken away."

Because Kendra and Ampata are people of color, they represent markers of difference in two ways. First, because they have abilities and experiences of normalcy Buffy thinks she does not have (Kendra, while being exotic, is, according to the show, highly disciplined and inappropriately aggressive and Ampata is both exotic and appropriately feminine), she is jealous of them. Since

Buffy ultimately remains on the show and Kendra and Ampata leave it, this jealousy necessarily creates an alignment to and an empathy for her position as what Clover calls "the final girl" or what I would call, given the series format of the show, *the perpetually final girl*. The show constructs her as even more marginalized than racially marginalized people; they have something she does not have. Of course, the marginalization of these characters' emotional experiences with regard to their own position, as well as simple character underdevelopment, contributes to their eventual elimination. Second, their physical differences from characters who make up the norm on the show are accompanied by moral differences (Kendra's inability to see the potential humanity in Angel and Ampata's willingness to sacrifice a human life to save her own), which justifies their elimination from the show and the repositioning of Buffy, whose angst has been made more complex and clear and whose moral superiority has been renewed, at the center of the show. Ultimately, the show recuperates heterosexual longing through the continual denial of a romantic relationship, which is forever denied Buffy. This longing is the primary basis for her feelings of marginality. It is this longing that ultimately is linked to her continual aggressiveness and to her physical violence against others.

No person of color acknowledged as such on the series has been able to remain a significant character. All characters of color (most of whom have been Black) have either died or have failed to reappear. In the very first episode, a Black actor plays a vampire. In the "Witch," a Black female student's mouth is sealed closed. In "The Pack," a Black male student gets hit by a ball while playing dodge ball and is therefore put out. We see an older Black woman get shaken about during a bus scene in "Never Kill a Boy on the First Date." Another Black male vampire appears in "When She Was Bad" and eventually is killed. An Asian or Asian-American women's musical group called Cibo Matto plays in that same episode. In "School Hard," Buffy saves a young Black woman from a vampire attack, and Xander and Willow lead her off to safety. Also in that episode, Spike grabs a Black man by his collar, then twists and breaks his neck. One of the detectives who takes Giles into custody in "The Dark Ages" is a Black woman detective. In "Killed to Death," there is a Black woman doctor who wrongly attempts to stop Buffy from going after an invisible monster who sucks the life out of kids in her hospital. And in later episodes in the second season, characters who look like they might be Asian or Asian American appear in vampireface and are then killed (e.g., "Bewitched, Bothered and Bewildered" and "Becoming, Part II"). One of the few characters of color who is neither evil nor killed is an Asian or Asian-American woman attracted to Xander in "Bewitched, Bothered and Bewildered"; she appears in the hallway scene in which he is fetishized and serves as a reminder that Sunnydale High School has a *diverse* high school body.

In most of these examples, Black characters are either helpless or in need of Buffy's assistance to rescue them from vampires. For them, the narrative logic is

"Someone has got to die." When these characters are in positions of authority, they either try to prevent the characters from solving the crime or do not fully understand the crimes they are investigating. Thus, even when they are the authorities, they need Buffy's guidance and protection. In general, characters who are not white are not central to the narrative and are useful only insofar as they somehow enhance some aspect of the main characters. Anything other than Anglo-European cultural values and logic is marginalized. The point made over and over again is that such characters are not logical, are emotional, and in general are not needed on the show.

And while many more background characters are played by actors who are people of color in the third season (some vampires may be played by Latino or Asian-American actors in these episodes), they are eventually killed or are simply used as background figures.

The longest-running character of color on the series besides Kendra is Mr. Trick, who premieres in the third-season episode "Faith, Hope, and Trick," and after appearing in several episodes as the faithful servant of the white master, the mayor, is killed by Faith in "Consequences." After his brief introduction, the actor playing Mr. Trick delivers an unusually lengthy (for a person of color) line. He says, "Sunnydale, town's got quaint, and the people call me sir, don't you just miss that? I mean, admittedly its not a haven for the brothers, only strictly the Caucasian persuasion here in the 'dale, but you know you just gotta stand up and salute that death rate. I ran a statistical analysis, and hello darkness. Makes D.C. look like Mayberry, and ain't nobody saying boo about it."[30] Here, Mr. Trick overtly clarifies the racial metaphor underlying the show's narrative by comparing African Americans in Washington, D.C., with vampires in Sunnydale and by conceiving of both as equivalent examples of "darkness." That Mr. Trick (who we see become a vicious vampire in one scene in that episode, in which he lurches out of a limousine at a drive-in cashier's window, pulling the cashier into the car) is played by a Black actor collapses together in one character the racialization of vampires and the racialization of actors who are people of color on the show.

Buffy relies on what have now come to be conventional depictions of racial (and other) marginalized characters, depictions that may appear to be harmless, if one simply blocks out the similar way marginalized characters appear in everyday news discourse.

CONCLUSION

In this chapter, I have examined the portrayal of characters the show itself depicts or defines as marginalized and different in order to flesh out the kinds of lessons *Buffy* provides viewers about contemporary society. Specifically, I argue that both popular media discourse about girl power and *Buffy* forward a problematic understanding of power and liberation when we take race into consid-

Mr. Trick in vampireface, illustrating perfectly the racial metaphor of vampires as people of color.

eration. In general, that discourse and *Buffy* encourage a certain kind of violent aggression deployed by white females. In order to promote this liberatory aggression, the media rely on racial hierarchicalization of people of color; on the show it means their subordination and eventual elimination. The question I would ask is, "Toward whom is girl power directed?" This study of *Buffy* answers that question, "Predominantly, people of color."

Thus, as media critics, we must remain skeptical of the kinds of liberation politics being taken up by dominant media systems. And by this, I am not suggesting reconstructing a Victorian, patriarchal society in which men in power discipline women's behavior. Rather, I am suggesting that we address particular liberatory discourses within a larger media culture. Contemporary media systems, themselves imbricated within a neocolonial market of products and profit, seek out such icons and themes as those in historical feminist struggles and projects and popularize them through processes of commodification. Thus, the proliferation of discourse about feminism into the general popular, corporate domain comes with great risks and expenses; it only makes sense that those who are most socially marginalized within society will become the scapegoats in the process of popular culture's championing of its version of white liberation.

I have chosen to focus on Kendra and Ampata through a process of a kind of resistant reading that recognizes their positions within assimilationist contexts. Devoid of their cultural politics, relegated to positions that contrast with the lead, white star, Buffy, each repositions white heterosexuality, white aggression, and empowerment for white females at the center of the text. By concentrating on Kendra, Ampata, and other marginalized characters on the show, I participate in my own version of resistant spectatorship, evading the spectator positions most rigorously forwarded by the text. This approach to television spectatorship is not new; resistant spectatorship is, by necessity, an effect of the social conditions circumscribing daily living, which includes watching television. My own experiences necessarily affect the ways I view television. Nevertheless, this approach to research, to examine characters neither the media nor the television show recognizes as important, is a creative method not undertaken by many within media culture research.

The very fact that media studies tend to concentrate on the characters at the center of the show—e.g., Buffy, Xena, Sabrina, and Ally McBeal—means that, as media critics, we, too, are imbricated in a system of power relations that may have effects on what we examine and what assumptions we bring to the act of watching television and studying texts. Furthermore, this fact also points to the processes of idea promotion that occur subtly within media culture, and the vigilance of the neocolonial rhetoric I see being promoted on television, in films, and elsewhere. When white women beat up "dark" people, and we are asked to cheer, what does this say about the state of affairs within U.S. society today? Whose ideas are being promoted here? And what does this reveal about contemporary social life and conditions? By examining television and understanding the history of colonial relations (and the role gender and race relations play within that history), perhaps we can begin to make sense of this phenomenon. The very notion that liberation and empowerment can be gained through images of women murdering people of color cuts too close to contemporary images of young boys taking out their aggressions and hostilities, because of their felt marginality, on those without guns. Indeed, it was very likely the fact that media executives realized what Clover has said, that boys can read themselves and their masculinity through images of retaliating girls, that led them, after the Columbine High School massacre, to pull the third-season episode "Earshot" and delay showing the season-ending episode "Graduation Day, Part Two," until summer, after the regular season had ended.

Perhaps a political project that simultaneously addresses race and gender, as well as sexuality and class, and that adamantly challenges oppressive media culture, no matter whose values are ostensibly being promoted, would be one way of addressing the kinds of ambivalent spectatorship issues related to living in contemporary U.S. society. Starting with the examination of characters marginalized by texts because of differences may be one way to approach such a project.

NOTES

1. One could, for instance, interrogate the racial politics of gender and whiteness on the show and examine changes in Buffy's hair color and clothing; Faith's (the third slayer) dark clothing, her sexuality, and marginality; and the show's overall ambivalence with regard to white privilege, colorblindness, and marginal/dominant positions within white culture. Indeed, some might argue that the show's overall concern with the various positions of power possible within white culture is a central organizing theme of the show.

2. While there is some popular discourse about actor Charisma Carpenter, who plays Cordelia Chase, being a Latina, I will not discuss her specifically as a character of color

or the actor's racial identity (for a discussion of this, please see, for instance, Meers and Yoo), because the show does not foreground the actor's racial identity. Despite her racialized Latina identity in other popular discourse, the show itself ignores this aspect of the actor's identity in constructing the character. The show simply portrays her as a popular, white, female student. In addition, for the same reasons, I will not discuss actor Sarah Michelle Gellar's Jewish identity. The show does overtly address character Willow Goldberg's Jewish identity, but does not generally do this in a way that ultimately marginalizes her. In fact, in the episode "Bad Eggs," Willow's status is arguably augmented by references to her Jewish-American identity. Because she is Jewish, she says she does not want to teach Christmas carols to the egg she is taking care of as if it were a baby. Xander immediately responds in culturally appropriate terms, even though somewhat derogatorily, by saying, "Then teach it that dradel song." Overall, I would argue that a white Judeo-Christian norm exists among the major characters, with primacy given to the "Christian" in the equation.

3. See Stuart Hall's discussion of the differences among resistant, negotiated, and dominant readings.

4. What concerns me about *Buffy* is that the show eliminates both the racially marginalized actors who play the roles of villains on the show, *and* the characters themselves are eliminated from the set, scenes, and narrative, often by way of a violent and brutal stabbing by protagonists on the show.

5. In her book, Clover focuses on horror films with primarily teenage male audience members, films that often have teenage females as protagonists. She inquires into this cross-gendered identification and finds that "gender displacement can provide a kind of identificatory buffer, an emotional remove that permits the majority audience to explore taboo subjects in the relative safety of vicariousness" (51). Furthermore, the girl who saves the day in such films as slasher movies may be, "on reflection, a congenial double for the adolescent male. She is feminine enough to act out in a gratifying way, a way unapproved for adult males, the terrors and masochistic pleasures of the underlying fantasy, but not so feminine as to disturb the structures of male competence and sexuality" (51).

6. See also Stuart Hall ("The Whites"). Hall refers to what he sees as

the "absent" but imperializing "white eye"; the unmarked position from which all these "observations" are made and from which, alone, they make sense. This is the history of slavery and conquest, written, seen, drawn and photographed by The Winners. They cannot be *read* and made sense of from any other position. The "white eye" is always outside the frame—but seeing and positioning everything within it. (38–39)

By making this argument, I am not saying that resistant readers cannot see people of color within racist contexts as empowered. I am suggesting that that empowerment has to be understood in relation to a visual culture structured around whiteness. Some readings resisting the structuring of whiteness see in debilitating images empowering ones for people of color, but even these resistant readings may rely on the oppressive structures already in place.

Because of the perspective of whiteness from which representations on television make sense, Herman Gray suggests African Americans often appear in assimilationist contexts—primarily surrounded by white people, devoid of relationships with members of their own communities, without their particular cultural politics, rarely aware of institutional racism even as they may be critical of personal racism, and in narratives that fail to address the contradictory aspects and therefore complexity of racialized experiences (e.g., 85–86). Thus, even when audiences read such images in resistant ways, there is much that is unstated and not presented by the texts that, were it present, would be available to supplement those resistant readings.

7. As Jenny Sharpe writes, for example, "The representation of the English lady as an institution that had been desecrated plays into a code of chivalry that called on Victorian men to protect the weak and defenseless" (76).

8. For two critical newspaper articles about *Time's* depiction of feminism, see Liz Braun and Paula Geyh.

9. Claire Bickley sees Buffy and Ally as "a pair of evil- and ennui-battling babes" (48). David Bianculli compares *Buffy, Xena: The Warrior Princess,* and *Hercules,* all "fantasy-world action series," and says they are capable of "generating laughs" as well as creating dramatic narratives (69). And an article in the *Sacramento Bee* talks about "Chicks Who Kick," arguing that the word *chick* is now "chic," and discusses *G.I. Jane, Xena: Warrior Princess,* and *Buffy* (Nauman, B1).

10. And while part of this larger cultural context, *Buffy* provides a counter to the ever-popular *Ally McBeal.* As Adam Rogers writes, "Buffy the vampire slayer could whip Ally McBeal's butt. Harsh? Sure. But where Ally deals with problems by emoting to friends and hallucinating petty slights [*sic*], Buffy copes by kick-boxing her problems and driving wooden stakes through their hearts" (60). Moreover, *Buffy* is one of the rare detailed explorations into teenage female angst ("Buffy the Vampire Slayer," 35). In her article, Susan Kittenplan writes about Sarah Michelle Gellar; Peta Wilson (Nikita on *La Femme Nikita*); Jeri Ryan (Seven of Nine on *Star Trek: Voyager*); Lara Flynn Boyle (Helen Gamble on *The Practice*); Roseanne (*The Roseanne Show*); Ana Gasteyer, Cheri Oteri, and Molly Shannon (*Saturday Night Live*); and Lisa Nicole Carson (Renee Radick on *Ally McBeal*) (510).

11. Michael Ventura discusses the popularity of *Buffy, Xena,* and *La Femme Nikita* among teens and argues that they realistically portray the heroic warrior needed to live through the unending hellish discomforts of the 1990s. While critical of *Buffy,* Jacqueline Reid-Walsh explains the popularity among female adolescents of such shows as *Sabrina, the Teenage Witch; Buffy; Dawson's Creek; Xena: Warrior Princess;* and *Clueless* because they portray strong, active female protagonists. In her article, Louise Brown compares *Sabrina, the Teenage Witch; Buffy the Vampire Slayer;* and *The Secret World of Alex Mack.* The article suggests teen girls' self-esteem drops as they enter adolescence and explains why these shows are popular with girls. An article by Jill Brooke on girl power and consumerism mentions *Dawson's Creek; Seventh Heaven; Buffy the Vampire Slayer;* and *Sabrina, the Teenage Witch.* Discourse on the Web also provides evidence of this larger discourse about *Buffy* and girl power, and there is a need for a detailed ethnographic fan study of *Buffy,* which this essay does not conduct. Literally hundreds of websites devoted to *Buffy* exist. See, for instance: http://www.culttv.com/html/buffylinks. html#gile for a nice list. In his research, Thomas Hine found more than 320 websites devoted to *Buffy.* Among the many elements of these sites, some encourage feminist, antiracist, youth-empowering, gender-bending, and artistic expressions.

12. Liz Braun distinguishes between middle-class feminism and feminism for the poor but does not address race. And while it does not offer a serious treatment of race differ-

ences, Debbie Stoller's article is rare in that it does actually acknowledge that concern over girls generally means concern over white girls. She writes:

> Whereas young girls of nine or ten are self-confident, happy, and assertive—made of more piss and vinegar than sugar and spice—at puberty, a majority of them claim to be "unhappy with the way they are," an effect which is more pronounced among white girls than it is among Black and Hispanic girls. (C13)

And, in discussing *Dawson's Creek,* Alyssa Katz writes in her article that "series creator Kevin Williamson writes the most perfectly pitched white-kid dialogue since John Hughes ruled junior Hollywood" (35), at least indicating clearly the target audience of the show.

13. I capitalize "Black" because the term was fought for as a term of identification, not unlike the term African American. I put "white" in lowercase not only because it was not the result of long-term social struggles, but also because recent studies suggest that whiteness is not a term generally used as an identity category by white people (see, for example, Nakayama and Krizek).

14. It is important to point out that when Spike is injured and thus uses a wheelchair, Angel goes on a ruthless campaign to humiliate him, both because of his injury and because he uses a wheelchair.

15. On the original U.S. *Mighty Morphin Power Rangers* television show, five vigilante youths wearing color- and ideologically coded suits use their sophisticated weapons and technology to police and punish the forces of "darkness" in order to protect Angel Grove (code for: Los Angeles) and their father figure, Zordon, from danger and destruction. And, in the Disney film *Pocahontas,* anxieties about the colonization of Native Americans by so-called "settlers" are resolved when Pocahontas gives up her language, her culture, and her ideals. Her culture is marked throughout the film as inappropriately masculine and patriarchal. In order to save her blond, white, male lover from death, she risks her own life and, in the process, sheds her culture.

16. Adam Rogers writes, "Originally targeted at male teens, *Buffy* has turned out to be the WB Network's strongest show among women 18 to 34; the median viewer age is 29" (60).

17. Fran Rubel Kuzui directed the film and is now a producer on the TV show.

18. By the third season, the review of past episodes strategy is common to all episodes, perhaps in order to provide continuity between episodes as they build toward the final episode in which the mayor reaches "ascendance" and grows into a large monster that Buffy and company blow up.

19. There is some precedence in the horror genre for making a case that vampires are racialized. In the film *Pet Sematary II,* a movie inspired by Stephen King's book of the same name, corpses come to life out of a Native American burial ground (Dwyer, 45). For an academic discussion of the racialization of zombies in *Night of the Living Dead,* see Dyer.

20. Barbara Lippert suggests Buffy offers an alternative because she slays rather than takes a boyfriend, suggesting she chooses her career over her relationship (24). In fact, in "Never Kill a Boy on the First Date," a first-season episode, Buffy's preparation for her date is depicted as excessive, and in the end she ends up apologizing for putting her desires to date above her job as slayer. This suggests, in fact, that *Buffy* is

deeply ambivalent about Buffy's desire to have a life versus her responsibilities as slayer. While Giles wants her to act more responsibly—i.e., practice more, read sometimes, and take slaying more seriously overall—she often does not and pursues her own desires (which Giles sometimes says are childish), so much so that at times she simply pouts when she cannot have her way. This reversion to childlike responses seems an outcome of being an eighteen-year-old adult and still having a controlling mother and father (Giles) figure.

21. In the third-season episode, "Faith, Hope and Trick," for instance, Willow is making fun of Giles to Buffy and does not realize Giles is in the room. She says he makes a "cluck, cluck" noise when he is mad but is just too English to say he is mad.

22. In the third-season episode "The Wish," a character named Enya, who is responsible for granting Cordelia's wish for Buffy never to have come to Sunnydale High School, is represented on later episodes as being too anti-male. Nevertheless, she ultimately becomes a semi-regular character when she and Xander start to have a romantic heterosexual relationship. And while Cordelia's mannerisms and behaviors (e.g., her excessive snobbishness, vanity, and irony) are sometimes met with irritation by the other members of the group, even those excesses are never characterized as too unredeemable for her to have to be expelled.

23. I am, of course, implicitly referring to the racist practices of Blackface and Yellowface, for instance—media strategies primarily used to allow white actors to play roles of Blacks and Asian Americans in derogating ways.

24. The contrast between *Sunny*dale High School, where the protagonists live, and the netherworld, where the monsters live, is constructed along a light/dark continuum. Of course, there are always contradictions in any kind of generalized claim. Spike's hair is white, and Drusilla, while a brunette, has pasty white skin (not unlike Willow's, by the way). Perhaps because of their unusual whiteness, they have some of the most powerful lines of vampires in the show and have a long-standing presence as well. One could argue that as they approach whiteness on a continuum from black to white, they get closer to having the amount of air time the main five or six characters have on the show.

25. Despite the disinterest the show ultimately pays to her, fans interested in Kendra have even created websites specifically devoted to her. See, for instance, <http://www.geocities.com/TelevisionCity/5636/kendra.html> and <http://www.gurpages.com/tv/amy_the_witch/kendra.html>.

26. In "Faith, Hope and Trick," Buffy et al. reason that Faith appeared because Kendra died.

27. In "Faith, Hope and Trick," being a slayer shifts from being a primarily racial marking to being a primarily class marking. At Joyce's request, Buffy invites Faith to dinner. Joyce asks Faith questions about slaying and, in a typical interlude in which Buffy and Joyce escape to the kitchen to have a conversation, Joyce asks Buffy if she could stop slaying, let Faith take over the job, and go on to college to have a more normal life. In this instance, based on Joyce's comments, slaying is coded as labor, labor that the less fortunate (e.g., Faith, who is not college-bound) might do so that those who want to achieve higher goals can. And while Buffy says she wants to continue being the slayer, she nevertheless does not challenge in any way Joyce's suggestion that Faith does not have the class potential Buffy does.

28. The name Ampata is very close to the name of a mountain, Mt. Ampato in the Andes, where the "Maiden of Ampato," "Juanita," is said to have been buried for five hundred years before being discovered by archaeologists (see Peter Maass, B1).

29. All references to Ampata, from this point on, mean the impostor the characters think is the real Ampata.

30. Of course, it is not *absolutely* clear what "death rate" Mr. Trick means: the death rate of Black characters on the show, which is high; the death rate of vampires Buffy and company kill; or the disproportionately high death rate of African Americans in U.S. society compared to that of other racial groups.

WORKS CITED

Bellafante, Ginia. "Feminism: It's All about Me!" *Time* (29 June 1998): 54–60.

Bianculli, David. "Buffy, Xena and Herc Doin' A Helluva Job." *Daily News* (New York) 13 October 1998, 69.

Bickley, Claire. "Girl Power Ignites the Tube: *Buffy the Vampire Slayer, Ally McBeal* Rule TV's Top 10 of 1998." *The Toronto Sun,* 31 December 1998, 48.

Braun, Liz. "Feminism at Work and at Play." *The Toronto Sun,* 5 July 1998, C13.

Brooke, Jill. "Girl Power: Teenaged Girls in 1998 Are Avid Consumers." *Adweek* (2 February 1998): 18.

Brown, Louise. "Sabrina, Buffy and Alex Give Preteens a Door to the Wild World of Super Girls." *The Toronto Star,* 25 October 1997, SW14.

Buescher, Derek T., and Kent A. Ono. "Civilized Colonialism: 'Pocahontas' as Neocolonial Rhetoric." *Women's Studies in Communication* 19 (1996): 127–153.

"Buffy the Vampire Slayer." *Nation* (6 April 1998): 35–36.

"Buffy the Vampire Slayer." [Ratings]. *Mediaweek* (3 November 1997): 18.

Clover, Carol J. *Men, Women and Chain Saws: Gender in the Modern Horror Film.* Princeton: Princeton University Press, 1992.

Diawara, Manthia. "Black Spectatorship: Problems of Identification and Resistance." *Screen* 29 (1988): 66–76.

Dwyer, Victor. "Buffy the Vampire Slayer." *Maclean's* (10 August 1992): 45.

Dyer, Richard. "White." *Screen* 29 (1988): 44–64.

Geyh, Paula. "Adapting Women's Movement to Suit Selves: 'Bad Girls' Champion a New Feminist Order." *The Plain Dealer* (25 August 1998): 5F.

Gray, Herman. *Watching Race: Television and the Struggle for "Blackness."* Minneapolis: University of Minnesota Press, 1995.

Hall, Stuart. "Encoding/Decoding." In *Culture, Media, Language.* Edited by Stuart Hall, Dorothy Hobson, Andrew Lowe, and Paul Willis. London: Hutchinson/CCCs, 1980, 128–138.

Hall, Stuart. "The Whites of Their Eyes: Racist Ideologies and the Media." In *Silver Linings.* Edited by George Bridges and Rosalind Brunt. London: Lawrence & Wishart, 1981, 28–52.

Hine, Thomas. "TV's Teenagers: An Insecure, World-Weary Lot." In *Reading Culture: Contexts for Critical Reading and Writing.* 3d ed. Edited by Diana George and John Trimbur. New York: Longman, 1999, 78–81.

Katz, Alyssa. "*Buffy the Vampire Slayer.*" *Nation* (6 April 1998): 35–36.

Katz, Jackson, and Sut Jhally. "The National Conversation in the Wake of Littleton Is Missing the Mark." *The Boston Globe* (2 May 1999): E1.

Kittenplan, Susan. "TV's Girl Power: TV Actresses." *Harper's Bazaar* (September 1998): 510.

Labi, Nadya. "For the Next Generation, Feminism Is Being Sold as Glitz and Image. But What Do the Girls Really Want?" *Time* (29 June 1998): 60–62.

Lippert, Barbara. "Hey There, Warrior Grrrl." *New York* (15 December 1997): 24–25.

Maass, Peter. "500-Year-Old Mummy Arrives in Washington to Wrapped Attention." *Washington Post* (14 May 1996): B1.

Meers, Erik, and Paula Yoo. "Killer Charm: *Buffy the Vampire Slayer*'s Charisma Carpenter Proves Her Name Was a Prophecy." *People* (8 March 1999): 79–80.

Nakayama, Thomas K., and Robert L. Krizek. "Whiteness: A Strategic Rhetoric." *Quarterly Journal of Speech* 81 (1995): 291–309.

Nauman, Art. "Is It OK to Call Women Chicks?" *Sacramento Bee* (31 August 1997): B1.

Ono, Kent A. "Domesticating Terrorism: A Neocolonial Economy of *Différance*." In *Enterprise Zones: Critical Positions on Star Trek*. Edited by Taylor Harrison, Sarah Projansky, Kent A. Ono, and Elyce Rae Helford. Boulder, Colo.: Westview, 1996, 157–185.

———. "Power Rangers: An Ideological Critique of Neocolonialism." In *Critical Approaches to Television*. Edited by Leah Vande Berg, Lawrence Wenner, and Bruce Gronbeck. Boston: Houghton Mifflin, 1997, 271–284.

Projansky, Sarah. "Girls Who Act Like Women Who Fly: Jessica Dubroff as Cultural Troublemaker." *Signs* 23 (1998): 771–807.

Ramírez Berg, Charles. "Immigrants, Aliens, and Extraterrestrials: Science Fiction's Alien 'Other' as (Among *Other* Things) New Hispanic Imagery." *CineAction!* (Fall 1989): 3–17.

Reid-Walsh, Jacqueline. "Power Girl/Girl Power: The Female Action Hero Goes to High School (A Review of the Television Show *Buffy the Vampire Slayer*)." *Journal of Adolescent and Adult Literacy* 42, no. 6 (1999): 502–503.

Rogers, Adam. "Hey, Ally, Ever Slain a Vampire?" *Newsweek* (2 March 1998): 60.

Sharpe, Jenny. *Allegories of Empire: The Figure of Woman in the Colonial Text*. Minneapolis: University of Minnesota Press, 1993.

Stoller, Debbie. "Brave New Girls: These TV Heroines Know What Girl Power Really Means." *On the Issues* (Fall 1998): 42–45.

Ventura, Michael. "Warrior Women." *Psychology Today* (December 1998): 58–61.

Wittstock, Melinda. "For Those Watching in Black and White . . . " *The Guardian* (London), 2 March 1998, 4.

8

Biology Is Not Destiny;
Biology Is Fantasy

Cinderella, or to Dream Disney's "Impossible"/Possible Race Relations Dream

Marleen S. Barr

When asked why she writes fairy tales, A. S. Byatt replies that the genre provides a "clear" narrative form that does not require devoting attention to character motivation. "Readers know what a fairy tale princess does," she says.[1] Her story "Cold" reflects this classification ease: "Princesses [. . .] are expected to marry. [. . .] In our country [. . .] princes are glassmakers and glassmakers are princes" (Byatt, 135, 163). In our country, fairy-tale princesses (such as Cinderella) who are expected to marry princes are white; it is automatically assumed that glassmakers of magical glass slippers do not have black clients in mind. Disney's 1997 *Cinderella* thwarts such clarity: a black Cinderella marries a Filipino prince. Disney's Other, unexpected princess and prince—fairy tale royalty of a different color—cloud generic normalcy, cause viewers to question immediate notions regarding race.

Cinderella rejects the white fairy tale protagonist as fixed definition. The program replaces this expected trope with the protagonist as racial Other; however, within this fantasy world, Cinderella is devoid of Otherness. In other words, despite the multiracial cast, race itself is never an issue within the fantastic premise of this *Cinderella*. Hence, Disney's mixed-race fairy tale milieu coincides with Herman Gray's category of assimilationist television discourse. According to Gray, there is in assimilationist shows an elimination or "marginalization of social and cultural difference in the interest of shared and universal similarity" (85). *Cinderella* especially manifests this assimilationist stance via fantastic biological identity. The program presents a tale of two families whose genes do not compute. A Filipino prince emanates from "Queen Whoopi Goldberg" and "King

White Male." (Goldberg plays Queen Mazie. I call her "Queen Whoopi" because, when watching *Cinderella*, I see real-life Goldberg rather than the character she plays.) Because viewers are so comfortable with Goldberg's presence, having her play the queen further downplays white discomfort with racial difference. The white evil stepmother engenders one white and one dark-skinned black daughter. *Cinderella* is assimilationist vis-à-vis the fantastic; Disney eliminates race's link to reproductive biology and makes an impossible genetic race-relations dream come true. As Disneyland, which is devoid of cars, provides a utopian suburban environment, *Cinderella* presents a utopian assimilationist community devoid of reproductive biology tenets and overt racism. The program's fantastic biology is a "signifying practice that celebrate[s] racial invisibility and color blindness" (Gray, 85). In *Cinderella,* impossible biology emphasizes that race-relations transformations are possible.

In terms of assimilation, the program is quite congruent with the notions of Farai Chideya, ABC news correspondent and author of *The Color of Our Future.* Chideya points out that "America is changing from black and white as rigid categories to a multiracial society." The multiracial crowd and ball scenes in *Cinderella* depict Chideya's description of the future multiracial America. The program's fantastically generated royal interracial family exemplifies an America that has moved "beyond the black/white paradigm." Chideya, articulating a "beyond race" position in which white is no longer a neutral, universal color of normalcy, explains that "although whites have been considered the absence of race, whites have race."[2] Within *Cinderella,* no one has race—that is, everyone is culturally white (assimilated into white middle-class norms) and fantastically devoid of biological identity.

In the spirit of this possible cultural and impossible biological eradication of racial difference, *Cinderella* proclaims, regardless of race, if the shoe fits, wear it. Instead of usual race and class issues, the program is about race and glass: its portrayal of race, like glass, is colorless. The most poignant moment in *Cinderella* occurs when Cinderella places her bare black foot within the magically custom-made glass slipper. The camera's focus upon her foot inside the transparent shoe enables viewers literally to look through racial stereotypes. The audience sees that a black foot belongs inside the glass slipper, that a black woman is a rightful fairy-tale princess. Like her slipper, black Cinderella, in terms of culture, lacks ethnic difference; for her, race is not a social impediment. Individuals who function as so many glass people inhabit her world. Her community acts as numerous window-panes who make it possible to see through racial stereotypes.

Cinderella, fantastic assimilationist discourse, proclaims that racial differences and racism are royal pains (in the glass?) that can be (impossibly) biologically and (possibly) culturally cast aside. The program enables viewers to see what exaggerated cultural assimilationism looks like. But the assimilation functions only within the fantastic world. Viewers initially do not see the Other protagonists as "normal"—as congruent with Byatt's garden variety fairy-tale characters. At the program's inception, the audience is curious to discern exactly how a black Cinderella functions. The shock of seeing the new Cinderella becomes acceptance: black Cinderella becomes a normal Cinderella. Hence, for viewers, assimilation is a delayed response. Viewers, who at first focus upon racial difference, eventually find that a black Cinderella can be a valid Cinderella. Ironically, then, viewers move beyond race by focusing upon race—that is, assimilationism functions in terms of opposition: Gray's notion of "universal similarity"—accepting the premise that, regardless of race, all Cinderellas are created equal—operates in terms of "black is beautiful." *Cinderella* is a 1990s television program that uses black female protagonists (cast in roles where few black females have gone before) to discuss race relations from the safe distance of the fantastic. Before closely analyzing *Cinderella* according to the opposition of at once moving beyond race and accepting that black is beautiful, I will briefly identify and situate *Cinderella* within a new late 1990s literary and television subgenre: the race and glass fantastic story.[3]

RACE AND GLASS: A. S. BYATT'S "COLD" AND JONATHAN LETHEM'S "THE GLASSES"

"Cold," which reflects Byatt's aesthetic appreciation of color and glass, is a race and glass fairy tale. The same holds true for *Cinderella*. The *Cinderella* glass slipper is iconic. "Cold" also positions glass as an icon: an illustration of a glass art work, "*Facon de Venise* goblet, 17th century," precedes "Cold." When it is time for fairy godmother Whitney Houston to create glass slippers, she could appropriately call upon "Cold" protagonist Prince Sasan, a glassblower. This prince with a "dark, secret face" (Byatt, 153)—a potentially black-skinned prince— marries the pale Princess Fiammarosa (an "ice-woman" who cannot survive in Sasan's hot country). Like the *Cinderella* protagonists, Fiammarosa and Sasan might be an interracial royal couple. In "Cold," as in *Cinderella*, glass facilitates successful interracial union. Sasan creates a cold glass palace for Fiammarosa to inhabit. Their children initially share much in common with Cinderella's stepsisters. One child is dark and one is white. And, then, in the interest of "shared and universal similarity," the dark boy becomes pale and the white girl acquires a striking dark characteristic: "In a year, or so, two children were born, a dark boy, who resembled his mother at birth, and became, like her, pale and golden, and a pale, flower-like girl, whose first days were white and hairless, but who grew a mane of dark hair" (Byatt, 181). Like the Other *Cinderella* prince and princess—like Queen Whoopi and King White Male—this interracial fairy-tale family lives happily ever after. Racists never throw stones at their glass palace.

Race initially is an issue in science fiction writer Jonathan Lethem's "The Glasses." Two white, white-coated opticians encounter a black customer who returns his glasses a day after buying them because they are, without logical cause, smudged. When the opticians refuse to believe the customer, he discusses race: "You couldn't see *black* for all the green [money] yesterday. Now I look black to you" (Lethem, 132). The customer's complaint: Green money only temporarily allows him to be treated fairly, as white. However, the marked glasses, not the customer's color, soon become the most important concern. The opticians agree to watch the customer's hands for as long as it takes the customer to prove that the smudge is not self-generating. As in the instance of the camera's attention to Cinderella's bare black foot, the fantastic, not race, is the focus of the opticians' gaze upon the customer's bare black hand. The fantastic, not race, causes the opticians to stare because, in an urban environment, encountering the racial Other is a daily occurrence.

The fantastic, not race, figures most prominently in both Cinderella's and the customer's situations. Cinderella, due to fantastic intervention, has a chance to go to the ball; the customer has a chance to prove that his glasses fantastically "smudged themselves" (Lethem, 132). As the opticians—who remind the customer of "Nazi doctors" (133)—prepare to watch the customer, race no longer colors their assessment of his veracity. The potential that the smudge is fantastic erases blackness as a marker of his trustworthiness. Because of the potential presence of the fantastic, as the opticians stare at the customer's black hands, these body parts become as colorless as his glasses, Fiammarosa's glass palace, and Cinderella's glass slippers. Cinderella, when describing her name to the prince, mentions her face's "smudges" derived from fireplace cinders. These smudges mark and name her situation, not her race. Cinderella and the customer, respective fairy-tale denizen and fictional character who inhabits a realistic world positioned on the verge of the fantastic, contend with smudges that are real. In the end, racism smudges (or marks) neither protagonist. Both share the colorlessness of glass.

THE "IMPOSSIBLE"/POSSIBLE: *CINDERELLA*

"The Glasses" ends by referring to time. "The second optician moved into the back of the shop, to call his wife, to say he'd be late" (Lethem, 133). When Disney CEO Michael Eisner introduces *Cinderella* at the beginning of the *Wonderful World of Disney,* on which program it was first broadcast, time is also on his mind. Explaining that this fairy tale has not recently been remade, he says, "We thought it was about time—whoa, time. That reminds me. I have to return the coach to Cinderella before it gets too late." In the manner of a boring vaudevillian forced to vacate the stage, Eisner abruptly fades from view. This abruptness is appropriate. It is too late for a white man to have the first word—the focus of attention and sole authority—regarding interpretation.

Eisner sits on Cinderella's all-important pumpkin. Here, a white man—a powerful CEO—appears in a prone, subordinate position supported by an object representing magic and transformation. Eisner's position "on top" of the pumpkin cannot keep the pumpkin down (relegate the pumpkin to ever-after vegetable mode); transformation happens—in literature, in television, and in life. Specifically, in regard to Eisner, this fact is a good thing. Eisner—a Jewish, white CEO of a corporation that manufactures fantasy and dream—epitomizes Hitler's worst nightmare of Jews' post–World War II future. An American Dream that incorporates both a beautiful black Cinderella and a powerful Jewish person is a final solution to Hitlerian racism.

Hemingway, Faulkner, and Fitzgerald now share some of their prestige with Toni Morrison and Alice Walker; Eisner yields center screen to Whitney Houston. The black fairy godmother's first word is "impossible." This word, a song lyric from the original Rodgers and Hammerstein *Cinderella* score, at once describes the aforementioned fantastic biology and counters the very possible occurrence of transcending racism. The black female *Cinderella* stars—Brandy, Goldberg, and Houston—are celebrities. The clock does not strike twelve in relation to their glamorous real lives. The male leads—Victor Garber (who plays the king) and Paolo Montalban (who plays the prince)—pale in comparison to the black women's real world fame. Houston's role exemplifies the once impossible becoming possible: a black woman can fill Billie Burke's shoes (as portrayer of *The Wizard of Oz*'s Glinda, the Good Witch of the North).

Houston's appearance, as well as the part she plays, evokes the fantastic. She articulates "impossible" while attired in a resplendent golden suit. Against a blue "sky" background, she "beams down" to Cinderella's community. This fairy godmother resembles a beautiful black science fiction alien. Houston's presence implies that black is beautiful, an implication that holds true in some aspects of American reality. Like Cinderella's pumpkin and mice, black women (at least young, thin, light-skinned black women) have been transformed by newfound social acceptance. Black female glamour is an established American cultural commodity.

Hence, this *Cinderella,* contrary to its title, is not "Rodger's and Hammerstein's *Cinderella*." It is a new *Cinderella* for the 1990s that depicts a dream that race does not matter. In reality, this dream comes true for Brandy, Goldberg, and Houston. When hosting the 1999 Academy Awards, Goldberg (evoking *Shakespeare in Love* and *Elizabeth*) appeared in whiteface as Queen Elizabeth. Only Hollywood royalty can host the Academy Awards; the Bob Hope of the '90s is a black woman. Goldberg exemplifies the great white/black hope of transcending racism. In Disney art and professional reality, Goldberg *is* a black queen in white face. *Cinderella* positions her as the black queen/Jewish mother who incessantly pushes the prince to get married. (*Cinderella* writer Robert L. Freedman goes so far as to have Queen Whoopi say, *"Oy."* Although, of course, the Jewish mother stereotype is racist, I think that Freedman emphasizes it simply to generate humor.) The *goyische* (non-Jewish) prince shares Portnoy's complaint. But Brandy, Goldberg, and Houston cannot justifiably articulate the marginalized

Other's complaint. Houston is a glamour queen; Brandy is a black American popular-culture princess. Black women performers have come a long way from the time when Marion Anderson was barred from singing publicly.

Comedic Queen Whoopi in *Cinderella* is no Queen Elizabeth in *Shakespeare in Love* or *Elizabeth*. She is, however, somewhat akin to them in that she is queen of a community that shares the bustling and exaggerated "another time, another place" quality of the *Shakespeare* crowd scenes. When a blonde woman who holds a child catches viewers' attention, the initial *Cinderella* crowd scene signals racial ambiguity; the child's race cannot be discerned. This crowd scene emphasizes clothing, not race. The camera focuses upon headless bottom halves of ornately clothed crowd members; skin color is not in the picture. Skin color has no relation to Queen Whoopi's important position in her community.

Cinderella first appears on screen as she watches a *Punch and Judy* show. She inhabits a community in which racist social codes do not pull strings. Cinderella's stepmother describes her stepsisters, Minerva and Calliope, by saying, "How can a mother choose between two such extraordinary daughters?" "Extraordinary" does not refer to the fact that Minerva is black and Calliope is white. Cinderella's race does not prevent her from marrying the prince, from escaping the female community that treats her as a maid/slave.

When Cinderella meets the prince, she addresses sex roles, not racism: "A girl should be treated like a person, with kindness and respect," she informs him. She turns first-wave black feminist Sojourner Truth's question—"Ain't I a woman?"—into a statement: "I am a lady." The prince, who appears within the community while passing as a "real" (i.e., not royal) individual, is also concerned with defining "person." Lionel, the royal butler, describes himself to the prince as a "real" (i.e., nonroyal or working-class) person and emphasizes that his status is not romantic. Jason Alexander plays Lionel in a voice that resonates with realism: he sounds like a thick-accented Jewish immigrant, a Jewish refugee. Jewish reality, then, is implied in *Cinderella*. The program's assimilationist stance does not apply to Jews, who remain apart: they do not take part in the romantic royal fantasy except as servants.

Screenwriter Freedman authors a dream come true of escape from the Jewish mother's unceasing voice. King White Male describes Queen Whoopi in terms of a sexist stereotype: "Your mother was talking. I was listening," he explains to the prince to indicate that he has no chance to get a word in edgewise. More than once, the Queen's talking binge rampage ends in a series of futile squeaks. This whimper is how the male Jewish screenwriter ends the world of the Jewish mother's incessant locution. It seems that jokes at the expense of loquacious women in general and Jewish mothers in particular are outside the boundaries of political correctness. Be that as it may, the stereotypical Jewish mother confronted with a Filipino son would certainly say *Oy*, squeak, and call for smelling salts. The fact that the prince is a *goy* named Christopher does not help matters. It is highly unlikely that a Jewish mother would name her son Christopher. The script emphasizes the prince's long list of names and specifically questions "Herman." What kind of name is Herman? I ask the same about "Whoopi Goldberg." Does adopting the name "Whoopi Goldberg" enable a black show business personality to de-emphasize the fact that she is black? "Goldberg" does not, after all, denote black culture.

The *Cinderella* script addresses sexual politics as well as Jewish ethnicity. The stepmother recites patriarchal law to her daughters: "Beauty knows no pain. [. . .] Men can't stand to be around smart women. [. . .] This is not about love. It is about marriage," she insists. Yet the casting of Bernadette Peters as the stepmother subverts patriarchal imperatives regarding women and aging. This actor, in her late forties in this role, is sexually attractive. Peters is far more glamorous than the younger actors cast as her daughters. Peters portrays the stepmother in terms of her sexuality. As she looks in a mirror and tells her daughters that "the prince should pick one of you for his bride," she suggestively runs her hands along her body. Peters implies that she is an appropriate match for the "twenty-something" prince. Why not? Her desire does not make her look foolish. Men, after all, routinely marry women who could be their daughters. And the step-mother's implied desire to marry the prince becomes overt when, in the end, she grabs the glass slipper and (successfully!) places it on her own foot. Although the shoe is too tight to wear, Peters's hair is just right. Both Peters and Houston have the same hair style, in fact: tightly curled, piled high, with a strong reddish cast. We see that in the fantasy world of *Cinderella,* ethnic hair is good hair—or racial difference cannot be assessed by hair.

Although, like the stepmother, the fairy godmother does not get a love interest in this retold fairy tale, Houston, too, does directly articulate her sexuality. Before doing her thing with the pumpkin and mice, she informs Cinderella that she is not an elderly, sexless frump: "If you would rather have some old lady in a tutu sprinkle fairy dust on your hair. . . ," she says to the surprised Cinderella. The sexy fairy godmother does act like the usual tutu-clad one when she sprinkles confidence and independence within Cinderella's thoughts, however: "You're on your own. I got you to the ball. The rest is up to you." Here, for the first time in the program, familial biology (albeit implied familial biology) is not

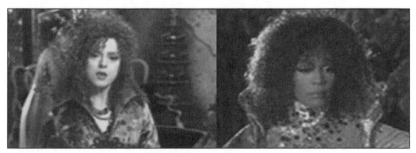

Ethnic hair is good hair in Cinderella.

fantastic: Houston resembles and acts as Brandy's appropriate mother, the beautiful black engenderer of a beautiful black "daughter." Appearing together on screen, Houston and Brandy picture black female nurturance and black female glamour's new, real generational continuity. It is not "impossible for a plain yellow pumpkin to become a golden carriage." It is not "impossible" for the exclusion Marion Anderson suffered to change: Diana Ross yields Houston who, in turn, yields Brandy. Transformation for black women is possible—and has occurred. Black female entertainment dynasties are now plausible.[4]

The fairy godmother might have inspired Byatt's Prince Sasan. When artificially altering the mice and the pumpkin, the fairy godmother acts in the manner of Sasan—who "had made an artificial world in which he hoped his wife could live, and could breathe, and could be herself" (Byatt, 178). She makes it possible for Cinderella to live, breathe, and be herself at the ball. The ball scene consists of the same interracial mix characterizing the initial crowd scene. Before the prince meets Cinderella, he enjoys dancing with a black woman. Here, again, *Cinderella* implies that black is beautiful. In addition to black people, a real female black voice is present at the ball. In the manner of Eliza Doolittle revealing her true lower-class origins in *My Fair Lady*, when she screams "Move your bloomin' ass!" at the Ascot Races, Minerva shouts these words in relation to the prince: "I want a chance at him!" Her mother places her white hand over Minerva's mouth. White culture, as black author Zora Neale Hurston asserts in *Spunk*, silences the essence of the black female voice.

Women's artistic voice is also silenced at the ball. Minerva, whose individuality survives her mother's attempts to make her conform to patriarchal rubrics, tries to impress the prince by reciting her poetry. "Don't you get it? It's poetry," she insists, as black and white royal guards remove her from the prince's presence. In a world where black women can be Cinderella, the queen, and the fairy godmother, guards remove the black female writer/literary critic (who happens to be fat).

Brandy's presence at the ball is in stark contrast to the loud and hefty Minerva. The fragile-looking, elegant, long-necked Brandy resembles a young, black Audrey Hepburn. Brandy's rendition of the ball scene evokes the transformed Eliza (portrayed by Hepburn) in *My Fair Lady*. The prince touches Cinderella's chin with a white-gloved hand. He is the possessor of white male power; Cinderella, who now wears a crown, is a black American princess. She is a prize that men want to win. This holds true for the king, a man more powerful than the prince, who is also attracted to Cinderella.

Color is emphasized at the ball. Lighting changes Cinderella's gown from white to blue to purple. Purple, in fact, is the predominant ball attire color. When Cinderella steps outside the ballroom and kisses the prince, the purple lighting that illuminates her face causes her literally to become purple, which we can read as liberatory through Alice Walker's use of the color as symbol of liberation in *The Color Purple*. But, despite the ball scene's emphasis upon the colors purple and white, Cinderella's color continues to be a nonissue. When she tells the prince, "I'm not what they think I am," he replies, "All that they are thinking is that you are the most beautiful girl at the ball. And you are." Again: viewers can accept that black is beautiful. The fairy godmother tells Cinderella to believe in herself, to trust the prince "to love you as you really are." The prince loves her—and viewers see that he loves her. The iconic clock striking twelve, not racial prejudice, is the fixed definition that temporarily thwarts Cinderella.

Empowered by the confidence her success at the ball yields, Cinderella finally confronts her stepmother. When the stepmother states that she cannot imagine Cinderella dancing with the prince, Cinderella simply—and assertively—asks, "Why is it so hard for you to imagine?" The stepmother's answer: "Because you're common, Cinderella. You can wash your face and put on a clean dress but underneath you'll still be common." Peters emphasizes the "c" in "common" in a manner that implies that the stepmother might have been about to say "colored"—to say "because you're colored, Cinderella"—reflecting a history of prejudice against symbols of racial (if not gender) equality such as black fairy-tale princesses. But derogatory racial utterances do not exist in this fantasy world, especially because the white speaker herself has a daughter of color. Cinderella does not have to wish/wash her color away, dream about possessing the bluest eye. Fairy tale—and speculative fiction—can change the aberrant into the usual.

Cinderella's black foot placed inside the glass slipper does not shock the audience. Lionel's Jewish accent describes the glass slipper in realistic terms: "A shoe made out of glass? Who dances in glass shoes?" He calls Cinderella's footwear plebeian "shoes," not elegant "slippers." Who dances in glass shoes? Black Cinderella. Moreover, when not dressed for the ball, Cinderella does not sport the highly coifed, if ethnicized, hair that her stepmother, stepsister, and fairy godmother wear. Instead, she wears long braids, cornrows, and a dull-colored, rough cloth dress. Cinderella's look thus attests to a history of working-class existence for black Americans—even enslavement, given her abusive treatment and overwork by her stepmother. And there are others in her world who also wear reality-based economic shoes and serve privileged masters: a noteworthy number of the prince's guards and servants are black. In such instances, race does matter in the fantastic world.

Ageism, as well as employment bias, is part of Cinderella's world. When the prince and Lionel inquire if there are any other women in the stepmother's house, she replies affirmatively. Her "yes" refers to herself, not to Cinderella. Lionel specifically says that he seeks a "young woman." "How young?" the stepmother asks. "Younger than you," is the answer she receives. The fairy tale has its limits. It should be no harder to accept as normal a sexy middle-aged Jewish woman than it is to accept a black Cinderella. Questioning age bias as well as racial bias should be a part of this *Cinderella*.

However sexy, the stepmother in *Cinderella* cannot possibly marry the prince. Desperate for the prince to marry one of her daughters, the stepmother begs him to consider that Calliope "is really much smarter than she looks" and Minerva "memorized *The Wreck of the Hesperus* in three languages." Desperation evokes references to the sisters' intelligence. They are allowed to be smart only when their cause as potential wives is absolutely lost, wrecked in all languages—"impossible."

As we are all aware, the glass slipper fits Cinderella's foot. Color is important in the culminating foot/slipper scene. Cinderella, at first, wears white slippers—literal bedroom slippers adorned with pink and blue decoration at the toe. She removes the bedroom slippers, whose colors symbolize racial whiteness and stereotypical female and male gender roles. Again, since Cinderella's foot is now bare, blackness appears behind the glass slipper (as black Cinderella appears behind the glass television screen—our celebrity-obsessed culture's place of primary importance). Cinderella's "slave" clothes—her "skin"-colored beige dress and brown jacket—give way to a white ball gown. The last scene shows white (white wedding clothes and a white coach) surrounding black Cinderella. In the end, the color white—not Alice Walker's liberatory color purple—prevails.

Byatt's Princess Fiammarosa casts positive light on this situation. Fiammarosa's achievement at once concerns color and transcends color—and is enhanced by glass: "Her greatest discovery was a sweet blueberry, that grew in the snow, but in the glass garden became twice the size, and almost as delicate in flavour" (Byatt, 182). The blueberry, an entity that is not white (and that is akin to the color purple), grows surrounded by a fantastic white alien milieu—and flourishes due to glass. So, too, for the delicate young Audrey Hepburn-esque black Cinderella. The fairy godmother informs her: "Now you can go wherever you want to go. Now you can do whatever you want to do. Now you can be whatever you want to be." Some black girls can be Cinderella. Some black girls can enjoy white privilege. Queen Whoopi, the black/Jewish mother, smiles approvingly at the black girl who marries the Filipino prince. The symbol of Cinderella's assimilationist victory: she holds a white bouquet.

The race and glass fantastic story climaxes as black Cinderella swaps white bedroom slipper for glass slipper.

The final image in *Cinderella* shows Houston ascending and appearing on top of the castle. She is ensconced above the turrets, which are the color purple. *Cinderella* announces that black women are above it all. Viewers who encounter the fantastic assimilationist *Cinderella* see that the reality of black women's social acceptability is paramount.

They also see that—in regard to interpersonal relationships—race, like size, ultimately does not matter. I asked Farai Chideya to comment upon *Cinderella*. What she had to say addresses this point about assimilationism: "The multiracial Cinderella starring Brandy was typical television fare on one level: sweet, syrupy, romantic. But on another level it was absolutely groundbreaking. By casting a black Cinderella, a Filipino prince, a black queen, and a white king, this television production showed America's children that families and romance need not be circumscribed by the boundaries of race. That's a vision of America's future . . . I hope."[5] Like my attention to impossible biology and possible social roles, Chideya also discusses *Cinderella* on two levels. She mentions what American children see. What the audience sees is all important.

When staring at the black fairy godmother positioned "on top," viewers simultaneously see race (a black fairy-tale character) and observe that race does not matter (viewers have spent two hours watching individuals of color functioning as effective fairy-tale characters). As Chideya explains, race is at once present and does not matter. One aspect of the assimilationist stance in *Cinderella*, reproductive biology, is fantastic: it is, as I have mentioned, impossible for a black woman and a white man to be the biological parents of a Filipino son. But another aspect of the program's assimilationism is very possible. Race does not have to determine familial (or any other) social roles. A black woman and a white man can adopt a Filipino son who, in turn, can marry a black woman. It is possible that society can change to the extent that, as in the *Cinderella* world, such a multiracially configured family will be thought of as normal. Currently, in America, there are places where families of diverse racial and/or ethnic composition can live happily ever after.

EPILOGUE: REALITY, OR WHAT FOLLOWS *CINDERELLA*

The commercials that followed the original November 1997 broadcast of *Cinderella* address the program and the issues I raise in this essay. A Game Boy advertisement portrays a gorilla's head accompanied by the words *monkeys, demons, dragons, evil,* and *jungles.* The juxtaposition of gorilla and these words combine fairy-tale tropes with the manner in which racist white Americans make gorillas a symbol for blackness. Racists can neither imagine nor accept a black Cinderella. They see the gorilla as Willie Horton—and as all black men. This attitude toward black men figures in *Cinderella*. A white man is the king; the only black men who appear in the program are servants, guards, and background dancers at the ball. In *Cinderella,* black men play no leading role, experience no transformation.

The State Farm Insurance commercial that follows describes none other than Barbara Jordan. Viewers are told that Jordan was "born black and a woman when it paid to be neither. State Farm salutes life's heroes because State Farm understands life." In *Cinderella*—and in the lives of many black men—if black men encounter pumpkins until the cows come home, transformation will not improve their situations. Racial transformation does yield Jordan, though. The commercial includes her voice declaring: "My faith in the constitution is whole. It is complete. It is total. I have finally been included in 'we the people.'" *Cinderella's* crowd scenes, ball scenes, and fantastic nuclear family biology portray an inclusive "we the people."

Finally, on its original broadcast date, Oprah Winfrey's *Before Women Had Wings* followed *Cinderella,* attesting that television's focus on black women is no longer an anomaly. Women, and black women in particular, can fly above many racist and sexist stereotypes. But, despite the biologically "impossible" and culturally possible racial transcendence *Cinderella* portrays, in reality, the WASP woman marries the prince. Or, more specifically, Diana Spenser married Prince Charles. Prince Charles would never marry a black woman; such a union would be "impossible." But Princess Diana, a real-world fairy-tale princess, did do the "impossible"; she provided a real example of how to add complexity to Byatt's notion that fairy-tale princesses are known entities. Diana divorced the prince and wanted to marry an Arab, a man of color. Despite (or perhaps because of) Diana's willingness to do the "impossible" in regard to royal family decorum, she and her lover are dead. We are left with "Long Live the Next British King." Who is to blame? Well, if—in regard to the patriarchal media establishment's obsessive commodification of celebrity women—the shoe fits, then the establishment should wear it. The true moral of real stories vis-à-vis real princesses: as Jack Zipes says, "Don't bet on the Prince."

NOTES .

1. This quotation comes from Byatt's reading at Barnes & Noble, Union Square, Manhattan (7 April 1999).

2. The preceding quotations come from Chideya's reading at Newseum/NY, Manhattan (20 April 1999).

3. My notion of the race and glass story coheres with work by black writers who discuss race in terms of colorless "elementals" (to use Byatt's term in her anthology title *Elementals: Stories of Fire and Ice*). For example, the title of James McBride's memoir is *The Color of Water: A Black Man's Tribute to His White Mother.* When McBride asked his mother what color God was, she replied, "God is the color of water."

4. This quotation comes from Chideya's reading at Newseum/NY, Manhattan (20 April 1999).

5. The May 1999 ABC telecast of *Double Platinum,* starring Diana Ross and Brandy, illustrates this point. Ross plays a singing superstar who encounters the daughter she left behind (Brandy). The character Brandy plays is herself an aspiring singer.

WORKS CITED

Byatt, A. S. "Cold." In *Elementals: Stories of Fire and Ice.* New York: Random House, 1998, 115–182.

Chideya, Farai. *The Color of Our Future.* New York: William Morrow, 1999.

Gray, Herman. *Watching Race: Television and the Struggle for "Blackness."* Minneapolis: University of Minnesota Press, 1995.

Hurston, Zora Neale. *Spunk: The Selected Stories of Zora Neale Hurston.* Berkeley, Calif.: Turtle Island, 1985.

Lethem, Jonathan. "The Glasses." *Voice Literary Supplement,* April–May 1999, 131–133.

McBride, James. *The Color of Water: A Black Man's Tribute to His White Mother.* New York: Riverhead Books, 1996.

Walker, Alice. *The Color Purple.* New York: HBJ, 1982.

Zipes, Jack. *Don't Bet on the Prince: Contemporary Feminist Fairy Tales in North America and England.* New York: Methuen, 1986.

Part III

Projecting the Future

9

Science, Race, and Gender in *Star Trek: Voyager*

Robin A. Roberts

Star Trek: Voyager is remarkable not only for the first female captain in a major role but also for the series' depiction of the intersection between science, gender, and race. More than any other science fiction television series, *Star Trek: Voyager* interrogates traditional science, exploring and exposing the ways that gender and race affect the practice of science.[1] The space vessel *Voyager's* Captain Kathryn Janeway is a leader *and* a scientist in charge of a ship that, as she boasts, has "research facilities [that are] the most advanced in Starfleet" (*Star Trek: Voyager:* "Innocence"). While *Star Trek: The Next Generation* and *Deep Space Nine* represent race primarily through male characters, *Star Trek: Voyager* especially features racially diverse female cast members. Since so many of *Star Trek: Voyager's* plots revolve around the captain and her interaction with female crew members, this series emphasizes how racial difference affects women and how the race and gender of the scientist affect the practice of science. Since the series' major female characters are all scientists and engineers, the interconnections between science, race, and gender emerge prominently in the characters of Captain Janeway, B'Elanna Torres, and Seven of Nine. B'Elanna Torres is the half-human, half-Klingon chief of engineering, and Seven of Nine is a crew member who is part-human and part-Borg, a machine species that assimilates organic life forms. Captain Janeway, by contrast, is European American and entrenched in the white male-dominated hierarchy of Starfleet.

As these descriptions suggest, I employ race here in two ways: first, in the traditional (and erroneous) sense of biological difference, usually noted by skin color (but in Seven's case, through visible machine implants), and second, in the sense of ethnic or cultural difference. "Race," then, both in the series and in this chapter, refers to a complex set of qualities and signifiers, including ethnic heritage, cultural knowledge, beliefs and values, and appearance. Depending on the context, one or more of these qualities may emerge as a defining aspect, either for the character or for others with whom she interacts. Janeway, B'Elanna, and Seven are visually marked as racially different, but these signs of race prove not as important as their cultural values, which are markedly different. Their differences emerge as they engage in the practice of science.

As Janeway, B'Elanna, and Seven interact, their conversations and actions evoke feminist approaches to science while demonstrating that race affects decisions that scientists make. Unlike any other television series, *Star Trek: Voyager* reveals the ways in which race complicates our understanding of both science and gender. Some feminist approaches to science reject its purported neutrality and expose the androcentric nature of scientific studies (Harding, Keller); other historians of science address its racial bias (Gould, Haraway). Through the "mulatta" perspectives of B'Elanna and Seven, and Janeway's receptivity to their views, *Star Trek: Voyager* both exposes bias and proposes a feminist alternative that acknowledges the triangulation of gender, race, and science. By exploring this triangulation and acknowledging its complexities and problems, *Star Trek: Voyager* alerts its viewers to the importance of considering not only gender but also race in any discussion of science.

To do so, however, *Star Trek: Voyager* literally leaves our world behind. Cast by a powerful alien seventy-five light-years from known space, *Voyager* journeys in the Delta Quadrant, completely isolated from the Federation (a political association of planets and cultures) and Starfleet (the quasi-military organization to which *Voyager* belongs). In the Delta Quadrant, the women literally occupy an alien space.[2] Janeway cannot turn to Starfleet for answers and guidance because she cannot contact Starfleet Command. The Delta Quadrant is not mapped by the Federation; it is *Star Trek*'s version of outer space, an unexplored territory. In this space women can create new rules and new understandings among themselves; they have an opportunity to confront racism and work out how to practice science without being constrained by a white, male-dominated hierarchy such as Starfleet. While Janeway belongs to this white, male-dominated tradition and often rigidly upholds her prerogatives as captain, she nevertheless bends hierarchical structures to work with B'Elanna and Seven. However, rather than suggesting a utopian communal relationship, the series instead points to the advantages and sometimes even the necessity for Janeway to heed women of color. That Janeway has appointed B'Elanna as chief of engineering, even though B'Elanna dropped out of Starfleet Academy, suggests the degree to which Janeway not only bends but breaks Starfleet regulations for both B'Elanna and Seven. The series, then, is not about abandoning racist and sexist structures but about how women can appropriate existing institutions. The show also emphasizes the effect of practicing science on the female characters' personal and professional lives.

While there are many episodes that feature either Janeway and B'Elanna or Janeway and Seven, this article will focus on two shows: "Dreadnought," in which an intelligent missile reprogrammed by B'Elanna threatens the ship and planets, and "The Omega Directive," in which *Voyager* encounters a particle that threatens to destroy the fabric of space. In both episodes, the captain disagrees with a female crew member about ethical and technological issues, and, in both instances, the crew member's gender and race difference affects the debate. These episodes suggest that the series can live up to critic Daniel Bernardi's expressed hope that *Star Trek: Voyager,* with its "multiracial cast complete with a female Captain (Kate Mulgrew) who literally takes charge of both the narrative and supporting characters, [may] be one of those rare challenges popular culture offers up to today's racial order of things" (21).

Star Trek: Voyager has a unique ability to deal with issues of race. Each *Star Trek* series, as Bernardi points out, "rarely depicts racism among humans, preferring to project it as a problem within alien cultures or between two alien worlds" (28). In its displacement of the category onto aliens, science fiction defamiliarizes the category, calling on the viewer to question assumptions and prejudices about race. Is race a social construction? Determined by culture? Filtered through biology? Episodes in all *Star Trek* series raise these questions. In *Star Trek: Voyager,* though, the frame is tightened, both because the actors who play crew members are more racially diverse and also because *Star Trek: Voyager* reflects the increasingly sophisticated discussions about race that have occurred since the airing of classic *Trek* in the late 1960s (i.e., the rejection of race as a biological category; the emphasis on biracial identity). The idea that women are separated from each other by race certainly never appears in classic *Star Trek.* While the original series did portray the first interracial kiss on television, only on *Star Trek: Voyager* do we have extended emphasis on how racial and ethnic differences affect female crew members' interactions and their scientific practice.

In his assessment of the changes from classic *Star Trek* to *Star Trek: The Next Generation,* Clyde Wilcox optimistically observes that "[t]he role of blacks has changed in the new show" (92). While there are a few more black performers in *Star Trek: The Next Generation,* the show's attitude toward race did not change dramatically. As Wilcox points out later in his article, "Although science fiction often seeks to extrapolate current trends into the future, the assumptions of a culture are usually projected as well" (99). As *Star Trek: The Next Generation* reflects attitudes toward race in the 1980s,[3] *Star Trek: Voyager* reflects the complex and contradictory expressions of race in the 1990s. That gender and race interact is part of this complexity, particularly the notion that race can separate women, preventing them from working together. That both gender and race are constructed is another key feature of contemporary attitudes reflected in *Star Trek: Voyager.*

As decades of scholarship attest, the categories of race and gender are socially constructed. Scientific research suggests that all racial differences among humans are superficial, with "no basic biological reality" (Marks, quoted in Boyd, 8a). And Bernardi explains in his discussion of race in *Star Trek* that race is "a historically specific system of meanings that has a profound impact on social organizations, political movements, cultural articulations, and individual identity" (5). Race, then, is about culture, a social reality (Omi, quoted in Boyd, 8a). Similarly, as Judith Butler describes, "gender is culturally constructed" (6). Whiteness presented as the default setting for the human race reifies white supremacy without overtly acknowledging the constructedness of racial categories. Similarly, the insistence that "man" includes "woman" linguistically elides the system of male dominance. Through the figure of the alien, *Star Trek: Voyager* engages the perspective of race and gender as fictional (cultural) realities. If either category persists in the twenty-fourth century, it is, as scholar Barbara Fields asserts in relation to race, "because we continue to create it" (117).

In *Star Trek: Voyager,* race and gender are presented and contested in the figure of the mixed-species female alien. The racial Other frequently appears in the myth of the tragic mulatta, the female figure of mixed race who ends up caught between two cultures. Bernardi discusses the biologically unlikely interbreeding of aliens (126) but does not focus on the special position of the female alien of mixed origin. Customarily represented as a white/black mix, the mulatta could feasibly exist in either world, but rather than seeing this flexibility as positive, realist writers and critics have depicted this hybridity as a psychological tragedy based upon life in a racist American society. Tragic mulatta narratives have a long history; African Americans and European Americans both have written them. As Nancy Bentley describes it, the liminal position of the biracial human is viewed with "a combination of sympathy, revulsion, and fascination" because the mulatta stands "precisely at the place where nature and culture could come unbound" (198). Mulatta narratives, then, function to reassure the reader that such categories as "white" and "black" can and will be enforced. By showing women of mixed race who cannot find a place in society, mulatta narratives reify the importance of racial distinctions, even as the figure of the mulatta herself acknowledges the arbitrariness and social construction of race.

Moreover, the mulatta's gender is absolutely central to her function as a reenforcer of racial distinctions. There are fewer fictional depictions of male mulattoes, reinforcing the notion that "all the men are black" rather than of mixed racial heritage (Bentley, 198). And mulattas are almost always a black-white mixture, shutting other races out of the idea of miscegenation. The mulatta represents race (often in conjunction with slavery) most powerfully because she is female and sexually desirable. As Bentley explains, "the Mulatta is granted her most pronounced symbolic power by virtue of her worldly suffering—her sexual exploitation and the betrayals and abuse she endures" (199). We can see echoes of this figure in *Star Trek: Voyager*'s characters B'Elanna Torres and Seven of Nine, but, in this postracist future, she is revised into a figure of power and strength.[4] Furthermore, as part-Klingon and part-Borg, respectively, both characters also carry signs of masculinity, for those species are presented in the *Trek* universe as aggressively masculine and warlike, with rigid hierarchies and dominating empires. Thus, B'Elanna and Seven's mulatta identities are both biracial and bi-gendered.[5]

While issues of race are perhaps more comfortably defamiliarized when placed in alien bodies, many alien species in *Trek* can reproduce with humans (Bernardi, 126). This simulated miscegenation reminds the viewer that since we have arguably yet to encounter any actual aliens in the world outside the screen, all televisual aliens must be read as ciphers for humanity. Through the alienness of B'Elanna Torres and Seven of Nine, *Star Trek: Voyager* can thus raise issues of racial construction and reinforcement. B'Elanna had a human father and a Klingon mother; and, as a child, Seven was taken from her human parents by the Borg and not only raised by these aliens but also altered by the machine components they implanted in her body. Seven especially points to the constructedness of race, as she is born human, made into a Borg, and then re-humanized while retaining some Borg characteristics.

Through these two women, as well as other aliens on *Star Trek: Voyager,* race is depicted as being about culture and identity. Its constructedness is also presented through special effects. As Neal Baker explains, "For *Star Trek: Voyager,* race is not only about color, it involves foam prosthetics, makeup and dental appliances. The constructedness of race is demonstrated, inscribed as just another special effect" (128). Seven, for example, shows how "white" can be reconstructed as another race through her mechanical appliances. B'Elanna's appearance also reflects her dual heritage. Roxanne Biggs-Dawson, who plays B'Elanna, is Puerto Rican, and her alien ethnic heritage is represented through her natural olive complexion and an added series of ridges on her forehead. The formidable presence of the crests identify her as Klingon. With her dark hair swept severely back and her large bushy eyebrows, B'Elanna's racial mix is physically emphasized. Playing the character with bravado and high energy, Biggs-Dawson emphasizes the torrid and energetic aspects of the character. Frequent angry outbursts toward the captain and her own lover, crew member Tom Paris,[6] exemplify B'Elanna's impetuous nature. These aspects type her as both Klingon and Latina.

Yet there is more to this character than stereotype. Rather than reproducing a simplistic identity politics, the show reflects a new sensibility in American society, shown in part by increased interest and awareness of multiracialism (represented by the call for a multiracial box on the next census, for example). *Star Trek: Voyager's* biracial female characters reveal that racial identity is complex and fluid, for B'Elanna and Seven struggle and change their sense of themselves as raced individuals. In both cases, biraciality is presented as a positive attribute. As viewers observe the play with ideas of race in the series, we must confront our own assumptions about race. When Janeway, B'Elanna, and Seven confront their own raced-ness, the viewers, too, must acknowledge their participation in the creation and re-creation of race.

Because she is played by Jeri Ryan, a blonde actress of European American descent, Seven's mulatta identity requires some discussion. Especially when compared to B'Elanna, Seven's "make-up" underscores the artificial, performative aspect of race identity. While Ryan is a model-perfect beauty and is presented as desirable, her upbringing by the Borg separates her inexorably from the other human crew members, with the possible exception of Janeway. The signifiers of her difference are the machine components visible on her face and hand, but the cultural difference is even more powerful and alienating. Seven's beliefs, values, and behavior make her uncomfortable company for the other crew members. Though she desires to be accepted, she cannot master the nuances of human culture. One recent episode, "Someone to Watch Over You," has the doctor character, himself a hologram, a computer construct, endeavoring to teach Seven how to "date." The doctor demonstrates his humanity by falling in love with Seven, but she is unable to reciprocate and abandons her "relationship lessons." Although Seven is colored "white," her culture makes her a classic science-fiction mulatta. That the machine parts were added biologically and through conditioning make her constructedness clear. Not merely a white sex symbol, then, Seven's biracial composition as human-machine hybrid and cultural outsider make it difficult for the viewer to maintain a sense of her as only an object of sexual desire.

In a different but parallel fashion, B'Elanna also represents the mulatta. In "Creole Identity Politics, Race and *Star Trek: Voyager*," Neal Baker explores how B'Elanna exemplifies a science-fiction version of "an individuated, French Caribbean identity in terms of hybridity and multiculturalism" (119). Baker's insightful analysis of B'Elanna's Creoleness demonstrates how hybridization is promoted through her character, yet he does not mention her gender, which is surely a crucial aspect of her character. That B'Elanna and Seven are raced *females* is critical to understanding the complex depiction of race, gender, and science that the show offers. These two characters function in this science fiction program, as Valerie Smith says the black woman does in literature, "as the locus where gender-, class-, and race-based oppression intersect" (44).

Comparing the female characters' depiction to the role of women in traditional science reveals their centrality to a critique of modern science and its exclusion of women. On the vessel *Voyager,* this critique focuses in part on the complex web of hierarchy and status in scientific institutions, indicated in part by characters' names and positions. I use B'Elanna and Seven's first names because that is how they are referred to in the series; this familiarity is part of the crew's intimacy and the demystification of the scientist. In contrast to other television and film depictions of the scientist, on *Star Trek: Voyager* we see the conflicts, doubts, indecision, and quarrels of scientists. Furthermore, the series focuses primarily on female scientists. The ship's doctor is a hologram, a computer projection that lacks legitimacy and power because he is only a program; his marginality is reflected in his lack of a name. The Vulcan, Tuvok, functions as chief security officer, not scientist, despite his high intellect and the fact that fans may expect him to be invested in science through his connection by heritage to the original *Star Trek's* Mr. Spock. That leaves the discussion of science to Janeway, B'Elanna, and Seven. While B'Elanna and Seven are the most accomplished practitioners of science on *Voyager*, neither has a university degree or the hierarchical status of "doctor." Both, then, exemplify the position of contemporary women in America, who are still a minority among scientists and who occupy a disproportionate number of support staff positions. Outsiders in the tradition of Barbara McClintock, the Nobel Prize–winner who was for decades ignored by the scientific establishment because of her unorthodox methods, both B'Elanna and Seven have to fight to have their voices heard.

When you compare Janeway to a rare portrayal of a female scientist in a mainstream movie, *Contact's* Ellie Arroway, Janeway's subversiveness becomes clearer. The few depictions of female scientists in television or film deal with European American characters and their struggle against male dominance, omitting any overt mention of race. In *Contact,* for example, a white female astronomer has spent years searching for signs of extraterrestrial life. When she finally hears the first signals from aliens, she and her coworkers contact other scientists around the world and release the information. Ellie has the racial privilege to earn respect enough to keep her lab until this point and, as a woman, sees science as collaboration. In contrast, her white male boss, who co-opts the project and the credit for discovering the signals, sees science as a means to power and for domination. He represents the greed of the white male scientific establishment in charge of grants and awarding credit for scientific discoveries. Because of his age and gender, her male boss is able to disenfranchise Ellie, and only the intervention of a powerful and incredibly wealthy magnate (also white and male) gives Ellie a chance to communicate with the aliens. The film presents the older scientist's gendered and racialized greedy individualism as corrupt, and justice prevails when he is killed by a terrorist (arguably a stand-in for racial Otherness). But while Ellie's pure-minded attachment to the truth is presented as admirable, the world is still not ready for her unflinching description of her experience with the aliens. Through the conflict between Ellie and her older male boss, *Contact* provides an example of how science can be practiced differently; the film associates scientific passion and purity with a female character. Ellie's search for the aliens parallels the passion evinced by Janeway, B'Elanna, and Seven, but unlike *Star Trek: Voyager, Contact* has no space for a raced female body.

Some explanation of "pure science" is necessary to understand Janeway, B'Elanna, and Seven's positions on science. In *Contact,* Ellie demonstrates a passionate commitment to the truth and faith in Others, the unknown aliens who have sent a series of plans to the human race. When Ellie faces objection to building the alien installation based on a perceived threat, she insists it be done because she values exploration and contact with aliens for their own sake.[7] At great cost to her relationships and to her financial and professional status, she chooses to single-mindedly pursue contact with aliens. That the aliens appear to her in the guise of her long-dead and beloved father reinforces the sense of personal connection that her scientific quest typifies. These qualities all represent "pure science," that is, not only science for its own sake, knowledge for its own sake, at any cost, but also science that stresses connection to others and desire for the Other. In Ellie's striving for "pure science," *Contact* exemplifies an issue that the female scientists on *Voyager* confront. In this way, Ellie from *Contact* prepares for the depiction of the more diverse female scientists in *Star Trek: Voyager;* the character of Ellie illuminates Janeway's, B'Elanna's, and Seven's struggles.

Star Trek: Voyager expands on *Contact*'s vision of the female scientist by presenting not just one exceptional woman but several, and they are not exclusively white. *Star Trek: Voyager*'s presentation of science as a worthwhile enterprise, one practiced by racially diverse women, affects how we look at science. Repeatedly through the series, conflicts between scientists generate the action. Problematizing the practice of science in this way demystifies its purported neutrality and objectivity. *Star Trek: Voyager* shows that science is affected by the race and gender of the scientist, leading to moral conflicts and dilemmas. But while *Contact* is set in contemporary America and is limited by its realistic setting, *Star Trek: Voyager,* set in a science fiction future, can imagine centuries ahead where diverse women can be leading scientists, and where contact with alien life raises issues of race as well as gender.

I discuss B'Elanna here as a scientist, a title I think she has earned, though others might dismiss her as a mere engineer, like Scotty in classic *Trek.* But part of the revaluation of science by feminists has included a rejection of the split between "pure" (theoretical) scientists and "mere" (practical) engineers. Sandra Harding, for example, criticizes the separation between "pure scientific work and the work of technology and applied science" (2). As the episodes I will presently discuss show, B'Elanna, Seven, and Janeway all blur the distinction between theoretical science and its practical applications, and the characters all take responsibility for their scientific work. In particular, because *Voyager* is stranded in the Delta Quadrant, far from any Starfleet help, Janeway, B'Elanna, and Seven operate independently and must do research in order to help the ship and its crew survive.

While Gene Roddenberry wanted a female in a command role in *Star Trek* from the very beginning, it took two decades of reassessment of science before a woman could be presented as a captain and scientist. Significantly, Kathryn Janeway is not alone on Voyager but has the help most particularly of B'Elanna and, more recently, Seven. The inclusion of B'Elanna and Seven makes for a more well-rounded depiction of women scientists, from three different racial backgrounds. While Janeway represents a captain steeped in white masculine Starfleet tradition and order, B'Elanna has rejected the hierarchy of Starfleet. Because the Federation and Starfleet (like the U.S. government and army) are dominated by white men, Janeway's position and racial heritage associate her with whiteness. B'Elanna's Klingon heritage and her former position as terrorist identifies her as outsider/Other, as does Seven's half-Borg quality. Since the Borg are the Federation's main enemy, Seven is not only a racial but also a political outsider like B'Elanna. Race, in this context, can determine political affiliation, and it does present loyalty problems for both characters. Significantly, both reject their organizations, the Borg and the Maquis, to belong to Starfleet and the Federation, which are racially diverse.

Though B'Elanna attended Starfleet Academy, she found its regulations irksome and joined the terrorist Maquis. The Maquis ship was transported by an alien to the Delta Quadrant, and *Voyager* followed. In the ensuing conflict, the Maquis ship was destroyed and the mysterious alien died, stranding both Maquis and Starfleet personnel seventy-five light-years from home. The two crews merged on *Voyager,* with the Maquis pledging to follow Starfleet protocol and command structure.

B'Elanna's considerable engineering expertise and scientific flair make her a natural for the position of chief engineer, but her resistance to hierarchy places her and the captain in innumerable conflicts. The tension between Starfleet's hierarchy and order and the Maquis's idealism and individuality is exacerbated by an internal conflict within B'Elanna's dual heritage. In "Faces," an episode from the first season, this conflict is externalized when B'Elanna (like Captain Kirk in classic *Trek's* "The Enemy Within")[8] is literally split into two people— one her timid human self, the other a violent Klingon. This "racial" divide appears also within her human heritage: as her last name indicates, B'Elanna Torres is Latina. B'Elanna, then, is "othered" both by her mixed heritage and her human ethnicity. So far, however, in plots, her racial identity has been presented through her bispecies alienness rather than her human ethnicity. But her appearance is markedly ethnic and alien.

B'Elanna's tendency toward violence and aggression and her warlike orientation are depicted as stemming from her Klingon heritage; they are presented as racialized masculine cultural characteristics that are valuable but that must be kept under tight control by B'Elanna herself or by the captain if B'Elanna oversteps her bounds. The Klingon side of B'Elanna is what has made her such a successful fighter and terrorist because she can harness these energies through her technological expertise. Through B'Elanna, the series presents the violent use of technology as an aspect of science: science can be a formidable tool, but it can also be a destructive power if not controlled. In her practice of science, B'Elanna points to a binary tension in her embodiment of race; however, this tension appears also in her gendering as she struggles to find and reconcile a feminine side with what is traditionally considered masculine—Klingon culture and the culture of science. As a member of the Maquis, B'Elanna has used her scientific expertise to kill in a conflict between races; as a woman, B'Elanna uses her scientific expertise to create a life form that she must destroy. In its exploration of these conflicts, the episode "Dreadnought" typifies the way that gender, race, and science are depicted in *Star Trek: Voyager*.

In "Dreadnought," *Voyager* encounters a "self-guided tactical missile" that is "adaptable, evasive, [and] armed with defensive capabilities." The captain assumes that the missile has been created by a traitor named Seska, but B'Elanna acknowledges her responsibility for the missile, called Dreadnought. Originally a Cardassian weapon, Dreadnought had been reprogrammed by B'Elanna with "one of the most sophisticated computer systems." Like *Voyager*, Dreadnought is lost in the Delta Quadrant, but in its attempt to make sense of its new surroundings, the missile has misinterpreted its location and behaves as though *Voyager* and local planets are the enemy. On its way to destroy planets and kill millions of people, Dreadnought must be stopped by the crew of *Voyager*; they struggle to dissuade and then disarm it. Because she created the missile, the responsibility is primarily B'Elanna's.

Race plays a central role in the creation and disarmament of Dreadnought. It was originally created by the Cardassians to expand their evil empire, then it was turned by B'Elanna, at that time a member of the Maquis, as a weapon against the Cardassians. Like B'Elanna herself, Dreadnought wrestles with questions of racial identity and loyalty. In its original incarnation, the vessel spoke with a Cardassian voice; when she reprogrammed it, B'Elanna gave Dreadnought her own voice. This literal echo reveals how the missile itself represents a struggle within B'Elanna. As she argues with Dreadnought, she is arguing with herself, in her own voice (and, at the same time, with her scientific acumen, which created a sentient machine). As B'Elanna explains to the captain, speaking of her reprogramming of Dreadnought, "Hell . . . I changed its identity." But she might as well be speaking of her own identity, from Klingon to human, from Maquis to Starfleet, from terrorist to scientist. As B'Elanna attempts to persuade Dreadnought that the Federation is no longer the enemy, that the planet Dreadnought has targeted contains innocent civilians, B'Elanna reenacts her own conversion process and her own internal struggle about loyalty and identity. While the missile seems to have an almost organic, preordained commitment to destruction, B'Elanna demonstrates that nonmorphological racial characteristics are qualities that are choices, not predetermined aspects. Unlike a machine, even an intelligent, self-aware machine, humans are not bound by their programming or controlled by their racial identities. When B'Elanna succeeds in destroying Dreadnought, she metaphorically destroys the prescribed mulatta fear that she is trapped by her racial duality. Significantly, it is after this episode that she journeys to the holodeck (a computer-controlled holographic playroom) to experience Klingon rituals and explore more fully her Klingon heritage. Since the holodeck is a simulation created and run by B'Elanna, these experiences, too, highlight the constructedness of race. In the holodeck, the player creates or recreates race and culture, interacting not with real people but simulations. Moreover, in confronting her Klingonness, B'Elanna metaphorically explores her gender, for it is the Klingon side that represents her masculine, aggressive, and warlike aspects.

In the aforementioned article exploring B'Elanna's "Creoleness," Baker argues that "Dreadnought" (in contrast to "Faces") deals ambiguously with B'Elanna's integration of her Klingon and human selves. But when you look at the progression of B'Elanna's character throughout the series, she appears to be working toward further integration of her Maquis past and her Klingon heritage. Using the holodeck to explore Klingon ritual is another example of how science fiction devices emphasize the constructedness of race/culture. B'Elanna literally plays with race. On the holodeck, B'Elanna controls the rituals (which involve fighting with deadly weapons). She can freeze the program, stop it, and resume it at will. She can thus safely explore Klingon culture and even invite others, such as her white lover Tom Paris, to participate, where such racial and gendered mingling would not be permitted by other Klingons. Klingon males have an extended and gender-segregated series of rituals and conflicts, so by including Tom, B'Elanna again transgresses race and gender boundaries in the utopian space aboard *Voyager.*

For B'Elanna, the issue of control emerges not only in terms of understanding and managing a biracial and bi-gendered heritage, but also in terms of understanding and managing science and technology from this hybrid perspective. Dreadnought exemplifies technology run amok, turned not once but twice from its intended purpose. The Klingon embrace of war manifests itself in B'Elanna's embrace of terrorism and her use of her scientific knowledge and engineering expertise in the service of war. Yet, now aboard *Voyager,* B'Elanna rejects a totalizing position; she will not use her knowledge of science to destroy others. Faced with Dreadnought again, B'Elanna berates her Maquis self: "I was so sure that I had thought of every possibility"; and she accepts responsibility for the weapon. "If anything happens, it's my fault," she acknowledges. In its dreadful specter of entire planets being annihilated, the episode warns of the dangers of technology and shows how humans cannot think of "every possibility." While science provides the answer and B'Elanna succeeds in undoing the damage she has caused, the episode calls for caution in the creation of new technologies.

It does so in part through the metaphor of mothering, a twist on masculine associations of science and technology. The parallel is established in the opening sequence, in which the doctor examines a pregnant ensign and discusses with her the choice of a name for the child she will soon bear. Then, small fragments of a destroyed ship are discovered, and Dreadnought appears. The juxtaposition of these scenes emphasizes how B'Elanna created new life when she reprogrammed Dreadnought, giving it a new identity, new voice, and new mission. Their conversations parody that of a mother to her child, such as when, for example, B'Elanna wishes Dreadnought "sweet dreams." And, as part of its education process, Dreadnought used to play games with B'Elanna. Furthermore, like a mother, in one scene B'Elanna laments to Dreadnought, "I'm hurt you don't trust me." In addition, the mother–daughter parallel is reinforced by Captain Janeway's relationship with *Voyager*. As B'Elanna prepares to die with Dreadnought if necessary, Janeway does the same with *Voyager*. If Dreadnought cannot be stopped, Janeway plans to put *Voyager* in its path, sacrificing the ship and herself to save the lives of billions on the threatened planets. While her behavior is traditionally expected of a captain, it is complicated by the femaleness of the captain and the femininity of the ship. Janeway orders the crew to evacuate *Voyager* and engages in conversation with the ship, which (like Dreadnought) speaks in a female voice. Unlike other *Star Trek* series, *Star Trek: Voyager* depicts the struggle with technology as a female struggle. Its successful resolution, then, validates an integrated, connected approach to keeping technology under control. This episode typifies a feminist approach to science, characterized by Evelyn Fox Keller, in the title of her book on Barbara McClintock, as "a feeling for the organism." In this episode, a feminine alternative to traditional, masculine, hierarchical science triumphs, leading to the survival of the crew and the ship.

What "Dreadnought" shows, then, is that it is possible to integrate the binaries of biracial and bi-gender identity through the aegis of science, which provides a space to explore and enact complex and contradictory aspects of race and gender. Through her control of the missile and its destruction, B'Elanna shows that women have the right and power to control their creations. Through her acceptance and integration of her Klingon and human selves, B'Elanna reveals that a biracial/bicultural identity need not lead to tragedy, as it does in the figure of the tragic mulatta. Significantly, B'Elanna achieves this resolution through the support of Captain Janeway, suggesting also that women should look to other women for assistance in working through issues of race, gender, and science.

In the first years of the series, B'Elanna and the captain struggle together repeatedly with scientific ethics, and they confront the race and gender issues brought up by these conflicts. More recently, this pattern has been reinforced

Captain Janeway and B'Elanna Torres consider their options in "Dreadnought."

through another female character, Seven of Nine. This half-human, half-Borg character, whose name alone indicates her "racial" separation, was assimilated by the Borg. Her name was changed from "Annika" to Seven of Nine, the latter a designation rather than a name. The change can be read as an allusion to the alteration in a woman's name as she adopts her husband's surname. Seven's nomenclature sets her apart from the rest of the crew of *Voyager,* all of whom, even the most alien, have names rather than number designations. Captured as a young girl, Seven has been turned into a machine, a cog in a huge collective consciousness. In other Star Trek series and in *Star Trek: Voyager,* the Borg have been depicted as an apocalyptic threat not only to humans but also to all organic life. When they encounter an organic species whom they consider inferior, the Borg fit the organic beings with machine parts, making them Borg. In *Star Trek: The Next Generation,* the Borg have been shown as male, but in one of the more recent films, *First Contact,* it was revealed that the Borg, as befits their hive mentality, are ruled by a queen. Bernardi reads the Borg as a "multiracial mass" that "threatens [the Federation's] all-too-white heroes" (87–88). While I agree with this reading, it is surely also significant that the Borg represent a feminine collective consciousness that threatens the very masculine individuality represented by Captain Picard and the predominantly male Starfleet hierarchy. That this feminine entity's science is superior to the Federation's is part of what makes the Borg so alien and powerful. Their "race" is partly feminine, a long-standing trope in science fiction, where, as Sam Moskowitz has commented "a male and a female are two completely different species" (90; see also Roberts, *Sexual,* 40–64).

The Borg's gender and race identity is complicated. Because they assimilate other species, they are in a sense hybrid, obtaining knowledge and experience from thousands of organic life forms. However, they are colonizers, taking knowledge and forcing the beings into a Borg mold (literally). The Borg emphasize the construction of race because they literally construct other races as their own, a classic assimilation model. Because they form a collective, they represent a feminine mass that threatens Western notions of the individual, who is putatively masculine. In the terms of Carol Gilligan and Blythe Clinchy, among others, women's psychology is marked by our emphasis on connection and relationship, while men's psychology emphasizes separation and individual achievement. Only in science fiction can psychological aspects of gender be embodied, through aliens. While the association of aliens with racial difference is more overt, the parallel to gender is also a recurrent theme in science fiction (Roberts, *New Species*). That the Borg ship is womblike, with individual Borg created in bins, reinforces its feminine aspect. But in its emphasis on machines, the Borg represent logic and the mechanical, which in Western society are seen as masculine. Seven of Nine, however, emphasizes the feminine side of the Borg; first, in her own biology, which is decidedly female, and, second, in her struggle with her mulatta status.

Seven of Nine is the first female Borg to be shown at length in *Star Trek*. Rescued by the crew of *Voyager*, she is deprogrammed against her will. As the series proceeds, Seven wrestles with what it means to be human. While the doctor has removed almost all of the Borg implants and she looks more human, Seven must still regenerate nightly in a Borg alcove in the ship's bowels. Alienated from the rest of the crew, Seven engages in frequent conflicts with Janeway. While her mentality is alien, the captain and crew rely on Seven for her scientific knowledge, gained from the collective consciousness of the Borg. Because of the Borg's superior technology and scientific advances, and through her retention of Borg science, Seven is the preeminent scientist aboard *Voyager*. In this regard, race is again inverted from its associations in contemporary science. While science and scientists are primarily white men in America in the 1990s, it is the raced female alien who is the outstanding scientist in *Voyager*'s twenty-fourth century. Not merely a data bank, Seven is presented as a passionate character who struggles with scientific ethics and racial and cultural conflict.

As briefly discussed at the beginning of this chapter, Seven's appearance emphasizes her racial difference. When we first see her in "The Gift," she appears more machine than human. Clad in metallic gray, she lacks hair, and one arm and one eye have been replaced with mechanical implants. Briefly, the camera looks from her perspective and we see the human crew of Voyager, wavering, out of focus, small. Detached from the Borg, Seven demands to be returned to the hive. Janeway refuses because the Borg would then assimilate the entire crew. Instead she offers Seven her humanity, which Seven rejects. Yet as Borg components are removed, Seven's humanity visually reasserts itself. Her human immune system regenerates, and, with the doctor's help, she grows hair, has her metallic eye replaced with a human-looking one; she even sports high heels and a form-fitting uniform that reveals her to be very mammalian. Furthermore, Seven has stereotypical European features and blond hair. Extremely attractive by contemporary standards that clearly hold in the Trek future, she soon has male crew members, especially Tom Paris and Asian American Ensign Harry Kim, gazing at her covetously.

Yet Seven remains alien, not accepting her humanness. Because she was assimilated at an early age, she has few social skills and no human cultural knowledge. Like B'Elanna, she remains a mixture, both literally (as part of her physiology remains Borg) and psychologically (as she struggles with human culture). Like B'Elanna, Seven engages in disputes with Janeway, especially in the area of science, revealing conflicts about ethics and morality. In her body, as the doctor notes, Seven reflects a struggle within human society. "A battle is being waged inside her body between the biological and the technological," the doctor explains as he attempts to reverse her Borg assimilation. In this character, race (through species) is used as a metaphor for conflict.

"The Omega Directive" is just one of many episodes that directly illustrates the intersection of science, gender, and race, yet it is significant in its focus on

Seven's relationship to this intersection. The title refers to a top-secret directive given to all Starfleet captains. A dangerous particle, the Omega, has the ability to destroy the very fabric of space, making warp drive impossible. The particle represents "a threat not only to the Federation but to the entire galaxy," and it is "the most powerful substance known to exist." All Starfleet captains are under orders to destroy any particles they encounter during their travels. Sworn to secrecy, Janeway at first tells no one except Seven, who knows of the particle's existence from Starfleet captains who have been absorbed by the Borg.

Bound by her orders, Janeway intends to destroy the particle, created by alien scientists to solve their planet's energy shortage. Seven, on the other hand, wants to preserve and study the particles, like Ellie in *Contact* wants to meet the aliens. Their difference is presented as a cultural disagreement. Seven criticizes Janeway's "ignorance and fear," arguing that the particle should "be harnessed, not destroyed." The captain expresses surprise at Seven's attitude, saying, "I didn't realize you had such a strong scientific curiosity." Those are terms that Janeway can recognize, but Seven asserts her difference in terms of Borg culture. Seven describes her interest in the Omega particle as "not curiosity" but "desire," explaining that "Omega is infinitely complex yet harmonious. To the Borg it represents perfection. I wish to understand that perfection." Seven's desire to view the Omega particle is unlike that of her Borg family, who wish to harness the particle as a weapon. Rather than domination, the feminized, biracial Seven seeks communion with the Other.

As in *Contact,* pure science is here depicted as a desire to observe and understand, despite considerable risk to self and others. But the Borg continually capture other species' technology, the better to continue their mission of domination and absorption of other, "imperfect" species. So Seven's "pure science" is mediated by the Borg tradition. They have obtained their scientific advances at great cost to other species and to themselves. Seven's position, then, is closer to the white male corporate executive's position in *Aliens;* he is on a secret mission to capture a deadly alien for its potential profit as a weapon of war.[9] Ripley, the film's female hero, on the other hand, calls for the destruction of the aliens, just as Janeway calls for the destruction of the Omega particle. Seven's and Janeway's arguments about scientific ethics thus raise the issue of how science can be used to dominate other groups.

If Seven represents pure scientific desire, Captain Janeway represents caution and curbs on science. Janeway says, "I now know how Einstein must have felt about the atom bomb or Marcus when she developed the Genesis device [reference to a female scientist from *Star Trek II: The Wrath of Khan*]. They watched helplessly as science took a destructive course. But I have a chance to prevent that from happening." Tuvok, her Vulcan chief of security, laments, "It's unfortunate we cannot study this phenomenon in more detail. We may not get another chance." Janeway responds, "Let's hope we never do," which prompts Tuvok to comment, dryly, "a curious statement for a woman of science." Janeway explains, "I'm also a woman who occasionally knows when to quit." She refuses to endanger the quadrant to study the particle, saying that to do so would be "arrogant and . . . irresponsible." Another alien outsider, Tuvok, presents the view already articulated by Seven, the position of pure science, unfettered by responsibility to others. This position is raced and gendered because it is presented as the Borg perspective—the Borg adopt this attitude as part of their complete lack of empathy or connection to others. From the perspective of psychology, the Borg represent a quality considered masculine, that of detachment and hyper-rationality.

Having Tuvok support Seven's interest in studying the Omega particle reinforces the racial aspect of this scientific conflict. From classic *Trek* on, Vulcans have been depicted as the Other—cold, dispassionate, and powerful. Furthermore, in the exclusive case of *Star Trek: Voyager*, the Vulcan is played by an African American actor. Having Seven present the case primarily, however, alters the reading from one of cultural difference alone. Because two female characters disagree about scientific ethics, the episode shows how cultural difference can divide women. Yet in the episode's resolution, the show suggests that even though two women may disagree radically, they can still work together and practice safe, effective science. In their feminist approaches to science, Seven and Janeway represent two positions: the former suggesting that feminist science would be practiced more purely, more perfectly, without masculine bias; and the latter, Janeway's position, arguing that the effects of science must be considered, that science cannot be isolated from its consequences. A compromise is achieved, suggesting that both feminist positions are valid and compatible.

Seven's attitude reflects the Borg willingness to sacrifice drones in the pursuit of any cause. Janeway represents a more feminist, site-specific response; she acts in terms of connection when, unlike Seven, she considers who would be affected by her decision to study the particle. In this regard Janeway enacts a feminine response as described by Carol Gilligan, an ethic of concern. Yet Janeway authorizes Seven to proceed with the construction of a chamber that might preserve Omega particles. Both women end up achieving what they desire. Seven captures the particle and, for 3.2 seconds, sees its perfection. Janeway orders the chamber destroyed, the particles are eradicated, and space is preserved. Together, the two reflect on the experience, with Seven entering a holodeck simulation of Leonardo da Vinci's studio that the captain uses in times of stress. The camera angle presents the two as equals. They sit down next to each other, eye to eye. In so doing, they represent the rapprochement of two different approaches to science. Their dialogue and ability to work together despite their cultural differences reflects how science can provide a nexus to negotiate, especially for women.

Star Trek: Voyager's triangular engagement with science, race, and gender emblematizes humanity's future. Through its futuristic setting, the series implies that it is race, gender, and science that should concern us now. W. E. B. Du Bois said that the color line would be *the* problem of the twentieth century, but *Star*

With Janeway's help, Seven studies perfection in "The Omega Directive."

Trek: Voyager demonstrates that it is the intersection of science, race, and gender that humans will have to continue to struggle with, even in the twenty-fourth century. While the show does not present a blueprint of how this intersection should be negotiated, *Star Trek: Voyager* creates a possible nexus in a space for diversely raced female characters to practice science. In this representation, the show is ground-breaking, and, in its optimistic representation of conflict resolution, *Star Trek: Voyager* suggests that women scientists, working together, can overcome the barriers created by race. In this regard, the series succeeds in "going boldly where no one has gone before."

NOTES

1. One of the last bastions of male dominance, and perhaps the most resistant to change, science is still primarily defined and populated by men. In 1992 women still received less than one-sixth of the bachelor's degrees in science. Although women have been earning a majority of all bachelor's degrees since 1983, we approach parity with men only in the biosciences. Women are much less likely to be funded in graduate school than their male counterparts, less likely to be awarded federal money, and more likely to have teaching assistantships rather than the more prestigious research fellowships (Schmittroth, 236, 247, 476, 576, 586).

2. *Voyager* has been sent to this remote part of space by an immensely powerful male alien who parallels the rich industrialist who helps Ellie in *Contact*. Both male figures enable women to leave normal space, and there the female characters are (perhaps ironically) freer from patriarchal constraints.

3. See Bernardi's discussion of race in *Star Trek: The Next Generation* and my discussion of gender and race in *Sexual Generations: Star Trek: The Next Generation and Gender.* In general, *The Next Generation* reflects a 1980s Reaganesque position in which racial inequities have been rectified.

4. For a comparison, see my discussion of the mulatta in *Star Trek: The Next Generation* in *Sexual Generations*. The figure there is far less powerful than in *Star Trek: Voyager*.

5. I am indebted to Jennifer Jones for this formulation.

6. When they are both transformed into aliens in another episode, the captain and Paris become "lovers" who reproduce a brood of young on an alien planet. This brief affair provides another connection between the captain and B'Elanna: their mutual lover, Paris.

7. While the aliens appear to her in the guise of her father, this manifestation is presented as a way to communicate and earn her trust. Although not a scientist himself, Ellie's father had encouraged her interest in the stars, and he presents an alternative to the evil patriarchs.

8. See Elyce Rae Helford's "A Part of Myself No Man Should Ever See: Reading Captain Kirk's Multiple Masculinities" for a perceptive analysis of this episode. Kirk's struggle with gender as discussed by Helford provides a model for B'Elanna's and Seven of Nine's struggles with gender and race.

9. I am indebted to Angeletta Gourdine for this formulation and many helpful suggestions as I revised this essay.

WORKS CITED

Baker, Neal. "Creole Identity Politics, Race, and *Star Trek: Voyager*." In *Into Darkness Peering: Race and Color in the Fantastic*. Edited by Elisabeth Anne Leonard. Westport, Conn.: Greenwood, 1997, 119–130.

Bentley, Nancy. "White Slaves: The Mulatto Hero in Antebellum Fiction." In *Subjects and Citizens: Nation, Race and Gender from Oroonoko to Anita Hill*. Edited by Michael Morrit and Cathy N. Davidson. Durham: University of North Carolina Press, 1996.

Bernardi, Daniel. *Star Trek and History: Race-ing toward a White Future*. New Brunswick: Rutgers, 1998.

Boyd, Robert S. "Science Rejecting Notion of Genetic Race." *The Baton Rouge Sunday Advocate,* 13 October 1996, 8A.

Butler, Judith. *Gender Trouble: Feminism and the Subversion of Identity.* New York: Routledge, 1990.

Clinchy, Blythe McVicker, et al. *Women's Ways of Knowing*. New York: Basic Books, 1997.

Fields, Barbara Jeanne. "Slavery, Race and Ideology in the United States of America." *New Left Review* 181 (1990): 95–118.

Gilligan, Carol. *In a Different Voice: Psychological Theory and Women's Development*. Cambridge: Harvard University Press, 1993.

Gould, Stephen Jay. *The Mismeasure of Man*. New York: Norton, 1981.

Haraway, Donna. *Primate Visions: Gender, Race and Nature in the World of Modern Science*. New York: Routledge, 1989.

Harding, Sandra. *Whose Science? Whose Knowledge?: Thinking from Women's Lives*. Ithaca, N.Y.: Cornell University Press, 1991.

Helford, Elyce Rae. "A Part of Myself No Man Should Ever See: Reading Captain Kirk's Multiple Masculinities." In *Enterprise Zones: Critical Positions on Star Trek*. Edited by Harrison Taylor, Sarah Projansky, Kent A. Ono, and Elyce Rae Helford. Boulder, Colo.: Westview, 1996, 10–32.

Keller, Evelyn Fox. *A Feeling for the Organism: The Life and Work of Barbara McClintock.* San Francisco: W. H. Freeman, 1993.

———. ed. *Feminism and Science.* Oxford: Oxford University Press, 1996.

Moskowitz, Sam. *Strange Horizons.* New York: Scribner's, 1976.

Roberts, Robin. *A New Species: Gender and Science in Science Fiction.* Urbana: University of Illinois Press, 1993.

———. *Sexual Generations: Star Trek: The Next Generation and Gender.* Urbana: University of Illinois Press, 1999.

Smith, Valerie. "Black Feminist Theory and the Representation of the Other." In *Changing Our Own Words.* Edited by Cheryl Wall. New Brunswick: Rutgers, 1991.

Wilcox, Clyde. "To Boldly Go Where Others Have Gone Before: Cultural Change in the Old and New Star Treks." *Extrapolation* 33, no. 1 (1992): 88–100.

10

The Construction of Feminine Identity in *Babylon 5*

Sharon Ney and Elaine M. Sciog-Lazarov

Babylon 5 speaks to us in many voices. It speaks to us in the voices of parents and children, of lost souls and prophets, of the wicked and the good. It even speaks to us in the voice of an ersatz God the Father Who ponders aloud which came first, the thought or the word. But first and foremost, *Babylon 5* speaks to us in the voices of men and women. More often than not, these voices do not offer us answers or solutions; rather, they ask us questions, and the questions are always the same. Who are you? What do you want? Where are you going? Why are you here? In the final episode, "Sleeping in Light," the immortal Lorien, first of all sentient beings, asks these four questions directly of the series' hero, John Sheridan. The latter's answer—"There's so much I still don't understand"— could be the cry of the viewer as much as of the character.

Understanding *Babylon 5* is a far from simple endeavor. The core events of the show take place during a five-year glimpse into the lives of the people inhabiting the eponymous space station between the years 2258 and 2262, with a prologue set in 2257 and an epilogue set in 2281. Its overarching tale of the "Shadow War" is a Jungian archetypal myth that pits patriarchal "order" in a cyclical struggle with "chaos" (Lang, 28–38). This age-old conflict between two elder races, the Vorlons (order) and the Shadows (chaos), provides the main impetus for story lines that seem to divide and multiply endlessly and range from hero quests, war stories, and political fables to melodramas and romances.

The choice of the biblical Babylon as the name of and the metaphor for this mythical struggle is particularly apt. Babylon was the center of the ancient world, as well as its source of confusion and "many tongues." It serves as both an icon of *heteroglossia* and the unifying symbol of a drama that its creator claims traffics unashamedly in "a hodge-podge of philosophical positions, biblical allusions, Jungian archetypes, hero-myth, Greek tragedy, socio-political extrapolation, comparative religions, [and] literary metaphor" (Straczynski, 22–23). At yet another level, Babylon means "The Gate of God." It is the way through which we pass and the way through which we ascend to the next level of existence. Like the biblical civilization, which God cast down for trying to rival Him, Babylon 5, the UN-like space station, suffers a similar fate before rising to new heights. As revealed in "Sleeping in Light," the story is told as a documentary after the facts, based on the records of those who lived them; and in retrospect the protagonists attain mythological status while the station itself becomes a character that paradoxically occupies a place that is both in the center and on the periphery. Babylon 5 is a trading nexus, a melting pot, and a meeting place, yet it resides in a barren solar system at the borders of all races. It is a place of communication and, in time, the source of the breakdown of communications. Anything can happen on Babylon 5. Normal rules collapse, power is up for grabs, and the fabric of social relations is malleable. Through its location on the borderlands of physical space and society, it becomes a place where culture is remade from an inert object into something under challenge, under the gun (Ortner, 181). Here, legends walk as real people among the populace, angels appear, and miracles can happen.

Within this framework, the fundamental questions of *Babylon 5* are bandied about incessantly. The Vorlons ask, "Who are you?" The Shadows ask, "What do you want?" The characters ask both questions of each other and of themselves. Everyone is caught up in the quest for identity and purpose, the same quest that lies at the roots of the feminist project.

Rephrasing this quest in terms of its consequences, Marleen Barr asks: "How can women co-exist with men, retain their female characteristics and function as powerful individuals?" (61). It is a question that reflects a very real concern of the feminist movement and of women in general. The Western cultural bias of casting gendered categories and associated roles and behaviors as binary opposites has routinely placed women on the negative side of the contrast. If men are powerful, women are weak; if men are active, women are passive; if men are dominant, women are subservient; and the social cost to women for escaping these biases is heavy. Inevitably, when women stray into the cultural territory of agency and power that men have staked out for themselves, they are forced to sacrifice aspects of their gendered identity, most notably their sexuality.

In our culture, where power is inexorably gendered, the speculative nature of science fiction can and should be used to project new ways of thinking about these issues. *Babylon 5,* with its strong female protagonists, takes up the challenge and demonstrates that this relentless opposition of power and femininity can be vigorously attacked through aggressive use of female characters in multi-dimensional roles. Though it seldom takes direct aim at the topics of gender identity, gender equality, or the feminist movement, these issues are strongly expressed in the subtext (Gordon, 196), although submerged by the series' aggressively egalitarian milieu. The principal female characters, both human and alien, occupy positions of power or authority or knowledge. Their place beside men as equals, and often as superiors, is accepted as a matter of course, and, superficially at least, their agency and competence are unquestioned. This is also true of the minor characters, whose skill and self-sufficiency create a rich feminist background for the three protagonists we will consider in this analysis.

First we have Commander Susan Ivanova, second in command of the Babylon 5 station, a near caricature of the driven professional woman who locks all intimate relationships out of her life. She answers the question "Who are you?" with the declaration "I am death incarnate." In telepath Lyta Alexander we find a woman who appears to embody an extreme vision of patriarchal objectification, who can only define herself in relation to others, and for whom the integrity of an independent self seems to have no meaning. Ambassador Delenn of the Minbari stands midway between these two extremes. A complex being who is whole in and of herself, she nevertheless chooses to reach out to Captain John Sheridan, seeing the possibility of creating something greater in synthesis with him.

Commander Susan Ivanova, Lyta Alexander, and Ambassador Delenn present us with three startlingly different answers to the question "Who are you?" While there can be no doubt that *Babylon 5* is, at its heart, a patriarchal myth, as are all of our myths, within this framework these three characters remain both powerful and sexual. But the question remains whether their "female characteristics" remain uncompromised, or whether, even in a feminist-oriented fantasy, patriarchal norms continue to thwart feminist aspirations and construct feminine identity.

SUSAN IVANOVA

Who am I? I am Susan Ivanova. Commander. Daughter of Andre and Sophie Ivanov. I am the right hand of vengeance and the boot that is going to kick your sorry ass all the way back to Earth, sweetheart. I am death incarnate, and the last living thing that you are ever going to see. God sent me. ("Between the Darkness and the Light")

Who is Commander Susan Ivanova, what is the source of her power, how did it come to be manifested so negatively, and what are her implications for the expression of gender in *Babylon 5*? Despite the assurance of her pronouncement of who she is, as we follow the story of the Earth Force commander turned rebel leader, we find a character threaded with contradictions. Commander Ivanova is at war with the universe and with herself. On the one hand, in the guise of her professional persona, she appears masculinized and militantly feminist. She is obsessed with control, aggressive, and uncompromising in her goal to pursue fulfillment in her career. On the other hand, as we follow her constantly thwarted pursuit of close personal relationships, we are presented with the portrait of a woman who is ineffective, insecure, and easily swayed by romantic gestures. It is in these excursions into Ivanova's off-duty hours that her feminine qualities surface. The divergence of characterization within two narratives, one heroic and the other romantic, is remarkable and raises issues as to how power and sexuality are gendered in *Babylon 5*.

Power and Patriarchy

Quite early, it is made clear that Commander Ivanova has achieved her professional success by actively rejecting the traditional female roles. Her brother urges her to stay home when she reveals her desire to join the military ("In the Beginning"). Her choice alienates her from her father, and even his deathbed apology, years later, is not enough to make up for his earlier lack of acceptance ("Born to the Purple"). When she astonishes her colleagues with an ex-lover who arrives unexpectedly on the station, determined to renew their affair, we discover that her excursion into a long-term relationship failed when she refused to subordinate her career to her lover's wishes ("The War Prayer").

It is ironic that in rejecting the demands of the men in her life, Ivanova pursues power from within a patriarchally defined military structure—the upper ranks of captains and admirals in *Babylon 5* appear to be an almost exclusively male preserve. Yet at the same time that she pursues power and affirmation within the confines of a male-dominated structure, her need to retain control over her life remains paramount. Her professional relationships with the men who are her superiors are often insubordinate and adversarial. For instance, she simultaneously accepts and rejects Commander Sinclair as a father figure, appreciating his support and advice, but baldly pointing out that she is not obligated to take it ("TKO"). She resists subtle discrimination, demanding and winning the right to lead the station's tactical fighter squadrons ("Believers"). She is also a rebel long before the rebellion begins, rejecting the chain of command (a transparent symbol of male domination) in situations in which she perceives it as an obstacle to her own best interests or her conscience. When she dismisses the crew and arms the station's weapons against the Psi Cop, Bester, to protect herself from discovery as a latent telepath, she turns a deaf ear to Sheridan's order to stand down. He has to talk fast in order to persuade her not to destroy Bester's ship ("Dust to Dust").

Ivanova more successfully subverts the military hierarchy and satisfies her obsession for control through the accumulation and careful dissemination of information. She makes a point of knowing everything that goes on around her. When Sheridan asks her how she knew about the Rangers, a secret "Army of Light" whose purpose is to defeat the Shadows, her response is: "Captain, when something happens on this station and I don't know about it, worry" ("Matters of Honor"). In this one phrase, Ivanova sums up her life and philosophy. Knowledge is the key that enables her to feel in control of any situation, but the information must be provided on her terms, not offered freely. Anyone who gives too much information is to be as mistrusted as those who offer none at all. For example, telepath Harriman Grey's reasons for joining Psi Corps are irrelevant to her and unsought; his offer of information about himself is quickly rejected ("Eyes").

Despite her continual resistance and secret networks, the true source of Ivanova's power and sense of self springs from her acceptance of her place in a patriarchal military structure. When she chooses to follow Sheridan and participate in his secret rebellion, she jeopardizes both. As the rebels encroach on the authority and legitimacy of the military hierarchy, Ivanova becomes more insecure, not knowing where she fits in anymore ("Messages from Earth"). Following Babylon 5's secession from the Shadow-dominated Earth Alliance, her self-assurance slips further when she dreams that she arrives at her duty post naked ("Sic Transit Vir"), but she reaches the nadir of her power when Sheridan's death leaves her in command. She deeply misses Sheridan, who, in her mind, has replaced the brother she lost, and rather than being energized to fight, she faces her greatest crisis and loss of faith in her ability. G'kar, the Narn ambassador aboard Babylon 5, comments:

> It is now seven days since we lost Captain Sheridan and [security officer] Mr. Garibaldi. And in a way I think we have also lost Ivanova. It is as though her heart has been pierced and her spirit has poured out through the wound. ("The Hour of the Wolf")

No other character reveals such vulnerability and insecurity.

Unlike Sheridan, whose power ultimately springs from his belief in himself and in his personal moral choices, Ivanova continuously looks outward for legitimacy—first from the chain of command, and then from Sheridan. While Ivanova reluctantly assumes command of the rebellion, she finds herself unable to appropriate his power for herself. She can only bring herself to pick up the pieces and, by doing so, becomes merely the custodian of his cause: "I wish it didn't have to be like this. What matters now is finishing the work he began. I have to let him go and just get on with the work. I think, I hope, that's what he would have wanted" ("The Hour of the Wolf").

Power and Sexual Ambiguity

Ivanova's masculine and feminine traits are separated and channeled by two intertwined narrative threads, one heroic and the other romantic. In her heroic role, Susan Ivanova is aggressively masculinized. She shows many characteristics typically associated with men. She is most often addressed and referred to in a masculine manner by her last name or title. She is a hard drinker (vodka, in keeping with her Russian parentage), enjoys a bar brawl using fists and bottles, and threatens all and sundry regardless of rank with everything from physical violence to cunning practical jokes ("Babylon Squared," "A Day in the Strife"). While her femininity is compromised in her heroic role, it surfaces in the romantic narrative of her personal life, but in highly trivialized circumstances. Off duty, she exhibits a penchant for feminine frills and jewelry. She is susceptible to her ex-lover's romantic gestures of flowers and an intimate dinner ("The War Prayer"). She enjoys wearing sexy lingerie and is upset with the captain when he barges in on her and fails to notice ("Lines of Communication"). A significant amount of time in one episode is devoted to a remarkable encounter with the recently transformed Delenn. At a loss how to deal with her newly acquired attribute of hair, Delenn shanghais the nonplused commander and presses her into service as a confidante and human beauty consultant ("Soul Mates").

The more Ivanova attempts to control her romances and her surrogate familial bonds with her colleagues, the more "feminized" her personal life becomes and the less mastery she has over her relationships. For example, in "The War Prayer" she succumbs to an ex-lover's overtures only to discover he intended to use her in a terrorist assassination plot. Later, Ivanova requires telepath Talia Winters to remove the pin and gloves that mark her affiliation and loyalty to Psi Corps as a prerequisite to pursuing a romantic relationship ("A Race through Dark Places"). That Ivanova is bisexual could potentially offer a feminist critique of the heterosexual imperative; however, Ivanova is no more successful in her sole lesbian relationship than in her heterosexual ones. For instance, immediately after she and Talia become lovers, Talia is revealed as an unwitting Psi Corps spy ("Divided Loyalties"). By far her most successful relationship is with John Sheridan. But even this safe, fraternal bond eludes her control when Sheridan puts himself in harm's way time and again, beyond her ability to protect him. After he is killed on Z'ha'dum and then miraculously returns from the dead, Ivanova distances herself, wary of being put through another shattering experience and feeling comfortable only when she can relate to him simply as a fellow soldier. In fact, her trust in her ability to control her personal relationships erodes to the point that she requires Sheridan to swear as one professional to another that he will not deprive her of her right to be part of the final battle with the Shadows ("The Long Night").

Susan Ivanova's feminine traits are ruthlessly compartmentalized, then trivialized, and in the process she is stripped of her ability to positively affect events. For example, when Ambassador Delenn asks about the nature of her "odd cramps" ("Soul Mates"), we witness Ivanova's response to a typical feminine encounter. Her embarrassment and unease at being questioned about such an intimate and ultimately feminine biological process is disproportionately acute. In another episode, when being pursued by a "male" alien ambassador, she literally fends him off with a song and dance lampooning sex and human intimacy. Yet, as he leaves the station to return to his home world, the alien promises, "Next time, my way" ("Acts of Sacrifice").

In the end, the only power left to her appears to be the power to withdraw. This process involves shedding her personal relationships, and, since these relationships reside at the heart of her femininity, she discards her outwardly feminine traits as well, becoming, in effect, "desexed." Yet despite her ambiguous view of herself, we are always aware of a powerful sexuality simmering just under the surface. In the universe of *Babylon 5*, where bisexuality is unremarkable, Ivanova is not forced to relinquish her sexuality entirely in order to reject her traditionally feminine aspects.

Death and Love and Ivanova

By severing herself from the personal relationships that harbor the feminine aspects of her identity, Ivanova consciously cuts herself off from the patriarchal fantasy of the romantic heroine, which demands that the heroine's relationship with the hero become the locus of her search for identity (Radway, 139). Ivanova's nonromance with the character Marcus Cole is an extreme example of her rejection of patriarchally defined feminine roles. She tells him time and again that she doesn't know "where he fits" in the scheme of things, by which she means the military chain of command. He in turn portrays his relationship to her in personal terms and produces a chart that places Ivanova in the center of his universe ("Messages from Earth"). As her relationship with Marcus progresses, the traditional romantic roles are inverted. Marcus takes on traits usually reserved for the heroine—passivity and virginity—while Ivanova appropriates heroic agency. By subverting the patriarchal structure in her search for an independent sense of self, her intertwined roles of hero and romantic heroine collapse in on each other, bending traditional gender roles in the process (Gonsalves).

It is Ivanova's fighting ability that stands as the purest, most blatant, most masculine, and most negative expressions of her agency. Commander Sinclair, Security Chief Garibaldi, and Captain Sheridan all take turns actively fighting their enemies, but Ivanova is acknowledged as their premier fighter pilot and leader of offensive missions. She, not Commander Sinclair or Captain Sheridan, is the one most consistently on the front line of battle. She chases raiders and single-handedly destroys a small fleet ("Believers"). She defends the station at the outbreak of the Narn/Centauri War ("Signs and Portents") and when the time comes to secede from the Earth Alliance, it is she who leads the fighter pilots in the battle to defend the station ("Severed Dreams").

All the men in Ivanova's life attempt to stand between her and what appears to them to be her self-made appointment with destruction. She perceives their actions as interference in her right to assert her individuality and control her own life. During the battle in "Severed Dreams," Sheridan orders her to eject from her fighter when it is critically damaged. At first she angrily rejects his order, replying, "I can handle it!" When he insists, she finally obeys, escaping just before the ship crashes. In another episode, Rabbi Koslov comes to her when she fails to return to Earth for her father's funeral and tries to persuade her to sit shiva (to mourn with family and friends). When she refuses, he points out that she cannot reject relationships without suffering the consequences: "You cannot run away from your own heart, Susan," he concludes. "Not even in space" ("TKO"). The theme of "running away" resurfaces when the immortal alien Lorien also advises her to consult her heart. When she responds that her head doesn't talk to her heart anymore, he counsels her to reconsider her decision and points out one of the notable distinctions between the First Ones and the younger races:

> We've lived too long. Seen too much. To live on, as we have, is to leave behind joy and love and companionship because we know it to be transitory. Of the moment. We know it will turn to ash. Only those whose lives are brief can imagine that love is eternal. You should embrace that remarkable illusion. It may be the greatest gift your race has ever received. ("Into the Fire")

Rabbi Koslov and Lorien, both patriarchal figures of immense power and authority, attempt to guide Ivanova onto the path of traditional femininity by encouraging her to embrace the passivity that is at the heart of the romantic experience—that perfect union where the ideal male, who is masculine and strong, yet nurturing, recognizes the intrinsic worth of the heroine, and where she is required to do nothing more than to exist as the center of this paragon's attention (Radway, 97). Very much aware of the self-destructive consequences, Ivanova pursues the only course left open to her in her struggle for an independent identity. After Sheridan is betrayed and captured immediately following the first battle of the Earth Civil War, she assumes the role of the avenger, defeating, then harrying the Earth fleet to destruction ("The Face of the Enemy," "Between the Darkness and the Light"). In doing so, Ivanova consciously adopts the role otherwise reserved for the men in the show: the search for something worth dying for.

In the end, however, her effort to define who she is in her own terms and control her destiny is thwarted. She is mortally injured in the penultimate battle and on the point of death when Marcus Cole discovers the existence on Babylon 5 of a banned alien machine. He rushes to her rescue and uses it to transfer his life force into her ("Endgame"). Upon her recovery, her protestations of grief and love are not nearly so convincing as her impotent rage. By this single act of self-sacrifice he has negated her illusion of control ("Rising Star"). Inevitably, it seems, the patriarchal fantasy of feminine identity is achieved, albeit in a strange and symbolic manner. Though Ivanova resists the patriarchal narrative, in the end she is robbed of agency and made a passive recipient. The transfusion of Marcus's life force has transformed her, and the message has been sent and received: power and agency are masculine prerogatives, and feminine identity can only be achieved through the intervention of men.

LYTA ALEXANDER

Al Bester: The Corps is Mother. The Corps is Father.
Lyta Alexander: In that case, Mr. Bester, I'm an orphan. ("Epiphanies")

Though raised by the Psi Corps, telepath Lyta Alexander uncompromisingly rejects Bester's spurious familial claim when he parrots the Corps' motto. However, despite this repudiation of patriarchal authority, Lyta is the epitome of eager submissiveness. As such, she is the painful embodiment of Everywoman, and her story is a study in the negation of agency and the feminization of victimhood. Set apart by both her telepathic status and her life experiences, she is a willing tool, trying to win acceptance by making herself a slave to the demands of others and accepting their right to manipulate her as they see fit. As her character develops, the tool becomes the perfect weapon: created by the Psi Corps, armed by the Vorlons, and primed by rejection. As with Ivanova, the distinction between power and control is cleanly drawn. Unlike Ivanova, the source of Lyta's power leads to a totally dissimilar outcome.

Controlling the Power

Disenfranchised, feared, and disrespected by nontelepathic humans, Lyta is forbidden to use her natural power freely. The Psi Corps badge that proclaims her separate but unequal status and the gloves that provide a physical barrier between her and the rest of the human race conjure a double image of alienation and bondage, of the Star of David and the Veil. In a portrayal of the traditional feminine role at its most soul-destroying, these two themes are played out through the metaphor of sexual abuse as the various factions seek control of Lyta and the use of her power.

As a classic "victim hero," Lyta is placed in a position of passivity or nonagency from the outset, and her subsequent choices and shifts of allegiance are the consequences of the bad things that happen to her (Ortner, 9). When she first arrives on Babylon 5, her status as a necessary piece of equipment is revealed when the station commander says, "It's about time Earth sent us a telepath" ("The Gathering"). After saving the life of the Vorlon ambassador, she is recalled to Earth, but her experience has changed her life, and she returns two years later, a fugitive from the abusive Psi Corps. She spends the rest of the series striving to win approval through service. Her allegiance is first given to the Vorlon, Kosh Naranek, and then, when he is murdered, to his successor, Kosh

Ulkesh. However, the Vorlons ultimately prove as abusive as Psi Corps, and she turns to Captain Sheridan ("The Summoning").

The link between femininity, bondage, and abuse is established following the assassination of the first Vorlon ambassador, when his replacement places stringent controls upon her life and turns her from a willing servant into a slave. Delenn is horrified to discover that Lyta's quarters are bare except for a bed— Kosh Ulkesh's one "concession to the human need for sleep." When Delenn questions whether the Vorlon can force Lyta to live like this, she receives the sad response, "Yes, he can." We next encounter Lyta when Kosh Ulkesh, a being of pure energy, is pulling out of her body, and we realize that she has been literally "possessed." He finishes, she staggers, and the symbolism of rape is established with her words: "You didn't have to pull out of me so fast; you hurt me." Her physical debasement eventually strikes a spark of rebellion, and the mechanics of her possession and the true nature of her relationship with the Vorlons are revealed:

> *Lyta:* I have a right to know. I let your people modify me [. . .] because I believed. [. . . But] with you it's as if I've been used and then thrown away when I'm not needed anymore. Dammit, I have earned some respect.
>
> *Kosh Ulkesh:* Respect? From whom? ("The Summoning")

For the first time it has been made clear to her that in trying to win the recognition she craves by debasing herself, she has only succeeded in lowering others' opinion of her. If she acts like a slave, she will be treated like one.

Her consciousness of use and abuse culminates during her long association with Sheridan. She risks her life, something she never did for Psi Corps or the Vorlons, by volunteering to test the theory that telepaths can defeat the Shadows ("Ship of Tears"), traveling to Z'ha'dum with Delenn and Ivanova in an attempt to save Sheridan ("Hour of the Wolf"), and intriguing with Sheridan against Kosh Ulkesh in order to lead the Vorlon into a deathtrap ("Falling towards Apotheosis").

In spite of her efforts, she is never really trusted or appreciated. While Sheridan's thanks for her efforts in luring Kosh Ulkesh into the trap are sincere, they are grudging, and he dismisses her attempt to rescue him as "foolish." Indeed, he quickly fulfills the role of an emotionally abusive husband or father. The one time she acts on her own initiative to keep the superweapons of Z'ha'dum out of the hands of Psi Corps, Sheridan responds angrily, threatening to withdraw his protection and let the Corps have her ("Epiphanies"). Even his defense of her to the Psi Cop Bester is based more on his hatred of Bester than his appreciation of her. As Sheridan consistently fails to treat her even as a human being, much less a trusted companion in the fight, she is left confused and frustrated ("Epiphanies").

Her usefulness apparently over at the end of the Shadow War, she is shunned by Sheridan and her former colleagues, turned out of her quarters, and left with no alternative but to accept Bester's offer and rejoin Psi Corps in order to keep from starving. In a further variation on the themes of abuse and domination,

Lyta, Delenn, and Ivanova on a mission to rescue John Sheridan: fulfilling the patriarchal myth of Babylon 5.

Bester states his request in simple terms: "There is no easy way of putting this. I want your body." Lyta is forced to sign a contract ensuring that upon her death her body will become the property of the Corps to do with as they wish ("Moments of Transition"). Nevertheless, when Sheridan asks for her help in his war against Earth, she agrees, even when what is required of her is repugnant and immoral: to sacrifice the lives of several dozen Shadow-programmed telepaths in order to assure Sheridan his victory. The impression is of an innocent who still wants to believe her efforts will be recognized, but she is in fact a victim of abuse who seeks the good opinion of the abuser and can only define herself in relation to him ("The Exercise of Vital Powers," "Between the Darkness and the Light," "Endgame"). The implications are clear: a woman who casts herself in the traditional role is by definition abused and objectified. Trained to fulfill the traditional female role, Lyta cannot overcome her other-directedness, and, even as she is forcibly marginalized and isolated, she continues to grasp at any request for help that comes her way. She never seriously considers refusing help. She wields enormous power but never uses it for her own gain or to punish others for their slighting or abusive behavior. It also never seems to occur to anyone, least of all to Sheridan, that her power is to be feared. Even Garibaldi, who has had firsthand experience of telepathic manipulation, uses her to convince a character named Byron and his colony of telepaths to be spies for the Alliance ("The Paragon of Animals").

Sexuality and Power Unleashed

Lyta's talent is a weapon, and her body, and by extension her sexuality, is a commodity. A defining moment of her function as eroticized object occurs immediately following her arrival on Babylon 5. The Narn Ambassador G'kar meets with her to discuss a "business proposition." He leers, offers to buy her "telepathic genetic material," and invites her to have sex with him. She refuses, but from that moment on her sexuality can be read as something that others "take" ("The Gathering"). Her relationship with Kosh Naranek, the first Vorlon ambassador, is equivocal. They seem to stand in somewhat of a parent–child relationship: he becomes her mentor and protector, and, as his aide, she is immune to persecution from Psi Corps ("Passing through Gesthemane"). At the same time, their relationship has a sexual component. The first time we see Kosh Naranek "possessing" Lyta, the look on Lyta's face is one of rapture ("Divided Loyalties"), a stark contrast to her relationship with Kosh Ulkesh. Her love for Kosh Naranek is a vital motivating factor in her support of Sheridan, who, she suspects, unwittingly harbors a piece of the Vorlon. The deciding factor behind her insistence that she, Delenn, and Ivanova go to Z'ha'dum is the possibility that she can unite once again with her beloved mentor ("The Hour of the Wolf").

Unable to extricate herself from the identity imposed on her by others, she does not perceive the possibility of being something more than an object until she meets Byron. He believes, if Lyta does not, that her power is innate, not something granted or taken away without her consent, and once she claims it for herself, she essentially steps outside the control of patriarchal authority as symbolized by the society of nontelepathic humans. Byron tries to show her that she has the right to demand acceptance on equal terms and that she is capable of rescuing herself.

Unfortunately, neither Lyta nor Byron is allowed to wholly reject the romantic narrative. Janice Radway summarizes the romantic narrative structure as follows: "The heroine is removed from a familiar comfortable realm, then builds a new relational self through interaction with the hero and discovery of her own sexuality" (134). Though the heroine may be raped and abused by others, only the hero can initiate her and bring her to an understanding of her own sexuality, a true understanding of herself and of her power (Cohn, 34). In his acquiescence in this instance to the role of romantic hero, Byron brings Lyta into this state of self-awareness. The issues are not so much ones of desire and love, but confirming where agency and power truly lie—with the man. Though he rejects Lyta's attempts to place herself in a parent–child relationship to him, he does not hesitate to undertake another role of the hero in contemporary romance: the agent of passage. Otherwise, Byron demands the freedom for himself and other telepaths to define themselves on their own terms. Byron is the only one to view his fellow telepaths as people in their own right rather than as tools ("The Paragon of Animals"). His philosophy is existentialist, and, of all those he encounters, it is Lyta who most needs to recognize and embrace this philosophy. He seeks to prove both to himself and to those who follow him that they are human beings who have developed special powers that demand appropriate recognition, and not merely in the form of discovering others' secrets for the benefit of whoever employs their talents. Consequently, Byron's worldview is shattered by his discovery during a sexual encounter with Lyta that their telepathic development was a result of Vorlon interference designed to enable their use as weapons in the Shadow War, and he begins a journey that will ultimately lead to his own destruction, as well as the final severance of any grasp of humanity Lyta has left to her. What she knew but sought to deny while in his presence is revealed to all, and, as he collapses and commits suicide under the weight of the revelation, Lyta's hopes of a new life for herself and other telepaths are reformed and refocused.

Compelled to reexamine her fundamental beliefs following Byron's suicide, Lyta liberates herself from victimization, but only insofar as she is empowered by his death in becoming the repository of his cause ("A Tragedy of Telepaths"). The change is apparent to everyone who comes in contact with her. When Vir, the Centauri ambassador's aide, and Dr. Franklin, the station's chief medical officer, ask Lyta to help them find out what happened to the crews of Centauri ships shot down by the Drazi, she demands a high fee for her services. Vir is stunned. In the past she would have done it for free. "Is it my imagination," he asks Dr. Franklin after she has left, "Or has she changed?" "Oh, she's changed!" comes the reply. Later, she frightens Franklin when she forces a would-be assassin on the Drazi homeworld to turn his gun on himself and pull the trigger. However, Franklin is quick to turn his fear to advantage, intimidating the other Drazi with the threat of Lyta's power ("Movements of Fire and Shadow"). But Franklin is deluding himself. He has no control over Lyta's actions. She is her own master and fulfills requests on sufferance, demanding a high fee directed toward the fund for seeking out a telepath homeworld. She has defined herself anew in terms of the needs of her own people and not those of the "mundanes," the Vorlons, or the Corps.

Once she begins to exercise her power independently, her sexuality is foregrounded. Her clothes and manner become more sensual as time passes. At the close of a business meeting with G'kar, the now-former Narn ambassador, she reminds him of the proposition he offered her when they first met. At the time he had wondered whether her "pleasure threshold" would be high enough to cope with him. As she exits, she assures him that it is he who could not cope and leaves the discomfited alien hopelessly lusting after her. As her power has been unleashed, so has her sexuality.

Having slipped outside the encompassing patriarchal structure, Lyta becomes a destabilizing force in both her relationships to individuals and to society. In "Darkness Ascending," Garibaldi wakes to find her sitting on his bed. She has been using him to investigate the powers given to her by the Vorlons. He wakes again to find the room empty and he is left to wonder whether or not she was really there. In addition, escalating terrorist attacks on Mars and Earth are traced back to Lyta, who is providing both funds and impetus. When Sheridan authorizes the new station commander, Captain Lochley, to arrest her, Lyta abruptly rejects the submissive, nurturing role that underlies patriarchal femininity and attempts to escape by callously using her powers to cause a surrounding crowd to riot. Only Sheridan, who has also been "touched by a Vorlon" and drastically altered by Lorien when he was brought back from death, has the power to stop her. She capitulates, but warns Sheridan that he cannot be everywhere. Lyta, the weapon, is no longer under his control ("Wheel of Fire").

Incarcerated and awaiting deportation to Earth, she strikes a last-minute deal for her freedom and accepts exile from human space. Unwelcome on Babylon 5, Lyta departs with G'kar, who hopes that he can help her deal with her anger against the human race ("Objects in Motion"). They leave Babylon 5 together, invoking patriarchal images of father/daughter and mentor/student, that imply Lyta is once more under guidance and control and can safely be allowed to wander. But when she holds out her hands and the restraining chains drop free of their own accord, we know this image to be a sham.

The barrenness of the patriarchal model of femininity is starkly presented through the character of Lyta, and her story stands as a scathing indictment of traditional roles for women and the consequences of breaching them—the danger of uncontrolled female power and sexuality. But the cost to Lyta for attaining an independent self-identity is too high. During a conversation with Garibaldi she explains how, during any war, there are small-, medium-, and large-scale weapons, the last being those used only when all else has failed. She explains how the Vorlons created such weapons in the form of telepaths. Garibaldi comments that the strongest of these weapons would be the telepathic equivalent of a thermonuclear weapon. Eyes glowing, voice calm, and her identity lost to the power that has possessed her, Lyta responds, "Pleased to meet you, Mr. Garibaldi." The weapon has announced itself and, in so doing, has finally put to rest the woman who once occupied that body ("Objects in Motion"). She is alone and truly an orphan at last.

AMBASSADOR DELENN OF THE MINBARI

Sebastian: Who are you?

Delenn: Delenn.

Sebastian: Unacceptable answer. I already know your name. Who are you?

Delenn: I am the Ambassador from Minbar.

Sebastian: Unacceptable. That is only your title. Who are you?

Delenn: I am the daughter of . . .

Sebastian: Unacceptable. What a sad thing you are. Unable to answer such a simple question without falling back on references and genealogies and what other people call you. Have you nothing of your own? ("Comes the Inquisitor")

When the Vorlons' Inquisitor asks Ambassador Delenn "Who are you?" the question is eerily appropriate. Who is Delenn? At first glance, she appears more contradictory than either Susan Ivanova or Lyta Alexander, vacillating between the extremes of vigorous action and utter helplessness as the series progresses. At the heart of her schizophrenic personality changes are the many roles she plays in *Babylon 5's* multiple narratives. She is co-hero and savior of the universe together with Commander Sinclair and Captain Sheridan in the overarching story of the Shadow War. She is the mentor in both Sheridan's and Sinclair's hero quests. She is the hero of her own tragic quest when she strives to bridge the gap between the Minbari and the humans but instead brings about the near destruction of her people. Finally, she is the heroine of a very traditional romance. As these disparate strands interweave, traditional concepts of gender are at once validated, blurred, and transgressed, strongly resisting the narrow confines of patriarchal femininity.

Androgyny and Femininity/Hero and Heroine

In the first year of the story, when Delenn is wholly Minbari, she is a quasi-androgynous and physically powerful figure. In fact, one of our earliest sights of her is when she rescues Security Chief Garibaldi ("The Gathering," re-edited version), carrying him to safety in a fireman's lift. Though identified as female and always referred to as "she," Delenn's costume of flowing tunic, trousers, and boots is ambiguous, and the features that humans would perceive as secondary sexual characteristics are de-emphasized. Exceptionally intimidating and inclined to act on impulse, she grabs Garibaldi's gun in an attempt to murder an alien of a race known only as "soul hunters" and subsequently steals the alien's collection of souls in order to set them free to be reborn ("Soul Hunter"). She is also fearless, arrogant, and sure of her beliefs, as when she steals and cremates the body of the Minbari war hero Branmer in order to prevent the warrior caste from using his memory to stir up hatred against the humans ("Legacies"). Though she most often acts as a mentor and adviser to Commander Sinclair ("The Gathering," "Parliament of Dreams," "And the Sky Full of Stars," "Grail," "Legacies," "Chrysalis"), she also issues him ultimatums and orders ("Mind War," "Grail"). Finally, she vows to follow her heart and defies the will of her peers in the Gray Council, the ruling body of the Minbari, seeing herself as the instrument of prophecy and destiny ("Babylon Squared").

In the second year, Delenn undergoes a metamorphosis. Using a forbidden alien machine, she changes into a half-Minbari, half-human female and is repudiated and stripped of her rank by her own people as a consequence ("All Alone in the Night"). At the same time, she develops additional feminine traits. The lackluster, ambiguously sexed clothes are replaced by close-fitting robes that emphasize her female characteristics. Most marked, however, is the development of feminine behavior typical of the romantic heroine. With her transformation, her social identity as a Minbari is destroyed, and she is transformed into a symbolic representation of the immature female (childlike innocence and inexperience) vis-à-vis human behavior (Radway, 123–127). For example, she is

reduced to tears by a human reporter ("And Now for a Word"), a condition un-
thinkable to imagine in Delenn prior to her metamorphosis. Paradoxically, two
other characteristics of the romantic heroine, rebelliousness and the determination to voice her desires and will, work to Delenn's advantage by harmonizing
with her heroic characteristics, and, as the situation demands, she has no trouble in effortlessly stepping out of her persona of romantic heroine and into her
role as hero.

Savior of the Universe

In the quasi-mythological narrative of the Shadow War, Delenn is the prime
mover for the forces of order long before the Babylon Station is conceived ("In the
Beginning"), and as such she is by far the most powerful character for the first
three years of the series. She succeeds her mentor, Dukhat, as spokesperson for
the Vorlons and possessor of their secrets. Consistent with this role, she always
seeks to be in control, and her power lies primarily in information and mental
strength. Using her special knowledge, she manipulates Sinclair and then Sheridan until her purpose is achieved: Sheridan is co-opted as her unshakable ally
while Sinclair returns to the past as the great Minbari hero, Valen ("War without
End, Part Two"). At the most dangerous moment of the Shadow War, it is she and
Sheridan operating as equal partners who drive the elder races beyond the rim of
the galaxy and break the millennial cycle of war ("Into the Fire").

When Delenn's power is at its height, her feminine characteristics and sexuality are at their most vibrant. Her robes swirl around her ankles, feminine and
glowing in jewel tones of deep crimson and blue, amethyst and violet. Her face
is vivid and her hair carefully coifed. She moves with a deliberate awareness of
herself. She also begins to play with human feminine behaviors, flirting with
Sheridan and trying out the effect of a slinky black evening gown ("A Race
through Dark Places").

Her power derives from too many sources, political and spiritual, to be
stemmed, regardless of the attempts that are made to strip her of her authority.
The Gray Council deprives her of her place among them, yet she still retains her
secret adherents ("All Alone in the Night"). She continues in her role as the
Vorlons' chief agent following her physical transformation. A leader of the Religious caste, she can never be stripped of her spiritual power, which transcends
mere politics. Male, female, or hermaphrodite, as the fulfillment of Valen's
prophecy, she also stands as the last great hero of the Minbari in her quest to
bring her people and the humans together in a permanent alliance, transcending gender in the process.

Soul Mates

For a time, Delenn's romantic and heroic traits mingle with little conflict, but
one significant change signals the beginning of the erosion in her authority and

power. In "Comes the Inquisitor," Sebastian is sent to test her fitness for her role in the Great War to come. He asks only one question: "Who are you?" and finds all of her answers unacceptable. She never actually answers the question because Sheridan arrives on the scene to save her. But when Sheridan also finds himself at the Inquisitor's mercy, she discovers that Sebastian's taunting question: "Have you nothing of your own?" is deliberately deceitful. Prepared to sacrifice her destiny in exchange for the life of John Sheridan, Delenn realizes in the act of self-sacrifice that without his presence, she cannot define who she is. Significantly, Sheridan also attempts to sacrifice himself for her. This is the first of many instances when both Delenn and Sheridan make a conscious effort to move beyond the limits of self, and the love that binds the two is often couched in transcendental terms. They are "soul mates"; they will wait for each other in "the place where no shadows fall." They are "star stuff—the universe attempting to understand itself." In the end it is the Inquisitor who names them both. They are the right people in the right place at the right time.

At first it is clear that Sheridan needs Delenn as much as she needs him. Especially in the context of their heroic battle against the Shadows, their co-dependency and equal standing are what enable them to win the war ("Into the Fire"). But in the context of their slowly developing romance, Delenn becomes less assured and in some circumstances more passive and easily swayed to follow another's lead. When she and Sheridan are forced to take their new ship, the *White Star,* into battle against the Shadows, it is she who is afraid and uncertain of what to do ("Matters of Honor"). That Delenn's growing dependency on Sheridan undermines her power and authority in their personal relationship is shown in the way she vacillates between aggressive, self-confident hero and passive heroine. Even her appearance undergoes a subtle change. Her sexuality seems to drain away, and her vibrant-colored garb and cosmetics fade to pastels and finally into self-effacing beige. Eventually, she can function as an independent leader only when physically separated from her lover. Each time they are reunited, her power dwindles while Sheridan's is enhanced.

When the two are apart, however, Delenn reclaims her status as hero. On patrol with a portion of the Ranger fleet, she wipes out a fair number of the enemy Drakh ("Lines of Communication"). She is fully prepared to sacrifice her life in order to put a stop to the Minbari civil war ("Moments of Transition"). Nevertheless, when she informs Sheridan that she must return home because the situation there is getting out of hand, she tells him, "What is left requires that you be dangerous, and I think you would be more comfortable doing that if I were not here." The irony of her statement is not lost on the viewer. Both Sheridan and Delenn are manifestly dangerous characters. The dangerous side of Delenn comes into play twice when Sheridan is threatened. On the first occasion, "Ship in the Night," she reminds his kidnappers, the Streib, of the cost exacted by the Minbari the last time they met. Her words then are echoed in "Severed Dreams," when Babylon 5 seeks to secede from the Earth Alliance. As the station appears doomed to fall and Sheridan is weakened, her own heroic characteristics come to the fore. She arrives at the head of a fleet of Minbari war cruisers, a classic invocation of the cavalry coming to the rescue. When the Earth-loyal ships threaten her, Delenn's response brooks no argument, while simultaneously reasserting her allegiance to Sheridan: "Only one human captain has ever survived battle with the Minbari fleet. He is behind me; you are in front of me. If you value your lives, be somewhere else." Mindful of Earth's previous encounter with the Minbari, the Earth ships promptly depart. Here we see another aspect of the relationship between the two. When they are together, Sheridan dominates, but when he is weakened, she is correspondingly strong. To take another example, when attacked by the battleship *Agamemnon,* Sheridan's former command, he is unable to order fire on his former subordinates. Delenn comes to the rescue with a plan of escape ("Messages from Earth"). On other occasions, Delenn can maintain power in Sheridan's presence only through subterfuge and her willingness to withhold information from him. She tantalizes him with the invitation to participate in the "Shon Fal" ritual, during which each partner is supposed to discover the other's pleasure centers. Subsequently, he is left bewildered and confused when he finds a group of Minbari present whose role is to sit outside the (thin) bedroom partition to ensure things do not go too far. Delenn dominates the scene, reversing the classical sexual roles by her use of information he did not have and her reliance on customs of which he was unaware ("Racing Mars"). Indeed, Delenn maintains a position of power as their relationship develops by evoking endless Minbari rituals.

However, when they have completed the requisite number and the marriage takes place, we seldom see her again on a completely equal footing with Sheridan. When raiders attack the station, he reacts in a traditionally protective manner, conveniently forgetting that in the past they led space fleets into battle together, and insists that she be escorted to a safe place. Delenn doesn't argue, but as soon as he vanishes down the corridor, she quietly dismisses her escort and goes about her business ("A View from the Gallery"). For the most part, she refrains from exercising her power directly. This newfound inability to directly exercise her power—or perhaps her preference to refrain from exercising it—points unerringly to the unequal balance of power in their married relationship. In order to do something she knows Sheridan will not like, as when she sends Lennier, her former diplomatic aide, now a Ranger, to track down unknown raiders to their base, she waits until Sheridan is gone or preoccupied and acts without his knowledge ("Meditations on the Abyss"). There are, nonetheless, occasional exceptions to this new behavior. The most significant is when she takes Sheridan to task on his treatment of Byron and his telepaths ("In the Kingdom of the Blind"). Thus it can be seen that it is not so much that Sheridan needs to be alone to be dangerous. Rather, one must be weakened or the pair separated if either is to do what must be done.

Delenn succeeds more surely than Ivanova in breaking down patriarchal stereotypes, but, in the end, she, too, succumbs, and in the role of the romantic heroine her identity is disassembled, then rebuilt along somewhat more traditional lines. Where Ivanova is straightforwardly aggressive, Delenn masters the art of passive aggression, using more subtle (and traditionally feminine) methods to achieve her goals. In some ways, Delenn's capitulation may be more an artifact of perception than reality within the *Babylon 5* universe. Her heroic roles as savior of her people and co-victor of the Shadow War conclude in the fourth season, and though she still functions in the roles of commander of the Rangers and vice president of the Interstellar Alliance, we seldom see her in these contexts during the fifth season. Her romantic narrative comes to eclipse all that went before, and she is visible to us only in the guise of the romantic heroine.

CONCLUSIONS

For centuries we have regularly traded our old myths for new ones, reinvented and reinterpreted them. We listen for the voice that is ancient in us, and recast our core myths in more contemporary clothing, to better understand them and ourselves. [. . .] The myth-maker points to the past, but speaks in the voice of future history; it is the collective voice of our ancestors, speaking through us, giving us a sense of continuity and destiny; it makes connections between those who have preceded us and those who will follow us. (Straczynski, 12)

The universe of *Babylon 5* speaks definitively to us in a male voice through the patriarchy inherent in its heroic and romantic narratives. The women have important and powerful roles, but in the end the men play an integral part in their search for and validation of their identity, power, and sexuality. Despite this, *Babylon 5* in many ways succeeds in presenting feminist ideals by allowing women to appropriate the traditionally masculine role of the hero as well as that of the heroine. In this way the series sets up a conflict through the interaction of the gendered personality traits demanded of these two roles and explores three very different responses to the question of whether women can retain feminine characteristics and function as powerful individuals.

Babylon 5's answer to this question is apparently yes—and no. The patriarchal fantasy of feminine identity is one in which men appropriate all of the power, and the battle lines are drawn around the nature of the romantic heroine, the traditional identity quest narrative of women. And, we would argue, this is an identity quest that women cannot and should not give up entirely, for within it lies essential elements of feminine identity—the articulation of interpersonal relationships, love, and family. Yet at the same time it is obvious we cannot live with this paradigm in its present form.

Ivanova rejects the romantic narrative and the other-directedness demanded of women in patriarchal culture. She defines herself as hero and achieves self-definition and agency, but only at the cost of close interpersonal relationships.

She becomes somewhat of a "female-man." Though her sexuality is not lost, it becomes ambiguous as her traditional feminine attributes are stripped away. However, in the end, she finds herself once more symbolically bounded by the patriarchal narrative through the sacrifice of her lover Marcus Cole. Left once more confused over who she is, she is impelled to recapitulate her identity quest in the years between her departure from Babylon 5 ("Rising Star") and her appointment as *Entil'zha* (leader) of the Rangers ("Sleeping in Light").

Lyta Alexander's quest for an identity takes her through the most abject of patriarchal narratives for women. Here, also, male intervention is necessary for Lyta to see herself as something other than an object. Yet, at the same time, this narrative departs from the traditional when, in his role as hero, Byron encourages Lyta to recognize the power within her without reference to anyone or anything else. For a time it appears that she has succeeded in shedding her victim role as her power and sexuality increase, but the true extent of her objectification is ultimately revealed and found to be insurmountable. Her rejection of and by the society of her birth, combined with the meddling of the Vorlons, the representatives of patriarchy, completely dehumanizes her. In the end, when she unequivocally rejects the nurturing qualities of femininity, she becomes merely a weapon—a thing, not a person, gendered or otherwise.

Finally, we have Delenn, who wholeheartedly embraces the role of heroine as well as that of hero. She steps from one role to another, losing and regaining her power, shedding one identity for another like a chameleon. As the leader of her people, she exercises undisputed power. As Sheridan's wife, she has power, but she cannot always use it and appropriates a passive-aggressive approach, which complements Sheridan's. A heroic character, secure in her identity, she deliberately reaches beyond herself for the validation of another. In the see-sawing of power between the hero and heroine there is no doubt the hero is favored, but, at the same time, Delenn's compromise does not go unrewarded. By recognizing his dependence on Delenn, John Sheridan also seeks outside himself for validation. In Sheridan's rite of passage through death and back to life, Lorien entreats him to accept the negation of self and simply "be" by finding something worth living for. In the end Sheridan's answer is simple: Delenn ("What Ever Happened to Mr. Garibaldi?"). If the heroine must look to another for validation of self, so, too, now must the hero.

Despite their divergent narrative developments, the stories of Susan Ivanova, Lyta Alexander, and Delenn have several elements in common, not the least of which are the quest for a uniquely female identity and the free exercise of power over their own lives. In all three, patriarchal notions of female identity contest with a deeply seated yearning for self-determination. Yet neither Ivanova's nor Lyta's quest ends on a positive note. Both women face very bleak futures and, as such, their tales offer a scathing indictment of either following the purely traditional role or seeking to abandon gender roles altogether. Thus, *Babylon 5* puts forward a positive case for the compromise position, as largely appropriated by

Delenn. That her effort is not entirely successful is neither a negation nor a criticism of *Babylon 5*. We are all raised to internalize our culture's norms, ethics, categories, and social behavior. The storyteller speaks to society at large. His role is to at once recapitulate and reinvent our culture while simultaneously grounding us in our past and offering up the possibility that we can remake ourselves without cutting ourselves off from our patriarchal roots.

"The secondary status of women is one of the true universals" (Ortner, 21). We each carry within us this particular piece of distasteful baggage from our patriarchal past, and the problem of how to get rid of it is an enormous undertaking. As Sherry Ortner suggests, "We are up against something very profound, very stubborn, something we cannot rout out simply by rearranging a few tasks and roles in the social system, or even by reordering the whole economic structure" (21). If we regard our culture as some kind of monolithic, immovable object, then indeed we are in a fix. This point of view sees subjects as "constructed by and subjected to the cultural discourses in which they must operate" (Ortner, 2), but in fact it is an open question as to what degrees cultural discourses "successfully impose themselves on real people in real time" (Ortner, 2). Culture is constantly "made" and "remade" by intentional actors whose goals are not necessarily consistent with what their culture demands, and so actors resist and negotiate the world. In other words, culture is more disjunctive, contradictory, and inconsistent than social scientists of the past have been trained to think.

Babylon 5 echoes these disjunctions and inconsistencies that make up the multiplex, polysemic nature of the real world. Gender and power become fluid, shifting as the characters pass from one role to another, imitating life in their ability to pick and choose their relationship to the community around them, depending on the context of their interactions (Rosaldo, 166). This is particularly true of Delenn. Of the three characters we have studied, Delenn most successfully negotiates the conflicts inherent in her roles as hero and romantic heroine, adopting whatever approach is most appropriate to the task ahead and surviving. Her approach is presented as a positive and effective compromise to the feminist dilemma.

As a whole, *Babylon 5* takes the feminist side on the battle lines drawn up between the patriarchal tradition and the feminist demand that women be equal in power with men and yet at the same time retain the freedom to display feminine attributes and an active sexuality. Despite its futuristic premise, the series is threaded with an awareness of the poor choices offered to women in the present day, and at the same time neither rehashes patriarchal homilies nor trumpets the feminist agenda. The concerns of the feminist movement are treated sympathetically, but though we are moved toward a greater appreciation of the arbitrary limits placed on women, a nonpatriarchal paradigm still proves elusive. However, as the series comes to an end, the male protagonists move to the sidelines and the women take center stage, perhaps suggesting the exhaustion of patriarchy. Delenn becomes the president of the Interstellar Alliance; Susan

Ivanova becomes *Entil'zha* of the Rangers; and Tessa Halloran, formerly known as Number One and leader of the Mars Resistance, succeeds Garibaldi as chief of Covert Intelligence for the Interstellar Alliance. In *Babylon 5*, then, we see the opening moves in a dialogue through which feminist thought and our patriarchal past can ultimately reach a compromise on the nature of gender, power, agency, and identity. Someday, the series suggests, women will be able say with confidence that they indeed co-exist with men, retain chosen feminine characteristics, and function as powerful individuals.

WORKS CITED

Barr, Marleen. *Alien to Femininity: Speculative Fiction and Feminist Theory.* Westport, Conn.: Greenwood, 1987.

Cohn, Jan. *Romance and the Erotics of Property: Mass-Market Fiction for Women.* Durham, N.C.: Duke University Press, 1988.

Gonsalves, Cynthia. "Gender Bending the Romance Genre in *Babylon 5*." <http://members.home.net/cynthia1960/b5romance.html> (January 28, 1998).

Gordon, Joan. "Yin and Yang Duke It Out." In *Reality Studio: A Casebook of Cyberpunk and Postmodern Science Fiction.* Edited by Larry McCaffrey. Durham, N.C.: Duke University Press, 1991, 196–202.

Lane, Andy. "Between the Essence and the Descent: Carl Jung and *Babylon 5*." In *The Babylon File: The Definitive Unauthorized Guide to J. Michael Straczynski's TV Series Babylon 5*. Edited by Andy Lane. London: Virgin, 1997, 28–38.

Ortner, Sherry B. *Making Gender: The Politics and Erotics of Culture.* Boston: Beacon, 1996.

Radway, Janice A. *Reading the Romance: Women, Patriarchy and Popular Literature.* Chapel Hill: University of North Carolina Press, 1984.

Rosaldo, Renato. *Culture and Truth: The Remaking of Social Analysis.* Boston: Beacon, 1989.

Straczynski, J. Michael. "Approaching Babylon." In *The Babylon File: The Definitive Unauthorized Guide to J. Michael Straczynski's TV Series Babylon 5*. Edited by Andy Lane. London: Virgin, 1997, 7–27.

11

No Ramps in Space

The Inability to Envision Accessibility in *Star Trek: Deep Space Nine*

Hanley E. Kanar

A standard gloss on the 1960s television show *Star Trek* is that it attempts to envision a utopian egalitarian society in future space. Subsequent criticism of that show illuminates the fact that the writers were unable to extricate vestiges of the racism and sexism that plagued their own social context. Later incarnations of the show, including *Deep Space Nine,* attempt to achieve the utopian vision sought in the original *Star Trek.* While these later shows are able to do away with some of the more obvious race and gender inequality, and despite the strides forward in the disability movement, representations of disability have changed little since the Trek of the '60s.

Though it saddens me, I have all but given up the hope that any mainstream media form will portray people with disabilities in a neutral way in my lifetime. This really seems to be asking too much, for reasons at once expedient, historical, and shortsighted. First, using disability as a metaphor for expressing pathological, psychological, religious, cultural, and sociological adulteration is too easy a linguistic and visual shorthand for media dispensers to forsake out of concern for literal accuracy.[1] Disability, like black hats and overflowing champagne bottles, connotes meaning beyond any obvious physical attributes, though admittedly without the camp that the aforementioned have to lighten their connotative load. In addition, offensive and limiting stereotypes about disability are not read as offensive to a majority in the same way that stereotypes about women or racial and ethnic minorities are read, though they are the same at root: they are demeaning, controlling, and reductive.

Second, there is evidence that negative stereotypes have been used in all of Western culture and civilization over all time to "fix" or stabilize identities and in this way control the "Other," or that which threatens self or group autonomy (Gilman, 12–20). Generally, stereotypes serve specific insulating and/or identification purposes for inclusive members of racial, ethnic, gender, or belief-identified groups, like religions or political parties, but this is different in the case of stereotypes about persons with disabilities, who occupy space both inside and outside of their primary group. Since there has never been a civilization or culture that does not include persons with disabilities, drawn as they are from literally every group that there has ever been, they are an exceedingly diverse bunch. Regardless of this, persons with disabilities, who do not necessarily identify with each other, have nonetheless been made a sort of universal Other in whatever cultural context they find themselves. Persons with disabilities are often seen as Other in the social group with which they most likely self-identify, while they may simultaneously view themselves as different from the group of disabled Others with whom they are seen as similar by the able-bodied in their primary group. People with disabilities can be members of minorities within minorities, a position both alienating and isolating.

Isolation of minorities is integral to controlling minorities and to perpetuating the negative stereotypes and perceptions about those minorities to both those wielding power and to those oppressed by it.[2] This is one of the reasons why segregation was employed by whites in power in the American South prior to the Civil Rights movement; simply put, segregation kept the African American Other from commingling with whites. Ending segregation started the process toward breaking down barriers between those who had white privilege and those who did not by, if nothing else, revealing and normalizing the presence of African Americans in places where they had not been fully seen. This is also why isolation of persons with disabilities has kept them from full participation in any community life. Physical segregation and isolation of persons with disabilities, from wheelchair inaccessibility to lack of deaf interpreters, has helped to keep the population of Others with disabilities invisible, contained, and nonthreatening; this is why attitudes toward persons with disabilities have been so slow to change. Prior to the 1990 passage of the Americans with Disabilities Act (ADA), persons who used wheelchairs couldn't assume that they could go to all public schools or even get on most public transportation buses, much less ride in the back.[3] The absence of people from public venues like schools or buses thus normalized their separation and isolation. For this reason, disability rights attorney Robert Funk and others advocate for mainstreaming persons with disabilities into public spaces rather than pushing for "special" or handicapped-only accommodations. "Special" but unequal and stigmatized accommodations have created a "dependent caste" stereotype that is self-perpetuating (Funk, quoted in Shapiro, 143).[4]

This configuration is further complicated because persons with disabilities are members and products of the cultures that define disabled persons like them as "less than." They are imbued from the time of their social birth with the same prejudices and stereotypes about disabilities that the able culture surrounding them imposes on them. In his essay "Communication Barriers between 'the Able-Bodied' and 'the Handicapped,'" disability scholar Irving Kenneth Zola elucidates this:

> While most minority groups grow up in some special subculture and, thus, form a series of norms and expectations, the physically handicapped are not similarly prepared. Born for the most part into normal families, we are socialized into that world. The world of sickness is one we enter only later—poorly prepared, and with all of the prejudices of the normal world. (144)

Furthermore, while individual persons with disabilities may be perceived as belonging to a "minority" because of some identifiability with another more commonly defined minority group, disability is rarely thought of as bestowing minority status. Says Martin F. Norden, author of *The Cinema of Isolation,* "Even today, most members of mainstream society seldom perceive people with disabilities as minority group members subject to alternating rounds of bigotry, paternalism, and indifference, in part because of the latter lack of an ethnic heritage and identity common to other oppressed groups" (12). Historically, then, the force of negative stereotypes and the isolation associated with perpetual Other status has been largely unchecked both inside and outside of various groups and cultures for persons with disabilities, with only the details varying between groups.

Despite the fact that medieval stereotypes about disability have been challenged intellectually and legally, the cultural shadow of these *memes,* or ideas central to core cultural beliefs, follow images of disability. This is especially true in mainstream media representation and particularly in film and television where a very narrow beauty standard is allowable, a standard that even able-bodied people have a hard time meeting and to which even children are made subject. According to Fred Pelka, a freelance writer on disability, "We live in a health chauvinist culture—a culture that often regards the disabled and ill as morally inferior to those who are able-bodied and healthy" (17). The popular media reflects this chauvinism, even as it reflects a heightened sensitivity about how the chauvinism itself is expressed, as in more visible disabled background and cameo characters but no disabled romantic leads. Regardless of the tempered or even glorified way that persons with disabilities are depicted, they are still isolated, set apart, and managed. This is because, at its core, health chauvinism is just a refined version of gender chauvinism. In fact, in the conclusion of his discussion of the depiction of persons with disabilities in film, Norden asserts that "stereotyping of physically disabled people is conspicuously linked to gender issues. The deeply rooted forces that have created our patriarchal society are intimately related to the ones responsible for its ableist perspectives" (315). It comes as no surprise, then, that women are more likely to be defined as disabled and "are generally more likely to be blamed for their own illness and disability" (Pelka, 19). This is particularly true now when "new age" philosophies, like those frequently lionized on television shows such as *Oprah* and targeted specifically at women, have as their core assertion that everyone is responsible for creating his or her own life situations, good and bad, regardless of any social or physical contingencies.

Finally, why should any media desist from using negative disability metaphors and images when the most visible among us Others, like celebrity cripple Christopher Reeve, reinforce these stereotypes, metaphors, and images by characterizing his current disabled state as a dreaded enemy to be escaped from and making phrases like "find a cure" a mantra or even a battle cry that he publicly encourages others to chant?

I do not blame Reeve for struggling with this, of course. He has had a terrible loss. I became disabled in young adulthood myself and I still leave an emotional light on for that elusive "cure," too, but I have had a bit more time to become analytical about the larger reasons why adjustment to disability is so difficult. Sure, the physical adjustment is hard. I remember being more comfortable in the body in which I was formerly situated, but my difficulty adjusting was not and still is not just about physical comfort. Yes, I was more mobile then, but aside from this, and dare I say more than this, I miss all that great social privilege that goes along with being able-bodied in this and in every culture that has ever been.[5] Understanding the encompassing jolt Reeve incurred with his throw from the horse means understanding that, along with losing his ability to walk, he has lost his membership the among ranks of the privileged able. Unfortunately, when Reeve chants for an audience (findacurefindacurefindacure), the audience hears only that he wants out of his current disabled physical circumstances, not that he wants to improve his social and economic circumstances. We have gotten to hear his firsthand analysis of what it physically means to be a person with a disability when compared with being a person without one, and his verdict is that only the physical part of disability is unacceptable (findacurefindacurefindacure). This is played for his audience as a single denotative note, a moan even—disability is bad and he wants out. Fine, understandable even. Reeve is dealing with a major loss, but his tone will modulate over time. It has to. There are day-to-day desires and necessities to attend to. His comfort and discomfort now need to be addressed. This is the reality of the physical circumstances that he and all persons with disabilities live with, cure notwithstanding, because disability is a polyphonic chord, not a single note.

Reeve's mantra makes hearing only one note of this chord (findacurefindacurefindacure) too easy. There are also connotative meanings to his mantra, the harmonics of a normal lived experience, that are lost but that also need to be heard. Imbedded in the mantra is the harmonic desire for acceptance, from ourselves and from the world. Imbedded in the mantra is the wish for a sense of true normalcy in our lives, however we find them, and that normalcy must be defined, for us as for everyone else, by its lack of comparative remarkability. When Reeve writes about the complex coping strategies he now has to use in order to perform what most people consider to be the most basic bodily functions, his ruminations are probably read with a sense of guilty but relieved remove. What echoes there for those who listen more broadly, though, is the clear desire to be seen as still being normal, of having normal needs that must be met regardless of the seeming inconvenience of method, of having the same mundane tasks to perform before the actual living of one's more important life can be lived, of not having to feel embarrassed or isolated because one is allowed to live like everyone else, in unremarkable peace. I hope that Mr. Reeve, myself, and everyone else who considers him- or herself to be physically inconvenienced or uncomfortable finds relief from physical discomfort. In the meantime, however, there are many things that need to be "cured" about disability, and I'm not talking about the physical body.

You may be wondering by now what all this has to do with *Star Trek: Deep Space Nine* (*DS9*). As I mentioned earlier in this chapter, I have given up hope that persons with disabilities will ever be able to find accurate polyphonic examples of themselves in the mainstream media. Most media-drawn characters are one-dimensional, with that dimension being either laughable, maladjusted, or heroic and obligingly uncomplaining (or artificially and temporarily so). I have not given up hope of finding them in science fiction, though. I remember seeing the bar scene in *Star Wars* and thinking to myself, What a wonderful world it would be if that many physically different persons could actually occupy a single space without tokenism or remark. Indeed, science fiction offers, if not an actual cure for the stigma of disability in film, then at least a place where physical difference can be downplayed and made unremarkable. Imagine my horror then, when I watched the *DS9* episode "Melora," to find that all of the imaginative forces behind this program could advance no further from their earliest disabled character, the hapless Admiral Pike from the original *Star Trek*, than to the similarly hapless character Melora Pazlar.[6]

The character Pike is rendered speechless and essentially bodyless—his mute head sits atop a movable box and he is reduced to yes/no answers that are communicated through two lights on the dashboard of his box. His only hope for salvation, even in a future that can dissemble and reassemble bodies into molecules for easy space travel, is to be essentially banished to another planet where the more advanced beings there can give him the illusion of wholeness, if only in a zoo-like atmosphere. This alleviates the crew of the *Enterprise* from having to accommodate the incapacitated captain and it makes acceptable the idea that the only way to live a meaningful life is to be able-bodied, even if this is only an illusion. The solution, arguably humanitarian if still segregationist, even provides Pike with an unfortunate female who, though not as limited by disability as Pike is since she can still walk, is written into the script as similarly in need of segregation (read as isolation, if the *Enterprise* is read as mainstream society) because she is ugly and old. For this female character, then, age and ugliness is coded as disabled so she is equally yoked with Pike and is therefore a good candidate for banishment in the Star Trek universe. In this way, Pike has a lucky Frankenstein; he a benevolent benefactor who only banishes him. He gets his bride this time, too. Science fiction TV had come that far at least.

But not a lot further. The writers maintained their inability to reimagine disability characterization for two *Star Trek: The Next Generation* (*TNG*) characters, the blind but technically sighted character Geordi and the token Klingon Worf. Arriving on the television screen after the flush of high-tech films like *Star Wars*, the character Geordi in *TNG*, though physically blind, is also technically sighted because Geordi wears adaptive equipment, a visor that allows him to "see" well enough to function as sighted. His disability functions more as a technical contingency, so his disability is in a sense cosmetic. The character Geordi is a benign version of the filmic disability stereotype that Norden calls the "Techno Marvel" (293). Functionally and visually, his disability is so minimal that the viewer perceives his adaptation to his bionic self as seamless and easy, obviating any need to address any of the difficult issues surrounding blindness in a sighted world. There are only scant references to his disability, those occasions when Geordi is separated from his visor and finds himself literally blind, but the shows always resolve with his "sight" being restored and Geordi returning to his "normal" life.

More ominously troubling in *TNG* is the character Worf, a Klingon warrior-turned-Federation-adherent. In an episode called "Ethics," the character Worf manages to combine and inflame some of the most hated stereotypes and feared realities of disability when he becomes paralyzed from the waist down. Worf's initial response to his paralysis is to commit ritual suicide, a response that is explained as expected of beings with disabilities in his culture because, "when a Klingon can no longer stand and face his enemies like a warrior, when he becomes a burden to his friends and family, it is time for *Hegh bat* [. . .]. I will not live as an object of pity or shame" (quoted in Vande Berg, 64).[7] This response is understood as backward by some of the *TNG* characters, but it is also understood as reasonable by them, most notably Captain Picard. Then a very risky surgery is proffered. When offered the choice between certain life, albeit as a paralyzed being, and almost certain death, but with the exceedingly slim possibility of nondisabled life as incentive to gamble, Worf elects to risk everything.[8] So terrible is the concept of life as a paraplegic that death and lifelong paraplegia seem equal in the abilities game of chance. Of course, Worf's gamble is rewarded, thus reinforcing that "findacurefindacure" mentality that sidesteps any discussion of what, outside of risking one's life, might be done in the enlightened future to improve the quality of the lives of persons with disabilities so that they might more often opt for life. Now we have spokespeople the likes of Jack Kevorkian, who, according to disability writer Marta Russell, "defines terminal illness as 'any disease that curtails life even for a day'" (39). Along with court decisions that rule that persons with handicaps will benefit from the option of having a physician-assisted death in order to "take the economic welfare of their families and loved ones into consideration," it is little wonder that the twentieth-century writers of *TNG* could not envision a better future for persons with disabilities (Russell, 39).

The *DS9* episode "Melora" revisits the familiar theme of the Pike saga, in that she is eventually banished (cleverly accomplished with her consent) to be with her own "kind," a whole planet of coded cripples all isolated from the mainstream. But rather than being old, mute, disembodied, bionic, or depressed, Melora is beautiful, articulate, sexually competent, and physically fit, even as we are encouraged to perceive her as disabled. Her voice could have been used to change the tone of stereotypes about disability and assumptions about universal handicap bitterness, her sexuality could have been shown to be as fundamental and unencumbered as that of other crew members, and her body could have been read as fit and attractive. In truth, the writers toy with addressing twentieth-century disability politics in this way, but they back off, their ambivalence about disability and normalcy overriding their egalitarian impulses. Instead of allowing the Melora Pazlar character to expand the repertoire of available disabled characterizations, her voice, like that of the disabled Star Trek characters before her, is used to reinforce and validate common stereotypes and misconceptions about persons with disabilities, the expression of her sexuality is stunted, and her body viewed as an unfortunate but fixable natural anomaly. If she consents to being "repaired" she could be included, first in the community of *DS9* and then more broadly as a symbol of the larger cultural inclusion that persons with disabilities require. When she would not be "fixed," when she objects to an offer to assimilate through medicine that will make her "able" but render her literally homeless and cost her her race identity, she is banished as quickly as Pike was banished and much more quickly than Geordi, who luckily regained sight, and Worf, who expediently risked death under the surgical knife rather than on the cutting room floor, where all disabled *Star Trek* characters go.

In *DS9* Episode 26, "Melora," the title character, cartographer Ensign Melora Pazlar, ostensibly comes to DS9 on a mission to chart the Gamma Quadrant. She is described as brilliant, as a super-achiever, but the representational reason for Pazlar's arrival on DS9 is to do another gloss on disability. Melora is from a planet with very low gravity, so her movements on the high-gravity station are labored and painful-looking. She does not have a disability per se, but the character is coded as a person with a disability because in order to move about with any ease at all, she has to wear leg and arm braces and use forearm crutches, making her appear to have had polio or some other muscle-wasting condition. To achieve any mobility that replicates the speed with which the other crew members move, she has to use a twentieth century–style wheelchair, and not a very high-tech one at that.

If these visual references to disability and personal discomfort and inconvenience aren't obvious enough, the dialogue immediately begins to reinforce other social stereotypes about disability, especially about the way it impacts on the able society when forced into inclusion mode. The episode starts with Lieutenant Dax and Dr. Bashir playing in the wheelchair they have fabricated for Pazlar's use. They are doing donuts in a hall and talking about her while they await her arrival. An astonished Dax says of the wheelchair, "I haven't seen one of these in three hundred years. I'm surprised that it was even on file in our data bank." Bashir replies, "It wasn't. She sent me the specifications." This begins a quite extensive sequence of references to the lengths that the crew has had to go to respond to Pazlar's perceived pickiness about accommodating her special needs. Numerous references to her "specifications," coupled with myriad beleaguered expressions, can easily be read as complaints about the lengths that they had to go to reasonably accommodate her.

For example, when Dax and Bashir run into Chief O'Brien on their way to meet Pazlar, Bashir quizzes him about whether he has accomplished the seemingly impossible task of making the station accessible and comfortable. An overworked-looking O'Brien, with an expression of sarcastic astonishment at the ridiculousness of the question, can only reply with a breathless sounding "no," a shrug, and a somehow explanatory "Cardassian construction!" Evidently, the ADA's architectural standards were repealed before the DS9 station was constructed since it seems to be not only inaccessible but also difficult to bring into compliance. The station's inaccessibility becomes a focal point later in the episode, but not in order to remark on the inexplicable failure to make a construction accessible in the future. This failure goes unquestioned as a policy point. In fact, having whole sections of the station left inaccessible seems to be a salient feature necessary to illustrate Pazlar's refusal to stay within the boundaries literally constructed to keep people like her in their place and to show the dire consequences of such a refusal.

Though there is considerable air time devoted to discussion about the crew working diligently toward following Pazlar's mobility design specifications, the able characters' responses to the demands of these fictional accommodation rules are consistent with the backlash experienced by persons with disabilities looking for accommodations after the passage of the ADA. In his seminal study of the disability civil rights movement, *No Pity*, Joseph P. Shapiro notes that there was considerable resistance to complying with the mandates described in the 1973 Rehabilitation Act and also to those of the ADA (71). Similarly, there is a limit to how diligently the DS9 crew is willing to work on an accommodation that will not directly benefit them, and there is clearly a limit to their willingness to follow Pazlar's specifications and their endeavors to fulfill her accessibility needs before they start giving each other exasperated looks.

There is great irony in this. Though Dax, Bashir, and O'Brien shake their heads and wring their hands over the architectural inaccessibility of DS9 and Star Fleet architecture in general, they also use Pazlar's willingness to struggle in this user-hostile environment without much complaint as a sign of her superiority. When Dax wonders aloud why they couldn't just use the transporter to move Pazlar around, O'Brien again rolls his eyes and says, "Makes sense to me, but she sent word that it wasn't acceptable." There is not even a glimmer of recognition in this discussion about why Pazlar would choose to travel with her colleagues instead of being molecularly disembodied and separated from them for their convenience. Bashir, the character designated to elevate the exacting Pazlar to near-saint status before she arrives onboard, gushes in rather breathy tones that it makes perfect sense to him. He lists Pazlar's accomplishments at the Academy, and these are numerous, but what really gets him is that "after she has her basic needs met, she refuses any special assistance. She's extraordinary." She is also a martyr.

This scene reinforces yet another cluster of stereotypes about disability and its intersection with able society. Clearly, there is a discrepancy between Pazlar's definition (read as all persons with disabilities' definitions) of a "reasonable" number of basic needs she can expect to have met and that of the crew. Also notable is the image of the "inspirational cripple," a term, notes Shapiro, that is "deeply moving to the nondisabled Americans and widely regarded as oppressive by most disabled ones" (16). Before Pazlar even makes her entrance, we know that she's a "worthy cripple," or one who "overcomes" her disability, and she is also a "super-crip," a brave and uncomplaining super-achiever. Both of these labels are ones that make dismissing the reality of life as a disabled person easy for able people, but they are also stereotypes that make just being an average person who happens to have a disability seem like a failure, or imply that being average is akin to not trying hard enough. Needing to be regarded as exceptional as a minimum requirement for inclusion is demanded only of people for whom some major physical and societal barrier, like stigma or disability, has also been erected.

On top of her "disability," Pazlar is also female. The character's voicing of her frustration at the constant barriers she encounters is written as hypersensitive and churlish, even as bitchy instead of justified. When she first comes aboard, she is not chatty or effusively grateful that they have made the station minimally accessible to her. On the contrary, when we first view Pazlar she is in the entryway, having just disembarked from her transport. She appears to be gasping for air, and she is holding onto the wall for support. We see that the weight of the gravity in the station is encumbering her every movement. She's wearing leg and arm braces and she has a cane, but still she gathers herself up to salute and report for duty in a very official way. When she finally sits in the wheelchair, or "trolley car," she doesn't go into a litany of girly thank-yous or crippled hyper-gratitude. No, Pazlar notices that the "trolley car" is different than the model that she specified and, exasperated, she comments on it.[9]

If her complaint had been received as a response to a mechanical miscue or even as evidence of Pazlar's irritable temperament, this scene would have just been a neutral character development. As it is written, however, Bashir says that he altered her design to "help" her, and this is where another core stereotype surfaces, but this is also where the writers of this episode display their conflicted views about disability, about the character, and about what she is to represent. Pazlar is the embodiment of what the nondisabled world views as the problem with trying to accommodate the disabled. Bashir is the key able-bodied foil in this episode full of able-bodied foils for the solitary "disabled" character Pazlar. It is through the able-bodied characters' actions that the writers attempt to show how difficult, if not impossible, it is to satisfy a disabled person's needs. This is shown over and over again through the rolled eyes and knowing sighs and glances written into the nonverbal dialogue given to able-bodied characters in this episode. This is also, however, where the writers unwittingly expose their own lack of understanding of the disability rights movement and of the way that persons with disabilities view the awkward and often demeaning gestures and comments of many nondisabled people. In trying to prove that it is difficult to accommodate disabled persons, the writers actually prove Joseph Shapiro's assertion that "Nondisabled Americans do not understand disabled ones" (3).

As the able-bodied character who has the most significant interaction with Pazlar, the Bashir character is unwittingly scripted to at once infantilize, lionize, and eroticize Pazlar. First, his paternalistic medical gaze probes the body of papers generated about her. This is done against her will. She had clearly drawn out limits or "specifications" regarding what she needed, as opposed to other

Regardless of the ignored specifications for Pazlar's "trolley-car," DS9 is not handicap accessible.

personal facts that she was unwilling to share, but he read her entire Star Fleet resume and personal data, and he read it as "disability" history. Simply having Bashir in charge of her accommodations medicalizes her before she even boards the station. Then he lionizes her by analyzing her Star Fleet accomplishments as "remarkable" but only in light of what he knows about her "disability" status. Next he infantilizes her to control the body that she inhabits by ignoring her brilliance and self-sufficiency and altering the specifications she has outlined about accommodations to "help" her. The assumption here is that he knows better what she needs than she does. Finally, he dominates her sexually and medically, a gendered double-whammy, by casting his masculine medical-gaze and his male erotic-gaze on her, thereby subduing the disability through sexual and medical seduction.

Norden notes that disabled women characters are frequently "constructed with a similar general purpose in mind: representing some force that able-bodied males find threatening, they are objectified Others to be gazed at" (317). Rather than allowing the Pazlar character to express the disabled point of view that persons with disabilities know what works best for them, or the feminist point of view that women know best what works for them, the Pazlar character is scripted to sound irritated and bitchy when she informs Bashir that she does not want his improvements because she has been practicing on the original chair design—her design. Bashir's response is scripted to sound placating rather than apologetic when he offers to convert it back to the original design, thus framing Pazlar as a malcontent rather than a clear-headed designer irritated with a deviation from her design. The ultimate evidence that the writers do not understand the disabled woman's point of view is that Pazlar is then scripted to sound martyred rather than resigned when she grits her teeth, refuses more of their assistance, and says, "No, I'll just have to adapt." Bashir and the other crew do not understand why their "help" offends her, nor do they explore this human-relations gaff, and she, though very articulate in other ways, cannot explain the disconnect any better than to bring up the seemingly accurate but almost meaningless chant: "No one can understand unless they've [*sic*] been in the chair." By making the gulf between them physical rather than personal and political, the writers widen the gap of understanding between able-bodied and disabled people and they lose the opportunity to explore the link between feminism and disability politics.

The inability to empathize or to see the similarity between social ills like racism and sexism and ableism is the crux of the conflict about disability rights and pride on *DS9*, and this is the same conflict that isolates people with disabilities in present-day society. As Shapiro points out, there is a "clash between the reality of disabled people and the understanding of their lives by others" (4). Pazlar does sound ungrateful, but what is she supposed to be grateful for? Reasonable accommodations? This is only the dismantling of a type of segregation. Medicalization of her normal activities? This is a violation and a reduction of her identity to her body parts. This is the type of voyeurism and reductivism that the Star Trek writers should be ashamed of themselves for using since they would never do this so blatantly to a female character if she were not disabled. The Pazlar character is like many in the disability pride movement who reject the medicalization and infantilization that seem to permeate much disability policy.[10]

Medicalization, like all stereotyping, is limiting and reductive, and outside of a necessarily therapeutic setting, it defines people as a set of ableist notions about normalcy. Pazlar, in her role as stand-in for all persons with disabilities, has been provided with an accommodation, but she has not been respected enough to be given the accommodation that she needs. Pazlar, as a woman, is not respected enough to have that accommodation be the limit of how her body becomes public grist. Pazlar is objectified on account of her body. As a "disabled" woman, she must take what she is given and "adapt" to whatever the male doctor and father-figure Bashir deems better for her than what she knows for herself.

Intertwined in the entire episode of exchanges between Bashir and Pazlar are keys to understanding current core-conflicted ideas about persons with disabilities and what they want and need. Pazlar's voicing of a desire to be self-directed echoes back at least as far as the 1960s, with the 1970 opening of the Physically Disabled Students Program, the precursor to the Independent Living Movement, chartered to be run "by disabled people; approach their problems as social issues; and make integration into the community its chief goal. Independence was measured by an individual's ability to make his own decisions and the availability of the assistance necessary" (Shapiro, 34). Writing Bashir's character to assume that he, as a physician, knows more about what Pazlar needs is to have missed this entire page of disability politics. Also closely linked in this episode of *DS9* are the gender politics that are inextricably tied to the disability politics. Disability, in the body of Pazlar, is subjected to the medicalized male gaze at the same time as Pazlar, the woman, is subjected to the medicalized male gaze. It is, essentially, the identical gaze.

To their credit, the writers allow Pazlar to reject the medicalization of her gravity-related inconvenience. She challenges Bashir's placement as her on-board mentor to Commander Benjamin Sisko, though her objections are dismissed. She rejects his and the rest of the crew's pseudotherapeutic administrations to her physical and even her psychological needs, but this is read by them as maladjustment. It is not until she develops a love interest in Bashir that the whole issue of her rejection of the medical model is defused, and not for her benefit. After Pazlar's initial complaint to Sisko about not needing a physician's care, Bashir declares that he is no longer her physician, but this is only a prelude to her later seduction. When Bashir and Pazlar become lovers, the ground is literally shifted. Their coupling takes place in Pazlar's room in zero gravity, but, despite the fact that the sex act is symbolized by them floating fully clothed with limbs intertwined before a vagina-shaped window looking out into space (!), it is the sole time when they are literally on equal ground. Prior to their coupling she is clearly his patient, prone on his examining table after her fall. After they are lovers she is again clearly his patient, prone on his examining table, when she is acquiescing to his medical experimentation. Once she succumbs to his medical and paternalistic ministrations, she literally lets her previously asexually coifed hair down into billows of Godiva-like blondness, teasingly covering her nakedness while she reclines, vulnerable and passive on the examination table. Her previous resistance to medical intervention is virtually gone.

The irony is that these attributes of strength are lost, or written out, when she hurts herself trying to get around in the inaccessible station. Her injury lands her at the mercy of *DS9* medicalism and paternalism simultaneously. Denatured and literally out of her element, she allows Bashir's medical husbandry in a bizarre deep space homage to feminine submission narratives.

Generally, though, Pazlar's initial resistance to the constant and overt attentiveness to her body is read as churlish, as "attitude." Her desire to take up more space than the engineers have made accessible for her results in her injury, in her being scolded by senior officers for trying to do things on her own, and by her blaming herself in embarrassment when she needs to be assisted after falling in an inaccessible part of the station. Even though she blasts the environment by asking, "What kind of an architect would deliberately design a raised rim at the entrance of every door?" she spends far more dialogue time deriding herself for the accident: "I wasn't paying enough attention to what I was doing." Of course, this injury is a necessary element to the rest of the plot because it winds her up in the infirmary where all of the rest of the interesting action about disability autonomy and pride intersects with medicalization, sexualization, and mantra chanting (findacurefindacurefindacure). While she is being attended to by the doctor, he mentions that he is reworking some old theoretical modeling that, with the aid of modern scientific applications, could result in Pazlar's neural pathways being altered, resulting in her being able to exist in high gravity without using any adaptive equipment. Eureka, a cure.

A Godiva-like Pazlar is rendered vulnerable to the medical and sexual gaze.

After this, much of the rest of Pazlar's screen time is spent naked and sheet-covered while she is being ministered to by the doctor/lover, who is trying out his theory on his beautiful blond guinea pig. She has been utterly quieted by the curative medical and amorous attentions of the male doctor, so much so that the narrative begins to resemble the structure of the "ideal romance" described by Janice Radway in her book on romance novels. Radway asserts that even though in the ideal romance structure the power differential seems to replicate a fairly ordinary patriarchal configuration, "it should be noted that she has become in-fantile in the sense that she is all passive, incomplete desire, yearning for the life-giving nurturance of a tender but all-powerful individual."[11] After Pazlar is dominated sexually, she is as willing as the female heroine of a romance novel to be infantilized. Not a single subsequent mention of her capabilities, her afore-mentioned brilliance, or even of the mission that sent her to DS9 in the first place comes back into discussion. Her feminine pliability supersedes the issues of her "disability." As "able" and medically and sexually objectified, Pazlar be-comes more valuable and acceptable to the narrative as a test subject for Dr. Bashir's efforts at "fixing" her body and the paper he will write about this ac-complishment than she is as a cartographer. When she first tries out her new "legs" by visiting the bridge, all of the other crew members stare at her newly "able" body appreciatively and then they all congratulate Bashir on the paper he is going to publish and, silently, on his trophy woman. This is supposed to be the dream of every crippled person and every ambitious doctor, right?

The crack in this perfection, in what is supposed to be every cripple's dream, begins to show when Pazlar has had a chance to live like an "able" person and decides that she might not like it. Again, the writers of *DS9* foray into a core tenet of the disability culture movement—the philosophical rejection of able as superior.[12] After sleeping in regular DS9 gravity, she is uncomfortable. She lit-erally aches. Furthermore, the process of altering her for "normal" society means that she can't go home again, can never float weightlessly again. She doesn't think she wants to go as far as rejecting her core self as a career move, and evidently love ranks behind personal autonomy, too. The viewer may be lulled into thinking that this is enlightened of the writers, since disability pride, like gay pride and race pride, includes the concept that people are fine the way they are. However, this is a false consciousness because in the Star Trek uni-verse the implicit credo is assimilate or die (disappear from the show). Gener-ally, though self-acceptance is seen as a worthy goal for most people, on *DS9* if self-acceptance means accepting or accommodating disability or difference, it is seen as subversive.

This is not obscure disability pride jargon or politics that the writers could not possibly know about, either. In deaf culture, for example, the cochlear implant, an in-dwelling hearing apparatus, is regularly trashed by deaf activists as a viola-tion of a deaf identity that ought to be valued rather than treated as a medical condition. Without the support of "disabled" activists, however, Star Trek universe characters like Pazlar, Worf, and Pike must reject their race and species identity if they are to assimilate and be accepted. Unless she becomes "able" she won't fit in, and she rejects the option, thus validating the tenets of disability rights philosophy while simultaneously damning herself to prime-time oblivion. There is no room on *DS9* for the difference of "disability." There is only room to exploit it with watered-down liberal condescension without truly exploring it completely. Remember, Pazlar's complaints about accessibility were seen as unreasonable. She was shown as overly sensitive and this was tied to being "disabled." Then, when she chose not to assimilate into ableness there, this was conveniently written off as validating her race identity instead of what it really was—invalidating her because of her "disability." The problem is that Pazlar did not need to have her race identity validated. She had a home planet to return to where everyone else would be just like her. Most persons with disabilities are Others everywhere but are not represented on *DS9* or anywhere else.

Because they cannot envision a way to keep a "disabled" character on *DS9*, the eventuality of getting rid of Pazlar is the stickiest problem for the scriptwriters. Her exit must be read as her decision, to soothe their liberal leanings, and it must be read as a difficult one so that all of the trouble that they have gone to make her appear to be changed by the love of a man is not watered down too much. To accomplish this, and to elevate Pazlar to hero status, they involve Pazlar in a crisis involving a crossover with another story line being played out in the same episode. The craft she and Dax are on to finally chart the Gamma quadrant is hijacked. Pazlar is wounded by the hijacker, but the drugs that she has only recently stopped taking to prevent her species change are still in her system and this residual prevents her from dying. Because she can function in low gravity while no on else on the craft can, Pazlar sneaks to the pressure controls, turns the gravity to low and presto, Pazlar saves the day using only her genetic heritage and ingenuity. This clinches it for her. How could she give up her weightlessness, the distinguishing feature of her race, when the writers have made her a hero for using it?

Even though the mandate of all Star Trek is to "seek out new life and new civilizations" and "to boldly go where no one has gone before," the writers and perhaps even the viewers really don't want just any of those new folks to come back and visit them. They are essentially slumming. By only occasionally including characters with disabilities in the cast, the writers perpetuate the image of disabled persons as Others and of disability as liminal, rather than the everyday occurrence that it actually is. Even though the writers give lip service to inclusion, the occasional use of characters with disabilities misses the ways in which this spottiness perpetuates the isolation of disability and misses critiquing the essential artificiality of the concept of minority altogether. Minority, as a concept only, exists in the contrived hegemony of DS9 or any other constructed hegemony, because it is kept alive artificially. If you ignore the contrivance of the idea of an ideal group, all beings are always doing the same things anyway whether they are dis-

abled or not. Disabled bodies and able bodies, multiraced and gendered bodies—
all of us engage in similar basic functions, in common biological, unremarkable
activities. Beings have to. In order to maintain the perception of the liminality of
disability on any of the Star Treks or in real life, though, a very high level of perceived and exclusionary conformity must be maintained. Though Melora Pazlar,
the embodied example of a disabled person, does all of the same things that all of
the other crew people do, she cannot conform and so she must be relegated back
to the margins. *DS9* functions like the Borg, the ultimate assimilation nightmare
characters, in that way. The ableist assimilation crew members mean her no harm;
they just want to improve the quality of her life by remaking her in their able
image. They need her to assimilate in part because it validates their self-defined
superiority and Pazlar, by not willingly coming physically over to their side, challenges the very idea that able is better. They cannot understand this, and in this
way the episode of *DS9* captures the essence of why able people do not understand the disability pride movement and why Christopher Reeve, with his findacurefindacurefindacure mentality, is their disabled ideal.

   DS9, like its relative *TNG* and their progenitor *Star Trek,* though genera-
tionally separated, all spring from the same shallow but fertile field of 1960s
liberal imaginings. As television offshoots of the more deeply seeded Civil
Rights, Anti-War, and Women's Liberation movements, the Star Trek family has
a lot of ground to cover. Staked by the sturdy-seeming textual duo of Infinite
Diversity in Infinite Combination (IDIC) and the Prime Directive, the members of this series family vows and even succeeds to grow where no television
series has ever grown and to yield what no television series has ever yielded—
a vision of a world where the inequalities, the insensitivities, and the violence
of the past has been overcome and where challenges to this newly conceived
status quo can be weeded out wherever they are found.[13] In a real world, where
the environment seems irretrievably physically and psychologically damaged,
the unblemished and emotionally expansive environment imaginable in outer
space is made easily accessible for us through the multiple Star Treks. Outer
space becomes the postindustrial, postnuclear, postmodern bucolic fantasy that
we seem to long for.

   There is much to suggest that this utopian image continues to have lasting and
valuable effects, or at least that it reflects a willingness to imagine and even celebrate the inclusiveness, acceptance, and diversity that is the desired outgrowth.
It also, unfortunately, reflects the general liberal myopia about the actual narrowness of the definition of inclusion it wishes to generate despite the "space" it
purports to operate in. It is true that the combined Star Treks do a good job of envisioning a diversity-packed utopia where a startling variety of beings, all hailing
from far-flung universes, commingle in working harmony. It is also true that in
this modeling even beings who have trouble behaving themselves in the polite society of the various Star Trek structures are graciously accommodated, right down
to their native cuisine. Yet these truths, however idealistic, do not alter another

truth—that the utopian society of the Star Treks, where the race, class, gender, religion, ethnicity, and even species differences that plague us now are problems only for those few left unenlightened, still cannot envision a way to comfortably include individuals who have disabilities.

Disability marks a bodily site where the need for IDIC occurs in a single individual rather than in a conflicting pair or group, thus complicating the equation otherwise more easily solved through some form of communication or understanding of a mind-set. The writers are so self-congratulatory about the breadth of their inclusion rhetoric, and this rhetoric is woven into each episode so seamlessly, that it is the inability to fit into what is depicted as "normal" or "polite" that most often becomes the topic of the episode. The underlying assumption of the rhetoric itself, the definition of "normal," is never questioned and it is especially not intended to be used to describe physical attributes, only behavioral ones. It is precisely the narrowness of this definition, not the breadth for which the Star Treks are so often hailed, that exposes the overarching queasiness about universal inclusion deeply imbedded in the social structure of the ostensibly boundless space of the Star Trek universes and in the world of the writers who envision it. Regardless of the quadrant, there seems to be no room for envisioning inclusion for persons with the type of physical differences we currently define as disabilities. Even in our best imaginings we are limited as to the extent that we care to make society accessible. In the Star Treks this means that unless you are bipedal, two-armed, and generally sighted, hearing, oxygen-breathing, English-speaking, and physically capable, you can't be mainstreamed into society. In the world that this fiction attempts to improve upon, retrogressively, things are not that much different.

NOTES

1. Susan Sontag argues that the "most truthful way of regarding illness—and the healthiest way of being ill—is one most purified of, most resistant to, metaphoric thinking" (3). I argue that we should enlarge on this discouragement of negative metaphoric speech by broadening it to include the word *disability* and words with literal meaning about the physical reality of disability. While some may construe this as oversensitivity, the constant reiteration of negative metaphors is not neutral speech any more than using racial epithets as metaphors would be considered neutral speech. The word *crippled* may not be necessarily a negative term in itself, but when the word is usually used as a word defining something that is worthless and nonworking or even dangerous, as in "crippled nuclear reactor," then negative connotations become part of common usage instead of occasional colorful speaking.

2. See Martin F. Norden, *Cinema of Isolation: A History of Physical Disability in the Movies,* 1–3. His discussion of social isolation draws on John McDermott's essay "Isolation as Starvation," in which he quotes McDermott as saying that "the most severe difficulty encountered by a human being is that of isolation from the flow of events.

This isolation prevents the making of relations and prevents recoveries and consequently growth" (215).

3. The current disability rights and culture movement, most recently represented in the news media regarding the 1990 (ADA), actually had its genesis much earlier, simultaneous with the foment of the other civil and gender rights movements in the early 1960s, arguably starting with the 1962 lawsuit filed by Edward Roberts, a quadriplegic, who sued the University of California and won admission. The fight for equal access to public transportation can be traced back to the 1983 founding of American Disabled for Accessible Public Transit, or ADAPT. This group specifically targets the adaptation of mass transportation so that it is wheelchair-accessible. This stance is distinguished from one that pushes for more handicapped-specific transportation. The rational for this is that the separate vans that are most often cited as handicap-accessible transportation actually isolate disabled riders more. Rather than simply waiting for a regularly scheduled bus along with nondisabled riders, handicap-accessible vans designed exclusively for the transport of disabled riders isolate and actually further restrict persons who use them. These rides must often be scheduled a day or more in advance and the riders must accommodate the schedules of other riders as well.

4. See Joseph P. Shapiro, *No Pity: People with Disabilities Forging a New Civil Rights Movement*. Shapiro cites Institute of Medicine statistics that indicate that 35 million Americans have disabilities that "interfere with daily activities like work or keeping a household" (6–7).

5. See *Beyond Ramps: Disability at the End of the Social Contract* and author Marta Russell's discussion of class privilege and disability. She asserts that economically privileged persons with disabilities most often argue for disability rights that reflect more their economic class status than their disabled status, as in Christopher Reeve advocating to Congress about getting the insurance company caps raised for the already well-covered disabled, not about getting reasonable and workable insurance for persons with disabilities. This is a good point as far as advocating for those with the least first, but Russell fails to comment on just how quickly one can fall from the privilege of having insurance to having none, effectively making all persons with disabilities vulnerable to living in a health-care vacuum. With most health insurance policies issued with a million-dollar cap and most acute care for paralysis patients quickly eating into that sum before the disabled person even leaves the hospital, that million dollars and that insured status quickly disappear.

6. For this essay, *DS9*, when italicized, will refer to the television series. When not italicized, DS9 refers to the space station on which the series is set. In addition, *Star Trek*, when italicized, refers to the original series; when not italicized, Star Trek refers to the multiple-series universe and cultural phenomenon of Trek.

7. Vande Berg discusses Worf's will to suicide because of his disability in terms of Worf's masculinity and his liminal position in the context of the show. I posit that his liminality is heightened when he becomes disabled, i.e., he becomes the minority within a minority that I discuss earlier in the essay. This is a position in which many persons with disabilities find themselves—they are culturally liminal in every way. The issue of Worf's damaged masculinity is important to this constellation of multiple liminalities, too, but it goes beyond the scope and female-gender focus of this essay.

8. This attitude is not solely fictional. In *Beyond Ramps: Disability at the End of the Social Contract,* Marta Russell discusses the support for doctor-assisted suicide and euthanasia for the elderly and disabled. She accuses former Governor Richard Lamm of "backhanded social Darwinism." According to Russell, Lamm "proclaimed that terminally ill and disabled people had a 'duty to die'" (29).

9. It is interesting to note that although they have been unable to modify adaptive devices like wheelchairs and leg braces much beyond what we have already, they are not above tinkering with the language and coming up with cute and ableist euphemisms for disability and disability related items. *Trolley car* instead of wheelchair is akin to the detested *differently abled* once used as a euphemism for disability or even the plainer term *crippled.*

10. See Janice Radway's *Reading the Romance: Women, Patriarchy, and Popular Literature,* 145.

11. See Douglas Martin's "Disability Culture: Eager to Bite the Hand That Feeds Them." This large article touches on several important aspects of the radical disability movement, including an interesting historical perspective on the genesis of the movement.

12. Russell, quoting disability historian Paul Longmore: "Being made over after the model of nondisabled people is exactly what people with disabilities can never do, can never achieve" (14).

13. "Infinite Diversity in Infinite Combination" is the Vulcan credo for tolerance, and the "Prime Directive" is the Star Fleet noninterference policy.

WORKS CITED

Funk, Robert. "Disability Rights: From Caste to Class in the Context of Civil Rights." In *Images of the Disabled, Disabling Images.* Edited by Alan Gartner and Tom Joe. New York: Praeger, 1986.

Gilman, Sander L. *Difference and Pathology: Stereotypes of Sexuality, Race, and Madness.* Ithaca, N.Y.: Cornell University Press, 1985.

Martin, Douglas. "Disability Culture: Eager to Bite the Hand That Feeds Them." *New York Times,* 1 June 1997, sec. 4:1ff.

McDermott, John J. *Streams of Experience: Reflections on the History and Philosophy of American Culture.* Amherst: University of Massachusetts Press, 1986.

Norden, Martin F. *Cinema of Isolation: A History of Physical Disability in the Movies.* New Brunswick, N.J.: Rutgers University Press, 1994.

Pelka, Fred. "Hating the Sick: Health Chauvinism and Its Cure." *The Humanist* 54, no. 4 (July/August 1997): 17–20.

Radway, Janice. *Reading the Romance: Women, Patriarchy, and Popular Literature.* Chapel Hill: North Carolina University Press, 1984.

Russell, Marta. *Beyond Ramps: Disability at the End of the Social Contract.* Monroe, Me.: Common Courage Press, 1998.

Shapiro, Joseph P. *No Pity: People with Disabilities Forging a New Civil Rights Movement.* New York: Times Books, 1994.

Sontag, Susan. *Illness as Metaphor*. New York: Farrar, Straus and Giroux, 1978.

Vande Berg, Leah R. "Liminality: Worf as Metonymic Signifier of Racial, Cultural, and National Differences." In *Enterprise Zones: Critical Positions on Star Trek*. Edited by Taylor Harrison, Sarah Projansky, Kent A. Ono, and Elyce Rae Helford. Boulder, Colo.: Westview, 1996, 51–68.

Yuker, Harold E. "Labels Can Hurt People with Disabilities." *Et Cetera* 44 (Spring 1987): 16–22.

Zola, Irving Kenneth. "Communication Barriers between 'the Able-Bodied' and 'the Handicapped.'" In *The Psychology and Social Impact of Physical Disability*. 2nd ed. Edited by Robert P. Marinelli and Arthur E. Dell Otto. New York: Springer, 1984, 139–147.

Index

Editor's Note: Generally, I find indexes confusing, inadequate, or excessive. Yet I believe they can be beneficial. Because this book is a collection of the writings of multiple authors, the odds are I have omitted terms some readers will consider absolutely essential and included others that could have been omitted. Nevertheless, to make this index as useful as possible, I have followed the rule of referencing only those terms, names, and titles that include some development or exploration of a point. Page numbers are given only at moments in the chapters where the reader can learn something substantive about the term, individual, or text. The single exception to this rule is where referencing multiple usages of a term by diverse authors will help to shed light on its complexity and multiplicity of meaning (e.g., *feminism, gaze, polysemy*).

About the Contributors

Linda Badley is professor of English, women's studies, and film at Middle Tennessee State University. She is the author of several articles on fantasy literature, film, and television and of the books *Film, Horror, and the Body Fantastic* and *Writing Horror and the Body: The Fiction of Stephen King, Anne Rice, and Clive Barker.*

Marleen S. Barr currently teaches science and technology studies at Michigan State University. She is a winner of the Science Fiction Research Association Pilgrim Award for lifetime achievement in science fiction criticism. Her forthcoming books are *Genre Fission: A New Discourse Practice for Cultural Studies* and *Future Females, the Next Generation: New Voices and Velocities in Feminist Science Fiction Criticism.*

Elyce Rae Helford is associate professor of English and director of women's studies at Middle Tennessee State University. Her research, teaching, and publications center on gender and race in contemporary feminist fiction and science fiction literature, television, and film. She is co-editor of *Enterprise Zones: Critical Positions on Star Trek* and is currently writing a book on depictions of feminist anger in popular film, television, and comics.

Hanley E. Kanar is ABD in American studies at the University of Iowa, where her concentration is on the history of medicine and women's body politics. She currently teaches college composition in the Chicago area.

Nicole Matthews teaches media and cultural studies at Liverpool John Moores University in the U.K. She has published on reality TV and feminist cultural studies and is the author of *Comic Politics: Gender in Popular Hollywood Comedy Film After the New Right.*

Farah Mendlesohn is lecturer in American studies at Middlesex University, London, where she teaches the religious history and race and ethnicity in the United States. She has published a number of articles on modern science fiction authors and is currently editing a collection of essays on Terry Pratchett (to be published by the Science Fiction Foundation) and is undertaking research for a book on early magazine science fiction (1926–1945).

Sharon Ney earned her doctorate degree in philosophy from the University of Durham, England, and has taught at the Universities of Durham, Leeds, and Michigan, Flint. She has given many papers on time and time travel, has an article published in the *Journal of Philosophical Research* entitled "Are Grandfathers an Endangered Species?" on the grandfather paradox, and was philosophy consultant on the Dorling Kindersley book *Young Person's Guide to Philosophy.*

Kent A. Ono is associate professor in the American studies and Asian American studies programs at the University of California, Davis. His research emphasis is on critical and theoretical analysis of print, film, and television media, specifically focusing on representations of race, gender, sexuality, class, and nation. He has contributed articles to various journals and anthologies, is co-editor of *Enterprise Zones: Critical Positions on Star Trek,* and has co-authored a book, entitled *Shifting Borders: Rhetoric, Immigration, and California's "Proposition 187"* (forthcoming).

Sarah Projansky is assistant professor of women and gender studies at the University of California, Davis, where she also teaches film studies. She is co-editor of *Enterprise Zones: Critical Positions on Star Trek* and has published in *Signs, Quarterly Journal of Speech,* and various anthologies. She is currently completing a book on representations of rape and postfeminism in contemporary film and television.

Robin A. Roberts is the author of a number of books on gender and popular culture, most recently, *Sexual Generations:* Star Trek: The Next Generation *and Gender.* She is professor of English and women's and gender studies at Louisiana State University.

Jessica A. Royer is an arts and features writer who has her M.A. in journalism from the University of Missouri, Columbia. She resides in the Chicago area and is writing for *Chicago in the Year 2000,* a documentary project to chronicle a year in the life of the city.

Elaine M. Sciog-Lazarov is a technical writer/editor and systems analyst who has an M.A. in social anthropology from the University of Chicago. She and

Sharon Ney are currently planning an extended series of essays on the cultural and philosophical subtexts of *Babylon 5*.

Leah R. Vande Berg is professor of communication studies at California State University, Sacramento. She edited a special issue on Disney for *Women's Studies in Communication* and is currently editor of the *Western Journal of Communication*. She co-authored *Organizational Life on Television*, co-edited *Television Criticism: Approaches and Applications* and *Critical Approaches to Television*, and has published numerous articles on gender, media, sports, and cultural values in anthologies and scholarly journals.

Rhonda V. Wilcox is professor of English at Gordon College (Barnesville, Georgia). She has published numerous articles on television, including *The X-Files, Star Trek: The Next Generation, Northern Exposure*, and *Buffy the Vampire Slayer*. She is the author of the television chapter in the third edition of *Handbook of American Popular Culture* (forthcoming).